Praise for
IN PURSUIT OF JEFFERSON

"Every schoolchild knows Thomas Jefferson wrote the Declaration of Independence, but I doubt even the most dedicated reader of travel literature knows he also published a compact guide explaining the architecture, people, food, and (especially) wines of Old World Europe to the citizens of the brand-new United States. This retracing of the Founding Father's life-changing time abroad is a very entertaining book about a very complicated man."

—Mark Adams, *New York Times* bestselling author

"*In Pursuit of Jefferson* is an endlessly intriguing and completely original portrait of a complicated man and the places that formed him. Derek Baxter is the perfect guide, pairing a wry, eager sense of adventure with meticulous research, ever mindful of Jefferson's instruction to 'follow truth, wherever it may lead'—even when those insights reveal a troubling side of the founding father and his legacy."

—Doug Mack, author of *The Not-Quite States of America*

"*In Pursuit of Jefferson* is an excellent historical travelogue focused on Thomas Jefferson's unique musings and wanderings across Europe. Derek Baxter is an unabashed fan of the Sage of Monticello and follows him on his journeys as he matures as a politician, naturalist, scientist, and observer of human nature. The glue that holds the book together is found in the timeless parallels of scenery and outlook that the author discovers along the way. Jefferson, though no Mark Twain, turns out to be the quintessential American abroad—a sometimes fumbling Founder infused with gusto, wit, and affection for most everyone and everything he meets."

—Philip G. Smucker, author of *Riding with George*

"In his debut book, *In Pursuit of Jefferson*, Derek Baxter tells the bitter-sweet story of Thomas Jefferson, or should I say, Baxter's own reckoning with this most revered—and contradictory—figure from American history. In crisp language that is often conversational, Baxter weaves history with geography, food and wine, and science to tell what is ultimately a story of acceptance. It is only after following Jefferson's 'hints' through Europe—not to mention the Paris of North America—that Baxter comes to accept Jefferson for who he really was—a flawed human who might still offer some 'hints' on how best to move forward today. It confronts the uncomfortable but relevant issue of Jefferson's involvement with slavery plainly and with heartfelt honesty. This is a fine work of historical travelogue that will appeal to anyone with an interest in history, geography, science, and self-discovery—an engaging read offering much food for thought."

—Darrin Lunde, author of *The Naturalist*

"Taking their cues from Jefferson's *Hints* to travelers and following in his footsteps, Derek Baxter and his family gained a deeper and more enlightened understanding of a flawed founder's life and enduring legacies. This is travel writing at its best, an impressively researched and well-crafted chronicle of self-discovery and civic engagement."

—Peter S. Onuf, Thomas Jefferson Foundation Professor
of History, Emeritus, University of Virginia

"This jaunty, inventive approach to an old question—who was Thomas Jefferson?—turns out to be a wise, readable, and altogether satisfying work... An unusually pleasing and affecting guide to Europe through the eyes of two tourists separated by more than 230 years."

—*Kirkus* STARRED Review

IN PURSUIT OF

Jefferson

Traveling through Europe with the Most Perplexing Founding Father

DEREK BAXTER

Published by Sourcebooks
P.O. Box 4410, Naperville, Illinois 60567-4410
(630) 961-3900
sourcebooks.com

Cataloging-in-Publication Data is on file with the Library of Congress.

Printed and bound in the United States of America.
SB 10 9 8 7 6 5 4 3 2 1

To William, John, Thomas Lee,
Liana, Miranda, and Nico,
my fellow followers of Hints.
I respect all of you,
admire four of you,
and love three of you.

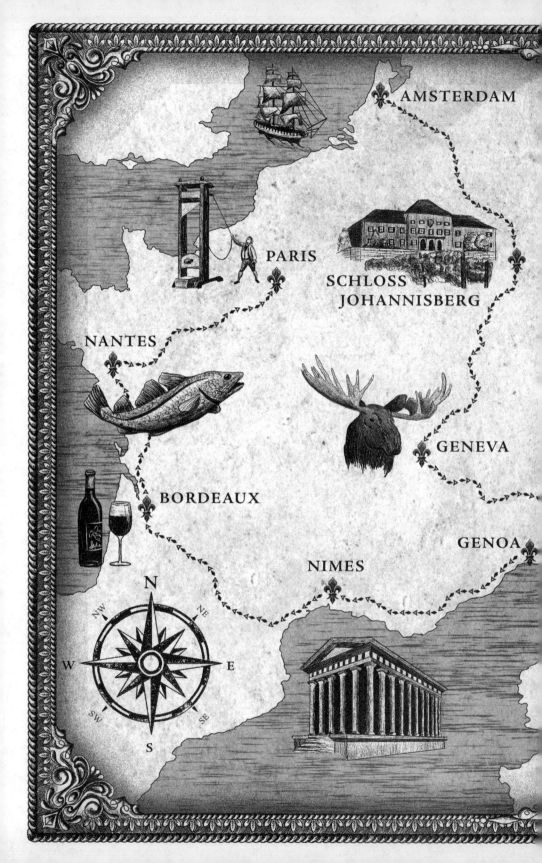

FOLLOWING THE PATH

HINTS TO
AMERICANS

OF THOMAS JEFFERSON'S

ROME

NAPLES

TABLE OF

Contents

CHAPTER ONE

The Starting Line

Napoleon loosens up to my left and Roman legionaries stretch in front of me, but I am the only Thomas Jefferson at the starting line. Not the spitting image of him, mind you. He was six foot two, straight as a gun barrel, with red hair and gray-green eyes, built like a fine horse with no surplus flesh, it was said. I am six inches shorter, with chestnut hair and an un-Jeffersonian beard and blue eyes, more of a donkey than a thoroughbred. I'm wearing a tricornered hat, colonial leggings, and a cape with "Thomas Jefferson" helpfully embroidered in gold lettering on the back. Instead of the small notebook with ivory pages he used to record his endless observations, I'm clutching an iPhone.

So the comparison is imperfect. But I doubt the costumed runners around me, preparing for one of the strangest marathons in the world, know what he was supposed to look like anyways. And I do have some things in common with my favorite Founding Father. We're both Virginians who made their way here to the Médoc, a sandy peninsula on the left bank of the Gironde estuary in Bordeaux in southwest France. We were both around age forty when we traveled far from home in search of something missing in our lives.

Let's start with Jefferson—he did come first.

You might think of Thomas Jefferson as the smooth, confident

Renaissance man who could do most anything, respected (even beloved) throughout America in his time as the leading voice of liberty. That wasn't the Jefferson of 1784. He sailed from Boston for Paris that year a broken man. Dark clouds hung over his political career; his time as governor of Virginia during the American Revolution, from 1779–81, had been a disaster. Jefferson was a brilliant writer and thinker but not the kind of decisive leader to guide a state successfully through war. He failed to prevent British troops from overrunning Virginia and, embarrassingly, had nearly been captured himself. Stung by fierce criticism from his political opponents, he announced his retirement from public life and didn't budge from this stance, even after the war concluded. Frustratingly, his greatest accomplishment to date—that he wrote the Declaration of Independence—was known only to a few. Other American leaders kept his authorship under wraps to make the document appear as the consensus work of the entire Continental Congress, not that of a lone genius.

Jefferson was sensitive, and the criticism hurt. But it paled in comparison to the tragedy he suffered in 1782. Martha, his wife of ten years, died some months after a difficult pregnancy. Jefferson was devastated. He had three daughters to raise by himself in a state that he felt had turned its back on him. He didn't know where to turn.

This is not sounding like a man who will be on the front of the nickel.

And he probably wouldn't be on it if he hadn't gotten on that ship to France. He brought his oldest daughter with him, entrusting his two younger ones with relatives, and began a new life. Jefferson spent five years based in Paris, a city—once he got used to it—that fascinated him. He haunted bookstalls, matched wits with other intellectuals in salons, viewed art, listened to music, planned social reforms, and became an expert on every subject that caught his fancy. He returned home in 1789 famous, a leader in government, brimming with observations on architecture, agriculture, gardening, politics, and more. Rather than mimicking what he came across in Europe, he planned to take the best of what he saw and improve the concepts in America. Jefferson had a purpose again—more purposes than any one man could hope to accomplish in a lifetime, in fact. Back home he would rise.

His greatest insights came on three trips he took away from the French capital, traveling the wide, wide world. The first was a two-month sojourn in England in 1786, where he assisted John Adams in diplomatic dealings but more profitably spent his time exploring the gentle English countryside.

The next was a three-and-a-half-month-long voyage to Aix-en-Provence in the south of France in 1787, ostensibly to take mineral waters to help heal a broken wrist. The trip was really an excuse to get away from his desk; Jefferson gave up on the treatment after just a few days and instead roamed across northern Italy and along the French Mediterranean and Atlantic coasts. Here in Bordeaux, where I am now, he tasted wines and made contacts with producers who would send him their best vintages for years to come.

His final journey was a seven-week work trip to Amsterdam in 1788. He left Paris for the Dutch port city heading east through what is now Belgium. When he finished his diplomacy, he returned via a leisurely route through Germany and Alsace, boating down the Rhine. "I am constantly roving about," Jefferson wrote to the Marquis de Lafayette (the French aristocrat who had fought in the American Revolution) about his travels, "to see what I have never seen before and shall never see again."

While on the road, he took copious notes on the people he met, from peasants to princes. He learned how to make cheese in Italy, discovered the sweetest figs in the Mediterranean, and found inspiration for the architecture of his home, Monticello, in Roman ruins and contemporary Parisian domes. He crossed the Alps while charting the elevations at which olive trees survived. He wrote lyrical letters on the road, sketched inventions from his carriage, made lifelong friends, and dreamed revolutionary thoughts again. Jefferson was back.

These travels meant so much to him that when two young Americans asked him what to do on their own trip through the continent, Jefferson responded with a five-thousand-word letter—in effect a small, unpublished guide—which he entitled *Hints to Americans Traveling in Europe.* Worrying that men in their twenties were apt to spend too much time studying the pleasures of spas and the "voluptuary dress and arts of European women," he crafted a sober travel regime with themes to explore and questions to answer, designed to keep them on the straight and narrow, turning them into mini-Jeffersons.

The original Jefferson had much invested in the success of this planned trip. The travelers, John Rutledge, Jr., and Thomas Shippen, were sons of acquaintances of his. They and other young men from the States had the chance to shape the just-started American Experiment. Europe was a vast tableau that Americans could mine for inspirational models and cautionary tales alike. But, he emphasized, a voyager must choose wisely. Jefferson's worst fear was that Americans would return home with a love for foppish aristocracy or smoky industrial mills. Better to find things that would help our country, like a useful new crop or building technique, or even a decent wine suitable for importing.

And so Jefferson set down a detailed itinerary, drawing from his own travels. *Hints* starts in Amsterdam, then sends the traveler south through Germany and Switzerland down to Rome. The route then tracks back north to the Alps and crosses France westward along the Mediterranean. It meanders northwards along the Atlantic coast and finally ends in Paris. Along the way, travelers were to focus on eight "Objects of Attention"—subjects worth investigating—during their journey. It's a fascinating read, strangely overlooked in many of his biographies. As far as I know, no one since those young Americans in 1788 has actually taken *Hints* and followed it.

Until now.

+ + +

A copy of *Hints to Americans* is stashed in the trunk of our rental, parked a mile or so from the starting line of the race. "I can't believe we're doing this, honey," says the racer behind me, my wife, Liana. Her eyes are flashing. Although she's a generally confident person—she's Cuban, as she'd be quick to tell you (or anyone), and Cubans are not known for being shy— neither one of us has run a marathon before. She's in costume, too, wearing a homemade colonial woman outfit, a bonnet, and a loose-fitting skirt.

"Well, we have to now. We couldn't leave if we wanted to," I reply. There are thousands of runners compressed around us, all waiting for the gun to go off. Nearly all are in costume as well: Vikings, chimney sweeps, knights, and so many others. Following the travel advice of a man who's been dead for nearly two centuries, while racing against cavemen and pharaohs, seems a dubious solution to my midlife crisis. But here we are.

For the last couple of years before this race I've felt stuck in a rut. I'm OK with my job as a lawyer dealing with technical matters in a government agency—it does pay the mortgage—but after such a long time there I've pretty much figured the work out. My days are the same. Get up, ride the commuter train, spend nine to five tapping on my computer and sitting in meetings, then take the train back to our town house in the northern Virginia suburbs, where we live along with our kids and Liana's parents. Repeat. Look forward to my next raise in precisely one year, ten months, and twenty-three days. I perform like a professional at the office, but deep down I know some side of me isn't being tapped.

At home I switch to being an overwhelmed father. We have two small kids: Miranda, age five, and Nico, age two. Both are joys. But by the time we get them to sleep I'm ready to crash myself, taking my vague dissatisfaction with my life to bed with me, still unexplained, unresolved. The roles I've backed into—dutiful employee, exhausted parent—seem as inflexible as the course of the stars in the sky.

Walking to the starting line: no turning back now.

When I'm riding the commuter train, my thoughts return to one of the last times I tried to find out who I was and wanted to be: when I studied at the University of Virginia, the school founded by Jefferson in Charlottesville. As a history major, I loved how the university's Grounds, with their serpentine walls and statues of the founder, made the past seem present. Understanding history gave my own life meaning; it situated me in time and let me appreciate how I was following in the footsteps of those who came before. Back then, I dreamed of being an historian and writer—I hadn't yet been convinced of the sensibility of going to law school.

For me, the only thing that could compete with history was travel. While history grounded me, travel allowed me to test my assumptions about the world, to discover what I shared with others and what made me different. I spent my third year in college studying abroad in Aix-en-Provence, Jefferson's destination when he went to take the waters on his 1787 tour of France. Called the city of a thousand fountains, Aix has been a university town since the Middle Ages, known for its elegant cafés, honey-colored Renaissance buildings, springs bubbling over moss-covered rocks, and winding streets, which led to surprises.

I took classes in an American school housed in what once had been an eighteenth-century chapel and lived with a French family who ran a theater. I studied in the cafés, joined a local hiking club, and went to concerts with my hosts' teenage son. French food was a source of constant revelation for me; I had my first encounters with the strong yet seductive flavors of truffles, escargots, and salt cod with tangy aioli sauce. Taking advantage of my twenty-year-old metabolism, I gorged on *pain au chocolat* as if they were about to be banned and lunched on baguettes stuffed with steak and *frites*.

Even better than the meals, if that were possible, was the town's past—whenever I had the chance of combining history with travel in some way, I was in heaven. On weekends I'd take the bus to the nearby Mont Sainte-Victoire with a small guidebook in hand until I finally located all the spots from which Cézanne painted the craggy white mountain, his greatest muse. For a paper for school, I sought out elderly French people and captured their recollections of the liberation by the Americans during World War II—it was the fiftieth anniversary of both D-Day and the Allied invasion of Provence two months later. One old woman clung to my arm and told me the story of how she, a teenager at that time, took in a young American parachutist ("he could not have been any older than you") who had crash-landed in the woods near her farmhouse.

Most enjoyable of all—although I didn't volunteer this when my fellow American students recounted their beery weekend escapes—were the quiet Saturdays I spent on my own with my favorite book, *Evocations of Old Aix-en-Provence*, a history of every street in the medieval-era town. I'd tramp down each *rue*, book in hand, visualizing what had once happened there: this lane was where tanners worked, here was the ancient Roman road out of town, that square was where hangings occurred. Acquiring this knowledge made me feel like I possessed a superpower; I knew what really had happened here, perhaps even better than the French themselves did.

On school breaks I slipped away to places new to me: Paris, Strasbourg, Corsica, Valencia, Lisbon, and Tangier, filling up my journals with impressionistic descriptions. Each trip I took during that unforgettable year fueled my drive to take another. I explored Prague and shared pints with Czech college students, listening to their stories about the secret police under Communism. And what about that time the boisterous Italian family gave my sister and me (as we backpacked through Tuscany) a ride in their VW bus high up into the mountains, singing at the top of their voices as they ascended, then invited us to join them in a cookout? Or that trip to the prehistoric caves of Lascaux with my friend Laura, a fellow student, where we picnicked on fresh strawberries and pâté sandwiches in a Cro-Magnon shelter we found in the woods? (Whatever happened to her? I looked her up: she followed her dream and now she's a writer.)

What I wouldn't give to travel like that again. That year wasn't just about encounters with history; it was also one of personal transformation as I learned to live with the unexpected. When I arrived, wearing my Reeboks and Orioles cap, I stuck out like a sore thumb, *un pouce douloureux*. I felt helpless, barely able to order food. By the end I was comfortably chatting with French students in cafés about the latest political news out of Paris, bringing food to my mouth with the fork in my left hand as they did. My crowning achievement came the night my host mother called home from her theater and, when I answered, thought for a few moments that it was her own son speaking.

Not to say that I had turned French—I did miss home—but my outlook on life expanded. There were different ways of doing things, I found out, and what to adopt and what to discard was up to me. At night I journaled about my new discoveries and plotted my next travels. The world was a blank canvas and filling it in was a joy.

Was all that destined to be a once-in-a-lifetime experience? Will I ever find that sense of wonder again? Recently, I returned to a long-discarded pursuit: spending nights reading travel journals, writings of the explorers, descriptions of long-ago trips to far-off lands. Yarns involving travel and history, tales of people conquering challenges, moving forward into the unknown, living the kind of life I once fantasized that I might lead.

And I might be reading them still if, surfing the internet late one night some three months ago, I hadn't stumbled across *Hints to Americans Traveling in Europe.*

Jefferson's itinerary fascinated me. A few of the places I had been to and would love to see again. Most I had not. Their names rolled off my tongue: Amsterdam, Heidelberg, Porto Fino, Vercelli, Carcassonne. How I would have made use of this guide if I had had it when I was a student in Aix—I would have put *Evocations* down and taken to the road with it in hand. I smiled when I saw the practical travel advice Jefferson included, too. Who knew a Founding Father gave tips on hotels? (Don't miss The Wildman in Koblenz but stay away from the "most unconscionable rascal" of a tavern keeper in Tains.) "Abundance, abundance to be seen here," Jefferson wrote in *Hints* on Genoa. He might as well have said that about the entire journey he designed, the best the Old World had to offer.

The eight "Objects of Attention for an American" particularly intrigued me; I was fascinated by which subjects Jefferson thought most useful for travelers to learn about, improving their minds so they could then better their communities back home. The fledgling republic back home was teetering financially. Many farmers hadn't recovered from the recent war; new ideas might help. Three Objects thus focused on economic issues, starting with agriculture, so important that everything in "near relation to it" should be investigated, including "useful and agreeable animals which might be transported to America" and plants of note. Jefferson separated the "mechanical arts" into two Objects of Attention. One consists of items that Americans necessarily had to construct themselves, like bridges. The other includes manufacturing, which the traveler need only pay a "superficial" view to since the new nation would likely be importing manufactured goods for the foreseeable future.

Three Objects belong to the realm of culture. Architecture was the most important of these, "worth great attention" since the new country was growing, and thus building, rapidly. Painting and statuary together form one Object, although Jefferson dryly noted that they were too costly for most Americans to afford. A surprising inclusion for me was landscape gardening, which he considered to be an art form "peculiarly worth the attention of an American." Since plants abounded in the New World, all a canny landscaper had to do was remove the weeds and *voilà*: instant garden.

The final two Objects deal with political issues. One recommends familiarizing oneself with the monarchies of Europe, but only as examples of the "worst part of mankind," dark reminders of what America broke away from. The other asks the traveler to investigate how governmental policies "influence the happiness of the people" by getting a first-hand look at how commoners live on a daily basis. Taken together, these missives make clear that anyone following *Hints* might enjoy the ride, but there was real work required on the road—Jefferson didn't do vacations.

But even more than the specifics of the guide, what captivated me most was the identity of its author. Since I was a boy growing up in Virginia, I had looked up to Thomas Jefferson and marveled at his many talents. I checked out biographies on him from the library and visited Monticello, only two and a half hours from our house, with my parents. When our fourth-grade class staged the musical *Tall Tom Jefferson*, I of course played the lead, my hair powdered, singing about wanting to be remembered as one whose heart did care. To me, he was the brainy Founder, the one who wanted to change the world. There seemed to be nothing he could not do.

I took my prom date to dinner at Gadsby's Tavern, where Jefferson celebrated his first inauguration as president in 1801, then on for a nightcap at, yes, the Jefferson Memorial. (Not surprisingly, she broke up with me not long after.) For college, I was torn between going to William and Mary—which Jefferson attended and where I could slip away after class to roam Colonial Williamsburg—or UVA, what Jefferson called his "academical village." Naturally, I picked the latter, often studying on the university's Lawn, sitting quite literally at the feet of my mentor's statue.

I looked up to him for writing the Declaration of Independence, of course, for voicing our national aspiration for freedom and sticking up for the common man. But his practice of slaveholding certainly bothered me. Having written that "all men are created equal," why hadn't he freed his own slaves? I couldn't explain that failure, that disappointing blot on his character.

But the rest of the package seemed worthy of admiration. I was especially in awe of how he seemed to do it all. Jefferson never settled. He wasn't locked into a routine or a single narrow career for decades. He had an insatiable curiosity and a desire to wriggle out of the traps set by the ordinary world. He elevated every situation he was in, looking deep into the subjects before him and turning himself into a Renaissance Superman in the process. Surprisingly athletic, he would measure his pace by an odometer, covering a mile in a brisk fourteen and a half minutes. Every day, he'd find time to explore his world, recording observations and musings: the weather, flora and fauna, snatches of music rattling in his brain, and ideas for a new America. Called a "walking encyclopedia," Jefferson could supposedly calculate an eclipse, survey an estate, tie an artery, plan an edifice, try a cause, break a horse, dance a minuet, and play a violin.

Playing the role of Jefferson as a boy, looking up to him as a man.
The bust of TJ is modeled after the 1789 sculpture by Jean-Antoine Houdon.

I stayed up most of the night I first came across *Hints* diving into Jefferson's travel writings online and plotting paths on Google Maps. What would I discover if I followed his itinerary? Adventure, new fields of learning, hidden truths? Would any of the subjects contained in Jefferson's guide inspire me—architecture, gardening, traveling itself? My purpose might be hidden in plain sight.

I dreamed of not a mere trip but a journey, a quest of discovery. Of sharing experiences with Jefferson that might lead to a deeper understanding about him. What I wanted to rub off on me was Jefferson's never-flagging sense of wonder about the world. Would emulating his desire for knowledge gained through travel tamp down my gnawing dissatisfaction? I wanted the wines, the Roman architecture, the Dutch canals. Even encounters with rascally tavern keepers would at least be memorable.

Most importantly, I wondered what I might find out about that truly uncharted and fearsome territory, myself. What would happen if I just picked up his guide and went?

I checked Jefferson's *Hints*. They had no expiration date.

By the time I showed up bleary-eyed to the office the next morning, though, I had mostly returned to my senses. Following Jefferson's travels was a pipe dream, wasn't it? I had had those before. Kicking the tires on other careers. Trying out hobbies, hoping they would push me out of my malaise. (Remember that banjo that's now in the attic? The Italian language CDs now gathering dust?) The latest idea sounds like a blast but totally impractical given my responsibilities. I had my moment—all those travels back in college—but I've long since grown up.

Someday I might just chuck it all in and follow *Hints*. Sure. After all, now it was just one year, ten months, and *twenty-two* days until that next raise.

Someday.

But still I kept returning to the internet after the kids fell asleep, fascinated by the destinations Jefferson set out in his guide. Weeks later, I came across a second surprising revelation.

One of the many practical difficulties that worried me about following *Hints* was making the same connections to subjects that Jefferson did. Take Bordeaux, for example. How would I access the ultra-exclusive wineries he recommended visiting? That's when I landed on a website for the Marathon du Médoc. Nearly ten thousand runners race in costume and drink wine at the twenty-one refreshment stops in vineyards along the route. It's the longest marathon in the world, the organizers wrote, tongue in cheek, because tipsy competitors don't run straight; they *faire le zig-zag*, adding miles to the requisite 26.2 (42.2 km). Even the food provided along the course was gourmet—steak, cheese, ice cream, and, at km 38, oysters freshly pulled from the nearby Atlantic.

All this astonished me. These vineyards produced thousand-dollar-a-bottle Bordeaux; they didn't allow just anyone to stroll up for a tasting, reserving visits for discriminating critics and big spenders (as Jefferson, who was both, did two centuries earlier). They even included the famed Château Lafite Rothschild, whose red reached a light "perfection" after repose, Jefferson wrote. They were an essential destination for an American Traveling in Europe. And now I knew that one day a year these vineyards opened their gates and uncorked their vintages for the commoners, *comme moi*.

The website for the Marathon du Médoc featured a cartoon logo of a smiling tipsy runner tripping past the grapevines, and it called out my name as clearly as Jefferson's *Hints* had weeks earlier. These wineries were not out of reach after all; I'd just have to pay a modest registration fee and run my way in. Wouldn't Jefferson have approved? He wanted to better the lives of the common man, his beloved yeoman farmers, not just the elite.

The theme of this year's marathon, the 2012 version, was history; 8,500 runners would dress as their favorite characters from the past. It seemed like a sign. The perfect link to Jefferson, the perfect entrée into this exclusive world of wine. I can't put this project off anymore—wait too long and this history-themed race will have passed.

It's more than that, though. Time won't wait forever. Dad, who worked so hard in a bureaucratic job for his family, finally retired a few years back, ready to get back to his gardening and canoeing and writing fun pieces to share with the family. Yet now he's having short-term memory issues. His own father died from Alzheimer's; the memory of his decline haunts us all.

I can't count on deferring my dreams forever, I thought. They might not be there when I'm finally ready. Or I might not be there to catch them.

How many times will your calling come for you? I stared at the cursor blinking on the screen, hovering over the Marathon du Médoc website. As midnight approached, my heart suddenly, decisively settled on an answer. Yes.

Over breakfast the next morning, I breathlessly told Liana about my plans—subject to her buy-in.

"Of course, you must do this," she said calmly. That's what I expected. From her own experience, she certainly knew something about the long road to personal growth.

Liana is three years younger than me and three inches shorter, with wavy brown hair and coffee-colored eyes. She clicks with people easily; by contrast, I can be a little reserved and detached, bemusedly observing the players in the game of life. She came over from Cuba at the age of twenty-three—how she finagled her way out is a complicated tale that deserves to be told over a beer. She arrived with a law degree earned in Havana and only a spotty command of English. Liana loves to tell the story of how when the Soviet Union, the benefactor of the Cuban communist regime, collapsed in August 1991, her middle-school Russian teacher overnight became an English teacher, a language as new to the educator as to her students. "Theee peen-seel eees rrrred," she would solemnly intone to her confused class.

In America, Liana had to start all over again. She worked part-time in a day care in Charlottesville, the city where we first lived together, while simultaneously enrolling at the Jefferson School taking English as a Second Language classes. And it wasn't just English: she had to learn everything from typing to driving to—unused to actually having a choice—picking out a bottle of shampoo from a supermarket shelf. Through sheer determination, she's advanced to a position as an immigration policy analyst. Her career is on the rise, thanks to her drive and high energy—while mine has glided to rest on a plateau.

"What about you, honey? Do you want to run a race while drinking?" I asked. I'm at least a weekend jogger; Liana's yoga won't help her much.

"Count me in. Bring on the wine," she replied.

We're not going to do the full *Hints* journey all at once, far from it. I'm not quitting my job, just taking a week's leave. I couldn't take months off work to do the trip from start to finish, much less afford such a splurge. Most obviously of all, we can't abandon the kids for that long. But there's no better place to begin following *Hints* than Bordeaux, one of Jefferson's favorite destinations.

If this trip goes well—if I find a glimpse of what I'm looking for, if I'm able to live a bit of what Jefferson did—then I'll find a way to continue on the journey, even if it takes me years to complete the whole thing. Later I can brainstorm how to chop the travels up into manageable segments, to figure out how to return to the Old World and what my itinerary should look like. And to start studying these Objects of Attention so I'll understand what Jefferson wanted me to find.

If not—if the trip feels forced or ridiculous, Jefferson's advice just too dated—then I'll stop and cut my losses. And at least we'll have had some good wine. So for me, this race is more than a marathon: it's a true trial run.

Liana and I booked tickets for five days in France. We spent a couple of months running, sometimes pushing the kids in strollers before us. I read some books on Jefferson and tried to get to know his world (basically I listened to a lot of harpsichord music). Then it was onto the plane, into the rental, and down here to the Médoc. We put on our costumes and arrived at the starting line. For the first time in over two centuries, Thomas Jefferson will be traveling through France.

CHAPTER TWO

Something New Under the Sun

"I'm so nervous!" says Liana at the starting line. "But it's a good kind of nervous." Her eyes sparkle as we bounce up and down in place. An official launches into an obligatory speech, for along with wine, cheese, and romance, France is known for its stifling bureaucracy, even at loose events like this. "*Messieurs, Mesdames*, welcome to the *Marathon du Médoc!*" Great cheers.

"A reminder that the winning male and female will each receive their weight in wine as a prize." More cheers. But then the tone turns ominous. "It is unexpectedly hot today. We ask you drink much water. It is greatly recommended." Silence. Don't tell the French to drink water.

The organizer explains that an extra half hour has been allotted due to the heat, but any runner who does not finish within seven hours will be disqualified, their complimentary bottle of Bordeaux revoked. A trio of volunteers called the Sweepers will run at the slowest allowed pace—fall behind them at your peril. I look at Liana. That's a long time for a real runner at a real marathon. Even Jefferson, at his rapid walking rate, could finish in that time. Nonetheless, our training didn't come close to this distance. And we do need time to drink all that wine.

The starting gun cracks, two fighter jets fly over, confetti rains down, and we surge forward: Vikings waving swords, Jesus carrying his cross, and a pair of extroverted Elvises. And one eager Thomas Jefferson.

Thronged with crowds, the narrow streets of Pauillac make for slow going. We take a last glance at the mighty Gironde; we're leaving this port town and won't see it again until we complete our marathonic loop. After just one kilometer comes our first break. A bemused volunteer pours us La Rose Pauillac in real stem wineglasses, and I gulp mine down. My kind of race.

"Take it easy, Derek," Liana says, the voice of reason. "We have to pace ourselves."

We run on hard-packed dirt through vineyards steaming in the growing heat, stopping to imbibe at châteaux that looked ripped from the pages of fairy tales. No experts, we nonetheless taste the wines on offer, trying not to drip sweat into the glasses. Then it's back to running alongside Crusaders with shields, kilted Scottish Highlanders, ahistorical penguins, and a man wearing a revolutionary red bonnet and carrying a guillotine on his back. Surrounded by these fellow travelers, I feel like a peasant on carnival day finally able to mock his lord. Château owner after owner personally hands us a glass of rarefied wine as if tossing liquid euros to the riffraff.

At km 12.5 we reach Château Gruard Larose, where we have an in. This is a rare Bordeaux winery open to the public, and the day before the race, having decided it was too late to improve our running, Liana and I had visited it to practice drinking. Patrick, the young guide for our small group tour, had a long nose that appeared to be genetically selected for sniffing wine. "The vines have to suffer," he said, explaining how they penetrate deep into the rocky soil in search of water, resulting in flavorful but not overly juicy grapes.

While we were tasting the wines (a little like black cherry, Liana pronounced), Patrick asked if anyone was racing the next day. We raised our hands, as did a Japanese man who would be running as a Buddhist monk. The other tour group members stared at us, dumbfounded, unaware of the madness that would descend on the Médoc the next day.

Drinking fine Bordeaux and listening to a band in the courtyard of a château—what kind of race is this?

"What are you going as?" asked Patrick.

"Thomas Jefferson."

"That's great! He came here to Bordeaux, you know. He took notes and included our winery. That was a help when it came to classify the wines in the classification of 1855. We got included." Jefferson ranked twelve vineyards in four different categories of quality, the first person to do so. His taste was on the mark. Some sixty-eight years later, Emperor Napoleon III established a list in a similar order to the Virginian's. The Napoleonic hierarchy became a nearly immutable law; there have been only two changes to it since. "We were ranked in the second category in

1855," Patrick told us with a resigned look. "We will never be first and we will never be third."

Jefferson's travels through southern France (as well as Italy and Germany) formed part of his quest for the perfect bottle of wine. This wasn't just so he could lay out the best table in America (although he would do that, too). Until independence, Americans had drunk only rough, overly sweet Madeira forced on them by the English and their restrictive trade policies. Now the wines of France were open to American importers. But which ones were the best? There were no printed guides; Jefferson would have to make discoveries for himself.

The grapes he selected might even be grown back in America. Jefferson worried that the fastest-growing drink in popularity back home was corn whiskey. He didn't want his beloved yeoman farmers going on benders; he imagined them sipping fine yet affordable wines by the fire at night, reading Virgil in the original Latin and discussing democracy.

So, Jefferson "rambled" through the vineyards as he put it, talking to vintners, observing winemaking, and finding deals. He recorded how women plucked snails off the grapes and how men grafted vines. He bought vine cuttings to experiment with in his garden and bottles to sample at home. These were the happiest days of his life, he wrote later.

After his trip, Jefferson would use his rankings of Bordeaux to guide his purchases, which he made directly with the winery wherever possible. Middlemen inevitably cheated the consumer, he wrote, adulterating wine, switching vintages and producers, and storing it poorly. Only the producer itself provided the genuine article, for it would be suicidal for them to do otherwise. He would travel home from France with 363 bottles in tow, mostly white Bordeaux. And that was just for his immediate use—the rest of his vast wine collection was shipped in crates.

On race day we run up to Patrick, who's observing the moving chaos. "Are you feeling good?" he inquires. He seems happy to see us.

"We're surviving; we made it this far," Liana replies.

We take quick sips of Gruard Larose and run on. All these small tastings haven't affected our running prowess, such as it is; the buzzy tease leaves us wanting more. Our wish is soon granted—two kilometers later is Château Lagrange, with its Roman-looking tower and, *bien sûr*, more wine.

It seems odd that there are châteaux cheek by jowl every few kilometers, like so many McMansions. As I sip on, epiphany strikes: they're not real. Châteaux demanded vast tracts of land, tended by peasants who would provide tribute to their lord. But the château-to-peasant ratio is all off here; the marathon is taking us to twenty-one of the great houses in just seven hours on foot, with dozens of others in sight on the horizon. Many must have been built expressly to impress wine buyers—like Jefferson back then and us today. My later research will confirm that; most châteaux in Bordeaux date from the nineteenth century, not the Middle Ages. If a newer winery doesn't possess one, it just hires an artist to sketch a make-believe castle and slaps it on its label anyway: *le marketing*.

My very first Jeffersonian observation! The old man would have been proud of me—empirical data led me to a new, even if fairly minor, understanding of something. Of course, I surely could have learned this on Google from the comfort of home. But until I got here on the ground, I hadn't even known to ask the question. I wish I could tell Jefferson himself about it; instead, I babble my ideas to Liana and into my iPhone for posterity.

My reflections on châteaux might be my only deep thoughts for the day, though; I'm not discovering any deeper truths about wine itself from the tastings. There are just too many of them, and running in leggings and a cape doesn't sharpen my appreciation. Even reaching the fabled Château Lafite Rothschild at km 26.5 comes as an anticlimax; my legs and palate alike are fatigued and losing sensation. The wine I sample barely registers with me.

But I don't care. A can't-believe-my-luck sense that I've found my golden ticket suffuses my body. I needed some *Hints* in my life, and judging by Liana's beaming face, it looks like I'm not the only one. I'm already inspired to return to France, not necessarily in costume, and discover more. *Hints* recommends fifteen wines to try on the road—I'll need more time and a better-trained liver for that challenge. And we can begin to make inroads on the more serious Objects of Attention.

As we run on, my thoughts drift to the prior travelers who followed this travel advice—the men for whom Jefferson wrote *Hints*. The Pennsylvanian Thomas Shippen left his law studies in London to team up with his friend John Rutledge, Jr., newly arrived on the continent from South Carolina and in search of adventure. Both had family fortunes to burn and a particular interest in learning about the women of Europe. They were later joined by William Short, Jefferson's private secretary, a Virginian in his late twenties. They strike me as the kind of young men I remember from my own days at the University of Virginia—Founding Frat Boys.

Jefferson wanted them to stay focused on his Objects of Attention and other investigations into culture. He was confident that Americans—open-minded and optimistic—would be receptive to the ideas they brought back home, which he hoped might even strengthen the fledgling democracy. "We can no longer say there is nothing new under the sun," Jefferson wrote later about the nation he had helped found, "for this whole chapter in the history of man is new."

The Boys visited some of the early wine destinations recommended by Jefferson but with mixed results. Shippen ran out of money and dropped out of the trip before Bordeaux. And the other two, exhausted and behind schedule, skipped the Médoc altogether. This fact makes me feel smug. Competitive as ever, I congratulate myself on doing a better job putting *Hints* into practice than they did, beating the Boys in a race they couldn't have known they were in.

The clouds float away, exposing a bright glare. "I am now in the land of corn, wine, oil, and sunshine," wrote Jefferson about the south of France. "If I should happen to die at Paris, I will beg of you to send me here, and have me exposed to the sun. I am sure it will bring me to life again." This sun seems intent on finishing us off, though. To our dismay, we find plenty of Bordeaux but no water. Organizers of a marathon in America would not have offered twenty-one stops with stem wineglasses. But they would have had water, and Gatorade, and phalanxes of green Porta Potties. The French can produce bureaucratic forms *par excellence*, but since the days of the Maginot Line, the French do style, the Americans, logistics.

"People are dropping like flies," Liana says, pointing out a medic attending to a dehydrated runner.

We feel like refugees trudging in advance of an invading army, no doubt German. Some runners are in fact dressed in World War I costumes with green capes, pointed helmets, and toy rifles, and they look like the war has gone badly. Desperate Vikings grab half-full water bottles lying by the road and drink from them. I forget about Jefferson and his cursed *Hints*. As wine swirls in our stomachs and mixes with the morning's croissants, the call of nature comes *à l'urgence*.

"I have to go," Liana says. We haven't seen a toilet in hours.

"Really? Are you sure?" I reply.

"I can't hold it. I can't concentrate anymore."

"What if we try that château up on the hill?"

We jog over to it. Liana knocks on the door of Château Montrose and pleads for a bathroom. A woman shrugs and points to the nearest vines. I stand guard as Liana hoists her skirts next to grapes that would soon produce a $250 bottle of wine. A trio of Crusaders do the same. "They dung a little in Médoc and Grave," Jefferson wrote, "because of the poverty of the soil; but very little, as more would affect the wine." To that I add: avoid the 2012 Château Montrose and its questionable *terroir*.

We pass a group of running Romans, who on closer inspection turn out to be British students. "Jefferson was always my favorite president," whispers a young blond conspiratorially. Are the English allowed to have favorite presidents? Then the grim Sweepers pass by in their scarlet capes, those sadistic volunteers running at the slowest allowable pace. The British Roman had told us how her cousins fell behind them and wound up in a van driven by scowling *gendarmes*, bused back to town, their prize bottles of wine forfeited. We pick up the pace and catch the Sweepers. Luckily, no officials had seen us, so we're still in the race.

Twenty-one miles into the race: refueling before the last push.

But by now, the small sips of Bordeaux no longer dull the throbbing in our knees or the blistering on our feet, and even the mild winey buzz has disappeared. *"Allez*, Liana!" call out the spectators, who look concerned. Her name is on her running bib, but I wonder why she is garnering such attention. Then I see that she's as bright red as a nice Cabernet Sauvignon. Despite all the pageantry and wine, it is still a marathon, our first, and doubts about this whole expedition creep in. How would it bode for any plans of following *Hints* if we fail on this inaugural leg?

We walk briskly. I know we're north of six hours into the race, closing in on the seven-hour limit. A tent with a flag proclaiming km 38 is a welcome sight. We're on the homestretch and it's time for the most famous stop on the journey—a table piled high with heaps of mottled oysters. A man with a proud white mustache and sun-browned arms shucks them at a snail's pace. I drink white Sauternes poured from a plastic water bottle. It tastes different from everything we've had before: tropical, like lychees and passion fruit. Jefferson loved this sweet wine so much that he would order it his whole life, sending bottles to George Washington as a present.

The lush Sauternes almost puts me in a trance. If only I could lie down, stop running, and drink some more, preferably listening to sitar music. I reach my hand out for seconds.

Liana shouts to me from the edge of the tent. I can't hear her but manage a Gallic shrug, smile weakly, and take another swig. Liana looks upset, as if she had eaten a bad oyster, and points dramatically at a hill as if to say *J'accuse!* I follow her finger: high, cresting a distant hilltop 100 meters ahead of us, run the three Sweepers. Behind them, a gaggle of runners practically cling to the trio's capes, begging for penance. The Sweepers and their acolytes disappear over the hill, crushing the juice from our dreams.

We are about to be placed in a van and hauled back to the starting line, my *Hints* test run a failure. On Monday I'll be back on the commuter train, getting to work by nine for another week of sameness. Just like those Bordeaux wines, I'll be confined in a classification that's impossible to break out of.

My mind flashes to Jefferson and the Boys. Am I really going to be leaving them so soon? I think about William Short and the advice he sought from his mentor. He, too, traveled to Bordeaux with a troubled mind, torn about his own future. Should he remain in Paris long-term or follow his dream of running for office back home? He was afraid that if he chose wrong, he'd have to resign himself to a life he hadn't wanted.

Consider carefully, Jefferson counseled in a return letter. He would be sorry to lose Short as his secretary, but the young man had to find his own path to "durable happiness." It won't be easy; it will certainly involve hard work. "This is not a world in which heaven rains riches into any hand that will open itself," Jefferson wrote. "Whichever of these courses you adopt, delay is loss of time. The sooner the race is begun the sooner the prize will be obtained."

Merde! I feel an almost electric jolt course through me. I'm not ready to abandon this race, this prize, this pursuit of happiness.

Without a word, Liana and I rush forward, revolutionaries storming the barricades. We put pain out of mind. We charge up the hill, surprising the British Romans, sweeping past the Sweepers. On a runner's high, blisters and heat forgotten, we clock our fastest kilometer as the grand Gironde comes into sight. My cape flies crisp in the wind, our hearts pound in unison, our minds drag our exhausted bodies behind them. *Allez*, Liana! She is purple like merlot and determined. Loud French music blares, people clap. The clock ticks seven hours. We cross the line holding hands.

We've finished the marathon. Now the hard journey begins.

CHAPTER THREE

Traveling like Jefferson

BEGINNINGS

"All things here appear to me to trudge on in one and the same round. We rise in the morning that we may eat breakfast, dinner and supper and go to bed again that we may get up the next morning and do the same: So that you never saw two peas more alike than our yesterday and today."

And so twenty-year-old Thomas Jefferson bemoaned his fate (which at the time was studying his law books and living at home with his mother and six siblings) to his college friend John Page. And that was how I, too, felt only six months ago, before running the wine marathon. Not anymore. I'm happy at both work and home, knowing that each night I can continue my training, my transformation into a Jeffersonian traveler. That's how I'm spending 2013, saving up for the journey to come and studying *Hints*, its themes, and its author. Playing the long game doesn't bother me; I've always felt that planning for a trip can be as fun as actually going on it.

And it's not all book learning. To truly understand why Jefferson valued travel so much, I'm heading to the Rivanna River in central Virginia, the scene of a trip that changed him forever—and began his lifetime of purposeful journeys.

"Thrown into the society of horse racers, cardplayers, [and] fox-hunters," Thomas wrote about his youth, he worried that he, too, would lead a wasted life. His aristocratic peers lived in luxury, never questioning their own provincial tastes and views. Their unwillingness to examine the obvious injustices of slavery particularly grated on him. Although his own family held around forty people in bondage, Jefferson railed against the "evil" institution in principle. Few planters shared his concerns. The most admired members of his society, he wrote, were those who "per-fumed most" and talked the "most nonsense." Thomas might have been seen as one of them, just another White plantation owner focused on the price of tobacco and the pedigree of his horses. But he was determined to be different.

In contrast to most of the Virginia gentry, Thomas's late father, Peter Jefferson, had led a rugged, intentional life. Although he had little formal education, he read constantly, always seeking to improve himself, becoming a self-taught yet noted surveyor and cartographer. His son saw him as a quasi-superhero, with unusual physical strength and "remarkable powers of endurance, untiring energy, and indomitable courage." The elder Jefferson traveled Indian trails along Virginia's borders and mountains, sleeping in trees to avoid "wild beasts," to prepare the definitive map of the colony. He hosted Cherokee leaders at his house, even though his surveying activities ultimately contributed to the dispossession of Native Americans from their land.

But in 1757 he died at age forty-nine, leaving his surveying equipment and book collection to Thomas, at age fourteen the elder of his two sons. "When young, I was passionately fond of reading books of history and travels," Thomas recalled later. He feasted on the stories of exploration his father handed down to him, like George Anson's *Voyage Around the World* and John Ogilby's foot-and-a-half-tall folio *Description of America*, chock-full of maps.

Thomas dreamed of creating his own narrative. He loved the outdoors and became an exceptional horseman but yearned for culture and learning. His favorite professors were British polymaths, ambassadors of the Enlightenment—the movement that rationally questioned dogma in science, religion, and government.

In 1763, the same year he complained about the drudgery of his life to his friend Page, the young Jefferson proposed to his friend that they embark on an overseas odyssey. The pair of them could go to England, France, Holland, and Italy (where Thomas would buy "a good fiddle") and finish in Egypt. But whether for lack of funds or will, they never went. Jefferson wasn't fazed. He found the perfect trip he could take on his own, a journey that had a serious point to it. Best of all, he could start right outside his own house, on the water.

Getting tobacco to overseas market was a major problem for Virginian plantation owners. Enslaved men labored behind oxen that slowly pulled thousand-pound barrels, packed with the plant, over muddy, poorly maintained roads. It was far more efficient to float tobacco downriver by boat to the Atlantic ports. The Rivanna River runs below where the Jeffersons lived in a wooden plantation house they called Shadwell, a few miles east from a mountain the family also owned and that Thomas would later name Monticello. Yet the river was filled with boulders. A pity, because it flowed into the broad James, which in turn flowed into the Chesapeake Bay, an otherwise excellent route for shipping the product.

But he heard that someone had successfully run the Rivanna on canoe. Could he do the same? If he proved it was navigable, even if rocks needed to be removed, he could promote the river as a new link in the transportation highway. Not only would selling tobacco become easier, so would ordering and receiving European goods—like the painted blue Dutch pottery Thomas's mother prized. His home in the mountains would join a greater network; it would become a thread in a ribbon of rivers, seas, and other waterways that connected Virginia to London, Paris, and Amsterdam, those cities he longed to see himself one day.

On a soft April day in 2013, I go with my dad to do our own version of Jefferson's pioneering trip. I couldn't ask for a better companion. Dad's an old Okie who grew up in the outdoors. Although he raised us in manicured suburbs, on weekends he'd take me paddling or tramping through the woods—Peter Jefferson had nothing on him. Now, we wrangle his beat-up aluminum Grumman off his SUV. The canoe still has a faint dent in the keel from where he wrapped it around a sycamore tree while floating in a flood four decades earlier.

This river seems a humble place to start, I think, as we carry the Grumman toward a muddy embankment, through a patch of woods, from which emerges, apparently, Gandalf the wizard.

"A fine day for a float!" the man says chipperly. He has a shockingly white beard, felt vest, and literal feather in his cap. He introduces himself as Bill, head of the Virginia Canal and Navigation Society. Society members, who are slowly gathering by the put-in, spend half their free time in libraries researching the history of the state's waterways and the other half paddling around, looking for finds. When I had learned they were planning a special canoe trip to commemorate the 250th anniversary of Jefferson's float down the Rivanna, I asked if I could come along. They had keyed it to Jefferson's 270th birthday.

Bill indicates two openings through the rapids before us. "The one on the left was built by a canal company in the 1800s. But if you go to the far right, you'll shoot the sluice that Jefferson made." We do, canoeing furiously past rock walls laid out by Jefferson—or, undoubtedly, his slaves.

Our small party floats downstream. Bill gestures to us to follow him; we paddle to the bank and get out. "Here are the remains of his canals," he says. We clamber over them; they're covered in vines like a forgotten Mayan ruin. Peter Jefferson first built a canal here to provide a water source for his flour mill, but a flood washed it away. Sometime after Thomas's 1789 return from Europe, he drew from his experience on the waterways of Holland and France to order enslaved workers to rebuild it to a new design.

After more paddling, we stop to lunch at Buck Island. Then, one by one, the canoes whoosh past a wing dam, a collection of rocks standing since colonial time that compresses the rushing water into a center channel. Paddlers yelp with joy. The river straightens out. Cows gaze placidly at us; a heron flaps its spindly wings like a pterodactyl, staying just downstream of us. Jefferson's early life was much like this—provincial. This could be any scene in the country, anywhere with quiet, small-town dreams. Whatever calling life had in store for him, it demanded he leave this corner of the woods.

We reach a long stretch of quiet river, those lazy spells when you drift under the overhanging branches and let your mind roam. I talk to Dad about Jefferson.

"Remember when we met Gorbachev?" he chuckles. When I was at UVA in 1993, twenty years ago, the school celebrated Jefferson's 250th birthday and they brought the ex-Soviet leader to talk on individual freedom. Dad had come down for it and we wandered Grounds to kill time before the speech. My father opened the door to Newcomb Hall and found himself face-to-face with Mikhail exiting the building with his bodyguards.

"What do you say to the man who brought down the Soviet Union?" Dad asks rhetorically. Like his father before him, he doesn't mind telling the same story over and over, building up to the punch line and dissolving in laughter. "I just looked at him in the eyes and said, 'Good job.'"

"Not bad if you only have a second to think of something," I reply. That's how I always reply. We paddle on.

"Dad, remember when we canoed below Great Falls a few years ago?" I mention after a spell. "I asked you why you didn't push me more when I was younger to find what I really wanted to do."

Dad on the Rivanna.

"Of course I do," he replies. That's reassuring, for he's been forgetting things lately. But that particular canoe trip was seared in my skull and apparently his, too. "Well, I told you the same thing I'm going to tell you today," Dad replies. "It's up to you. You've always wanted to do so many things. And you still can. It's always been up to you."

Suddenly, Bill gestures to us. Two other canoeists are circling something underneath the water, fighting to keep the current from sending them downstream. "Here's what we call the lost narrow boat," he says. Below we can make out white oak planks and an iron keel submerged in the river bank. Canal Society members had found the nineteenth-century boat years earlier and pleaded for it to be removed, but the landowner didn't want his farm disturbed. Each year the rushing water robs a bit more of the hull.

The boat was undoubtedly piloted by a slave, I think as we paddle to the take-out. When he wrote about navigation, Jefferson omitted who would be doing the navigating. As a young man, he fancied himself an abolitionist, in theory if not yet in practice, and was embarrassed by his actual occupation, plantation owner. Was Jefferson eager to travel to Europe to run away from his shameful participation in slavery? This is a tricky question to answer. Trying to understand his psyche can be treacherous. His character, John Adams wrote, was like "the great rivers, whose bottoms we cannot see and which make no noise."

But even if I haven't yet figured out Jefferson and his perplexing contradictions, at least his youthful voyage down the Rivanna has taught me a good first lesson about how he liked to travel. He started by dreaming big, poring over all those books on the explorers and drawing inspiration from them. And although he wasn't able to fulfill his plans for a grand European journey as a young man, he devised a trip close to home, a challenge that he was able to accomplish.

I've also learned something else from running this river and spying the lost narrow boat: when you travel, go slow, with your eyes wide open, ready for the unexpected. And don't be afraid to interrogate the motives of even Jefferson himself, my guide.

His Rivanna journey—which he finished unscathed—made a name for him. Jefferson petitioned the legislature to authorize the removal of boulders from the river, garnering support from neighbors. On the heels of this success, he won a seat in the House of Burgesses at the age of 27. Canoeing his river might have been a small dream, but it presaged a lifetime of bigger ones. When he ran for president decades later, he recorded his life accomplishments. Clearing the river was first on the list. Writing the Declaration of Independence was second.

In a roundabout way, his travel down the Rivanna paid off in another way as well. As a new member of the House of Burgesses, he traveled often to the seat of colonial government, Williamsburg. While in the capitol, Jefferson met a young widower, Martha Skelton, and fell in love. They seemed a mismatch. She was a petite brunette with a "lithe and exquisitely formed figure" and a strong personality, as a family member later wrote. Jefferson was then a lanky, awkward, mild-mannered red-head. But they shared a love of both music and the world outside their colony. They both adored the books of Laurence Sterne, who wrote a simultaneously comical and poignant novel about traveling through France.

Their marriage was one of "uncheckered happiness" together, Jefferson wrote. Yet they shared pain as well. She fell ill, often in connection with childbirth (it's unclear today precisely what medical condition she suffered from). Only two of her six children—daughters Martha, nicknamed Patsy in her youth, and Maria, who went by Polly—would survive past age three.

Despite these personal tragedies, Jefferson's star rose. He traveled to the Continental Congress in Philadelphia in 1775 as a Virginia delegate and authored the Declaration of Independence the next year. Yet he repeatedly asked to be released from his post so he could return to tend to Martha, who was in poor health.

In 1776, Congress requested he join Benjamin Franklin in Paris to convince the French to enter the war on the American side. Here was a ticket to the greatest city in the world, for a high public end no less, exactly what the young Jefferson had dreamed of on the banks of his river. But he declined. Instead, he was allowed to resign and go home.

In 1779, Jefferson was elected governor, busying himself with projects for educational and legal reform. Although the Revolution was in its fourth year, Virginia was relatively calm; fighting had occurred mostly to the north and south of his state. But enemy forces landed in the last days of 1780. As Governor Jefferson struggled to call up the militia, the British overran much of the state. In June 1781, dragoons charged up Monticello Mountain and nearly captured him. Jefferson escaped on horseback, taking back roads he had discovered as a young man, fording the James River to safety.

His political opponents charged him with weakness and mismanagement. Incensed by the criticism, Jefferson swore off politics. "I...have retired to my farm, my family and books from which I think nothing will ever more separate me," he wrote. Congress again asked him to travel to Paris; he again declined, remaining with his wife. "I lose an opportunity," he wrote wistfully, "of combining public service with private gratification, of seeing count[ries] whose improvements in science, in arts, and in civilization it has been my fortune to [ad]mire at a distance but never to see."

The Americans and French won at the Battle of Yorktown later that year, ending hostilities. A grand victory—which Jefferson celebrated in private at Monticello. He was "folded...in the arms of retirement," he wrote, his childhood dreams of travel buried deep inside. Jefferson's world would be bound by his little mountain and twisty river, a small life but, with Martha, a happy one.

This quiet domestic existence lasted for a year. He busied himself with his plantings and working on a geography of Virginia that would have made Peter Jefferson proud.

But in the fall of 1782 came the cataclysm. Martha died.

POINT OF VIEW

After another difficult childbirth, Martha Jefferson had spent the summer fighting fever, one from which she never recovered. On her deathbed, too weak to speak, Martha took up pen and paper. "Time wastes too fast," she scrawled, a passage from Sterne's *Tristram Shandy* that she and her husband knew by heart. "The days and hours of it are flying over our heads like clouds...never to return." Jefferson finished the lines, about the dread of an "eternal separation" from a loved one. Later, on another day, these words finally came to pass. He was left in a "stupor," he wrote, "as dead to the world as she was whose loss occasioned it." He stayed in his library for weeks, pacing all night until he would collapse and go to sleep on a cot. Finally, he emerged to ride "incessantly on horseback" over his mountain, with Patsy trailing behind him on what she called these "melancholy rambles."

Hoping to outrun his grief, Jefferson accepted a post as peace commissioner in France but before setting sail, learned that the Treaty of Paris was signed, putting a definitive end to the American Revolutionary War. Good news for the new nation, less so for the aspiring peace commissioner. But he didn't give up. Biding his time until he could go abroad, he won a seat in Congress, meeting in Philadelphia.

From Monticello, the direct road to the capitol lay to the north, yet as he departed in October 1783, Jefferson set out to the west. He was taking the long way: over the Appalachians, then north up the Great Wagon Road through Virginia's Shenandoah Valley to Harpers Ferry, and then northeast across Maryland and Pennsylvania. If he couldn't travel in Europe, at least he would get to know his own country better. Little did he know when he left that fall day, he wouldn't see his home again for over six years.

He had earlier received a simple questionnaire from a French diplomat seeking information on Virginia. This was just the excuse the overachieving Jefferson needed to delve into the geography, people, and political institutions of his home state. Working off notes he had taken out of personal interest over many years "on loose papers, bundled up without order," he produced a full-length manuscript that he entitled *Notes on the State of Virginia*, the most complete natural history of the state ever written. By traveling through the Shenandoah with his scientific instruments, he could collect more data to add to it. As with his Rivanna River journey two decades earlier, then, his travel would be purposeful.

Ours will be as well. Two hundred and thirty years later, Liana and the kids and I set out on his trail.

◆ ◆ ◆

I've spent much of the six months since my canoe trip with Dad studying Jefferson and his world. My mood's noticeably brighter now that I have this mission. I feel recharged at the office, too. Since I now have this other intellectual outlet, this additional path to self-realization, I can better appreciate my work and see its value. We're saving up for a trip abroad next year, and in the meantime I'm traveling in my mind, thrilling to every discovery I make in my research. Finding that my children are eager to join in this quest makes me even happier. Miranda is now six, with sandy brown hair, always cheerful. Nico's three, with dark hair and nonstop energy. Both have inherited my round chipmunk cheeks and inquisitive nature.

Two young explorers on Jefferson's trail.

I deemed them still a little young to go on a full-fledged *Hints* expedition abroad (next spring's trip will be only Liana and me). But in the meantime we've been exploring Jefferson-related sites on the East Coast to better understand how he traveled before arriving on "the vaunted scene of Europe." At Colonial Williamsburg, we took a carriage ride down Duke of Gloucester Street, moving as slowly as Jefferson once did (although I doubt his daughter leaned out to wave to tourists). "I feel very royal," Miranda pronounced. Afterward, I conferred with the wheelwrights at the woodworking shop, who taught me about the carriages that Jefferson favored: a sleek phaeton when he was young, a sturdy landau he designed himself as an old man.

When I was on a separate trip scouting out Jefferson sites in New York City, my favorite moment came when I pulled into a street parking spot in Washington Heights and scattered a flock of pigeons, startling Nico, who shouted "What chicken doing?" His exclamation proved he was neither a pigeon-recognizing city kid nor a chicken-aware country boy but a child of the suburbs. Yet both he and his sister discovered new terrains this past summer, urban and rural, and I wonder what effect all these explorations will have on them as they grow up. Will they fall in love with history and travel as I once did?

Now we're exploring the Shenandoah Valley. I happen to be thirty-nine, the same age as my mentor when he journeyed here in 1783. We first tramped through Grand Caverns, part of Cave Hill, located on the other side of the Appalachians from Monticello. Jefferson wriggled into a different cave in the hill's extensive subterranean networks, drawing a map of it and taking scientific readings that he would add to *Notes on Virginia*. After overcoming their initial fear of the yawning dark entrance, the kids found the array of stalactite, flowstone, and crystals fascinating, especially those named today after characters they knew (Snuffleupagus, the Burger King man).

Today we've arrived on a warm fall day at Harpers Ferry National Historical Park at the northern end of the valley. Here Jefferson had one of his greatest traveling insights, which he described in *Notes on Virginia*. When standing "on a very high point of land," he wrote, "on your right comes up the Shenandoah [River]," alongside a mountain, seeking an opening. "On your left approaches the Potomac, in quest of a passage also. In the moment of their junction they rush together against the mountain, rend it asunder, and pass off to the sea." The "wild and tremendous" foreground contrasts with the distant view of "a small catch of smooth blue horizon, at an infinite distance in the plain country, inviting you, as it were, from the riot and tumult roaring around, to pass through the breach... That way too the road happens actually to lead."

For Jefferson, the view was not only sublime, "worth a voyage across the Atlantic," but instructive. Studying it, he realized that "the mountains were formed first, that the rivers began to flow afterwards," eventually breaking through the rocks and even tearing a mountain "down from its summit to its base." This insight led him to conclude that "this earth has been created in time," that is to say, over time, rather than instantaneously as held by the prevailing interpretation of the Bible. This was Jefferson the traveler at his finest, combining empirical data with lyrical turns of phrase while drawing a greater truth out of the whole.

With this example in mind, the Baxter Expedition is ready for an ascent. A brochure touts a shale formation called Jefferson Rock, accessible from the town via a trail, stating that this is where he stood when he famously viewed the two rivers merging together. "Let's find this rock!" Miranda cries. We follow a series of stone steps and enter a woods of tulip poplars. A train calls in the distance. We're on a hill rising from the point where the two rivers join together; slowly the trail climbs up. It doesn't take long for the second-youngest traveler in our party to change her tune.

"I'm tired," she announces. "Can we go get ice cream now?" From his stroller, Nico seconds the proposal.

"Family rule: history first, treats later," I reply. Liana and I endure the increasingly vocal protests and, after a mercifully short hike, arrive at Jefferson Rock, a slab of grayish stone teetering on top of another, larger one. The setting is gorgeous: fire-red leaves, lazy water rolling far below. A sign confirms that "Jefferson wrote about the view from this rock." Excited, I look for the two rivers crashing together, but although I can see the Shenandoah clearly, I can only make out the Potomac far in the distance. That's odd. The waterways couldn't have changed course that much in two centuries. No, this site must be too far along the Shenandoah River side of this hill and not high enough to provide the right vista.

I'm still turning this disappointment over as we return to the town and encounter two park rangers. I ask them about what we just saw—could there have been some mistake? Was that really where Jefferson witnessed the confluence of the rivers?

The younger one bristles at the question. "There were only a few houses at the time, just Harper's and some warehouses," he says. "So you could see a lot more back then."

"You know, I'm not sure that was it," I persist. "I thought we were too far on the Shenandoah side."

"You need to look when there aren't so many leaves on the trees," the ranger replies defensively. He's clearly not used to visitors questioning one of the park's foundational stories. His white-haired companion has no such qualms. He smiles mischievously and adds, sotto voce, "Of course, the church has just as good a view."

Following this tip, we ascend a flight of stone steps to the old Catholic church and see the rivers coming together as promised—a pleasant view, although not exactly worth a voyage across the Atlantic. (I'll concede that it's worth a climb up some steps.) I notice a nearby two-story building with a balcony, Harper House. I had come across it in my research; it was built by Robert Harper, the town founder, in 1782, and likely where

Jefferson stopped during his visit. Later, I'll find the smoking gun: in an 1809 letter to a friend, Jefferson confirmed that the sight he described could be seen only by ascending the "height back of the tavern." I'll have to remember: don't always believe stories told about a place. When in doubt, check the source materials. Thankfully, Jefferson left a half-century's worth of meticulous records of where he went and what he spent money on.

Floating the Rivanna gave me a good first lesson in traveling like Jefferson: dream up a grand trip, but if you're not ready to take it, find an alternative. Move slowly and curiously, with an open mind. In Harpers Ferry, I've learned how, at his best, he made observations that combine empirical data with memorable descriptions, uncovering hidden truths about the world while he was at it.

To that tall order, I'll add: question received wisdom, even about Jefferson's own doings. I don't care what they told me—that wasn't his rock.

+ + +

When Jefferson arrived in Philadelphia, his first order of duty was tracking down Congress, which had skipped town. Following threatening protests by Revolutionary War veterans demanding their back pay, the legislature decamped to the presumably safer town of Princeton, New Jersey. Jefferson caught up to it there only to watch Congress leave again the next day, this time for the port of Annapolis, Maryland, where it would stay put for six months until it packed up and moved once more.

In 1783, the national Congress was not even the most powerful legislative body in the new nation—collectively, the state assemblies were and would remain so until the Constitution took effect later in the decade. The Articles of Confederation had created a weak national government. As there was no executive branch, Congress coordinated overarching issues itself, appointing a president with little power and a secretary of foreign affairs. The legislative work frustrated Jefferson. "Our body was little numerous but very contentious," he wrote; it sometimes failed to produce a quorum. In the spring of 1784, Jefferson boldly proposed that slavery be abolished in states formed from the Northwest Territory west of the Appalachians; his motion failed by one vote. "Thus we see the fates of millions of unborn hanging on the tongue of one man," he wrote of the missing representative whose voice was needed to pass the motion, "and heaven was silent in that awful moment!"

He himself, though, had brought an enslaved man, Robert Hemings, to serve him in Annapolis and also receive training as a barber. Jefferson held hundreds of other enslaved people—including Robert Hemings's younger siblings James and Sally—on his plantations back in Virginia. Coming across references to his slaveholding in my research always dismays me. Still, my focus is on learning about Jefferson the traveler, not the slaveholder. (Only later will I understand that ignoring the massive role that enslaved people played in nearly every aspect of his life, including his travels, is a mistake, one I will have to try to rectify.)

In May 1784, Jefferson's lifetime of waiting ended. Congress requested that he assist Benjamin Franklin in Paris in negotiating treaties of commerce with other nations. He traveled from Annapolis to Boston, then sailed on July 5 with everything needed for an ocean crossing: questions for the ship's captain on fishing and whaling, a thermometer to take daily readings, a pocket telescope to look for gannets and auks, and a copy of *Don Quixote* to teach himself Spanish on the way. With him came Patsy and his enslaved servant James Hemings.

Jefferson's boyhood dreams were finally coming true. Little did he realize that his long-awaited arrival in Europe would be closer to a nightmare.

＊ CHAPTER FOUR ＊

Paris, Springtime

Their landing was bumpy. Although the Atlantic had been placid, the English Channel was violently choppy and Jefferson's daughter Patsy took ill. After docking in Le Havre on July 31, 1784, less than four weeks after leaving Boston, he found that he couldn't grasp the spoken French of the porters. They ripped him off, charging nearly as much for bringing his baggage from the ship to a hotel as the ocean crossing itself had cost. Incredibly, Jefferson sent James Hemings to ride ahead of their carriage to arrange for hotels along the route to Paris, even though Hemings spoke almost no French.

In Paris, when Jefferson asked for the Hôtel d'Orléans, where wealthy American visitors stayed, he was brought to an establishment of that name on the Right Bank of the Seine. It was an expensive carriage inn, catering to short-term travelers, in the fancy new Palais Royal development. The neighborhood filled with crowds of pleasure-seekers during the day and prostitutes and their clients at night. After nine days, he finally realized he had been taken to the wrong place; the Hôtel d'Orléans he wanted—roomier, quieter, and a third the cost—was on the Left Bank.

Jefferson might have been an impressive traveler back home, but until now he had journeyed only through American states—backwater provinces in comparison to Paris, which considered itself to be the cultural capital of the world. Here he faced greater challenges: a language he couldn't understand, customs he couldn't decipher, and "rascals," as he put it later in *Hints*, preying on unwitting visitors. Unlike in America, there was a wide selection of hotels, taverns, and attractions to spend money on. Guidebooks pointed out where to go and what to avoid, but Jefferson didn't own any yet. He persisted with the trial-and-error method he used back home—with an emphasis on the error. Just because he fancied himself a world traveler didn't mean he was any good at it. Not yet.

The winter of 1784 Jefferson again became ill, attributing his maladies to the "seasoning" all new residents of the capital went through. And he was homesick. Not long after his arrival, he wrote that he couldn't wait to return to Virginia. "I am savage enough to prefer the woods, the wilds, and the independence of Monticello," he added the next year, "to all the brilliant pleasures" of Paris. He encouraged James Monroe to join him abroad: "It will make you adore your own country" even more, he wrote, from its soil to its climate, liberty, people, and customs. Traveling, he concluded, "makes men wiser, but less happy."

But when the sun chased away gray skies in the spring of '85, Jefferson began roaming the city on foot, alone. Leaving his Right Bank three-story house (which he had moved into in October 1784), he trekked up and down the Seine, tucking into forgotten quarters and looking for finds, especially books. "The object of walking," he wrote that year, "is to relax the mind. You should therefore not permit yourself even to think while you walk, but divert your attention by the objects surrounding you." Following these Zen-like perambulations, he felt "perfectly reestablished," his perceptions of the Old World slowly changing.

In his wanderings, he kept returning to the Palais Royal, the site of the hotel mix-up. If there is any one place where Jefferson transformed himself from an amateur to a global traveler, it might well be here. King Louis XVI's rakish cousin Louis-Philippe II had established the neighborhood, adjacent to the Louvre, as an upscale real estate development earlier in the decade. Its arcades were enclosed, a welcome change from filthy streets and careening carriages. Behind the innovative plate-glass fronts of store were furs, leather goods, books, jewelry, paintings, and much more. Prices were fixed; no unseemly bargaining here. The complex had countless cafés and hair salons, gambling dens and museums, gardens filled with strolling musicians, and the finest dining in Paris. It was the place to see and be seen. There were also mimes, but no place is perfect.

TJ gone French, as painted by Mather Brown in 1786.

One of his trips to the Palais Royal ended as embarrassingly as his hotel fiasco had. The smartest man in Virginia, Jefferson was used to trouncing opponents in chess. But at the Salons des Échecs chess club, it took him only minutes to lose to a stranger. He bought a guide to the game from this club but never tried to play there again. He was now a small fish in a very big pond.

When Liana and I arrive in the City of Lights—that metropolis of 2 million Parisians and their poodles, a center of world fashion and gastronomy—we very much are, too. After a year of preparation, now, on this mild spring day, we're ready to begin our *Hints* journey in earnest.

After arriving and checking into a boutique Parisian hotel that was once the home of a Jefferson acquaintance, the playwright Beaumarchais, we taxi to the Palais Royal for lunch at Le Grand Véfour, which dates to 1784. We're ushered inside to a dining room with plush red carpet, no music playing, and only a handful of diners whispering to each other. Brass plaques behind the seats indicate famous past diners, from Napoleon to Victor Hugo to Jean-Paul Sartre. Liana sits where Empress Joséphine once did.

Frugal as ever, I'm worried about the cost. The waiter hands each of us a menu. I look at the prices and almost gasp. "I'm not sure we can afford this," I say to Liana.

"Why, how much is it?"

"What are you talking about? It says it right there. In euros!" I whisper. We finally work out that only my version of the menu includes the prices—the establishment assumed that I was paying and that my female companion didn't need to trouble herself with the cost. They failed spectacularly on that last assumption. Just like I avoid the sight of blood whenever possible, I try to slip high restaurant bills to Liana without reading them, dodging the sense of guilt and worry they bring me. Liana always rolls with it.

"Should we leave now before they bring us anything?" I ask, slightly panicked, attracting quizzical glances from other diners.

"Derek, we came all this way and you said this place has a Jefferson connection. Let's just enjoy the moment."

She has a point. And the Jeffersonian answer to most any question involving money was: yes. For the ambassador, Paris was a nonstop splurge; he blew way past the modest allotment Congress gave him for salary and expenses, paying for personal items and entertaining on his personal credit, absorbing staggering costs.

Our waiter brings us *escargots* and *terrine de fois gras* on fine china to start. He leans over to place the dishes on our table—and I, wanting to show that I'm both a helpful and regular guy at heart, even when at a break-the-bank restaurant, reach up to receive them.

"It is not necessary, monsieur," the waiter says, guiding them to their place himself. Liana shakes her head at my *faux pas*. If I keep up this bumbling, I might not have to worry about the cost—we'll be asked us to leave.

Jefferson had certainly made his share of mistakes at the Palais Royal. But he kept going back there: to shop, attend the theater, view art, visit a wax museum, and especially to dine. He even proposed developing his own enclosed shopping arcade in Richmond, Virginia, which he predicted would be "very highly advantageous to the proprietors, convenient to the town, and ornamental." Sadly, his prospective business partner didn't bite. Although Jefferson pioneered both the French fry and the dollar, he couldn't complete the holy American trinity by also founding the mall.

He also found a bookseller he liked in the Palais Royal. "Every afternoon [he] was disengaged, for a summer or two" prowling the city for books and buying thousands, including many travel narratives. He discussed ideas with new friends in the intellectual salon culture of Paris. And he finished his manuscript on his home state, incorporating the notes he took while traveling in the Shenandoah Valley, with William Short's proofreading assistance. Jefferson turned out a full-fledged, encyclopedic treatment of what he called his "country," publishing *Notes on Virginia*, the only book he ever wrote, in Paris in 1785 and London two years later. I imagine him bringing his finished writings to his printer in the winding medieval streets of the Latin Quarter, only a short walk from Notre-Dame Cathedral, so far from where he started it at his desk in his quiet Virginia home. In his entry on the Rivanna River, he proudly noted that the waterway was "navigable for canoes."

As our dinner progresses, we realize how far we've come from our modest town house in the northern Virginia suburbs, too. Our waiter brings us a rack of lamb in a rich sauce, and succulent scallops, accompanied by a fine Alsatian white and a Burgundy red. After hours of this, he pushes a cart groaning with dozens of cheeses toward us. "You can try them all if you want!" he says, explaining their qualities. We're the last diners left. In this house of formality, he even lets his guard down and gives us some pointers about Paris. We end with complimentary glasses of brandy.

"That was the best meal I've ever had," Liana says, carefully shielding the bill from my view. "What a spectacle. The way they kept bringing us new plates and catered to all our whims."

"We were the center of attention," I say.

"I felt like Joséphine," she replies. I smile and take her hand. Dining exquisitely with your partner on a soft spring day in Paris—we're far from the first couple to discover this experience, but it's one of the great life moments you can have.

Le Grand Véfour has yet another satisfied customer.

If the spring of 1785 brought Jefferson comfort—his illness gone, his adjustment to Paris complete—the next three springs would bring him adventure. He spent March of 1786 exploring England and March through June of 1787 traversing the south of France and Italy. Each time he left Short behind to run the embassy in his absence, Benjamin Franklin having long since returned home. Jefferson was no longer bad-mouthing his new home much. The Old World held temptations and corruption, to be sure, but a grounded man like himself could resist them. And he loved the neoclassical mansion he had moved into on the Champs-Élysées. Jefferson had come full circle: he wanted to extend his stay.

His third and final journey in Europe came most unexpectedly. The ambassador had an emergency to fix: America was broke. Earlier in the decade, French and Dutch bankers had loaned the shaky U.S. government the money it needed to survive. But by February 1788, the Americans had stopped even paying interest. The financiers of Amsterdam finally demanded payment, sending Jefferson into a panic. His country was facing "something like a bankruptcy," he wrote; even the embassy in Paris was running out of funds. Someone needed to renegotiate and buy some time. Yet finances were one of the few things he hadn't mastered. The problem "press[ed] on my mind like a mountain."

Then came a stroke of good luck. The one American diplomat with a head for money, John Adams, was preparing to sail home from London after a decade in France, the Netherlands, and England. Before he departed, protocol required that he take official leave from The Hague, the Dutch political capital, where he still held credentials as an ambassador. Adams, Jefferson learned, was already on his way to this ceremony. If the Virginian could catch up with him and explain the extent of the crisis, surely Adams would find a solution with the Dutch bankers.

Jefferson had only a "very few hours' warning" of his trip, he wrote. But by now he was a veteran traveler, with everything he needed at the ready: his carriage, a small ivory book for taking down travel notes (which, in the evenings, he'd transcribe into a journal, then wipe the ivory clean), maps, a portable copying press for duplicating his letters, a thermometer, a compass. Instead of reading *Don Quixote*, this time he'd pore over maps and guidebooks: a Sancho Panza move.

The passport given to Jefferson by King Louis XVI in 1789.

"Some preparation seems necessary," he wrote once, referencing the need to educate citizens so they could participate in a democracy. He would apply this same sentiment to travel and virtually every other subject he considered. In contrast to his rocky arrival in France four years earlier, this time he had done his homework. As he would advise in *Hints* a few months later, before leaving, he first purchased a map of the country he planned to visit, the Netherlands. He now knew that, as he'd put it in *Hints*, "on arriving in a town, the first thing to do" is to buy a more detailed city plan and a book of the place's "curiosities." Never again would he be fleeced by porters, stay in the wrong hotel, or fail to understand an urban layout. Not to say that Jefferson held inflexibly to a scripted itinerary; he'd change his schemes based on the weather or what he learned from innkeepers and other travelers. But he'd arrive with an idea of how to get there and where to stay: lessons for us to learn from.

✦ ✦ ✦

Our stomachs bloated and minds content, we amble over to a bench in a courtyard surrounded by the arcades of the Palais Royal. From here we'll walk through the nearby Tuileries Garden to what is now called the Place de la Concorde. Jefferson strolled the mile from his Champs-Élysées home to that square often, counting how many steps it took him (820 "double steps"). I'm about to do the same, quite literally walking in my hero's footsteps and, although his house was torn down long ago, see where he lived and wrote *Hints to Americans Traveling in Europe*.

But first we need to let that meal settle. Liana explores a fashion boutique while I sit in the courtyard, still in my dinner jacket, and pull out a small red journal (made from paper, not ivory) to capture what we've experienced, to record moments of this trip of personal discovery.

What to do with these notes? Jefferson turned his jottings into his only book. But I'm neither an expert traveler nor a trained writer. Do I need to be, to create something lasting out of my journey?

Liana strolls up to find me scribbling away. "You look so happy," she says.

CHAPTER FIVE

The Earth Belongs Always to the Living

GULP DOWN CULTURE

"When you are doubting whether a thing is worth the trouble of going to see, recollect that you will never again be so near it."

Hints to Americans

Hints begins in Amsterdam, a bustling port city of 250,000 in 1788. On the quays, dockworkers unloaded ginseng, mahogany, books, stockfish, calico, and Mocha coffee, flotsam and jetsam washed up from all over the world. Boats carried the goods to warehouses, gliding along the concentric rings of canals, the odor of tar, pitch, cinnamon, and tobacco in the air. Captains with Javanese monkeys celebrated the end of their trips in taverns, while outside dissidents, schemers, merchants, and princes moved in a cacophonous yet ordered riot.

Jefferson visited in March of that year on a diplomatic mission. But it wasn't all work; he also wandered the city in search of discoveries. What did the Dutch do that no one else did? For one thing, design objects ingeniously and practically. He noted how canal boats eased their way over locks, bridges swiveled, windows opened to allow air but not rain in, tables folded to small dimensions, aviaries permitted birds to stretch their legs in a small courtyard, and outdoor lanterns lit both the street and the main room of a house at the same time. He sketched the most beautiful house in town, ate oysters, bought a waffle maker, and sailed up the Zaan River past windmills. When the bells of West Church played a catchy melody, he transcribed the notes. As a traveler, he was never more on top of his game.

Arriving here, Liana and I have our work cut out to live up to this example, and I've pulled some of Jefferson's practical, "how-to" travel advice out of his guide to help us. Ambitiously, I also want to cover several of *Hints'* Objects of Attention at once. We locate our accommodations, an Airbnb by the old walled botanical garden, as our anticipation builds about what we'll discover here. A cozy restaurant, a treasured memento, a new friend? Or will we remember crowds, lost luggage, sold-out attractions? Travel is the pulling of a slot; that's part of its allure.

"Go to the top of a steeple to have a view of the town and its environs," advises *Hints*. "Walk round the ramparts when there are any." That's a Jeffersonian technique: first gazing down on a city like a hawk, then getting to know it at ground level. We ascend the tower of Zuiderkerk, one of Amsterdam's oldest churches, overlooking Jefferson's own hotel. Below us, cyclists stream past brick town houses along the canals. Here's a city to make our own.

Down below, we stumble into a small celebration of the eve of King's Day. We grab plastic cups of beer, listen to a band, and buy an orange flag. In Rotterdam, fifty miles from Amsterdam, Jefferson encountered a predecessor of this festival, the celebration of the birthday of the prince of the House of Orange. The fireworks were "the most splendid I had ever seen," he wrote, "and the roar of joy the most universal I had ever heard."

But the partying came with political overtones. Each province in the Netherlands had a legislative body, but many posts in both the assembly and executive branch were effectively hereditary. Rotterdammers were firm supporters of the House of Orange, a dynasty that had dominated this semi-democratic form of government for centuries. In 1783, however, a faction of Dutch calling themselves the Patriots, inspired by the American Revolution, called for a true republic, winning majorities in Amsterdam and other cities. Aided by Prussian soldiers, the prince struck back in 1787 and reoccupied most of the country by force, overwhelming the "legitimate authorities" of the country, as Jefferson put it. The ambassador fretted that the resurgent Orangeists might retaliate against the Patriots, who included many of the financiers. Despite the kerfuffle over the loans, Jefferson knew his country needed the reformist bankers' support.

The day after the celebration, Jefferson found Adams, who quickly resolved the financial issues. The Dutch capitalists were filled with "immeasurable avarice," Adams observed; they preferred to keep lending money (for two additional years, on new terms) rather than pushing the United States into bankruptcy. "[B]y this journey, our credit was secured," Jefferson wrote, satisfied. Crisis averted, he celebrated by securing a private loan for himself. Now he could experience Amsterdam as a traveler—and shopper. Although he worried about America's long-term financial solvency (not to mention his own), Jefferson had a proposed solution: debts should be canceled each generation, allowing people to start over, not burdened by the mistakes of their elders. "The earth belongs always to the living," he proclaimed in 1789.

Jefferson wasn't the only one wandering the city. Over the last century, young, aristocratic males—often British—had followed a loose itinerary called the Grand Tour from northern Europe to Italy. They spent their days inspecting art, their nights reveling, and their mornings nursing hangovers and complaining about the locals. They returned with souvenirs: Roman relics, paintings of themselves in front of ruins, and, sometimes, syphilis. While pilgrims and explorers had long roamed the world, these men were among the first "tourists"—a new coinage—traveling to broaden their horizons while simultaneously enjoying themselves. A small industry catered to their needs; guidebooks provided information on hotels and destinations.

Jefferson wasn't interested in a standard journey, even if he rubbed elbows with Grand Tourists along the way. Americans should visit quarries, canal locks, and the homes of farm laborers. Don't just smile at Roman ruins but measure the circumference of their columns. *Hints* demands engagement. That's where his eight Objects of Attention come in: challenges for travelers, not tourists.

Having scoured *Hints*, I've found a promising Object to explore here. Although Jefferson begrudgingly gave them their own Object of Attention (Number Six), he deemed painting and sculpture to be art forms "too expensive for the state of wealth among us." *Hints* proclaims that "it would be useless therefore and preposterous for us to endeavor to make ourselves connoisseurs in those arts. They are worth seeing, but not studying." Not a quote I remember from my survey History of Art class.

Yet, a light, superficial understanding of a subject? I can handle that. Plus, Liana loves paintings, so we enter the castlelike gates of the Rijksmuseum. We spend hours studying the Dutch past preserved on canvas: fish frozen in mid-flop, ruddy-faced skaters gliding, a fleet of ships eternally entering a harbor. *The Night Watch*, the fourteen-foot-tall masterpiece of a militia preparing to patrol, transfixes us. "This is so Rembrandt," Liana whispers. "Look how he brings the scene to life and contrasts it with darkness. He captured it the way we would today with a phone. It's just crazy."

Jefferson probably saw the painting, which then hung in Amsterdam's

City Hall, but wasn't a fan of Rembrandt, or of Rubens, whose work he considered too florid. Jefferson liked his art practical, conveying historic or biblical scenes directly, without fuss. We debate his tastes at the museum restaurant over tangy mackerel and beets. "Should we keep going?" I ask Liana as we end with a brownie with meringue and celery-root ice cream (rich but not overly sweet).

"No, I'm having art fatigue," she replies. "I just want to walk a bit." *Hints* advises travelers to see things that you might never have the chance to see again, while acknowledging that you sometimes have to take a break. "But there is an opposite extreme too," Jefferson cautioned. "That is, the seeing too much. A judicious selection is to be aimed at." He detested private guides, who "lead you through all the little details in their possession, which will load the memory with trifles, fatigue the attention and waste...your time," thinking that the more they show, the better tip they'll get. Liana and I only have an audio wand, but the point is a good one and we leave.

In the park outside the museum, protesters chant against climate change. We talk with a young woman about why the Dutch are so concerned about the issue. (Uh, because the country is flat as a pancake and next to the North Sea.) Jefferson would have enjoyed this experience as much as the art galleries themselves. "In the great cities, I go to see what travelers think alone worthy of being seen," he wrote, "but I make a job of it, and generally gulp it all down in a day." What he really wanted was a taste of real life.

So do we. And where else to find it than on King's Day, when the whole city takes to the street.

MEET THE LOCALS

"The...public markets to be frequented; at these you see the inhab-
itants from high to low."

Hints to Americans

"Do you want an orange garland? I'll give it to you for a euro because
you look cheap."

Of course I want one; it matches my shirt. Liana is already decked
out like the love child of a pumpkin and a carrot, but she buys a pair of
oversize plastic orange sunglasses from the street seller. "Today we will
call them rainglasses," he says; it's heavily cloudy. It's not even 10 a.m.,
but similarly colored partygoers are already out, celebrating the House
of Orange—a family which was politically powerful in Jefferson's time
and, since 1815, has served as the Netherlands' monarchs. Not only will
there be music, drinking, and pot—lots of pot—but the city turns into a
giant yard sale, with a quarter of residents laying out junk and treasures
alike on blankets. Private sales of goods are normally strictly regulated,
but the authorities make an exception on King's Day.

Jefferson wanted to blend in, just like we do. His official business in
Amsterdam concluded, he didn't assert his rank as a diplomat; on the
road, he presented himself only as a "foreign traveler." Jefferson wanted
to know how people really lived and understand their worldview. To
avoid standing out, he swallowed his distaste for the royalists and wore
an orange ribbon in public.

But it wasn't all sociology for him; as he poked around Amsterdam,
he also looked for deals. I walk around with Jefferson's shopping list, curious if I can find the same goods today: hyson tea, a letterpress, paper,
quills, sealing wax, sheet music, toothpicks, ironware, a waffle iron,
books, maps, and porcelain cups (which he smuggled back to Paris

without paying duties). We start in Jordaan, an old working-class neighborhood colonized by hipsters. Guys in orange bathrobes drink beer, a trio of locals dressed as giraffes amble by, a Muslim woman in a flashingly orange head scarf sells knickknacks. The geriatric couple in front of us abruptly and inspirationally enter a sex shop. Below us, canal boats pump techno music while a man drops his trousers and urinates into the water.

On the Herengracht canal, we see a sign proclaiming "Love Is Gin." I buy a glass to test the philosophy and chat with the seller sitting behind the table while Liana tries on his wife's old clothes, which hang from a rack. He works in marketing for a multinational ice cream company by day, he tells me; at night he returns to his seventeenth-century town house, which shares old beams with that of the neighboring town house, once the home of Jefferson's banker.

The only thing we didn't see on King's Day was the king.

"Why is today so popular?" I ask. "Why is everyone selling things?"

"It's the only day all this buying and selling is allowed!" he laughs. From there, we wander down to Bloemenmarkt, the flower market, with bulbs in all shades. (Jefferson would plant striped and ruffled parrot tulips at Monticello.) In front of where his hotel once stood, a man sells one-hitters to people dressed in tiger suits. A sign reads "Just a Fun Time, Not a Riot."

We follow the sound of a thumping rhythm to a side street where a group of revelers dances to a conga band. Liana immediately starts shaking it. "This is great!" she shouts over the music. "These people are from the islands! I feel right at home." She misses her homeland so much that whenever she finds an expression of Caribbean culture she latches on to it. "Who would have thought we'd find all this in a cold country!"

"Do you realize we've seen so many people drinking and partying but no one fighting all day long?" she asks after we leave, squeezing my hand. Nor have we exchanged a cross word with each other, even when lost. Maybe it's the good feeling in the air. More likely, the weed. But this is controlled Bacchanalia, staying within a semblance of order and politeness. Even when accepting craziness, the Dutch demand mutual respect.

Weary from all the miles we've walked, we collapse into a café by the Keizersgracht canal. Jefferson downed fifty oysters in one epic night near here; we opt for a bowl of mussels. *Hints* recommends drinking local, as taverns often overcharge for foreign wines, so we order Heinekens.

Object of Attention Eight is Courts (the royal kind, not courts of law), and here *Hints* doesn't pull any punches, proclaiming that "[a] slight acquaintance with them will suffice to show you that, under the most imposing exterior, they are the weakest and worst part of mankind." But my slight acquaintance with the Dutch monarchy—through attending this festival—hasn't given me that notion. The struggles between the Orangeists and Patriots seem long-forgotten. We've seen occasional pictures of the king on display, but this festival appears to mostly be an excuse to party and show some national pride.

Will these impressions suffice? What should a Jeffersonian do here— conduct a survey of people's views?

"That's my third penis of the day!" says Liana as a man pees in full view of the diners.

Maybe another time.

✦ ✦ ✦

We've found all of the items Jefferson bought here, including sheet music in a store bursting with instruments, mysterious maps, hyson tea (which he loved for its "strength and flavor"), even quills. Amsterdam's still got it. We celebrate with gooey *stroopwafels*, chocolate oozing out of the wafers. The waffle iron was Jefferson's most popular purchase from this trip— Monticello cooks would serve up waffles for years to come. Liana and I return into the orange scrum and buy a few things ourselves: a shimmering sweater for Miranda, a stuffed lion for Nico, and a wooden candelabra.

But there was a darker side to Jefferson's shopping spree. He purchased on credit, yet was already deep in debt. Although he talked up the cause of abolition, how would he ever free the people he enslaved, the source of his income, if he kept sinking further into the red? He struggled with the contradiction. "I am miserable until I shall owe not a shilling," he wrote in 1786, "the moment that shall be the case I shall feel myself at liberty to do something for the comfort of my slaves." That moment had not come. The persons he had enslaved must have been worrying what their master was up to in Europe; if he died, or faced financial collapse, they might be sold and families separated.

Jefferson returned from Amsterdam to Paris in May 1788, to find John Rutledge, Jr., and Thomas Shippen waiting for him. Rutledge was the twenty-one-year-old son of a prominent South Carolinian planter and ex-governor; in his portrait, he has what looks to be a bouffant haircut, shaggy muttonchops, protruding nose, and slightly goofy expression. He had just passed the bar in his home state of South Carolina and come to Europe to meet up with his friend Thomas, the twenty-three-year-old son of Jefferson's doctor back home, who was studying law in England. They were planning a Grand Tour—and who better to ask where to go than the American ambassador.

Jefferson liked nothing better than giving travel advice; he reassured Dr. Shippen that his son would return home "charged, like a bee, with the honey of wisdom." But the press of work delayed him. Finally, their time and budget slipping away, the two young men reluctantly departed. William Short hoped to join them once Jefferson had caught up on things.

William Short, following Hints *to a Roman temple.*

In June, the ambassador finally committed his travel pointers to paper, claiming they were "scribble[d] very hastily and undigested." Given the great French and Dutch roads and postal system, it took only a few days for the guide to reach Amsterdam. And a good thing, too. For, *Hints*-less, Rutledge and Shippen were getting into all kinds of trouble.

They had gotten bad advice from the Marquis de Lafayette to travel in military uniform, even though the young men were civilians. The gambit worked at first; they were saluted and shown deference. But suspicious Rotterdammers almost threw them in jail for spying. Like Jefferson had, the Boys joined the animated crowds of royalists who forced everyone to wear an orange ribbon. When the German ambassador refused, Shippen reported, a mob nearly threw him into the water until the prince permitted him to walk around "unoranged."

Without direction, Shippen and Rutledge came up with their own Object of Attention: Partying. "Temptations…seduced us from our original plan," Shippen wrote. They went to Spa, in what is now Belgium, a resort town most certainly not on Jefferson's itinerary. For centuries, Spa had welcomed visitors with warm baths, gaming houses, and optional "services" not offered at reputable spas today. The duo was fulfilling Jefferson's travel fears: that a young male abroad would fall prey to the "glare of pomp and pleasure" and acquire "a fondness for European luxury and dissipation." Worst of all, he wrote (misogynistically enough), an unwary American might be "led by the strongest of all the human passions into a spirit for female intrigue," even toward "whores destructive of his health." Rutledge and Short later corresponded about the hazards of catching venereal disease while on the road.

Hints, then, came not a moment too soon. After receiving it in Spa (forwarded from Amsterdam), Rutledge thanked Jefferson, telling him how much he "prized" it and promising they "shall leave this heavenly place the day after tomorrow." Shippen pledged to record his own travel notes in the same "style and manner" as the guide. "Your advice on the subject of our future travels appears to me so excellent," he wrote back, "that it must be something very extraordinary which can prevent me from pursuing it."

A week later, the Boys were still luxuriating in the baths.

KEEP MOVING

"You shall hear from me on the road."

Jefferson to Short, leaving Amsterdam, March 29, 1788

Instead of heading back to Paris through Belgium, Jefferson sailed south on a flat-bottomed, square-rigged *schuyt* to the medieval city of Utrecht. This was one of his favorite travel hacks, returning via a different route to discover new places. *Hints* recommends the "remarkable pleasantness" of Utrecht's canals, so Liana and I clamber aboard a vessel moored in its old town. Mechanical Arts, Object of Attention Two, mentions boats as an example of "things necessary in America." I hope to get a flavor for how this one works on these waterways.

"Welcome, welcome," says the captain—a man with a white beard, square jaw, and hawklike nose—and we soon set off. He launches the long canalboat, sharing observations as he goes, first in his native tongue, then in halting English for us, the only passengers who aren't Dutch. "This is the old course of the River Rhine," he says as we pass under a bridge. "The water is coming from Switzerland. They dammed the river because farmers were not happy with the overflowing. So the main river now goes in an arc to Rotterdam."

We glide along past old warehouses. I'm glad we're traveling slowly. Travel has changed so much since *Hints*—Jefferson never even set foot in a train. Today, autos, planes, television, the internet, and a thousand other innovations have brought the world closer than ever before. But our powers of concentration and observation seem to have deteriorated as a result. When do we have the chance to putter along at four miles per hour, truly looking at what's around us?

"In this area were found, and you still find, artists and book writers," the captain tells us "It's very special." He points out the brick sculptures on the canal walls, each illustrating a trade. "This one is of a woman selling fish, because this was a fish market. Up there is a fireman, where the fire insurance was sold." We drift past a stone baker holding bread, a blacksmith hammering away, and even a child holding a plate of food, indicating the presence of an orphanage.

The old city slowly turns into countryside, with fluttery apple blossoms and sheep looking at us curiously. If it weren't for the thatched farmhouses I might think I was back on the Rivanna. "Here they have left the area wild, as it was before the dykes," he explains. "There are little pools—these are interesting for animals. Dozens of white geese have nests here." We dock for lunch at an island with a sprawling restaurant, the air redolent of pancake syrup. The skipper tells me of his days working in an industrial plant. Semi-retired, he's finally found his true love: slowly working his way down this river and back up it again. "I count the ducklings each morning," he says proudly and points out a beautiful old beech. "I'm in love with that tree. They said ten years ago it would be gone in five years. And it's still here."

When we're back on the water, a wiry Dutch passenger with curly blond hair asks if he can take the wheel and the captain happily obliges. The amateur steers true for about ten minutes, then hands it back over, having made it look easy. I think back to my canoeing history with Dad; can't I keep a boat straight? I request a turn and the captain consents, wandering off to chat with other voyagers.

At first, the boat seems to steer itself; we cruise straight past scenes of bucolic splendor. I'm so glad we've come here; this is exactly the kind of experience I dreamed of. Then a canoeist comes around the bend. "Pass him on the left," the captain calls out nonchalantly. But swiveling the wheel sends the boat toward the bank. I yank the helm the other way, overcorrecting, pointing us directly toward the now ashen-faced paddler. Finally, I stabilize things and pass him on the right.

This no longer is a pleasure cruise; I'm suddenly aware of the damage my lack of expertise can do with a thirty-foot boat. I lurch along, hoping for the captain to relieve me. A duck skitters in front of us, left, then right, then flying away when it can't figure out where I'm going. Ahead of us is a bridge with a nightmare in its shadows: a flotilla of canoeists. My anxiety spikes. I zigzag my way through them, somehow avoiding carnage.

"I'll take it now, skipper," the captain says kindly, and I slink back to my seat. In letting me steer for as long as I did, he's taken the notion of Dutch tolerance to the extreme. A few passengers applaud, perhaps for my bravery, more likely out of relief that I've stopped. I sidle up to the other amateur pilot. "That was harder than it looks," I say, looking for sympathy.

"It was OK," he replies.

"What do you do, anyways?"

"Oh, I'm a boatbuilder."

The captain guides us back into Utrecht, past more carvings on the canal, each one illustrating a chosen vocation. If he had his own carving, it would be of him piloting his boat, counting ducklings, and checking in on his beech tree, for he's found his calling. I envy him, as I'm still searching for mine.

+ + +

Somewhat paradoxically, a state of constant motion can lead you to introspection. Left alone with your thoughts, confronted with new experiences, you might come back a changed person if you're open to the possibilities. While on the road, Jefferson wrote to a friend about a night spent in an inn filled with "noise, dirt, and disorder." On reflection, he realized the beauty in a moment when a traveler with "all his effects contained in a single trunk, all his cares circumscribed by the walls of his apartment, unknown to all, unheeded, and undisturbed, writes, reads, thinks, sleeps, just in the moments when nature and the movements of his body and mind require." In this "little cell," Jefferson understood "how few are our real wants, how cheap a thing is happiness, how expensive a one pride." His letter echoed a scene in *Tristram Shandy*, the fictional travel narrative that he and Martha had loved. Now he was living out these dreams himself.

Once the Boys wrenched themselves away from the pleasures of Spa, they, too, began a journey of transformation. The sheepish Shippen assured Jefferson he spent "so long on top of [a] steeple," taking in the view as his mentor wanted him to. Despite Jefferson's advice to "see, not study" paintings and statuary, the young man, making up for lost time, spent an entire day in the Dusseldorf museum recommended in *Hints*— even prevailing on the custodian to lock him in there when the worker left on an errand. While Shippen appreciated the Flemish works on display, he fell in love with the "delicacy" and "inexpressible softness" of the Italian tableaux. "Thus you see Sir," he wrote to Jefferson, "I am become an Italian before I have reached Italy."

As the Boys made their way south through Germany, William Short got permission to join them. Later in the trip, he wrote enthusiastically to Jefferson about the Italian paintings he viewed and the "different shades of perfection" of each one. These letters helped changed Jefferson's mind on the possibilities of art. In Paris, Jefferson purchased a copy of a canvas by the Dutch artist Goltzius and commissioned others from Italy that hang in Monticello's parlor today.

I love the stories I've uncovered about the Boys' adventures out on the roads with *Hints*. They were still in their twenties, the ideal time for personal growth and change. I even feel a little jealous of them— just as I still feel wistful when I think back to my time at UVA, when I was immersed in history, and my year abroad in France living with the unexpected. Back then I read and wrote and hopped on trains when I felt like it, loving every minute.

Enough. Those thoughts always leave me frustrated. Here in Amsterdam, we've had an unforgettable time. I've found Jefferson's practical travel advice—to "gulp down" culture, meet the locals, and keep exploring rather than getting bogged down in any one place—helpful. But although I've learned a bit about Dutch paintings, royalty, and boating, I've also discovered the difficulties in grasping an unfamiliar subject when you're just passing through. At Harpers Ferry, Jefferson, the master traveler, lyrically offered up insights about the very origins of the world. My observations of stoned, urinating partygoers don't quite compare.

As a Jeffersonian with training wheels, I conclude, it's time for a course correction. I won't attempt to follow *Hints'* itinerary from start to finish, trying to find everything Jefferson recommended along the way. That would stretch me too thin. Instead, during my next trip (in a year's time, to places still to be determined), I'll just pick one theme and dig deeper into it. I'll still visit spots that Jefferson recommended, but will take more leeway in crafting my own itinerary based on the subject in question.

Before leaving Amsterdam we visit the Noordermarkt, a sprawling market with cheese, old records, clothes, and a book stand. To my surprise, it prominently displays a paperback copy of *Tristram Shandy* by Laurence Sterne, which I haven't read yet.

"You should look for the blank page," a Dutch customer tells me as I thumb through it.

"Why the blank page?"

"Ah, you must read the book to find out!"

"And the marble page!" the seller chimes in. "This is one of the classics of English literature. It's mind-boggling. It was the first postmodern book; then that style went away. We don't learn from the past enough."

I buy it and start leafing through it in a café while Liana finishes her shopping. Maybe this is a sign. Sterne's comical book, based in part on his own travels, inspired Jefferson to dream big; Jefferson, in turn, inspired me. Their collective travel reflections, cast into the world centuries ago, washed up in the Rivanna River, the port of Amsterdam, and a million other places, voyaging still.

Why not write a book about my own trips? You never know where it might wind up. Whatever the obstacles, this is my journey, and only I can record the moments of my path on it. Perhaps that's the missing piece in my search for my true calling. It's not just the places and history embedded in *Hints* and Jefferson's travel journals that speak to me, it's shaping these lived experiences into a story—my story.

Jefferson didn't want people encumbered by the debts and errors of the past. Nor should I feel burdened by whatever regrets I have about choices made years ago. So what if I didn't launch into a lifetime of history and travel after college? I'm here now, notebook in hand, embracing the pursuit. This is my time. As Jefferson said, the earth belongs always to the living.

CHAPTER SIX

Rambles through the Vineyards

THE MOSTLY SOBER MONKS OF BURGUNDY

Emerging from behind stone arches, the monks enter into the great room, resplendent in scarlet and gold-tinged robes, medals dangling impressively around their neck. I squint at my program. Oh, they're actually members of the Confrérie des Chevaliers de Tastevin, a group of amateur lovers of Burgundy who like to dress up and hold ceremonies. Fake monks. Yet another item to add to the long list of things I don't understand about wine.

This charity auction is certainly in an evocative place, the Château du Clos de Vougeot, where monks made wine from the Middle Ages to the French Revolution. A gentleman in an elegant suit announces the barrel of wine he's auctioning off. Although everything's in French, a language I understand, it all sounds Greek to me. A wine being sold, I learn, has a robe with flavors of resin and tar. Is that a good thing?

A small candle burns, functioning as a sort of timer while attendees raise their hands. It goes out after less than a minute. The auctioneer solemnly lights a second one; hands wave again. As the third candle is extinguished, the auctioneer nods at the highest bidder, who now possesses a medieval-looking oak barrel in exchange for around 5,000 euros.

"I hope he likes it," says my father, sitting next to me. Mom hushes us so we can watch the next bid.

Why did he pay so much? And why does another barrel of wine, which began life "friendly" but became more structured as it aged, go for even more? Everything seems as foreign as if I've been dropped in the middle of a ceremony of an unknown religion.

I don't have a clear idea yet on how to approach wine, our marathon notwithstanding. The few times I've tried swilling, sniffing, and spitting, I've felt self-conscious. Where are the notes of quince or leather or pencil shavings? What I really need is a Wine for Dummies course, but instead here I am in Burgundy, a three-hour drive southeast of Paris, on the other side of the country from Bordeaux. Talk about starting at the top—my wine education has begun in two of the most prestigious and complex oenological regions in the world. It's like signing up for an intro to physics class and finding out the lecturer is Albert Einstein.

My parents are most unexpected winetasting companions. There was no wine on the table in our Arkansas mobile home when I was little. Dad, square jawed but soft-spoken, had grown up in Oklahoma with sweet tea and Bud. Mom, bookish and sincere, was from San Francisco, with hard-drinking parents; I never saw her touch the stuff. After Dad got a job as a civilian at the Pentagon when I was six, our family fortunes improved. Now eating out—still a rare occasion for us back then—meant Red Lobster rather than McDonald's. Today, in their retirement, wine does appear at their meals. Their preferred winemaker: Trader Joe's Red Blend; their favorite vintage: whatever's on the shelf.

But I give them credit for bringing me here. In the year since Liana and I visited Amsterdam, I read up even more on Jefferson. Yet other demands pressed on my time, too: buying a new house, moving the kids to a new school, tackling work assignments. Despite my resolve, my momentum on this project was slipping a little. More troubling, I still didn't have a clear idea as to what I wanted to do in my next segment of *Hints*.

My parents knew of my interest in returning to France, though, and when they planned a trip of their own to Burgundy, Mom offered me a free ticket to join them as their travel companion and interpreter—just like I had been all those years ago when they visited me during my year studying abroad. Afterward, I could meet up with Liana for a short excursion of our own. The more I considered it, the more I liked this plan. And having learned from my last experience, I figured that one subject to investigate per trip was plenty. In Burgundy there was no question what it would be.

Although wine was not a full-fledged Object of Attention in *Hints*, it was a running theme in the guide, which lists thirteen specific varieties to investigate. Wine was important to Jefferson, and I want to figure out why. Drinking seems fun, if not frivolous, and as far as I know, Jefferson was neither. Yet he spent an inordinate amount of time puzzling out wine's mysteries.

Like everything else he was interested in, Jefferson sought to learn all he could about wine. He didn't just take a bottle or two home from his own travels; since middlemen often cheated the consumer, Jefferson made direct contacts with producers so he could import his favorites later. He dreamed of American farmers growing these European grape varieties, jump-starting a new industry. "We could, in the United States, make as great a variety of wines as are made in Europe: not exactly of the same kinds, but doubtless as good," he wrote.

Once he became a wine expert, he considered how he could change American's relation to the drink. Virginians thought nothing of downing shots of peach brandy each day—before breakfast. They had to drink some kind of alcohol after all; untreated water carried diseases, although the reason why it did so (bacteria) was not well understood. Even children drank watered-down beer or cider with breakfast. The main wine consumed was sweet, fortified Madeira, over 20 percent alcohol.

"The delicacy and innocence" of French and Italian wines, he wrote, "will change the habit from the coarse and inebriating kinds" known to his countrymen. Unlike Americans, the French "do not terminate the most sociable meals by transforming themselves into brutes." To that end, he resolved to promote lighter European wines, serving them at the President's House and Monticello his entire life, campaigning for low tariffs when they were imported and talking them up to anyone who would listen. "No nation is drunken," he wrote, somewhat counterintuitively, "where wine is cheap." Only when prices were reasonable would the middle class choose wine, and in moderation, over the "poison of whisky."

Jefferson developed his own classification of the four flavors that appealed to him and his winey followers: dry, sweet, acidic, and silky, with the last of these meaning dry with just a touch of sweetness. He sometimes also enjoyed "rough," or tannic, wines himself. And he dreamed of a style of wine which he never did find in Europe: rough yet sweet. It all adds up to six possibilities for the American palate—which I'd be hard-pressed to accurately distinguish right now.

Perhaps watching these wine experts do their thing will help. So here we are, looking at candles burn down and buyers mysteriously drop thousands of euros on wine that used to be friendly and now tastes like fur.

Another candle extinguished, another sale made, a new barrel announced. I look to my right. To my horror, Dad's hand slowly, insistently creeps higher.

"Dad!" I hiss, grabbing the offending hand. We're here to observe, not pay thousands of euros for a barrel full of wine we can't truly appreciate anyway. I had just instructed him not to bid on anything.

Both Mom and I had noticed how Dad's memory was going. Not

too bad, but noticeable. Even if this trip doesn't bring me expertise in wine, it's a chance to better understand how Dad is doing. This latest near-mishap proves how much I'm needed here. And I wonder, again, if I, too, will face memory problems in older age—another reason to make the most of the time I'm given.

But he just laughs in a low voice. "That got a rise out of you," he drawls, chuckling at his joke.

The candle goes out. We're not going home with that barrel of wine, thank God. Yet there are plenty of surprises to come.

Jefferson's Tasting Notes: Red Burgundy

- *Flavor profiles:* Dry; Chambertin, Vosne, and Vougeot "the strongest," Volnay "the lightest"
- *Pairs with:* duck and "good wheat bread"
- *Enjoy:* in the shadow of an abbey

Burgundy does not cater to the casual tourist; few wineries offer tasting rooms open to the general public the way they do in, say, California. So we sample local vintages in shops and restaurants, drinking smooth wines—even a newbie like me can tell that these are good, tasting faintly of berries. We pass an afternoon in a museum filled with weathered barrels, old presses, and displays on the history of these vineyards.

Although we see no more monks, real or otherwise, after Clos de Vougeot, we're spending our sojourn in Burgundy constantly in their shadow. The candlelit auction gave me the impression that winemaking was spiritual, esoteric, filled with secrets. At the museum, I learn how monks had pioneered a new approach to grape cultivation that was more scientific than mystical. The Cistercian monks of Burgundy discovered that to make good wine, you had to understand soil, climate, and topology. Over the centuries they recorded which grapes performed better on which plots, selecting for the best results. Some said they were so obsessed with the qualities of the soil that they would pick up a clump of dirt and taste it.

These monks pioneered the concept of *terroir*, the effect of geography on taste. Among other finds they made was that pinot noir was the preferred grape for reds in their region and chardonnay for whites. Following their lead, Duke Philip the Bold of Burgundy declared the grape Gamay, a higher-yielding but less noble competitor, to be a "vile and disloyal" plant, banishing it from his duchy to maintain standards.

Only a few years after Jefferson's visit, the monks' estate was nationalized during the French Revolution and sold off. Today the twelve holy hectares that the monastery once controlled have eighty separate owners. It's like that throughout Burgundy—hundreds of different proprietors, most with small acreages. This system couldn't be more different from the sprawling landed estates of Bordeaux, each its own fancy brand; here it's the descendants of peasants who are in charge. Burgundies are plenty expensive and exclusive, but they show off more variety and funk than Bordeaux—they're more Greenwich Village than Upper East Side.

We spend happy days making these discoveries. Each night we recap our adventures over dinner at the house where we're renting rooms, with wine pairings offered by our host, Jean-Paul, a tall and lanky man with a kind face. But although we return there each day, Dad can't find the way. "Where am I going?" he asks every few minutes behind the wheel.

His voice sounds as lost as he is. I'm surprised and confused by this recent change. Mostly, I want to stop the car and hug him and tell him it's going to be OK, but it's clearly not something he wants to talk about yet. We've always been close, our canoe trips just one thing we shared among hundreds. There were the countless afternoons he threw me batting practice as a kid, Saturdays he played board games with my sister and me, nights spent cooking special meals for the family. I don't want to lose him.

Toward the end of our stay, over duck *à l'orange* served by Jean-Paul, we review our wine expedition to date. We've enjoyed our share of Burgundies, but something seems missing. What would Jefferson do?

When he traveled here in 1787, he wrote that he rode an old horse, "put a peasant on another and rambled through their most celebrated vineyards, going into the houses of the laborers, cellars of the *vignerons*, and mixing and conversing with them as much as I could." He mapped Burgundy, noting where reds and whites came from. Jefferson's advice for someone on a fledgling trip of wine discovery was clear, then: start with the grape itself. But to visit vineyards there today you need an in.

"Maybe Jean-Paul can help," Mom suggests. He's already showered us with attention, so I hate to impose further. But as he serves us brandy-washed Chambertin cheese, I mention my interest in seeing grapes in action.

"Of course! All you have to do is ask. My brother Marc owns a small vineyard, you see," Jean-Paul says cheerfully. "I will give him a call and make the arrangements." Satisfied, I stumble up the stairs to my room, my gut bursting from another day of hard research.

That night I struggle to fall asleep, replaying the drive back to the B and B. I stare in the dark at the faded wallpaper, thinking about Dad. Someday will he forget this whole trip? Soon I'm sobbing convulsively, shaking, burying my face in the thin pillow so no one will hear.

◆ ◆ ◆

The man trundling a wheelbarrow filled with vine prunings coming up the hill has to be Marc, as he looks like a shorter, craftier version of

Jean-Paul, with a much bigger honker—a bit like the French comic book hero Asterix. After introductions, he takes us out to see his babies.

"These are pinot noir grapes," he says. In the right conditions they can yield an elegant, delicate wine with hints of berries. It's March, though, so the buds aren't out and we can only imagine how the grapes will look in their September glory. The tree branches hanging over the fields are bare, with clumps of mistletoe, enveloped by gray mist. We tramp along, smelling the damp vegetation.

Marc gestures toward another field. "I have—how do you say—forty-five acres, in about twenty-five to thirty different places. Few people here have one vineyard all together. There have probably been grapes here since the twelfth century. The monks from Cîteaux already knew the right variety." His ancestors had made a simple wine here, selling it out of barrels to local laborers. But Marc saw the possibilities of this land, just as the monks had long ago, and has worked to increase the quality of his product.

"Pinot noir is in the right place," Marc goes on. "The stones in the soil make the vineyard roots go deep, ten meters deep. They're impossible to uproot." I can see why as we walk across the rocky ground. "The stones are hard for us but good for the grapes."

Jefferson took notes on these rocks, too. Also visiting in March, he recorded how workers were "now planting, pruning, and sticking their vines." Marc has just finished doing the same. "Each of these vines is like a different country," he tells us and waits for our questions.

Embarrassed at my lack of knowledge, I'm not sure where to start. Dad doesn't mind, though. "How much wine can you get out of this?" he asks.

"For every two vines, I get a bottle," Marc responds. "We could produce more if we wanted to. But there's a balance between quality and quantity—and quality comes first!"

"We have to graft all our vines," he continues. "We do that because of you, the Americans! You brought phylloxera over here, which killed our grapes! We must graft as a result." As I had learned at the museum, the pest phylloxera was accidentally brought to France in the nineteenth century, causing devastation.

Dad, a longtime gardener, contemplates the vegetation between the rows of grapes. "We have the same weeds back home."

"Maybe you got them from us!" said Marc, laughing. "That would only be fair."

"When do you pick the grapes?" he asks.

"That causes a lot of stress," Marc says, shaking his head. "You have to decide and tell people two weeks ahead to get twenty to forty pickers. Then there could be a storm."

"Does the quality of the wine change each year?" I venture.

"Yes, I want it to change," he says. "Shall we produce a standard wine? Or one that changes by the season, is more complex?"

Marc leads us to the cellar for a tasting. He swirls the wine in the glass to get some air in it, holds it to the light to examine its color, smells it, then tastes. Although he looks as intent as if he's listening to complicated jazz, he seems neither overbearing nor pretentious. I don't feel foolish when I copy his gestures.

"Your pinot noir, is it dry?" I ask.

"Naturally," he says, not unkindly. There's the first of Jefferson's six flavor profiles, I think. He sips on a chardonnay and tells us the faint citrus taste comes from all the rain they had that year, making that vintage more acidic.

"Which wine do you like better?" I ask.

He laughs. "We have an expression in French: don't be both a judge and a party. I can't pick between them—it's like picking between your children."

Marc leaves, and my parents and I finish up our glasses. The next time I'm at a fussy winetasting that makes me feel I need a Mensa certificate to participate, I'll remember him. Behind each glass of wine, somewhere there's a farmer.

Burgundy gave Jefferson a teachable moment, too, as he experienced the monks' *terroir* firsthand. He was no wine expert until he got to France—he developed his palate glass by glass. It was here that he, too, first learned about the lifestyle of wine producers. A grape cultivator near Volnay told Jefferson he was able to put good wheat bread on his table and a bit of salted hog, since his red wines sold consistently well. Growers in nearby Montrachet, however, made do with rye bread because they made white wine, which failed more often. "On such slight circumstances depend the condition of man!" he wrote.

As for me, I haven't just learned something about wine, I see my traveling companions in a new light. It dawns on me that Mom planned the whole trip to help push me along in the pursuit of my dream. And that even with his short-term memory beginning to fail, I should never underestimate Dad.

I raise a toast to a good start. There's still much to learn, though. Unfortunately, just like Jefferson, I'll run into trouble when I take my wine tour to Germany.

Jefferson's Tasting Notes: Rieslings of Schloss Johanissberg

- *Flavor profiles:* not too acidic; the best riesling in the world
- *Pairs with:* smoked ham from acorn-fed pigs; note that smaller hogs make the "sweetest meat"
- *Enjoy:* while avoiding rascally tavernkeepers

The author in a staring contest with a riesling from Schloss Johannisberg.

A BUMP IN THE ROAD

Cresting the hill in our shiny rented Volvo, I see what I've been waiting for: the Rhine River, far below a series of ridges dripping with grapevines. I point it out excitedly. Liana does the same when she spots the distant tower of a castle—is it the same one Jefferson sketched in his travel journal? The scene looks ripped from the pages of the Brothers Grimm.

After parting with my parents, I met up with Liana in Germany yesterday, renting a car and reaching our hotel just before ten at night. Cheap as ever, I had declined the rental insurance, a fact that Liana chided me about during the drive. Unlike in France, where I spoke their language, and Amsterdam, where they spoke ours, communication is harder for us here. We had to negotiate with a surly German waitress in the hotel restaurant who wanted to close the kitchen; she reluctantly provided us with *flamme* pizzas, thin, with *crème fraîche* and onions.

Jefferson toured here in 1788 after his trip to Amsterdam. Since he couldn't speak German, he tried talking in English, French, Italian, and even Latin, to no avail. He sought out the site of a Roman battle against the Goths but wound up in a place a hundred miles away.

But he did find wine. "Here the vines begin," Jefferson wrote, "and it is the most northern spot on the earth on which wine is made." The Rhine is the birthplace of riesling, a crisp, acidic white wine grape. Jefferson sang its praises and stuffed *Hints* with riesling recommendations. In Jefferson's time and for long afterward, this wine was as pricey as a fine Bordeaux. But its reputation eventually slipped as producers aimed for high yield over quality. By the 1970s and '80s, "riesling" meant virtually any cheap, saccharinely sweet wine coming out of Germany. It's making a comeback, though. Have new winemakers atoned for the sins of their predecessors?

As I drive, I spot the wine village of Rüdesheim below us. "Its fine wines are made on the hills about a mile below the village, which look to the south," Jefferson wrote. I notice a small strip of asphalt after a curve—the perfect spot to pull over and admire where the fine wines are made. Wasn't that what Jefferson always did—go to the highest point he could find to get a bird's-eye view?

Crunch. That must have been the small barrier I eased the car over. No matter. The view admired, I drive down into the town and park.

"Honey, look at this!" Liana says, aghast, when she exits the passenger seat. The cheap-looking plastic splash guard under the Volvo is hanging akimbo.

I spend a long time on my cell phone with the rental agency and wait for a mechanic to arrive. Burly, with a goatee and a prominent crack that shows as he wriggles under the car, he barks at me and yells at a British family trying to squeeze past him into their own vehicle. I remember Jefferson's admonition in *Hints*: if you happen to meet the most "hackneyed rascals of the country," don't judge the national character based on them.

After a short while he gives up. "Go to a garage," he spits out.

"What do I do with this?" I ask, indicating the bent piece of plastic. Wordlessly, he opens the hatchback and slides the splash guard, covered in oil and mud, in the interior; it stretches nearly to the dashboard.

There's a particular repair shop I'm supposed to go to. But we have a cruise booked today, and tomorrow, Sunday, the garage will be closed. What would Jefferson do if he had a few days in Germany—burn one of them getting an inessential part of his carriage fixed? Or drink a shit ton of wine (for research purposes)?

An hour later we're on the Rhine, the splash guard nestled in the Volvo where it will remain for the rest of our trip. The water is gray and choppy, with foamy whitecaps, splattered by falling rain. Logs float alongside our boat. Despite the dismal weather, we see what Jefferson saw when he cruised the river in "a small but dull kind of batteau, with two hands rowing with a kind of large paddle, and a square sail but scarcely a breath of wind." Above us are terraces, with riesling planted up to nearly the top of the cliff, crested with a thick band of fir.

Here, Jefferson bought cuttings of riesling vines to plant when he returned to Paris. But his experiment would only be for his personal amusement, not as a test for his fellow American farmers. Having seen too much poverty in vineyards as he traveled, he concluded that winemaking was too risky an enterprise—"a species of gambling," he wrote to a friend back home, "and of desperate gambling too." The problem was not just that rain or hail sometimes ruined vintages. Fine weather also caused economic damage—if everyone had a bumper crop, the price of wine would go down and "you are equally ruined." The only hope was the rare "middling crop." The vine was "the parent of misery," he concluded. "Those who cultivate it are always poor." Better to simply buy wine rather than produce it.

He left open the possibility that things might change. If America depletes its soil and has laborers needing work, they might be employed in "barren spots" growing wine grapes. That at least would be "something in the place of nothing." But, he added, "that period is not yet arrived."

Liana and I do like the rieslings we order. You don't need to be a sommelier to understand that they're acidic—Jefferson's second flavor profile. But at one place, a glass of riesling puts Liana on guard. "It has this aftertaste of alcohol, almost like the smell you get from gasoline," she tells me, and when the waiter returns ask, "Is this off?"

"No, it's supposed to have a little taste like petrol," the waiter responds cheerfully. "We like it that way." Who are we to complain, I think later as I slide into the Volvo next to my traveling companion, a four-foot-long oily piece of broken car.

The crowning moment of Jefferson's trip, as I hope it will be for ours, was his visit to Schloss Johannisberg, a castle once owned by Benedictine monks. *Hints* pronounced its wine "the best made on the Rhine without comparison." We park by a pink château on top of a hill and walk in. From my online research, I understood that tastings and tours were available.

The man behind the counter thinks otherwise. "No, if you haven't prebooked, we cannot take you today."

"But I'm following Thomas Jefferson's travels!" I blurt out. "He came here. And I really want to see this place."

The man shrugs. "I'm sorry, but I have no information about Jefferson's visit. Good day."

And so our tour of mishaps thuds to a fitting conclusion; I can't get in to the one place I most wanted to visit. Why hadn't Germany gone as well as Burgundy had?

Liana tugs on my sweater. "Honey, it's not the end of the world. The Schloss has a restaurant." It's noon; we stuffed ourselves on our hotel breakfast spread not long ago. And the place is packed. But Liana insists. Our waitress is friendly and Turkish, with flowery tattoos on her neck. She guides us to a hidden table.

"We're not here to eat, just to taste," I tell her. She doesn't mind and brings us wines by the glass: a DIY tasting. We journey into the pale gold, shimmering offerings. The Silberlock "smells sweet like honey, but then it's dry," Liana says. She's more artistic than me, appreciative of aesthetics, so I pay attention to her reactions since my knowledge is still a work in progress. Their half-dry Rotlack Feinherb has citrus notes with peach coming on at the end. "This is summer," she smiles. Suddenly hungry, we order plates of schnitzel and steaming calf liver.

Our final glass of wine is a showstopper. Jefferson wrote that the owner of Schloss Johannisberg, the Baron of Fulda, had rendered its wine "stronger" since 1775, with its price doubling. That year the messenger sent by the baron with orders for the harvest to commence had been delayed for a week. When the harvest finally occurred, fungus had shriveled the grapes. Yet the final product proved unexpectedly sweet: Jefferson's third flavor. Today there's a statue of the messenger outside the winery, an ode to lateness.

We sip this sweet Gelblack, unctuous and nectar-like, and idle away the afternoon, chatting with the waitress, gazing at barges chugging up the Rhine below us, our problems melting away.

The Boys, though, were not impressed when they arrived at Schloss Johannisberg, finding its wine too expensive. Jefferson decided that riesling was just too much for Americans to enjoy anyway; the national taste wasn't ready for an acidic wine to be popular. Comparing rieslings to more commonly accepted wines would be like comparing "an olive to a pineapple," he wrote. Unlike in Burgundy, he couldn't find a good importer of Rhineland wines. If he wanted to drink rieslings later, he'd have to grow the grapes himself. He told a German friend that if he visited him in Virginia, Jefferson would offer him a glass of his own Monticello riesling.

Alas, it was not to be. None of the European varieties he brought back would grow successfully. Jefferson, sometimes cited as the Father of American Wine, couldn't make the stuff. Yet another contradiction for a Founder full of them.

"Germany was...interesting," I say to Liana, as we drive to the car rental agency, where she pays through the nose for my blunder without telling me the cost.

"You got what you needed here, didn't you, honey?"

We did discover new wines. And learned that the right glass at the right time can make cares go away. But I still wonder if there's some quality of these wines we're trying that I'm missing. "Yeah, I guess," I reply. "I don't know. I wonder if I should talk to someone before we do this again. To a pro or something."

"I know! Why didn't we think of this before?" She beams and says one word: "Fernando."

CHAPTER SEVEN

Jefferson's Dream

Jefferson's Tasting Notes: American Scuppernong

+ *Flavor profiles:* a **"fine aroma and crystalline transparence"**
+ *Pairs with:* a pepper-and-okra soup
+ *Enjoy:* with persistence and hyperbole

Three months later, Liana and I pull up to Barboursville Vineyards, in central Virginia, on a fine early summer day. The man who comes out to greet us has succeeded at something Thomas Jefferson failed at: growing wine grapes on American soil. In his fifties, Fernando Franco has a bushy mustache, friendly smile, and smooth manner that reminds me of a Latino Lando Calrissian. Although we haven't seen him in years, Liana and I knew him when we lived in Charlottesville, marveling at his salsa moves.

Fernando hands us glasses of his Barbera, and we admire the vines before us in the late sun. He came to the U.S. from El Salvador with a degree in agronomy, fleeing his country's civil war—which he doesn't talk much about. He worked in California until the owner of Barboursville, the Italian winemaker Gianni Zonin, hired him in 1997 as their viticulturist, in charge of the harvests.

"Gianni bought this land after he visited here in 1976," Fernando tells us. "He was the first to plant European grapes here in Virginia in modern times."

"Was he inspired by Jefferson?" I ask.

"Sure, he was a big fan. That was one of the attractions Barboursville had to him—Jefferson designed the house." Fernando points out crumbling towers to the north, rising like a Roman ruin out of the vines. They're all that's left of the mansion Jefferson sketched out for his friend James Barbour; it burned down on Christmas Day 1884.

If I were an award-winning viticulturist who lived next to the
ruins of a house designed by Jefferson, I'd be smiling, too.

We head out in his pickup for the vines. "Why did Jefferson fail at growing wine grapes?" I ask.

"Here, I'll show you." Fernando jams on the brakes and hops out. He picks up a clipping of a vine root from the ground and hands it to us. "In America we have the phylloxera louse. It's like a little aphid. It reproduces on leaves and feeds from saps of roots and leaves. After some years, there are several million holes. The osmotic pressure is lost, the plant can't bring water up.

"European vines don't know what to do," he explains. "But American vines have been living with this for thousands of years. They know how to heal these holes. So, we graft European grapes onto American rootstock." He mimes a slice onto the American root with his knife, showing us where a European vine could fuse with it, uniting Old World and New. "Jefferson had no idea about this. He put his grape cuttings in the ground without grafting, and they eventually declined and died."

Jefferson wasn't just beaten by a louse alone. He also didn't know how to protect his grapes from deadly May frosts. Fernando, of course, has technology at his disposal that Jefferson couldn't have imagined. In spring, he constantly monitors the weather. "At three a.m. one night, I woke up and saw that the temperature had hit freezing," Fernando says. He and his crew rushed out and set controlled fires in between the vines to generate heat. "The buds were already up—I thought we might lose the crop." He called in helicopters to push warm air down onto the grapes, saving them.

Without the benefit of modern tools and experience, Jefferson's dreams of making wine at Monticello—as a personal pursuit rather than a model for other farmers—came crashing down. He was ahead of his time, with a brilliant vision but not the means to execute it. But he didn't give up without a fight. As an old man, after years of trying to grow European grapes, he experimented with American varieties, claiming that the scuppernong—which some say has an off-putting foxy taste— was an "exquisite wine" that just needed time to mature. Sensing he had few harvests left in his future, he promoted native grapes to others so they would keep trying after he was gone.

Even though he had "sunk a good deal of money" in his elusive project of "introduc[ing] the culture of the vine," he wrote, Jefferson remained optimistic. He never relented in his push to change the national taste away from whisky, that "bewitching poison," and highly alcoholic Madeira. His persistence served as an example to future winemakers in Virginia. Until Prohibition, there was a thriving wine industry in Virginia using local grapes. On the back of every bottle of Barboursville wine is the phrase "Jefferson's Dream."

"Now how about we taste some!" Fernando smiles. He drives us back to his cottage, nestled at the edge of a row of vines. I ask about Jefferson's classification of flavors. How would Fernando group his own wines under them?

"Most reds are dry," he says. "Try this one." He hands me a glass of Cabernet Franc. "Acid, that's also easy to detect. You've already had one—that Barbera we tried is high in acidity."

"How about sweet?"

Fernando goes into his kitchen and emerges with a long, thin bottle of Paxxito. "This is Italian for 'little grapes.' We air dried them to allow their sweetness to come forward." The wine tastes of golden apricots.

"What about silky? Jefferson said that's one that's mostly dry, with a little sweetness."

He thinks it over and comes back with a Viognier. "Maybe this one. You're going to love it." We're consuming wine at a dizzying rate. But didn't Jefferson drink three or four glasses a night?

The Viognier goes down exceedingly smooth. "I taste flowers and honeys," says Liana. "And look at that beautiful color." It looks like amber.

"The color comes from the ripeness of the fruit," Fernando replies. "When the grapes are ready, they're yellow, just gorgeous." I nudge her— we can look for Viognier along the Rhone, its homeland, where we're going soon with both my parents and our kids. Fernando also tells me about the "rough," or tannic, wines I can find when we return to France.

"OK." I throw out the final challenge. "How about this one: rough and sweet."

Fernando's stumped. "We don't have any like that here." He pauses. "Did you say that Jefferson had a wine like that?"

"Well, no. He wanted to find a wine like that."

"Ah-ha!" says Fernando triumphantly. He instead gives us a glass of Nebbiolo, with "*un aroma de* smokiness," he says, blending languages. By now we're all starving. Fernando looks in his icebox and finds a rack of lamb, which he puts on the grill. In his bachelor pad he can't rustle up any sides, so the menu starts and ends with grilled lamb and wine. No one complains.

As the night goes on, we open up more. I tell him my dream of continuing down the trail of *Hints* and making new discoveries. And the obstacles I've encountered along the way, finding the time to prepare for and take these trips and saving up for them. Not to mention the promise I made to myself to share my experiences on the page—how will I get started on that? Following the footsteps of a polymath genius can be frustrating; no matter which subject I engage with, there's always so much more to learn. Clearly, I'm no Jefferson. I still don't really understand wine, for example.

He nods pensively. "This is a blessing," he says, gesturing toward the vines, the wine in our glasses, everything around us. "Here is what you need to know: all my work in the vineyard is an expression of love, of the *amor y cariño* we put into it. Remember, this is where wine comes from." He pauses. "I share this blessing with you, with Liana, for your journey."

Finally, we're done. Except we're not, because Fernando brings us the wine of the night: an Octagon, Barboursville's signature Bordeaux-style blend. And the merry-go-round of drinking and sharing starts over. Liana and I had planned to stay elsewhere, but there's no question of getting behind the wheel now; we can barely stagger up the stairs to Fernando's guest room.

The next morning, I wake to cicadas screeching outside, hardly audible over the cymbals crashing in my head. I look over my tasting notes from the night: neat at first, by the end, sprawling and emphatic. The last from Fernando: "I embrace mortality, now I can die in peace."

Only later do I discover that Jefferson cut his wine with water.

Jefferson's Tasting Notes: White Hermitage

+ *Flavor profiles*: "silky"—dry but also "sweet and luscious"
+ *Pairs with*: a nice piece of fish with aioli
+ *Enjoy*: on a pilgrimage

FIND YOUR WINE

"Try this rosé," René says. "It's not candied. It's the real McCoy." Tall and lean, with a graying goatee, he runs this vineyard near the Rhone, the great river that flows south from the Alps to the Mediterranean. I'm impressed by his English and his enthusiasm for my Jefferson wine quest.

Walking through a vineyard, tasting wine—haven't we seen this movie before? Yes, but not here, not with René's wines, our portal into the land and culture of Provence in southern France. In August, following the visit with Fernando, the band got back together: My parents, Liana and I, and the kids are all staying in a farmhouse on the grounds of a vineyard near the town of Vacqueyras where I can find the half dozen Provençal wines in *Hints*. Since our Burgundy trip, Dad's upped his game, buying higher-quality bottles. Each Sunday dinner we've compared them and talked about this trip, the culmination of our wine journey.

My children couldn't be more excited to be here on their inaugural Jefferson trip abroad. Miranda's now age eight and Nico's five. They're currently in the process of inspecting the farmhouse's pool while Dad and I walk the vineyards with our host.

"We went organic years ago," René continues as we hike up a hill. "We were scared. Everyone told us that the insects would eat everything. But we have birds—birds with huge stomachs because they feast on the insects." He keeps slugs away with crushed eggshells and ashes. At the summit, René pours us a peppery vintage. "This one is delicious served with guinea pig."

He pauses, noting our confused looks. "Ah no, I mean guinea fowl." Maybe his English does need a little work.

We are tramping through the *garrigue*, the fragrant Provençal under-brush, with rosemary and thyme. He hands us glasses of his last wine, which has hints of those herbs.

"Here's one your hero, Thomas Jefferson, would have liked."

I smile. I am proud of Jefferson—he took an often-overlooked subject, wine, and considered it from every angle: aesthetic, economic, scientific, poetic. These wine trips, thanks to Jefferson's *Hints*, have brought me both pleasure and useful knowledge. Drinking with the winemaker by an old Roman wall: a moment in my personal pursuit of happiness.

But it passes all too quickly, for I take leave of René abruptly; we've got to get out on the road to find more wines. I hardly see the vineyard or our farmhouse in the days to come, as I lead my family on a quixotic quest for the missing Jeffersonian wine flavors—three left to find.

We encounter a pair of them at Hermitage, traditionally held to be the birthplace of syrah, a powerful, brooding red—checking the box of a tannic (i.e., "rough") wine. Jefferson, ever the iconoclast, preferred the region's whites. I've done my homework this time, booking us into an exclusive wine restaurant and a tour of Jefferson's favorite vineyard. At the end of lunch, I surprise the waitress by ordering Viognier—not a traditional dessert wine. She brings it out with a conspiratorial wink. "It's one of the secrets of the house."

The Viognier is silky, as Fernando promised—there's the fifth flavor—but the white Hermitage we have on the tour after lunch is the King of Silk, smooth, "sweet and luscious," as Jefferson said. White Hermitage was Jefferson's go-to for great occasions: he recommended it to everyone from James Monroe (when congratulating him on being elected president in 1816) to a colonel he met taking the waters of Warm Springs, Virginia. Days later, Jefferson's new friend received a basket of white Hermitage by post.

The wine formed part of Jefferson's broader campaign to popularize light European blends. Washington and Adams made guests at their large dinner parties drink a series of toasts in the English style with drinks high in alcoholic content, bringing all to the verge of drunkenness. By contrast, Jefferson would gather no more than a dozen people, seated without regard to rank, around his table. They served themselves from dumbwaiter carts they could access themselves, taking only as much as wine as desired. His guests left enthused about the light drinks and their civilized host, who drank in moderation and asked questions more than he talked.

When Jefferson's budget dried up in his retirement years, he switched from Hermitage, "the first wine in the world without a single exception," to the bargains he found in the south of France—the "most elegant *everyday*" wines. Trying one Provençal wine, sent to him by an old wine-seller friend in 1817, brought him back to the moment when he first had it in a cellar in Marseille three decades earlier, he wrote. This taste memory prompted Jefferson to recall that it was time to restock his wine cellar. Even Jefferson's Proustian moments were practical.

I keep pushing on to find the last, elusive flavor Jefferson had dreamed of: rough yet sweet. At the market in Aix-en-Provence, a few blocks from where I once spent my junior year in college abroad, we stroll past sunflowers and shiny eggplants and try sizzling donkey sausage with a dry, aromatic rosé. In the hills of the Luberon, at the same restaurant where I took Mom when she visited me two decades ago in Aix, we sample the local wine, Le-cul-du-loup (Wolf's Butt). It tastes better than it sounds. "Don't wait twenty years for the next visit!" the owner calls out as we leave.

Jefferson searched for new flavors his whole life, too. His budget constrained, he sought after the bargains he remembered from his trips. He never got back to Europe but kept traveling through their wines: Hungarian Tokays, Italian Chiantis, sweet Sicilian Marsala. Not wanting to let him down, I keep piling up the kilometers on our rental, trying ever more obscure wines, still looking for The One. I always have more places to investigate, flavors to compare, wines to bag: I've turned into an alcoholic Captain Ahab.

"Derek, we're just going to stay here today," Mom says. They're tired of the road and the bottle. Miranda stays with them while I drag Liana and Nico off to the famed wine town of Châteauneuf-du-Pape. Jefferson passed through there but didn't mention their wines. What did he miss?

Powerful juice. We try it at a winery where the owner brings Nico a coloring book and a fine stem glass filled with water. The Châteauneuf is surprisingly smooth, despite tannins that slap your face. But it's not the missing taste, I conclude. We walk on the round, heat-retaining pebbles in the vineyards until Nico pulls us up short. "My knees are tired, my eyes are tired from seeing, and my nose is tired from smelling all the lavender," he says in a small voice. We go home.

"Why were you gone so long?" Dad asks when we return. He announces that tomorrow we're staying in. On our last day here? Just when I finally "get" wine and have so many places still to see? That night I walk alone among the vines, trying to calm down.

✦ ✦ ✦

The next morning, we walk to the local bakery for piping-hot baguettes and flaky croissants. Miranda's in heaven. "I love this bread; it's so hot and crusty," she says. "And I love that we can walk through this old village to get it." Dad plucks figs from the trees at the end of the lane. "For later," he says mysteriously.

So, we're staying in. There are certainly worse places to be stuck. Vacqueyras is small, but we kill time watching wedding guests exit the Romanesque church, throwing white petals at the bride and groom as they climb into a vintage Alfa Romeo. We linger over lunch at a small bistro. Dad buys provisions for the night.

Finally, we make the farmhouse ours, reading, taking a dip in the pool. In the late afternoon Dad begins feverish activities. He announces he's making roast pork with rosemary, thyme, and figs from the vineyard, in a recipe of his own inspiration. He plucks some grapes from the bower by the door to make a reduction sauce.

"Derek, how about a wine?" he says.

I fish out a bottle from this very vineyard out of my suitcase.

Baxter's Tasting Notes: Vacqueyras

+ *Flavor profiles*: cherries and herbs of Provence
+ *Paired with*: Dad's Provençal pork
+ *Enjoy*: with people you want to remember forever

The pork comes out of the oven to oohs and aahs. If Dad's lost a step, it doesn't show in the kitchen; he still cooks like nobody's business. We eat on the veranda as darkness falls. I uncork René's wine, the color of rubies, and sip: plum, pepper, a whiff of *garrigue*. Was the missing taste right in front of us all along? Not quite; it's not tannic. But memorable.

"This is pretty far from Oklahoma, Dad. What would your folks say?"

He laughs. "We didn't do anything like this back then. We didn't even have a pizzeria in our town. The first pizza we ever had I made myself when I was sixteen. And they loved it. So, they might not be too surprised."

"How about you, Mom? Maybe this place looks like California—you tell me."

Then it hits me. The missing flavor: a California zinfandel. No wonder I haven't found it here; the taste Jefferson thought we might like wasn't in Europe after all, but created by Americans. Although the zinfandel's origins lie with Italian primitivo grapes, it was Jefferson's winey descendants in the nineteenth century who made it what it is today: bold and brash, with tough tannins and sweet jamminess. Jefferson's favorite might have been silky, but he knew how Americans would like it: rough and sweet. He was a prophet.

I laugh and drain my glass. And realize how far I've come, too. Not just in oenological knowledge, but in a true understanding of what wine can do. It's brought us all here, hasn't it? With moments we never otherwise would have had together. And it has given us stories we'll dine out on for years: Dad nearly buying a barrel of wine from the monks. Our DIY tasting in Germany. These wines of Vacqueyras, perfect with guinea pigs. And, back home, a friendship rekindled with Fernando, who grows grapes with love. We'll relive these moments every time we open a wine from one of these places, uncorking memories in a bottle.

I feel that I'm stumbling closer to Jefferson's true message about the meaning of wine. It wasn't the statistics and classifications and campaigns. Good wine elevated his meals, giving a touch of culture and conviviality to an hour of life. Wine brought Jefferson back to a time and place—especially to his great journeys of discovery through Europe—but when he couldn't find or afford his old favorites, he found new ones and encouraged others to do the same. He used the drink to bring people together and put them at ease. "I find friendship to be like wine," Jefferson wrote, "raw when new, ripened with age, the true old man's milk, and restorative cordial."

We polish off the bottle and watch the rows of grenache vines fall asleep, drenched in starlight.

"Look, Grandpa," says Miranda, wide-eyed, gesturing to the vineyard enveloping us and giving him a hug. "You'll remember this for the rest of your life."

For as long as we're given, we all will.

CHAPTER EIGHT

Sitting in an English Garden

"I don't really like immigrants." The portly photographer leers at us and clicks away as the horse procession draws nearer. "Well, you lot are okay. Americans. I mean I don't like the kind who stay."

Even though it's the Fourth of July, a year after our last trip, Liana and the kids and I are watching the most British thing imaginable here in the gravelly courtyard of St. James's Palace in London: the changing of the guard. "It's the King's Troop Royal Horse Artillery today," the photographer says in what I take to be a Cockney accent, although admittedly I categorize all English accents as either Cockney or Posh. "Not the Queen's Life Guards, the ones with the big plumed white hats. They go seaside in the summer. Would you believe they take their horses with them?" *Click click click.*

The Captain of the Artillery barks a command and the guards raise their sabers. My inner revolutionary impulses rise. Isn't this what we broke away from in 1776? Even though we share a language, more or less, I feel out of place when Cockney Photographer starts slagging off immigrants again. He's exultant—his countrymen voted for Brexit eleven days ago, on June 23, 2016, and some "We Want Our Country Back" posters still hang on the walls.

Now in my fourth year of this journey, I'm ready to start putting some Objects of Attention in the rearview mirror. In fact, I have one in mind—the pursuit of which will begin here in London but take us far afield. Before getting going on it, I humored the kids by bringing them to some tourist attractions in the capital, pretending that they have a normal father who's taking them on a normal vacation for a few days anyways. Even then I couldn't help myself, sneaking in little Jefferson hits here and there. A quick jaunt to an ancient pub in Shadwell, the dockside neighborhood in London where his mother spent her childhood. A meander over to Golden Square, where he stayed during his five-week diplomatic mission aiding John Adams, the regular ambassador to England, in 1786. And now here to watch the changing of the guard, where one of us anyway is reliving a touch of the experience Jefferson had in this very place.

Jefferson came to England from Paris in 1786 to help hammer out America's first commercial treaty with Britain. Also on the agenda: persuading the sultan of Tripoli's representative to prevent pirate attacks on U.S. ships and negotiating a commercial treaty with Portugal. Adams presented his colleague to the court at St. James. Of course, Jefferson had called the king a tyrant. Bygones?

Hardly: the king literally turned his royal back on the pair of ex-rebels. "It was impossible for anything to be more ungracious," Jefferson wrote later. "I saw at once that the ulcerations in the narrow mind of that mulish being left nothing to be expected on the subject of my attendance." Jefferson's anger at the English nationalism he encountered went far beyond my discomfort at the photographer's prattle. And from there his trip only got worse.

Jefferson believed that the English had pioneered the very concept of liberty, which the colonists brought to America, but had lost sight of it in recent years as the monarchy became more corrupt. To him, London was a fallen city. Swelled by recently arrived peasants from the country-side and cloaked in what Adams called an "ominous" cloud of smoke, it had roughly eight hundred thousand inhabitants and not enough room for all of them. Jefferson hated the crowds, and they seemed to hate him back. With the most "wretched" architecture, the city "fell short of my expectations," he wrote. Some English statesmen, for their part, thought it was just a matter of time before the American project failed and the upstart rebels begged to be let back into an arrangement with the mother country.

I sympathize with Jefferson, our "apostle of liberty." Here, sur-rounded by the trappings of monarchy on our Independence Day, I feel like I'm behind enemy lines. I wonder what Jefferson did after this humiliation besides fume. If he had sought solace with a walk, I imag-ine he would have done so among the formal shrubberies of nearby St. James's Park, which would not have cheered him up much. It might have been a garden in England, but it was not his true love: an English garden.

Landscape gardening was so important in the eighteenth century that Jefferson ranked it as an art form alongside painting, sculpture, architecture, music, and poetry. Landscapes gave landowners a way to project an image of themselves to the world, so they were curated as carefully as an Instagram post today. While Americans back home were debating whether to ratify the Constitution, and the French argued over the new form their government might take, Jefferson waded into another controversy raging: French or English gardens?

The dominant landscape garden in Europe had been formal and French. Gardeners in France saw nature as messy, in need of correction. They laid out gardens in geometric shapes, with right-angle paths and embroidery-pattern box hedges, water spouting out of artificial foun-tains, and shrubs tortured into the shapes of balls and animals.

The English garden was an antidote to all this artifice. Although composed, it celebrated nature's organic power, with a touch of the wild, uncontained by the straitjacket avenues and shrubs of kings and lords. English gardens featured circuitous walks with subtle political messages coded in the Roman temples seen along the route. Even leaving the branches of a tree unclipped symbolizes freedom, wrote one eighteenth-century politician and garden designer (an idea I've embraced in my own backyard, perhaps to the extreme).

For once Jefferson preferred something English to something French. He adored this nod to nature, of liberty within order, so much that he left the stalled diplomatic negotiations to tour gardens instead. In his rented carriage he moved fast, sometimes accompanied by John Adams or Adams's secretary and future son-in-law, William Stephens Smith. Since Jefferson carried a detailed printed description of the gardens, Thomas Whately's *Observations on Modern Gardening,* he only had to record his own aesthetic judgments and "such practical things as might enable me to estimate the expense of making and maintaining a garden in that style." Back home, inspired by his journey, he would take the English garden to new heights—but also change it and make it his own. He made Gardens Object of Attention Four and informed the Boys where the best natural-style gardens were on the continent—the "finest...out of England," that was. For the really good stuff, they'd have to read his account of his 1786 tour, which he wrote up as a sort of prequel to *Hints,* calling it *Notes on a Tour of English Gardens.*

As we walk away from the palace, I find the perfect moment to announce an exciting opportunity for our family. In reshaping the American garden and turning it into an art form, Jefferson thought big. I've resolved to as well: I'll visit the same nineteen gardens that he did. Afterward, I can visit Jefferson's mountain again and understand it, and him, better. Surprises await—not all of them pleasant, especially for my understanding of Jefferson's character. But on this balmy Fourth of July,

I put on the face of a father offering ice cream cones in one hand and puppies in the other.

"Kids! Guess what we'll be doing next?"

"What, Dad?" asks Miranda as Nico looks up expectantly.

"Only the best part of the trip! We're going to be visiting nineteen landscape gardens!" Silence. "And, if we want, their stately homes, too!" I add, still grinning.

I take their stunned silence for assent. In the morning we're off to find our first lost garden. I will remember this precise moment years later, when the bills for my kids' therapy come due.

✦ ✦ ✦

My first misgivings occur when a golf ball whizzes over our heads. We're tramping through Moor Park, once a fine garden but now an exclusive golf course in the northwest suburbs of London. When we arrived, a few minutes earlier, a large sign at the entrance reading PRIVATE PROPERTY left us temporarily crestfallen. But behind it I spied a shabby wooden sign, reluctantly stating, in small letters, "Public footpath. No straying or loitering." This ancient easement gave us our way in. Will we find a landscape garden hidden somewhere on the estate?

In between two holes, the path narrowly weaves through a tangle of brambles, seemingly left there to dissuade the riffraff from this walk. "*Ai!*" yelps Liana, followed by a string of curse words in Spanish. "It feels like someone is striking little matches on me!" She's stumbled into a patch of stinging nettles. We wait for a far-off golfer to swing, then take the kids' hands and scamper across the green, still on our public path. A BMW roars past us on the road to the club. "Let's get out of here, Daddy," Miranda pleads, introducing a theme she will explore with increasing conviction as we travel on.

My plan, such as it is, is to find what Jefferson would have seen at these gardens so as to decode the landscape of Monticello on my return. The word "plan" might be a bit ambitious. My technique mostly involves tracking down where the garden was last seen and showing up to see if it's still there. Naturally, it would help if they behaved and actually remained gardens.

A wild boar bolts from a copse of trees and stampedes across the green. I take Nico by the hand and keep marching along the thinly marked easement. Finally, we reach the manor house, with its manicured lawn. Here Jefferson, accompanied by Smith, noted the estate's small lake and clumps of fir trees, suggesting that the whole panorama could use more water and a stronger sense of unity. To these thoughtful suggestions, I would add: also, don't turn the whole thing into a golf course. Liana complains about her hand, so we abandon our garden search and return to the car.

I might be a fortysomething Virginian, like Jefferson was on his tour, but unlike him, I'm no amateur botanist. Do I even know what to look for? This gardening business is new to me. When my parents spent summer nights weeding their vegetable plot, I inevitably disappeared into the air-conditioning. Nor are Liana and nine-year-old Miranda garden lovers, although they are troopers. The only person happy with this first foray is Nico, now six. "This is my style, Daddy!" he says cheerfully. "I like the boring stuff!" He announces that he'll be writing his own book about how William Stephens Smith liked the gardens.

The next two landscapes are also challenging: a once-proud estate with a lake is now a humble suburban park with a tiny pond, another a mere cluster of trees and shrubs. "I hope we see gardens next time," says Liana on our return to the hotel.

Be careful what you wish for.

Like father, like son.

THE PLANTS: KEW GARDENS

The first thing any self-respecting garden needs is plants. If our first few landscapes proved to be ghosts of their former selves, Kew Gardens, in southwest London, makes up for it by bludgeoning us over our heads with three hundred acres containing over fifty thousand kinds of plants, two thousand of which are trees from across the globe. It features a string of gigantic greenhouses, each a garden in its own right, growing delicate Alpine flowers and monstrous water lilies with ten-foot leaves, all patrolled by the garden's own police force, the Kew Constabulary. It was already the premier world garden in Jefferson's time, with fifty-six hundred plants, many collected by the great Sir Joseph Banks. Banks and his successors demanded botanical oddities from explorers and armies across the British Empire, testing tea, rubber, and other specimens at Kew for replanting elsewhere in the colonies.

Overwhelmed, we start by touring the complex on board a small train. "Our mission is to take the planet and make it better for future generations," says a genteel, white-maned conductor-guide named Tom.

"We have a stock of rhododendrons which we sell," he says. "Explorers sourced them in the nineteenth century and brought them to us. Those are their descendants in flower over there."

"I can't believe we came to England to see redwoods!" says Liana as we pass some.

Tom points out tulip poplars—from America, he informs us. With their exotic flowers and bold colors, plants introduced from America like tulip poplars, red cedars, dogwoods, and rhododendrons proved to be big hits in eighteenth-century English gardens. Jefferson saw the opportunities presented by this craze. Gardens are "peculiarly worth the attention of an American," he wrote in *Hints*, "because it is the country of all others where the noblest gardens may be made without expense. We have only to cut out the superabundant plants."

"Here is Syon House," Tom announces. Across the Thames stands a gleaming mansion with a pleasant lawn. It's our next stop after Kew, but I wasn't expecting a sneak peek. "This is the best view you'll see of it," he continues. "That's where they take the pictures that go in the magazines.

"And here's King George's Palace. He stayed there when he was mad, you know." The king's mental health declined not long after Jefferson's visit. Jefferson happily wrote in 1788 that the king was now considered a "furious maniac" and had to be confined at Kew. "Queen Charlotte would picnic there in spring among the bluebells," Tom went on. "George kept flocks of merino sheep. He was called Farmer George by the locals. He had a menagerie here with buffalo and wild tigers and kangaroos, which bred so rapidly. He'd offer a kangaroo or two to guests at the end of the evening," he pauses dramatically, "an offer they couldn't refuse."

I ask Tom what else we should see, and he turns the question over philosophically. "I like to sit and rest and watch the world go by with a glass or two of chilled white wine." A few hours later, after we're tired from exploring, his advice sounds like pure genius. But now we're behind schedule. I expected us to be at Syon, which we had seen from the train, by now. Unless. Unless that glimpse we caught of it, that brief yet enlightening glimpse, was all an expert garden tourist needed to add Syon to our count.

I bring out my dog-eared copy of Jefferson's and Adams's notes on gardens. They would resolve the question as to whether it was time to call it quits today. "John Adams wrote that Syon had 'A Repetition of winding Walks, gloomy Evergreens, Sheets of Water, Clumps of Trees,'" I read. "But he did like the lawn."

"We saw that lawn. It was OK for a lawn," says Liana. "What about Jefferson?"

"Let's see… He wrote nothing. He went to Syon and wrote not one word about it."

So, we take Tom's advice and repair to the garden restaurant to eat roast chicken and asparagus, drink a luscious chardonnay, and listen to birdsong.

✦ ✦ ✦

Jefferson participated in the exchanges at Kew—he received seeds from Banks via an intermediary—and cultivated his own network of plant-loving Europeans willing to make trades. But, without an army of explorers at his disposal as Banks had, Jefferson often had to resort to a more prosaic way of obtaining plants: buying them. Just before he returned to France, he stopped at a London nursery and stocked up on American specimens for his Paris garden and for exchange with French friends.

I want to see an example of a plant emporium, so after a restful, garden-free night we visit another place on Jefferson's list, Hampton Court Palace, upstream of London on the Thames, during its world-famous flower show. The annual festival attracts over 140,000 attendees over the course of six days, serving as proof that in Britain, gardening is sport. Flower fans tailgate and barbecue in the parking lot. We wander past immaculately arranged displays of foxgloves, water lilies, and azaleas and booths showing off the skills of landscape gardeners. We hear oohs and aahs and "Come look at these" as we round each corner. Nico's transfixed, smelling a nursery's collection of lavender. "Like Provence!" he says chipperly.

Our fellow festival-growers are part of the great British middle class, masters of their own small plots. Victory gardens—squares of cabbages and tomatoes tended by ordinary citizens—famously helped get the nation through World War II. Although a display on "Grey Britain" frets that home plantings have declined by 10 percent recently, you wouldn't know it here, where gardeners are rock stars. Bands play, and food sellers hawk sausages and gin-and-tonic ice cream. And everywhere people buy foliage, trundling back to their cars with air plants and hydrangeas in their arms, pulling carts filled with roses.

Yet as important as plants are, they're just one player in a carefully fashioned landscape. Although beautifully designed, Kew was primarily a living botanical collection; Hampton's gardens, Jefferson wrote, were "old fashioned." When we finally see our first proper English garden, with follies scattered across the grounds, it almost takes our breath away.

THE FOLLIES: PAINSHILL

In landscaping, a folly is a structure meant for decoration rather than utility. The very concept must have seemed antithetical to Jefferson, who ordered his daughter Patsy to not waste any hour of the day, who kept five books open simultaneously on a stand in his library, and who calculated the amount of pea seeds it took to fill a pint jar (2,500). Mr. Rationality would never go for *une folie*, as the French would say, a delightful, crazy idea just for the pleasure of it. Would he?

I'm still getting to know Jefferson, apparently: my guess was dead wrong. As I read his *Notes of a Tour*, I discover how seriously he took his follies, recording and rating dozens of them across England. The Whately guidebook he carried listed buildings as an essential element of any self-respecting garden, along with ground, wood, rock, and water. Jefferson would design many such structures for Monticello: a Chinese pagoda, a Gothic temple, a replica of the Pantheon, an artificial cascade and grotto. Most lived only on paper.

Landscaping was one of the few areas where he permitted himself to embrace hints of Romanticism, exploring an individual, emotional response to nature. But even Jefferson's frivolities were still grounded in the Enlightenment, inspired by classical building designs. Eager to understand this contradictory side of Jefferson, we search for the follies that inspired him.

We find our first not far from Kew—at Chiswick, the original English garden. Inspired by his travels in Italy, the owner, Lord Burlington, wanted to create his own Renaissance back home. In the 1720s he hired painter turned designer William Kent, who, in the words of an admirer, "leaped the fence and saw that all of nature was a garden." While Liana and Miranda take photographs, Nico and I stumble upon a full-on Ionic temple, which would fit in at the Roman Forum but seems out of place near English oaks. The same goes for a gigantic, severely classical archway standing pointlessly in the middle of the field, and random obelisks, which Jefferson found "useless," showing "too much of art." Kent had lifted motifs directly from the ancient world and plopped them down in the English countryside, violating Whately's command that garden buildings should seem "casual, not forced."

We also visit nearby Twickenham, another milestone in folly history. When Alexander Pope wasn't writing poetry, he mused on landscapes, reminding designers to "consult the genius of the place." Hardly anything is left of his own garden today, now the site of an academy, not normally open to the public for tours. But the Head of Prep School takes us to their crown jewel, now being restored: a grotto. Pope went crazy blinging out his artificial cave, tacking shells, marble, and arrays of gleaming stones on the walls. It's so kitschy that we feel we've stumbled upon a Disneyland two centuries before its time. Too much folly.

But in Surrey, just southwest of London, we discover Painshill, which does everything right. We climb up a steep embankment to behold a lake below us, nestled in a valley framed by cedars of Lebanon and vineyards, a painting for us to step into. We find a faux ruined Gothic temple and an ersatz medieval abbey, its walls tastefully crumbling. In the distance we spot a Turkish tent with flaps of canvas, white with blue trim, flowing around a stone interior.

Painshill, the quintessential English garden.

A squall comes down and we take shelter in the woods. It passes quickly. "Ooh, how nice!" exclaims the lady behind us as we emerge into a meadow now doused by sunlight. Before us the Chinese Bridge spans an arm of the serpentine lake fed by the River Mole. Swans float by, frogs chirrup, and birds launch into song as we cross the bridge onto a small, *Wind in the Willows*y island.

"You wouldn't think all that rain could fall, and then it's sunny and all that steam comes off the water," says a smiling guide on the outside of the grotto. She leads us in through a dark tunnel to the cavern itself. Light filters in through cracks and windows, bouncing off the grotto's walls, gleaming with a thousand crystals. Of course, the whole thing was contrived "so cleverly that nature itself would have been deceived," wrote a princess who visited in the nineteenth century. Jefferson dryly noted the grotto's cost: a staggering 7,000 pounds, the equivalent of well over $1 million today.

We finish our walk under the gaze of the large Gothic tower looming in the distance. We've given up on finding the Doric temple that Jefferson liked so much. Nor did we find the hermitage, which in the eighteenth century featured a hermit hired by the owner to add ambience to the place (but who kept slipping away to visit the local tavern). Instead, we just linger at the Chinese Bridge counting dragonflies.

"I love this place," Nico says contentedly. "Can we move here?"

Something about the setting of rolling lawns and evergreen woods allows me to accept these follies on their own terms. I want to believe in them. The experience reminds me of Monticello itself—a Virginia plantation house was not supposed to be perched on top of a mountain; all the rest were nestled next to rivers. Although the house is not a folly in the architectural sense of the word, Jefferson's decision to live on a mountain did give him a slightly delirious sense of delight. From it he could see fog blanketing valleys, distant mountains "looming," and, he wrote, the "workhouse of nature" fabricating its rain, snow, and thunder below.

Yet Monticello was also a folly for its sense of foolishness. Enslaved workers had to blast and level the top of the mountain to build the mansion and then spent decades hauling everything that was needed up the slopes—including water, for the mountain's springs were scarce. The house was immensely impractical and costly, in time and painful labor.

We cross the bridge to walk back to our car. "How many gardens have we seen already, Daddy?" asks Miranda.

"Five."

She does the math. "*Fourteen* more to go?" Her face turns ashen. We'll have to up our game; Jefferson set the bar by seeing seven in one day while traveling in a carriage (although he had only John Adams rather than two children to contend with). After visiting his last garden on the outskirts of London, Jefferson helped Adams finish a draft of the commercial treaty and they sent it off to the British foreign secretary. With nothing for them to do but wait for a response, Jefferson proposed to Adams that they leave the city and explore rural England. So we, too, set off, with questions in (at least my) mind: How did these gardens treat the two diplomats? How will they cater to their visitors today? And, as Miranda puts it: will there be ice cream?

CHAPTER NINE

Behind the Fence

THE VISITORS: LEASOWES

The Leasowes, near Birmingham, was the farthest point of the garden-themed journey of John Adams and Thomas Jefferson, from London through the countryside, and ours as well. Staying in the Talbot Hotel—where the diplomats lodged—helps set the mood for us. Wooden beams support our room's ceiling, the floorboards tilt, and the tarnished mirror on the wall looks old enough for Jefferson to have gazed into it as he applied his pomade. The clerk at the reception assures us our particular room is not haunted.

"Are we done with the gardens, Daddy?" Miranda asks sweetly. We saw several more en route and the botanical enthusiasm of three of the four members of our traveling party is, in my professional opinion, lagging just a tad. I at least am looking forward to seeing the Leasowes, as Jefferson was, for it was one of two *fermes ornées*, or ornamental farms, that he visited, agricultural operations that projected beauty. I already looked the place up online and discovered that it's now a municipal park rather than a restored landscape garden. At least it's not a golf course.

Not long before Jefferson's tour, some garden owners began issuing tickets to limit the crowds and keep the lower classes out. But not all had adopted this system yet. A servant at one garden near London denied

Jefferson and Adams entry because the owner, who had the sole power to admit visitors, was off at the races, leading Adams to rant that such gardens were nothing more than "Ostentations of Vanity." At another, the Catholic owner left curious instructions that only foreigners could visit his garden, since his countrymen (mostly Protestants) kept vandalizing it. When the servant at the gate barred Jefferson entry, he had the perfect one-liner in response to the servant, which he must have been dying to use for years: "But I am not an Englishman."

*Miranda eating crisps in a garden café, hardly containing her
excitement for the horticultural experiences that await.*

Still, landscape designers now were not only trying to please the aesthetics of the owners and their friends but also those of countless visitors. Landscape garden tours became the trend, with the high society cruising in their fast-moving, spring-cushioned carriages over new, smooth roads, ticking gardens off their lists and kick-starting Britain's internal tourism industry along the way.

Creators of gardens came up with tricks to keep visitors pleased beyond showcasing interesting plants and unusual follies. The greatest landscaper of them all, Lancelot "Capability" Brown, crafted garden walks that gave the visitor an ever-varying series of vistas: undulating hills wrapping around serpentine lakes, fields dotted with clumps of woods. He invariably added what he called "eye-catchers" in the distance—a folly or grove of magnificent trees that beckoned the visitor to draw closer to see them better. Brown designed nine of the nineteen gardens Jefferson saw. But not this one; a poet-farmer, William Shenstone, created it himself.

On a fine July afternoon, we drive the few miles from our hotel to the Leasowes, spotting a ruined castle across the road—once a great folly, but now privately owned, separate from the park. We amble up to a small visitor's center in the parking lot, sadly closed. A hulking man walking a gigantic German shepherd approaches us, both of their sets of eyes fixated on mine, and I begin to worry.

"Welcome," he says, breaking into a toothy grin. "First time here?" He works in building contracting, he tells us, and comes here every chance he gets. "It's lovely," he keeps repeating. "You need to visit the pool. You'll see herons there! And wild garlic—we've had it since early May. First you cook the leaves, then later you cook the flowers. And be sure to fill up with raspberries! I've just had me fill. You can get a meal out of it. That's my secret. Quite lovely."

We walk off, following our volunteer guide's instructions on the old circular path—an idea Jefferson would take back home. In Shenstone's day, the path here had benches and statues strategically placed for the visitor, with uplifting quotations in Latin, creating an ensemble of pastoral poetry. We find the pool, filled with swans, and smell the wild garlic. From the top of a hill, we catch a glimpse of smokestacks from some old factory, relics of the Industrial Revolution. Not the eye-catchers Shenstone would have liked.

Although Jefferson loved the idea of ornamented farms, he found this particular one little more than a "grazing farm with a path around it." And even this effort, he wrote, had "ruined" Shenstone; "it is said that he died of the heartaches which his debts occasioned him." Nonetheless, he had gotten the idea of how he might refashion his own plantation for his genteel visitors. Maybe he could do better. Surely the effort wouldn't bankrupt *him*.

"I'm so sick of trees," Miranda says. Who can blame her? We have a long dinner at a country inn and retire to our hotel (after, ahem, seeing one more garden).

To tell the truth, many of the landscapes are already running together in my mind. I have the recipe down: start with plants, add in some follies and a winding path to connect them, mix in a serpentine lake, sprinkle with eye-catchers to taste, and repeat. I wonder if Jefferson had to keep checking his notes to keep the gardens straight, too. Of course, some stand out because of the degree of difficulty we had in accessing them, like the one on a BBC Intelligence Services compound or one that was so grand that Tony Blair, who lives on the estate, resides not in the mansion but in the carriage house.

The most memorable ones we've seen, though, are more than the sum of their parts. Landscape designers famously modeled gardens after paintings, and their elements—rocks and earth, woods, water and follies—are akin to the colors on the palette board and the thickness of brush strokes. A truly exceptional landscape uses them to tell a story. Jefferson discovered this at one of the last stops on his tour, and we do as well.

THE STORY: STOWE HOUSE

In the 1730s, Lord Cobham, a Whig and member of the political opposition, made his Stowe House garden in Buckinghamshire, some sixty miles northwest of London, not only an aesthetic masterpiece but a political statement. To point out the decadence of the crown, he and his family constructed three didactic walking circuits: the Path of Vice (featuring ruined temples and headless sculptures symbolizing the corrupt

Tory regime), the Path of Virtue (showcasing statues representing examples from Classical Rome), and the Path of Liberty (reveling in the true natural state of Englishmen).

After we arrive, a young blond woman in the reception area hands me our tickets and indicates our walking options. "My favorite is the Path of Virtue."

"The right answer," I note. She blushes a little. There are kids present.

But we start our Choose-Your-Own-Adventure on the Path of Vice, advertised as an "easygoing walk." Doesn't vice always start out that way? We pass the Temple of Venus and its statue of that sultry goddess. The prudish Adams thought the temple's suggestions of "Mysterious Orgies" might give "artificial Incitements" to sin rather than serve as a warning.

We cut over to the Path of Virtue, a "steady stroll." We emerge from woods into a semicircle with carvings of Saxon deities for each day of the week, like Woden for Wednesday, emphasizing the English heritage of liberty. Cawing crows alight on the statues, ringed by box elders casting paganlike shadows.

Finally, we tackle the Path of Liberty, a "vigorous ramble," for freedom must be earned. We arrive at the Temple of British Worthies, a half-circle amphitheater with busts of English heroes. There are great artists, such as Shakespeare and Milton, and also champions of English freedom: King Alfred the Great, the unifier of Britain in the Middle Ages, and King William III, who came to power in the mostly bloodless Glorious Revolution in 1688, establishing a constitutional monarchy and a toleration for dissent and reason.

Jefferson couldn't have been more excited when he walked this trail. He had long followed in the tradition of the "country Whigs," the rural, radical branch of the English political party, reading their newspapers and books. Like them, Jefferson believed that no regime could take away a people's natural rights. The Saxons had once lived in a state of primordial freedom, which they had fought to maintain over the years despite threats from Normans and later from the corrupt Hanoverian line of kings. These pure Englishmen had brought the spark of liberty over to the New World, "unassisted by the wealth or the strength of Great Britain," Jefferson wrote. It was now up to American farmers to "keep alive that sacred fire."

Jefferson created his own hall of fame later at Monticello, starting with busts of his "trinity" of British heroes (who were also portrayed at Stowe): John Locke, Francis Bacon, and Isaac Newton. Jefferson's hall also displayed portraits of Washington, Franklin, and other "American worthies," illustrating how liberty had passed to them from England. Including to the man whose marble bust he placed in Monticello's entrance hall (a certain Jefferson, Thomas).

"They should have a Path of Crazy," yells Nico, running ahead of us through a pasture smelling of freshly cut grass. After chasing him down, we end our visit with tea and shortbread at the Temple of Concord, where we admire an exhibit on Capability Brown, who got his start at Stowe and served as its head gardener for nearly a decade.

We look out on green hills flecked with grazing sheep set off by groves of trees and temples. Jefferson praised Stowe's lines of sight, noting the contrast between hills covered with trees and a valley clear of them. And he loved that there were no unsightly fences. Instead, a four-mile-long trench known as a "ha-ha" kept livestock away from visitors. The ditch wasn't visible until someone walked right up to it, prompting the (easily amused) observer to exclaim "ha-ha!" in delight. Stowe pioneered the use of the ha-ha in England; Horace Walpole, a fellow Whig politician and garden designer, wrote that it was the "capital stroke, the leading step to all that has fulfilled" in the realm of landscapes. I'm happy to encounter it as well, since I read that Jefferson created a ha-ha back at Monticello, which I'm eager to discover.

Yet even though Stowe presented a seemingly timeless vision of the countryside, the nursery of English liberty, the reality was messier. Ordinary folk weren't welcome at Stowe. Due to technological advances, large landowners like Lord Cobham dramatically increased agricultural production in the eighteenth century. Encouraged by this, they snatched up common lands and claimed the land of poorer farmers who, under new laws, lost their land if it wasn't enclosed by hedges. The great landowners drained and improved their now sprawling estates, renting parcels out to unemployed small farmers, who became their tenants. Lines of trees screened these farmers from the view of visitors.

Lord Cobham even forced an entire village to relocate in service of his landscape. He defended his new estate ruthlessly—according to local stories, he pressed charges against two poachers who killed a deer on his land and had them hanged. In a clearing in the woods, he placed his newest statue: the pair of thieves fatefully carrying the deer on their shoulders. Did we just walk down the Path of Hypocrisy? Our Founding Landscapers failed to note any disconnect. Adams rated Stowe as "superb," and Jefferson had it near the top of his ratings, too.

When our own garden tour comes to a merciful close, Miranda and Liana rate Kew Gardens as their favorite, I pick Painshill, and Nico announces he liked them all. "They're so peaceful," he says. "I like to sit in them and look at the flowers and think." Like Jefferson and Nico, I've collected my favorite elements of the gardens we saw: circuit walks past grazing pastures, the contrast of woods and fields, an emphasis on American plants, follies, ha-has, and, above all, the need to use these elements to dialogue with the visitor. Truly, gardening in England, Jefferson wrote to a friend when his trip was done, "is the article in which it surpasses all the earth."

His trip might have been a diplomatic bust—the English reacted to the draft commercial treaty with derision—but on his return to Paris,

Jefferson redesigned the garden in the back of his mansion to add serpentine paths, a pond, and a small hill with a winding ascent. Later, back home at Monticello, he would create his signature landscape, inspired by English gardens but telling an American story. Until I return to Monticello, though, I don't realize just how many competing narratives this landscape tells.

A STORY SUPPRESSED: MONTICELLO

In the fall I take a tour of the Monticello grounds led by archaeologist Fraser Nieman. Even though the English garden had gone "far beyond my ideas," Jefferson wrote, he would take this living essay on nature and liberty even further himself. Like "the leaves of the trees, which the winds are spreading over the forest," Americans were heading west and turning the rugged nature they found there into cultivated farms. He wanted his own landscape to reflect this "empire of liberty," celebrating nature and its new democratic masters.

We walk on one of the "roundabout" roads Jefferson developed to encircle the mountain, connected by diagonal paths, a route which reminds me a little of the Leasowes. Jefferson hinted at a *ferme ornée*, Nieman tells the group, but he never had the funds to fully execute his vision. The woods were "wild," a visitor, Margaret Bayard Smith, wrote in 1809 as she made her way up the mountain for the first time in a carriage, "with scarcely a speck of cultivation." Like Capability Brown had, Jefferson screened out views of fields and houses so that only the savage forest could be seen. Smith felt shivers of terror as the carriage almost overturned on the rough road. Then, suddenly, she saw tamed fields, a "sublime" contrast.

My own touring party emerges to see these reassuring, rolling pastures, symbols of American progress as well. This was all by Jefferson's design. His walk varied his "rich profusion" of views, he wrote, with "mountains distant and near, smooth and shaggy" emerging and disappearing from sight, as did "a little river hiding itself among the hills" and cultivated fields seen between thickets of trees. This contrast between woods and fields makes me think of Painshill. But those were benign, Winnie the Pooh–type woods; Monticello's wilderness has more of an edge to it. Even today there are occasional black bear sightings.

Nieman shows us the grove. "[S]hade is our Elysium," Jefferson wrote. He pruned the lower branches of trees and removed shrubs so that only a high canopy remained. Visitors could walk and admire the American trees that were so prized in England: the tulip poplar and white oak, the Juno and Jove of our forest, as he put it, growing free. Until Jefferson could get Doric columns built, four tulip poplar timbers from these woods held up Monticello's pediment, symbolically uniting house and garden. He dreamed of keeping an American elk here and told visitors of his plans to turn springs into cascades and to build temples and grottoes: a garden in his mind.

His landscape was always a work in progress, like the American experiment itself. "I like the dreams of the future better than the history of the past," Jefferson wrote. Monticello's panoramas still display his vision, the tale of freedom-loving farmers conquering a savage wilderness. He intended the project of his home and grounds, his life's work, to serve as a mini-morality play, to show other Americans how they, too, could tame the land with grace. Jefferson's western-facing vista gave his visitors a view of alluring purple mountains and the virgin territory beyond.

We walk down from the lawn and see the Palladian pavilion towering over the kitchen garden. We stop at Mulberry Row, the center of the plantation's light industrial activities, screened from the house by mulberry trees, a sunken lane hidden from visitors. As Fraser concludes his tour, I ask him about Jefferson's ha-ha. "Where was it, anyway?"

He pauses, not expecting this. "Right here. It separated the lawn from Mulberry Row."

What Jefferson did suddenly becomes disturbingly clear to me. The ditch Jefferson made his slaves dig not only kept out pigs and cattle, it symbolically placed the enslaved workers in a different, less-than-human sphere. Our investigation had led me to what Jefferson had most wanted to keep hidden, the ha-ha he wanted no one to see.

The landscape here is so beautiful it makes it hard to remember slavery. That was exactly what Jefferson wanted. He hid his status as a slave owner as much as he could. "I do not (while in public life) like to have my name annexed in the public papers to the sale of property," he wrote. Jefferson would be horrified today at tour guides leading groups down Mulberry Row, a circuit that focuses not on his landscape but on the enslaved gardeners themselves.

Why does the ha-ha discovery surprise me? Jefferson's life was nothing but contradictions. The man of the people who lived extravagantly, a deficit hawk who ran up such staggering debts that Monticello had to be sold after his death. The slave owner who wrote that all men are created equal. So a beautiful landscape, ostensibly in celebration of liberty, that conceals the work of the enslaved workers who built it? That sounds about right. It's a bitter note to end this journey on. But it's necessary to fully understand a truth that lies behind Jefferson's vision. The eye-catchers in the distance dazzle, but they coexist with the cruelty underlying this ditch.

Below the ha-ha is the vegetable garden. Jefferson had walled it off with a ten-foot-high wooden paling to protect it from deer and thieves. Today it's once again an achingly beautiful, thousand-foot-long spread of dangling scarlet runner beans, spooky towers of hops, shiny red Texas bird peppers, and pale green sea kale, open to the world.

Behind the fence, shielded from the view of visitors, enslaved gardeners also grew plants from their ancestral homelands: okra, eggplant, sesame, watermelon. They intermixed these with fancy French figs and Mandan corn and Arikara beans sent to Monticello by Lewis and Clark—a far cry from the cold weather English plants still favored by other Virginia planters. This hidden experiment was an American Kew Gardens, testing out food for a new land and fusing cultures along the way. Jefferson organized the plants, with their shocking colors, into an aesthetically harmonious scheme that only he and his Black gardeners would see.

Beyond the kitchen garden, wedged between Monticello's rolling fields of wheat and tobacco, screened off to visitors by trees, were the small personal plots of enslaved families. They worked them late at night and on Sundays. Gardening was a small salvation: the Jeffersons were long on dreams but short on potatoes and cabbages, frequently running out of the practical necessities of life. Enslaved gardeners grew these staples, stored them in root cellars, and sold them to their hungry White masters in the dead of winter. Ingenuity and know-how earned them a little money and a hard-fought sliver of autonomy.

If only visitors could have seen these slave gardens, Jefferson's showy landscape would have been more authentically American. Just as Stowe hid the lives of English tenant farmers, the vision Jefferson projected at Monticello wrote African Americans out of the picture. Jefferson's obfuscation was worse; the displaced English farmers were free, no matter how hardscrabble their lives were, while his laborers were bound to his mountain in perpetuity. Jefferson missed the compelling story unfolding right under his nose. These hidden gardens tell of secret collaboration, a means in which African Americans could grow their own plants and make a little money on the side, turning the tables on an inhumane system, if only slightly.

At first, I didn't think Jefferson's slave-owning had much to do with my own travels. After all, I was tramping through the French and Italian countryside, in places that had no slaves in the eighteenth century, following trips made by Jefferson in which he journeyed either alone or with only a French valet. But now I realize slavery could never leave Jefferson's mind, not when he examined English landscapes, not when he created his own. Whether he mentioned them in *Hints* or not, enslaved African Americans would play a role in executing all his plans, from agriculture to architecture. Without slaves, Jefferson could go nowhere.

✦ ✦ ✦

But in the end, Monticello is not the final garden on our tour. Our own is.

I haven't immediately become an avid gardener after the trip; I'm anxious to get back on the road. But I can't do these travels forever; I'll eventually visit the places in *Hints* and give due attention to all eight Objects of Attention. And then what? Will I retire to my garden with the kids, content, changed somehow?

Inspired by our journey, I begin to think about our own land. Even understanding the dark underside of some of the landscape gardens we saw, their beauty is undeniable. The pain they caused—to tenants in England and slaves in Virginia—shouldn't be separated from them. But this poignancy means we should look harder at them to honor the gardeners who created them—geniuses in their own right as much as their designers were.

So our family plants a patch full of native Virginia plants close to the house. Nico asks for space to create his own garden, which he plants with our help. His plot has a curving bed of flowers, a birdbath, and whimsical gnomes to catch your eye. I couldn't rate it any higher.

CHAPTER TEN

A Continued Feast through Italy

The auctioneer is having a hard time getting takers at three euros until Liana raises her hand. Someone bids above her, at three-fifty, but she keeps waving. We now own a box of fifty peaches from the Po Valley for only four euros and Liana is elated.

"What are we going to do with fifty peaches?" I grumble. We're going to be in a car for the next week.

"Eat them!" Liana says merrily.

We're in Eataly, a cavernous warehouse in Turin stuffed with fresh, local produce, including peaches similar to the ones Jefferson loved. He traveled south into Italy in 1788 on a "continued feast on objects of agriculture," looking for new foods "susceptible of adoption in America," investigating pasta-making machines, Parmesan cheese, and rice. Back home, he would serve surprised guests with macaroni, Chianti, garlicky dishes, and, most shockingly of all, tomatoes, which some Americans considered to be dangerous—aphrodisiacal if not poisonous.

The warehouse stands in the shadow of the Alps. Jefferson crossed over them in a carriage on his forty-fourth birthday, seeking "curious and enchanting objects." The town of Saorge, built hard on a mountainside, enthralled him; it looked as if the stone buildings were "hanging to a cloud." "Fall down and worship the site," he wrote in *Hints*. "You never saw, nor will ever see such another." *Hints* sends the traveler through this Alpine pass with instructions to look for speckled trout in the rivers and to "watch where you lose and where you recover the olive tree in rising and descending the several successive mountains."

Traversing the Col de Tende pass, Jefferson wrote, leads to a view of the distant plains of Lombardy, with their rich, "dark-colored" fields "sometimes tinged with red, and in pasture." They have been farmed since Roman times, a breadbasket that inspired Hannibal to cross the Alps with his elephants. With agriculture in mind, Jefferson described the quality of the soil he examined ("black and rich"), the "abundance" of figs, and the blossoming of almond trees. He noted the Italian method of planting corn, of hoeing, and of using rice beaters with ribbed bumps "not unlike the jaw-teeth of the mammoth."

He had entered one of the great world food cultures. Not that he didn't appreciate what he ate in Paris. But Jefferson saw Italy as "a field where the inhabitants of the Southern states may see much to copy in agriculture." The climate of the Italian Piedmont, the hilly land sloping from the Alps to the flat plains in what is now northwestern Italy, was close to that of his own Virginia Piedmont.

His pursuit of Italian food would even lead him to break the law. The next time he crossed the Alps on his return to France he'd be on the lam, moving fast, "traveling through the night as well as day without sleep," as he wrote later. Jefferson would turn into a rice smuggler.

Approaching forty-four myself, I've taken Liana, Miranda, and Nico on our own summer of discovery in France and Italy. I have two Objects of Attention in my sights—Numbers One, Agriculture (including "new species of plants"), and Five, Architecture. By now I've covered three Objects briefly in Amsterdam (Painting and Statuary, Courts, and Mechanical Arts), one ad nauseam in England (just ask Miranda), and, of course, the subject of wine. Five years into my odyssey following *Hints*, I'm confident enough to tackle a pair of important topics simultaneously, even ones I didn't previously know much about. (The stories of our adventures in architecture will follow those of our agricultural and gastronomic experiences.)

Liana, lovely in the olives.

We began this leg of the journey with our own magical two days in the Alpine village of Saorge, swimming in the biting-cold "gurgling stream" Jefferson found, looking for trout and making our own olive elevation charts. We're also preparing for two weeks of travel through Italy—nearly the same amount of time Jefferson spent there. He sorely wished to stretch it out further, but he was lucky to make it to Italy at all. He had gone to the south of France to soak in a hot spring in an attempt to heal his broken wrist. His excuse for leaving his diplomatic post in

Paris was that he could make detailed notes about the French seaports and trading opportunities.

Yet how, in good conscience, could he travel to Provence and not go just 150 miles farther east? Raised on classical literature, Jefferson grew up devouring the histories of Tacitus and Livy's tales of Cincinnatus, the statesman-farmer, loving Italy from afar. As a college student, he had taught himself the language, studied with an Italian violin master, and planned a trip there with a friend. He named the Virginian summits he owned in Italian (Montalto and Monticello—the big and little mountains) and recorded the names of his garden vegetables in Italian (*cipolle bianco di Tuckahoe*—white onion from Tuckahoe). He just had to set foot in the land of the classics and the *dolce vita*.

So, he concocted a reason for the journey. He had discussed with John Rutledge's uncle Edward, a farmer and botanist, the difficulties that rice planters in the Carolinas had in marketing their product in Europe. Italian Piedmont rice was more popular, but was it a different variety or just processed differently? He decided he had to "sift the matter to the bottom by crossing the Alps into the rice country." And he would ask for forgiveness, not permission, informing Secretary of Foreign Affairs John Jay of his detour only when he was back.

This was a risky proposition. So as to prevent the competition from learning the secrets of their production, the consequence for smuggling unprocessed rice out of the Piedmont, ruled by the Kingdom of Sardinia, was the death penalty. If Jefferson wasn't careful, the next letter he might send to Secretary Jay might be written behind bars.

He could only make a short voyage to the northwest of Italy, a "peep… into Elysium," as he put it. *Hints*, though, encourages the traveler to go beyond this limited itinerary, to Florence, Venice, and Rome, promising that it "gives infinite pleasure to apply one's classical learning on the spot." Cruising in our rented Audi down the slopes of the Alps, I come up with an idea: our trip, too, will be a "continued feast," each stop like a course of an Italian meal. We'll head south to Naples, then tack our way back north again to the Piedmont region and the Mediterranean coast. I'm not trying to recreate a particular meal he had course by course but in search of Italian foods and ingredients that held meaning for him. It will be the journey Jefferson would have taken if he had spent two weeks in a hatchback rather than a carriage.

Eating our way across Italy—here, finally, is an Object that Liana and the kids can get behind without reserve. All we'll have to do is loosen our belts, track down some food recommended by Jefferson, and savor it. Repeat. It already sounds more popular than last summer's Endless Garden Tour.

Will there be more to it than the delicious meals though? Jefferson spent so much energy both in the garden and at the table that I'm hoping this trip will give me a different lens into his life and mind. Here at this warehouse, I'm about to discover that this seemingly simple pursuit of food will lead me to question how to interpret Thomas Jefferson's principles today. And realize how hard it is to drag this man of the eighteenth century into the twenty-first.

ANTIPASTI: TOMATOES IN OLIVE OIL

A waiter wearing a black Eataly shirt that reads "Food and Fashion—Italians Do It Better" brings us a platter of starters. I have the *straciatella* soup, with egg drops and meat broth, a plate of crusty bread to dunk in olive oil, and a salad of greens and tomatoes drizzled with even more oil. We eat melon with prosciutto so soft and piggy we expect it to squeal and walk off the plate. Liana tries smoky octopus accompanied by an audacious pairing of pea puree. The kids wolf down French fries cooked in more *olio d'olivo*.

This smooth, nutty olive oil is a revelation to us, accentuating the flavor of everything it touches. "This is very virgin," Liana pronounces. Jefferson would have concurred. "What a number of vegetables are rendered eatable by the aid of a little oil," he wrote, although this produce would have been pretty damn edible anyway. I wash the *antipasti* down with a cherry-tasting Nebbiolo, which Jefferson discovered near here, finding it "superlatively fine," sweet and brisk. If the meals that follow live up to this start, discovering Jefferson's epicurean side will be almost criminally pleasurable.

Eataly is in an old vermouth factory, perhaps the very one where vermouth was invented just two years before Jefferson's visit. It not only sells prepared meals but fresh, organic produce, meats, and pastas, mostly from the surrounding region. Our *antipasti* cleared, Liana and the kids leisurely sample cheese and honey at stalls and buy provisions for our drive ahead. I instead try what Jefferson said was "the favorite beverage of the civilized world," setting up camp with an espresso in Eataly's Learning Center and leafing through the manifestos I find there.

We're in one of the citadels of the Slow Food movement. It all started in the 1980s when an Italian activist from this region launched a campaign against a planned McDonald's near the Spanish Steps in Rome. The changing face of Italian agriculture following World War II had long disappointed professor Carlo Petrini. Long lunches, fresh produce, recipes handed down through generations—all were on the way out. Instead, multinational conglomerates consolidated food sectors and pushed the same products across the country: Parmalat in dairy, Monini and Carapelli in olive oil. Italians bought processed goods in supermarkets, flown in from distant lands, used microwaves, and binged on fast food—just like Americans. Petrini worried that as traditional foodways disappeared, so did consumers' connections to the earth and those who worked it.

This particular McDonald's, flush by an iconic emblem of Italian architecture, was a Golden Arch too far. The fight against it turned into a movement, promoting the radical notion that diners should take their time, understand where their meals came from, and savor the flavors. Each Slow Food branch maintains its own Ark of Taste, a living list of local food threatened by extinction. In 2007, some allies of this network established Eataly as a place for consumers to buy local, fresh, natural groceries while having a bite to eat or a drink. Today there are Eatalys all over the world, but we are in the mothership, still the biggest.

I feel confident that Jefferson, that old revolutionary, would have shared our excitement at being here. Eataly combines two of his greatest loves. He sought to elevate daily life, passing hours with guests at the table (and with those wines we now love). He shared with his guests fresh asparagus, anchovies, gumbo, and Creole stews. Really anything except the bland, boiled British food normally found on the tables of the ex-colonialists.

But like the Slow Fooders, Jefferson also wanted his purchases to support farmers and build a more egalitarian society. America needed the help; the Revolutionary War had left the new country with ravaged fields, rampant inflation, and a shaky, unstable government. As he traveled through Europe, he observed the soil, climate, and crops grown in different regions, assessing the factors that made peasants' lives pleasant or miserable. Jefferson argued that landless Whites in Virginia should receive fifty acres of land (he didn't include Blacks in these plans), and he didn't want them to plant tobacco on it. Jefferson's long years of cultivation of the cash crop had brought him frustration. The plant was extremely labor-intensive; it "impoverished" the soil, he wrote, and did not have the side benefit of providing food for workers. Tobacco planters rarely managed to crawl out of debt they were "immersed in" to their British creditors. If American farmers could produce a special variety of Piedmont rice, say, they could grow the struggling nation's economy and democracy in turn.

My family is still off exploring the pleasures of Eataly, so I leaf through my tattered copy of *Hints* and other Jefferson writings to prepare for the road ahead. The meal and dark espresso have left me feeling content; I'm sure I'll find confirmation that I am in the most Jeffersonian of spots.

Jefferson's love of vegetables? Check—we're in the right place. Although not vegetarian, he dined mostly on plants and just added meat as a "condiment" to his dish. He worshipped peas: hotspurs, marrow-fats, and many others. He sowed a thimbleful of lettuce each Monday of the year, trying out Aleppo, Tennis Ball, Marseilles, and Brown Dutch. Jefferson experimented with Spanish tomatoes and recommended spicing up dishes, like the venison his cooks prepared at the President's House, with garlic and basil. He grew Italian peaches, the juicy *San Jacopa* and the luscious *Poppa di Venere* ("the nipple of Venus"). So yes, he would have adored the *antipasti* we had scarfed down.

Jefferson's search for crops that American farmers could grow? That's the point of Object of Attention Number One: Agriculture. The olives he encountered in the Mediterranean particularly inspired him. In the rocky, poor soil of the Alps, olives were the thing that "contributes the most to the happiness of mankind," he wrote, supporting whole families that sold their oil. After his trip to Italy, he sent olive trees to South Carolina, imploring planters there to plant this "richest gift of heaven," as he did at Monticello.

This was part of his process of scientific observation, like noting when peach trees bloomed and when asparagus came to table in the life-long Garden Book he kept. Although Jefferson's olive trees eventually died, he experimented with sesame oil as a substitute. "The failure of one thing," he wrote later of his checkered gardening record, can be "repaired by the success of another." He recorded where different crops performed best and the results of his experiments with crop rotation and fertilizers, searching for the most rational way to produce the food he wanted.

But I pause as I come across a note that doesn't quite ring true with everything surrounding me. As president, he received Arikara beans from Lewis and Clark, collected from the Sioux. He loved them. They became his second-favorite green bean.

So, logically, he abandoned planting them.

Second-best still meant loser in the mind of an Enlightened logician. "I am curious to select only one or two of the *best* species or variety of every garden vegetable and to reject all others from the garden to avoid the dangers of mixture and degeneracy," Jefferson wrote, emphasizing "best." As much as he enjoyed the Arikara—its taste might have been the best of the many beans he grew—he judged it inferior to the gray snap bean, since the latter grew in only eight weeks. Why risk cross-pollination? Jefferson was no traditionalist. Once he discovered the Platonic ideal of beans, growing anything else would just be a waste of time. As important as flavor was, so were efficiency and productivity. A farmer had to learn how plants grew and then "turn the greatest quantity of this useful action of the earth to his benefit," he wrote.

Wasn't that the opposite of Slow Food? I thought I'd find this movement, and its return to a simpler time, to be aligned with Jefferson's approach. Yet if he had an Ark of Flavors, they were all ones chosen by him. Sentiment played no role in his rationalist selection.

"Look what we found, honey!" Liana says, returning from her shopping spree with olives and olive oil, soft Taleggio cheese, and a bag of organic *orecchiette* from the town of Gragnano, near Naples, the historic epicenter of Italian pasta. And, for good measure, a can of manure, advertised tongue-in-cheek as coming from an authentic Italian rooster, entitled Real Shit. The kids can't contain their laughter even as I put that one back on the shelf.

We load up our car, with the now forty-nine peaches perched precariously on top of the hatch's parcel shelf, and I take a last glance at the purplish Alps. I see, a block away, a conventional Pam supermarket, stocked with industrially grown food. And next to it, as if the rest of Turin were giving the middle finger to Eataly, is a McDonald's, doing brisk, greasy business.

How could people blessed with living so close to the original Eataly choose to shop at a standard grocery store and eat at Slow Food's mortal enemy? But something gnaws at me. As much as Jefferson would have loved the flavors in this warehouse, wouldn't he also be intrigued by the large, perfect-to-look-at produce grown with chemical fertilizers, on sale in the regular supermarket? Wouldn't even the machinations of McDonald's food engineers fascinate this man who measured everything? I could see Jefferson being more interested in the technology of supermarket checkout lines or the distribution system of bringing McValue meals to modern-day yeomen than in smelling Real Shit in a can. And judging by the foot traffic, a regular supermarket and regular fast-food restaurant are the everyday flavors of many Italians' Ark.

I stuff *Hints* into the glove compartment. Did we just spend the last two hours in the wrong place? We might find the origins of Jefferson's favorite Italian foods, but before I turn him into an advocate of Slow Food, I might need to rethink my assumptions about him—and not move so fast.

PRIMO PIATTI: MACARONI

The kilometers click by in our Audi, smelling of forty peaches, as we head to the farthest point south of our journey before we loop back north. We're on the trail of the Gragnano pasta we had seen in Eataly. Jefferson never made it out of the Italian Piedmont region, but William Short and John Rutledge did, reaching Naples. Short had a special quest to fulfill there: Jefferson had commissioned him with buying a macaroni mold.

We arrive in Gragnano, a dozen miles south of Mount Vesuvius. It's slow driving down the crooked streets. Laundry flops from windows, and people mill about everywhere. "It's like Cuba!" Liana says. Short found the scene less romantic, scandalized by the "ill clad dirty" crowds of Neapolitans and the women picking lice off of each other in "a warm part of the street." Naples kept expanding in the centuries to come, eventually absorbing Gragnano and its cluster of noodle factories. Now most pasta is made elsewhere in heavily industrialized plants (Italy has 120 manufacturers, which together produce more than a ton of pasta per day), but Naples remains the place "most famous for the excellence of that article," as Short put it. I've arranged for us to tour one of the few artisanal production houses that remain, La Fabbrica della Pasta.

Gregorio, our twentysomething bearded guide, meets us at the door. "I love it. Everything smells like pasta," says Nico as we walk inside.

Gregorio shows us old equipment, starting with copper pots like the one his grandfather had. "He needed a large one; he had twelve children!" If the Roman gods had created an ideal place for pasta production, they might have come up with Gragnano. He tells us about the pure water in nearby mountain streams and the fertile plains where peasants grew durum wheat. Mixed together, water and wheat flour formed the paste that would be molded into the proper pasta shape. He shows us a centuries-old iron box with holes for the pasta to squeeze through. It looks a little like the mold Short procured, a round iron box in which paste was inserted and then pushed, by a screw turned by a lever, through "the underpart" of the box, "perforated with holes," as Jefferson wrote.

"Feel that fresh breeze!" says Gregorio as it comes through the open window. "That's why our pasta is artisanal. That same breeze dries it." In the old days, once shaped, pasta was set out on wooden cones in the street to absorb the mountain winds and drafts from the Gulf of Naples.

A manager, Egidio, wanders out of his office. "The story of pasta here goes back five hundred years," he says. "The Arabs brought semolina, a paste made from durum wheat, to Sicily. Durum is the right kind for pasta—you use other wheat for bread. And it stuck."

Gregorio explains the history of pasta in Gragnano.

Although Jefferson didn't necessarily want to turn Virginia farmers into pasta makers, the possibilities of growing wheat intrigued him. Just a month before he wrote *Hints*, he observed from his carriage window a French farmer laboring behind an inefficient plow that put too much weight on the oxen's neck. On the back of a piece of paper he promptly designed a geometric, "mathematically perfect" plow. Wheat, he wrote, "diffuses plenty and happiness"; it failed less frequently than tobacco did and required less intensive labor throughout the year. And if Europe plunged into war (it would), prices would rise "and this single commodity will make us a great and happy nation."

But the very April day in 1787 that Jefferson was describing the "olives, figs, oranges, mulberries, corn, and garden stuff" of the Genoa region, a desperate farmer back home wrote him a letter. A "pernicious Insect" was devastating wheat crops back home; the "little Enemy" devoured grains and then hid in the stalks. The destruction was so total that James Madison wrote to Jefferson in alarm as well. Later, in 1791, Jefferson and Madison embarked on a tour of New England, driven by

James Hemings, on the trail of this wheat fly, *Mayetiola destructor*, probing its origins and weaknesses. The only solution they found to the crisis was planting in the late fall.

Despite the problems with this pest, back at Monticello, Jefferson would switch his staple crop from tobacco, that culture of "infinite wretchedness," to wheat. President Washington personally gave him "the best kind" of wheat he had ever grown, which yielded "plump" grains, Jefferson wrote. Still not satisfied, he'd then try growing Sicilian wheat.

Wheat required only one-fifth the labor as tobacco. Jefferson designed a complex system for harvesting the grain, involving a foreman constantly sharpening scythes and handing them to enslaved field hands so they would never stop working. He envisioned his wheat-harvesting operation as a perfect "machine," always in equilibrium. Growing wheat never consistently brought him more profits than his tobacco had, though; nor did processing wheat in the grain mill he established on the Rivanna River when he was president.

Once again, these musings bring me back to the depressing fact that Jefferson's plans invariably revolved around enslaved labor. This held true for the kitchen as well as the farm. Even as the ambassador traveled through Italy, his enslaved servant James Hemings was training, by Jefferson's design, under the Prince of Condé's chef at a château north of Paris. Before this, Hemings had spent a year studying with a cook who lived near Jefferson; now he was learning from a true culinary master. Jefferson's Italian friend Philip Mazzei, who lived in Paris, wrote to him that the cost proved more than expected—complaining that Hemings had assented to the higher price, assuming Jefferson would shell out the extra money.

Despite the ambassador's "grumblings," he did; he wanted to be able to continue eating gourmet cuisine back home. He might have to pay through the nose for the lessons, but back in Virginia, he wouldn't have to pay his own chef, who was bound to him for life with no say in the matter.

What did Hemings think about the apprenticeship? And about Jefferson's travels more broadly? It would be up to James to figure out the new pasta machine, discover how to best cook a new variety of rice, or come up with a recipe for peach ice cream. Did he see his new role in the kitchen as another burden to be dealt with or a means of leverage to improve his condition? Unlike Jefferson's, his thoughts haven't been recorded and saved for posterity. The more I'm able to learn about the enslaved people essential to Jefferson's projects, though, the more uncomfortable I feel on this journey—which I'd intended, perhaps naively, to be a joyous, uplifting one, filled with personal growth. Can I separate out the story of the cook from the story of the meal?

I still don't know. I came to learn about food, simple as that might sound. There's an undeniable legacy of injustice underpinning Jefferson's history. But as important and tragic a subject as slavery is, I'm trying to stay focused on *Hints*. So for now, rightly or wrongly, I keep traveling on, my mind on the suggestions in the guide. I can't help but feeling, though, that I might be missing a greater story not contained within its pages.

On display on the shelves of La Fabbrica della Pasta's small store are hundreds of pastas: familiar lasagna, penne, and linguine, but also *ruote* (wheels), *ocche di lupo* (wolf eyes), and *strozzapreti* (priest-stranglers), not to mention chocolate pasta, gluten-free pasta, and fiery pepper pasta. Jefferson's enslaved chefs served one or more of these shapes— who knows which ones—in a dish he called "macaroni" (the word then for any type of pasta) when he returned with an Italian recipe he had copied in his own hand. Many guests had their first macaroni at dinners hosted by President Jefferson. One diner, surprised by the steaming bowl with long strands of something in a strong sauce, asked if he was eating elongated onions.

The smell of wheat permeates the factory as Gregorio takes us deeper into it. Four brothers from a pasta-making family bought and revitalized it in the 1970s; one still works here. They have thirty-two secrets to making their pasta, Gregorio tells us.

"Can you tell us any of them?" I ask, lowering my voice a little.

"I don't know them myself," Gregorio responds. But he's willing to take us on a secret-free tour of the factory, although he asks us to not take pictures. We put on scrubs and hygienic caps and enter a room where a worker is mixing the pasta, which is then pushed through a machine and a bronze die to form its shape. Gregorio hands us a yellow tube of raw pasta and we eat it. It's a little moist and chewy.

"Next, we'll dry it," he says. "With food, fast isn't good, right?" he quizzes us Americans.

"Bleah!" said Nico, agreeing as enthused as if he were at a church revival. Gregorio fist-bumps his little convert. "But I like Chipotle," Nico adds quickly.

"Here is the drying cell," Gregorio continues. "We'll only take a quick look. Industrial makers heat their pasta at 150 degrees Celsius for two hours," he says. "This destroys the biological elements. We heat it at 40 degrees Celsius for forty-eight hours." Gregorio opens the door, revealing a small room with noodles on shelves. A blast of heat hits us in the face.

"After two days in that hell, we bring it here," he says, taking us into the recesses of the factory. "Our pasta must relax, get colder gradually, and gain weight little by little. That's a difference with industrial production."

The tour over, Egidio the manager comes up and tells us about one of the four brothers who still runs the factory. "No one else can do it."

"What happens when he goes on vacation?" I ask.

"Easy. He never goes. Well, he went once. Someone else tried to make a very simple kind of pasta. We had to trash it and give it all to the pigs. Even when he leaves, all this is in his head. One thing I've learned from him is that you have to warm up the water for the flour to forty-five degrees Celsius. It's cold when we get it." And with that we learn our first—and last—of the thirty-two secrets.

Gregorio shows us a sample of their pasta and pasta from an industrial producer, each left out for the same number of days. "Go on, touch them," he says. Theirs still feels soft to the touch, but the other pasta is hard as a rock.

"What do you think about the big producers?" I ask, trying to provoke him a little.

Gregorio shakes his head. "I can't say anything more about them; there are children here."

The divide between slow food and fast, artisanal and industrial, didn't exist in Jefferson's day. As he traveled around Italy, almost everything he ate was local by necessity, brought in from a small radius of farmland surrounding the towns and cities he stayed in. There wasn't refrigeration, good food distribution logistics, or mass production. In fact, Italy itself was not united—Jefferson journeyed through five different small kingdoms, duchies, and independent cities.

Nor was food homogenous. Scientific breeding of animals and selection of crops had started in England—Jefferson was a proponent—but was still in its infancy. How could he have predicted that globalized sameness would displace this patchwork of regional specialties? I cling to my belief that if Jefferson were squeezed in the back of my Audi with our now thirty-five peaches, he would have loved La Fabbrica della Pasta. Surely, he would have prioritized quality and support of the little guy over the behemoths. Right?

That night we cook in the kitchen of the villa we've rented for a couple of nights from Airbnb (we have the bottom floor). Liana brings out a steaming bowl of *tagliatelle* and we dine *al fresco*, watching the lights twinkle below us in the Bay of Napoli.

The lights we can see, anyway. Our view is mostly obstructed by the rental car of the family staying on the top floor, whom we've only caught glimpses of so far. For some reason they parked their vehicle right by the outdoor table. "These people really have no respect, do they?" I complain, louder than I intended. "What were they thinking?"

A couple of minutes later, the driver, a man about my age with spiky hair, hustles out of the house and moves the car, apologizing. He introduces himself as Mathieu from France. I'm suddenly more embarrassed than he is; I hadn't realized he'd hear what I said, or even that he spoke English.

Not for the last time, I count myself lucky to have married a people person. "Come join us," Liana says sweetly. "We've made plenty." Mathieu declines but Liana insists. I shouldn't have been surprised. Cubans rival Italians in their love of food; when they're not eating, they're talking about what they just ate. As Liana was growing up, a cardinal rule in her family was to share whatever they had on their table with any unexpected visitors, even if it wasn't much.

Eventually Mathieu and his wife, Rachel, with wavy hair and a broad smile, join us at the table with two kids and two bottles of wine. We're soon comparing travel notes and laughing. Thanks to a meal, I've gone from cursing at someone to becoming fast friends with him, all in one night.

But in a true Italian feast, as we'll find out, pasta is only a precursor to a *secondo piatti* worthy of a king. And it's time to discover the ingredient so prized that, to bring it home, the ambassador turned into a smuggler.

CHAPTER ELEVEN

The Rice Smuggler

SECONDO PIATTI: VEAL OSSOBUCO WITH RISOTTO ALLA MILANESE, MILAN

No one else is idling in their vehicle; the young woman in a beat-up car outside the Famagosta train station on the outskirts of Milan has to be the one. The whole thing feels slightly illicit, but that's what it takes to learn how to make cheese around here.

Elisa is in her late twenties, slightly built, with a round face. I've come to her to because of our *secondo piatti*, a local specialty, veal *ossobucco* with *risotto alla Milanese*. Whether or not Jefferson had it, rice and cheese were high on his mind when he was in Italy, and that's what makes this dish. Elisa couldn't help with the *ossobuco*, the stewed meat, which I'd eat elsewhere, but she both grows rice and conducts cheesemaking workshops. I found Elisa on a site called Withlocals, a Dutch company that advertises itself as a peer-to-peer network "connecting travelers with locals through food and experiences," and was the only one to sign up for this workshop. She's the perfect accomplice for my investigation into Jefferson's rice-smuggling caper. I'm solo today; Liana and the kids are hanging out with an Italian schoolfriend of hers and his family.

But first the cheese. Elisa drives me to Zipo, her small family farm in Rozzano, where Jefferson also took a day trip to watch cheese being made. In his time, it was a farming town eight miles southwest of Milan; now it's within the city limits, a mix of industrial plants, houses, and a few remaining farms. Elisa keeps hers going by the strength of willpower. Her father works as a dentist, her older sister a nuclear engineer in the States. When Elisa left school, she decided to do something different, using the family land as a working, not decorative, farm. She leads me into an old brick warehouse, and I put on a smock.

In front of us is a vat with a white, rubbery substance in it. "I got started early," Elisa explains. She's filled the vat with 220 liters of milk and added an enzyme to make it coagulate. "It's 38 degrees Celsius. Touch it," she says. It feels pleasantly warm. Then she hands me what looks to be a sword. "It's time for the *prova*, the test. It's our tradition. Tap the cheese with the sword, and if it bounces, we can get to work."

When I do it springs back at me, so I proceed to cut the milk in a checkerboard pattern. Next Elisa hands me a long wooden instrument with a steel basket at the end, which I use to swirl the nascent cheese around and around, separating the chunky curds from the liquid whey. The smell is sweet and warm, the repetitive swirling motion Zenlike.

Elisa then shows me how to pour half the curds from the vat into small baskets as the whey flows down the table and drains onto the floor. "I use the whey for some cheeses," she explains, "but not for the *primo sale*. It's fresh and young." While she heats the vat up to 45 degrees, I rake and pour again. This time Elisa asks me to mix fennel into some of the baskets; it's an ingredient in the *primo sale* Zipotta, named after her farm. Normal *primo sale* is ready for eating as soon as it settles, but the fennely Zipotta will age for a month and turn yellowish.

Elisa notes the cheeses we have just made in a small notebook, adding the quantity and today's date. "This one I'll call *primo sale Derek*." She'll place it in a hand-designed wrapper and sell it at a farmers market.

"Do you ever make Gran Padano cheese?" I ask. Gran Padano is hard and salty, a close cousin to Parmesan, the King of Cheeses.

Making primo sale Derek.

She's looked into it, she responds, but there are too many restrictions. "Cows can only eat hay and grass, for example, for their cheese to qualify. But sometimes ours eat other things." When Jefferson observed cheese-making in Rozzano, he recorded the name of the cheese as Parmesan, for the Parma region where that style had originated—"but none is made there now," he was told. It certainly is today, and Jefferson's cheese couldn't get away with being called Parmesan now unless it was made in that region. Jefferson noted that the Parmesan milk cows only ate hay and grass, similar to what Elisa had said about Gran Padano today. He described the milking, the churning and skimming of the milk, the addition of saffron for color, and the aging process. He even described how "they make a poor cheese for the country people" from the whey and buttermilk left over from the Parmesan. Although he never did produce it himself, he imported Parmesan cheese and served it at the President's House.

Elisa places some cheese in a large cooler outside the warehouse. An older gentleman comes up and removes some. "I work on the honor system," she says. "My neighbors come here, take milk and cheese, and leave the payment in that box."

We walk out in a pleasant breeze to Zipo Farm's rice fields, flooded to keep pests and weeds, which are not water resistant, under control. Pigeons coo and cars hum on the nearby highway as we stroll. "We will harvest all this rice in September when it's nice and golden," she says. "Look there!" she cries out, pointing to a crumbling irrigation ditch. "That's from *nutrias*. I hate them so much."

This takes me aback. Elisa has been so calm until now and she's losing it over some inoffensive animal. In Spanish, I recall, "nutria" means otter.

"Really, nutrias aren't so bad, are they?"

"No!" she spits out. "Disgusting! Disgusting creatures!" She looks as if a nutria had fallen into her vat of fresh *primo sale* and was now swimming laps. Noticing my puzzled expression, she pulls out her smartphone and I learn that in Italian the term refers to the nutria rat, or coypu, a furry rodent with huge, canal-destroying teeth.

Rice fields inspected and nutrias cursed, we return to the warehouse to see her old rice husking machine. It isn't husking season, but she shows me how it works. A similar machine was what turned Jefferson to a life of crime. When he realized that the Italian husking equipment was similar to what was used in the Carolinas, he zeroed in on the rice itself. After recording the dates of sowing, weeding, and harvesting, the depth of the water in the fields, and the characteristics of the rice, he finally deduced that it was a different, better variety from that of South Carolina and that the Carolinians simply had to have it.

Jefferson filled his pockets full of contraband and wrote casually in his notes: "Poggio, a muleteer, who passes every week between Vercelli and Genoa, will smuggle a sack of rough [unprocessed] rice for me to Genoa; it being death to export it in that form"; the Kingdom of Sardinia went to extreme lengths to protect the secrets of its production from its competitors. Jefferson hadn't practiced law in over a decade, and it showed: he had just written a confession. But both the rice kingpin and his human mule got away scot-free. No one checked them on their return journey, and Jefferson made plans to send the hot goods on to South Carolina, where it could be sown.

It's time for lunch. "White or red?" Elisa asks. It's warm and not even noon, but I appreciate that the question isn't whether I want wine but what kind. I ask for white. She brings out a carafe and a board of three cheeses, including *primo sale Derek*, the freshest of the three. The knowledge that I've just helped make it and communed with the cows behind its origin makes it taste like the best cheese in the world. I gaze at the family's thirteenth-century house and ask her how old the warehouse is. "Only from the seventeenth century," she shrugs. She leaves and then returns with a steaming, creamy bowl of *risotto alla Milanese*, leaving it next to the bottle of Zipo rice, which I'll take home to relive this experience someday.

The rice affair was only a highlight in a lifetime of plant exchanges. Back in Paris, Jefferson was at the hub of a network of amateurs who sent each other seeds and cuttings, roots and vines. In the garden behind his Champs-Élysées mansion he grew corn and riesling grapes among many other botanical specimens. He even asked James Madison to take time away from what he was working on to send him two barrels of Virginia apples. The fruit arrived in a mush from the crossing, which prompted Jefferson to cancel his additional request for live opossums. (Madison must have been relieved; his other duties included writing and defending the U.S. Constitution.) Once home, Jefferson kept plant seeds collected from all around the globe in vials carefully labeled in his cabinet, never giving up on his search for the perfect specimen.

I finish Elisa's risotto while wondering whether local food was ever the same after Jefferson and his fellow travelers began these exchanges. How can the efforts of Elisa, with her honor-system cooler, compete with international distribution networks? How can Slow Food be more than an afterthought in this globalized world? This trip is stuffing me full of calories and unforgettable flavors, but not yet with answers to my questions on how to interpret Jefferson's guide.

Elisa returns and sits down next to me. "Tell me more about your book," she says, innocently uttering one of my favorite sentences to hear in the world. Back home, I had started slowly turning my travel notes into a manuscript. I spill everything: the wine marathon, the boat trips, Jefferson's rice smuggling. She listens quietly.

"When you finish it, we can have a reception right here," she finally says. "How about in front of our old house in the garden? I'll provide some cheese for you for free."

I stare. She must not understand that this writing idea is still little more than a glimmer in my mind, a labor of love that I'm figuring out one page at a time. But I think of her example. Elisa transformed herself from a dentist's daughter in an obscure suburb to an artisan cheesemaker and rice grower, preserver of a thousand years' worth of foodways. She believes in the power of the ancient foods she makes and in her ability to get them out into a world dominated by multinational food conglomerates. Now she believes in me as well.

Likewise, Jefferson turned a short trip into an opportunity to learn about Parmesan cheese and smuggle rice, hoping to transform what Americans grew and ate. Even those Italians who had dreamed up food as complex as salty Parmesan cheese and creamy risotto were on to something. Maybe I should dream big, too.

DOLCE: VIN SANTO AND CROSTATA

Alessandro is in his late forties, short with a bulging nose. Seated behind his desk in a casual business shirt and jeans, he talks rapidly, waving his hands as if trying to annihilate a swarm of flies. His English might be spotty, but he more than makes up for it with his hands; he's Italian to the nth degree, owning the stereotype. Around us are cases of wine that each feature a drawing of a farmhouse and the name of Alessandro's winery in script, Il Monticello.

"The house was built around 1800," he tells Liana and me while the kids run among the olive trees. "But the property was called Il Monticello for many years before that. Forever," he says. Despite this pedigree, the name presented him with legal difficulties when he tried to market his wine in the United States.

We're staying on his farm perched on a small mountain, as the name promises, overlooking hills of olive trees and grapevines and a splotch of blue far below us: the Mediterranean. We're only a few miles from La Spezia, a town listed in *Hints*. Even without that justification, I would have jumped at coming here—I have such a weakness for the name alone that I would have booked us into Monticello Slums and Dumpsters for Rent. That Agriturismo Il Monticello is a lovely, old yellow house, with the smell of thyme in the air, is a bonus.

All around us stand Razolla olive trees, an ancient Ligurian variety that Alessandro uses to make olive oil, fruity and green, with notes of spices. The olives are handpicked, as traditional as can be, but he also measures the oil's acidity with more modern instruments. "In Italy we must have the taste," he says. "The pig, the grape, and the cheese: that is what we like. The difference between tomatoes from a little farm and the store is incredible. Tomatoes from the farm don't just taste like water. I only eat eggs grown by my friends. We want to look at our farmer in the face." Sure enough, later in our conversation, a customer comes up and places a small order. Alessandro ships a hundred thousand bottles of wine across Italy, he tells us, but some people like to look their wine-maker in the eye.

Galileo inspired him, he says. Alessandro holds an advanced engineering degree and looks to science and empirical data for guidance in running his vineyard and farm. "In Italy, if you ask students what they like, 99 percent say history and art. Only 1 percent pick math and science. But math is incredible—it is behind the formation of clouds, flowers, the sounds of the guitar," he tells us, illustrating these phenomena in turn with his gestures. "All this is math.

"We use technology but we also respect nature," he goes on. Alessandro's family made traditional Vermentino wine for generations, but its taste was rough and it sold only locally. When he and his brother revitalized the vineyard, using stainless-steel tanks and precise temperature controls, they produced wine at an entire new level.

Now he's applying his scientific knowledge against a small but deadly opponent, powdery mildew. Vintners typically blast grapes with as much copper mist as possible, which kills the mildew spores and protects the vines against further infection. "But we don't want to use too much," he tells us. Although he has yet to find a better substitute for copper, he monitors his grapes closely so as to spray only the minimum required. "My computer model shows when the attack will come. I measure precipitation, leaf wetness, air temperature, and relative humidity. Then my computer indicates the spores are flying." He waves his arms—spores closing in on unsuspecting grapevines. "And then comes the copper!" Imaginary copper sprays through the air. He sits down triumphantly.

"He's like a modern-day Jefferson," Liana whispers as he goes into the back to get us some bottles. Alessandro's love of both technology and nature intrigues me. Can an interest in the latest scientific methods be deployed in the service of traditional foodways?

Late in the day Liana serves up local anchovies and cooks up steak to go with our Gragnano pasta. "This is so good," Miranda says. "This pasta is so much better than what we have at home. Everything's been so good on this trip."

We pop open Alessandro's dessert wine, *vin santo*, tasting of apricots, figs, and honey. It pairs well with the last of the *primo sale Derek* and fruit tarts known as *crostata*. I think of our journey and Jefferson's. Unfortunately, the planters in South Carolina decided his smuggled Italian rice was inferior to their own stock. They even asked him not to send any more so it wouldn't run the risk of hybridizing with their own rice growing in their wet fields.

Although frustrated, Jefferson turned over a new question in his mind. Why grow rice in water at all? Stagnant water was not only the ideal breeding ground for nasty aquatic rats, as I've learned, but also a disease that killed "numbers of the inhabitants annually with pestilential fevers," Jefferson wrote. The culprit, not identified for another century, was malaria borne by infected mosquitoes that bred in standing water. Jefferson began searching for rice that grew in drier climates. Over dinner with the prince of Vietnam in Paris, he asked him for rice; it never came. William Bligh sent him a sample from Timor, collected after his crew mutinied, but Jefferson was unable to cultivate it.

But in 1790, a ship's captain and friend of Jefferson's, on a terrible mission to enslave Africans, was able to buy red Guinean rice for him. After planting, it thrived in a field near Monticello and, spread by Jefferson, "succeeded...perfectly" in Georgia. This was a boon for White planters, but it also fueled their demand for more slaves. When Jefferson ran for president, he listed the introduction of upland rice as one of his accomplishments. "The greatest service which can be rendered any country is to add a useful plant to its culture," he wrote about his rice sleuthing.

Jefferson loved to make decisions based on science, with its efficiencies and promise of progress. He sought the most rational solution to agricultural problems: if one variety of bean proved to be the best, others must be eliminated. He ordered his enslaved workers to work together as a "machine" to harvest monoculture plantings of wheat. Yet at the same time, wasn't he our Founding Epicurean? A lover of enlightened order who still found room for beauty and grace in his own life, as well as at his table? Even after weeks on the road, I'm still going around and around on the question of how to apply his philosophy to the great debates over food today.

As I had with his landscape gardens, which projected a vision of liberty while hiding the contributions of Black slaves, I keep running up against Jefferson's contradictions. In his own days he was known for saying different things to different audiences. The historian Joseph Ellis famously called him an "American Sphinx," with layers of interior defenses which he didn't allow others to penetrate. Although I'm hoping that following in Jefferson's footsteps will help me understand him better, I'm left again with the realization that solving the puzzles left by this most confounding Founder won't be easy.

Maybe this particular circle can be squared. I've seen examples of people keeping old flavors alive using new technology and artisans squeezing their way into distribution systems. Eataly has nearly forty branches across the world and more planned, even if some big producers are now on their shelves, too. Although Elisa sells her cheese and rice at a snail's pace, she's found a way to share her experience with global travelers like myself on the web. Both Egidio and Alessandre are exploring foreign consumer markets, smuggling the tastes of their ancestors into the twenty-first century. I like these possibilities.

Ultimately, though, the safest conclusion to the dilemma of where Jefferson would fall on these questions is: it's complicated. And perhaps unknowable. Putting Jefferson down on either side of a debate he didn't even know existed doesn't do him justice. He flagged issues and themes and gave us his principles; isn't that enough? If some of his values conflict centuries later, it's our job to struggle with them; he can't do our thinking for us today.

Still, I give him credit for sparking my interest and sending us on this trip. Those were some damn good hints. Our quest has introduced us to old foods that are new to us: artisanal *tagliatelle* and fennel-specked Zipotta cheese, silky-smooth olive oil and *risotto alla Milanese*. And it's opened the kids' eyes even more, to potato pizza, *spaghetti carbonara*, and fried zucchini flowers. Miranda, in particular, was impressed by the mind-blowing array of ingredients on display at Eataly. None of us yet know that she'll embark on her own cooking experiments back home.

Thanks to Jefferson's example, we've made life moments here by the Mediterranean. "If any person wished to retire from their acquaintance, to live absolutely unknown, and yet in the midst of physical enjoyments, it should be in some of the little villages of this coast, where air, earth and water concur to offer what each has most precious," he wrote as he concluded his Italian journey. "The earth furnishes wine, oil, figs, oranges and every production of the garden in every season. The sea yields lobsters, crabs, oysters, tuna, sardines, and anchovies."

I'm not ready to retire. But, if my experience is any guide, I can recommend lingering at the Ligurian coast over a dinner *al fresco*. And talking to your friends and loved ones as you dine, savoring what the air, earth, and water have offered, and appreciating the people who brought it to you. My own Hints are to sip *vin santo* as the kids run in the orchard, to watch the sun set over the vines and light up the silvery olive trees as it slips down to the sea.

And, for God's sake, help me finish this box of peaches.

CHAPTER TWELVE

Remedial Education

THE NAKED TRUTH

Moonlight spilled over the University of Virginia Rotunda, helping me to find it in the dark. Jefferson designed it with a brilliant white dome capping a structure of red brick and marble capitals carved in Carrara marble, an example of harmonious Classical architecture and pure beauty. He also had practical functions in mind, planning for the interior dome to be painted blue to serve as a planetarium and designing flues and underground brick tunnels for the chemistry lab on the ground floor. His structure has long stood at the heart of student life: commencements, protests, rallies, celebrations, graduations.

When I was a student, the Rotunda served a different purpose: its steps were where I placed my neatly folded clothes before running naked down the university's lawn.

I flew down the two-hundred-yard terrace that started at the Rotunda's base, my bare feet lightly grazing the cushioning grass. Others were doing the same. UVA has long held a requirement that students have to streak the Lawn before graduation—one not enforced by the Registrar but by the social code of students. In my final year at school, 1994–1995, streaking had become so popular that authorities strung a series of chains at intervals across the Lawn in an ultimately futile effort to halt this sacred tradition. The Friday night after they went up, a hundred students raced toward the barriers like naked lemmings and hurdled the waist-high chains in the dark, with most eluding both the campus police and an embarrassing visit to the hospital.

Sprinting to the statue of Homer at the far end of the Lawn, I focused all my attention on the uneven ground rather than the illuminated buildings on either side. But, truth be told, I never gave the structures a second glance when I walked by them in the daylight either. I managed to spend my years at the school completely missing out on Jefferson's architectural lessons.

If Monticello was Jefferson's "essay in architecture," as he put it, the buildings of the University of Virginia were his travel journal, the equivalent of *Hints* written in stone and brick. As an old man, founding and designing the state's first university in his retirement, Jefferson scattered buildings along the school grounds like so many Easter eggs, homages to structures he had observed or encountered in the books he bought in Paris. Decades earlier, he had fallen in love with buildings "by the accidental circumstance of his purchasing a book on Architecture when at college from an old drunken cabinetmaker," William Short wrote. This prize was likely the masterpiece written by Palladio, the sixteenth-century Venetian architect who repopularized classical Roman architecture. But purchasing Palladio was expensive (unless the seller was drunk). Years later, Jefferson would make things easy for his own students: rather than studying plates in a manuscript, they just had to open their eyes to the buildings surrounding them.

His teachings started with the Rotunda itself, a massive building half the diameter of the Pantheon in Rome, built with ideas borrowed from other grand domed structures Jefferson came across in Europe. South from the Rotunda stretched the grassy Lawn, with ten pavilions lining it, five on each side. Jefferson intended for a professor to live on the second floor of each and give classes on the ground floor. He also wanted them to serve as "models in architecture of the purest forms" for students, with "no two alike." The first students were literally surrounded by Jefferson's vision; they lived in fifty-four rooms in between the pavilions and behind a Tuscan colonnade with simple round capitals capping the columns.

But for me, they were just old buildings behind which police might be lurking with flashlights to harass streakers. I didn't even realize they were supposed to show different styles.

To be fair, his ideas were lost on most Americans at the time as well. Jefferson thought the state of architecture in America was atrocious. Virginia's public buildings, he wrote, were "rude, misshapen piles which, but that they have roofs, would be taken for brick kilns." As for the private houses, "it is impossible to devise things more ugly, uncomfortable, and happily more perishable." There were few trained architects in the new nation; workmen did not know what architectural orders were, much less the "first principles" of the building arts.

This gap troubled him deeply. It was not just a question of aesthetics: he believed that buildings should express a nation's core values. He wanted his own students to understand the noblest sentiments of the old Roman Republic—democracy, order, and harmony—in a new, American setting. Architecture is "worth great attention," he wrote in *Hints*, making it Object of Attention Five. Since the American population was growing so rapidly, there was an opportunity to build and rebuild with "taste." He hoped that his university would help instill it in a new generation of citizens.

He had high hopes for UVA as an alternative to the smaller William and Mary, his own alma mater, which he thought emphasized religion to the detriment of modern science. Jefferson wanted his secular, Enlightened school to give out merit scholarships to deserving White males in the Commonwealth, forming a democratic, republican vanguard (albeit one limited by race and sex) for the new nation. "This institution will be based on the illimitable freedom of the human mind," wrote Jefferson, lines now inscribed above a doorway to classrooms. "For here we are not afraid to follow truth wherever it may lead, nor to tolerate any error so long as reason is left free to combat it."

In the early days of the school, though, William Short (who, long after his travels in Europe, visited Virginia at Jefferson's invitation) worried that no one would understand this idea of "exhibiting models of architecture for the instruction of the rising generation." He was right. Inebriated students turned the Lawn into a site of carousing, gambling, even dueling—virtually everything except architectural appreciation. The sons of plantation owners barked orders to slaves and bossed around their professors. When UVA expelled three students for acts of violence, the eighty-two-year-old Jefferson, rector of the university, was left speechless, overcome. One of the delinquents was his own great-nephew.

Jefferson couldn't believe that his students had ignored what he had built for them: friezes (decorated horizontal bands) inspired by Rome, colonnades and what he called "cubic" architecture taken from Provence, innovative designs borrowed from Paris, and an opportunity to reflect on the social and political messages of buildings themselves. And not just at UVA: within roughly seventy-five miles of the school were his other great masterpieces, the Virginia State Capitol, Monticello, and his retirement home at Poplar Forest, lessons hiding in plain sight.

But if Jefferson had created an "essay in architecture" for his students, I, too, had failed to understand it while at university, literally naked in my ignorance. It wasn't just that I was oblivious to the UNESCO World Heritage Site where I studied every day; I hardly noticed buildings at all, any more than I did electricity pylons. I didn't even know the name of the style of the 1940s rambling brick home I grew up in in northern Virginia (ranch). Rather than resembling Jefferson's ideal student, I felt more akin to his drunk cabinetmaker's drinking buddies.

And so here I am in France, two decades later, *Hints* in hand. I'll have to learn architecture the hard way, with my clothes on.

FOUNDATIONS

"Come on, bull! Bull, be brave!" It's a little disturbing to hear Nico's cheers, but I chalk up his allegiance to sympathy for the animals rather than hostility toward the teenagers risking their lives in the arena. Fortunately, the event we're watching, called *la course camarguaise*, is more humane than traditional bullfighting—a contestant plucks a rosette ribbon from the *taureau's* neck with no swords involved and everyone lives to fight another day. But I'm more interested in the setting than the show: the ancient Roman amphitheater of Arles, in Provence.

We're sitting in a stone oval in the clear light. Like Jefferson, we've come here to tour Roman buildings, the bedrock of his architectural vision. He visited many on his 1787 trip to the south of France. "For me, the city of Rome is actually existing in all the splendor of its empire," Jefferson wrote to a friend back in Paris. To give news from this classical setting, "I should tell you stories a thousand years old."

Provence might seem a strange place to encounter these buildings, but the region got its name from being Rome's first province, conquered in 125 BC. It's littered with ancient theaters, temples, and bridges, preserved in the dry air. Jefferson's hero, the Renaissance architect Palladio, had traveled there as well in search of inspiration.

The amphitheater, after restoration, might look even more Roman now than when Jefferson was here. He recorded that it was surrounded by buildings and occupied by a thousand people living in houses constructed inside that obscured the original seats. He nonetheless measured arches, calculated the arena's diameter, and studied the columns. The Romans employed five different styles of columns, each with a different form and level of ornateness and status. These, Jefferson concluded, were Corinthian, the second-most elaborate of the five orders.

Inside the arena, the young men in the sand have more pressing concerns than architecture: the one-ton bull periodically charging at them. Whoever grabs the rosette from its horns gets the value of the current purse. Local businesses keep adding to the initial prize of 20 euros. "Five euros additional from the bar, which has fresh drinks," the announcer calls out. "Two more from the ice cream salesman! And two more from our local deputy!" I half-expect prosthetic-limb salesmen or funeral directors to start chipping in, out of self-interest if not civic pride. The crowd, except for Nico, cheers as the moves become riskier. "Two more euros from the french fry salesman! Five from the *Journal de Provence!*" When the purse reaches 190 euros—for a particularly nasty bull that jumps over the wooden walls and cavorts around the inner perimeter of the stadium below the seats—a brave teenager swoops in and grabs the rosette. He just avoids being gored and can now buy that game console he was dreaming of.

A charging bull will give you that extra spring in your step.

We wander around the rest of the afternoon in the shadow of the amphitheater, ending by dining on a nearby street. Literally on the street; since the restaurant is full, they've set up tables and rickety chairs in the middle of a cobblestoned lane. We periodically shift around to let a moped squeeze buy us. The *plat du jour* is *taureau à la planche*. Surely the bull we watched today couldn't have been grilled that quickly, but I now have an inkling where he'll wind up in retirement.

As dramatic as the day has been, it's the gracefulness of the Roman building itself that forms the most lasting impression. The amphitheater's 120 arches stand against the sharp azure sky. The grand exterior arcades, a series of contiguous arches that pedestrians could walk under (and perhaps shop in the stalls beneath them), perfectly blend form and function. Jefferson added a similar arcade at UVA, linking the Pavilions and student houses, allowing professors and students to walk and talk while sheltered from rain and snow.

To the extent I'm able to understand what these buildings are saying, I have a UVA professor to thank. When I was a student I had never heard of Richard Guy Wilson, although he was the dean of the architecture school at the time. But before our trip, I had attended a lecture by him on Jeffersonian architecture, one of his specialties. He looked exceedingly professorial, with a bow tie and tweed jacket, although he sprinkled his conversation with mild swear words. Students liked to call him RGW.

"Jefferson took from Palladio and the Romans ideas of balance, the hierarchy of orders, symmetry, and a love of geometry," RGW said. He talked about the classical meanings Jefferson sought to imbue not only in the buildings he designed himself, but also the ones he shepherded through to completion in Washington, DC, while in government— including the U.S. Capitol.

"His travels were important," the professor said. "Thomas Jefferson was willing to change his mind." He rattled off a list of buildings that provoked transformations in Jefferson's ideas. Following his time in Europe, the ambassador became one of the most important architects in American history. The notion that his journeys brought Jefferson to a different place in his architecture intrigued me, although the lecture didn't fully explain how that occurred. What the professor did make clear was that to understand a building you have to go out and see it in person, on-site, and reach your own judgments. As he would often say, "I haven't seen all the damn buildings, but they're all worth seeing."

Since traveling through Provence had changed both Palladio's and Jefferson's perspectives, now it's my family's turn to hopscotch around the region, viewing "antiquities from morning to night," as Jefferson had put it. One visit includes a walk under the symmetrical arches of the Pont du Gard, a Roman aqueduct bridge, led on by Nico giving chase to a dragonfly. In the Pont du Gard museum, we read quotes from famous visitors, including Jefferson's hero Jean-Jacques Rousseau, who, after viewing the aqueduct, wrote rapturously, "Oh, how I wish I was Roman!"

All our Founders did. They looked back to the Roman Republic like we look back to the Founders themselves, today (but a thousand times more so). Sculptors made Jefferson, Washington, and the rest look like Roman heroes; downtown D.C. today looks like you took a wrong turn off of the Roman Forum. Seeing these classical buildings in their natural habitats reminds me how odd it is that the style caught on in the States, two millennia later. We've gotten used to having our banks sprout columns, but we should remember how hard Jefferson and crew had to work to install this fetish in our culture. What would our public buildings be like today if the Founders had enjoyed dressing up like King Arthur's knights or constructing buildings that looked like Viking longhouses?

Instead, they saw the Roman Republic as an example of civic virtue, an example for those creating the first large-scale republic in the New World. When the Founders viewed classical buildings, it sparked nostalgic daydreams of their childhood Latin readings and reminded them of the values of strength, balance, and sacrifice for the common good. The Romans' architectural contributions were not just symbolic, though. They pioneered the use of arches, domes, and vaults, deploying reinforced concrete to build on a great scale, creating symmetrical yet muscular structures.

Before he went to Provence, Jefferson hadn't seen Roman buildings in person, but he had devoured books about them and copied them into his own early designs. For a lover of geometry like Jefferson, as RGW pointed out, classical structures provided him with a profusion of shapes to play with and mathematical equations to calculate.

When the Virginia State Legislature wrote to him in 1785 asking him to design a new state capitol, Jefferson insisted that it follow a classical model, one that had the approval "of all the judges of architecture who have seen it." With the help of a Parisian architect, he worked off the design of the Maison Carrée, a temple in Nîmes some twenty miles from Arles. Its columns standing symmetrically on all four sides, the temple was "the most perfect" classical building still standing, he wrote.

But Jefferson didn't create a carbon copy of the Maison Carrée. He doubled its size and reduced its rows of columns from three to two, so as not to darken the interior light of the bureaucrats inside. Instead of stone for the exterior, Jefferson recommended bricks covered with stucco. Worried that Virginian stonecutters couldn't fashion complicated Corinthian columns (with their acanthus flowers), Jefferson reluctantly swapped them out for the simpler Ionic, featuring scroll-like volutes (resembling curled ram's horns) on the top of the column. And instead of a Roman god in the middle, there would be a statue of George Washington, which people could view from an interior balcony.

"Jefferson threw tradition to the wind sometimes," RGW said in his lecture. "You weren't supposed to have a second-floor balcony on a Roman temple." Nonetheless, this was the most important building Jefferson ever designed, he said, inspiring American public architects to look to classical examples for centuries to come. Building this version of the Maison Carrée in America—while Jefferson himself was still in France—was an ambitious undertaking. Without trained architects in America, building contractors constructed based on sight, at most following simple drawings. Jefferson developed detailed work plans, perhaps the first in the U.S., and mailed them off before his trip to the south of France. Now he could see the original inspiration in person. So can we, if we can track it down.

The Maison Carrée and a model of the Virginia State Capitol (made by Jean-Pierre Fouquet based on the design of Jefferson and Charles-Louis Clérisseau).

The Maison Carrée has more or less stayed put for the last two thousand years, but finding it in Nîmes's dark, twisty streets proves to be a headache. I take a wrong turn and get caught in the traffic of yet another summer festival. As I turn onto rue Corneille, my rearview mirror seems to be glowing. I look closer: it's illuminated by the reflection of a white, gleaming temple, shining out harmony.

We park and wander up, the streets packed even at ten at night. It was indeed the "most perfect example of Cubic architecture," an amalgam of mathematical equations. Although its name translates as "Square House," it's actually a rectangle with pediments (decorative triangular gables) perched above six columns at each end. Miranda, who has studied geometry considerably more recently than I have, identifies squares, triangles, and "tons of cylinders," building blocks Jefferson used in many designs, including in his UVA Pavilions.

Outside a band plays Cuban songs, and Liana starts shaking it to a *guaguancó*. We find a small restaurant still open, right behind the temple. I order a Provençal-style pizza with whipped salt cod and a carafe of slightly fruity Costières de Nîmes and stare at the temple. When I turn back, both kids are slumped on the table next to their cheese pizza, asleep.

As for Jefferson, he was so enamored by the Maison Carrée that he gazed at it day and night, "like a lover at his mistress," he wrote. The workers of Nîmes must have thought he was depressed, contemplating suicide even, he wrote, since he barely moved for hours. But no, he was, he wrote, in "love...with a house!"

The temple stood as an affirmation of Jefferson's childhood studying Latin and his years of idolizing ancient Rome and its architecture. Yet when he turned to building in earnest back home, Jefferson never again simply copied Roman structures. He realized he could do more. He had started by parroting a building from the past when he designed the Virginia capitol but wound up making significant changes. He'd need to make even further adjustments when he turned to designing residences; homeowners didn't necessarily want to live in ancient period pieces.

How could he update Roman architectural ideas? Which other architects should he look to for inspiration? These questions weighed on his mind when he took his three-week detour from Provence to Italy, the sojourn that turned him into a rice smuggler. Ancient Rome gave Jefferson his architectural foundations, but it was time to search for a new superstructure. Having seen the architecture that inspired him in Provence, we're on to Italy next. There are more damn buildings worth seeing.

THE VILLA THAT DIDN'T BITE

As Jefferson traveled in search of inspiration, he noticed that many of the best examples of Italian architecture all used the same secret ingredient: Carrara marble, white with blueish-gray veins, included in everything from the columns of the Roman Pantheon to the chiseled arms of Michelangelo's *David*. When Jefferson commissioned the statue of Washington for the state capitol, he ordered a depiction of the general with a plow, sword, and bundle of rods carved out of a massive block of Carrara.

The Boys, unlike Jefferson, spent months touring Vicenza, Naples, and Rome before reaching Carrara, viewing ruins and taking lessons on architecture. William Short in particular enthused about his growing "passion" for buildings. While Short was still in Rome, Jefferson wrote and asked him to fulfill a "little commission." Jefferson had visited Genoa, the famed Mediterranean port city, the year before, meeting with artisans and recording the price of Carrara marble. Now he sent Short a design he had made of chimney pieces with friezes and cornices.

Like the Boys, we, too, had first tramped across Rome in the stifling heat, admiring the Pantheon and the Roman Forum, with its hodgepodge of buildings from different epochs. "It's all jumbled up!" Miranda exclaimed when she saw it. And now we head to the quarries to see this architectural performance-enhancer ourselves.

The town of Carrara is nestled in the Apuan Alps, overlooking the Mediterranean coast and the old road linking Genoa and Pisa. We find the road to the quarries and keep going up. Finally, we reach a low-hanging building advertising tours, don green hard hats and orange safety vests, and climb into a 4X4 covered in grayish-white marble dust. Since a large group of equally large Germans take up the middle seats, we're consigned to the far back, facing each other in a compartment without seat belts. The tattooed driver cranks up loud and dubious Italian rock music to put him in the mood for what appears to be a murder-suicide mission, hurtling around curves and shooting past trucks groaning with their loads.

I look out the window, a mistake. We're only inches from the edge. Far below us is a quarry that resembles an Incan temple, with huge blocks of marble resting on top of each other, and far below that a dot of blue, the sea. I glance at the rest of the family; their faces are as white as stone. "This is so scary," Nico says. "Are we going to make it?" Finally, at the top, we breathe a little easier and get out to look around, leaving the driver to sit sullenly in the 4X4, plotting the descent.

"This is a working mountain," a young guide explains over the crashing of rock into trucks and the warning beeps of heavy vehicles backing up near us. American safety inspectors would not approve. "Each one of those trucks carries thirty-five tons of marble. The purest, the whitest, is ninety-five percent calcium carbonate, and we can sell that at five thousand euros a ton.

"Here we have thirty quarries still active," she continues. "And this mountain over here has been excavated ever since the year 0 BC." We watch a diamond-tipped drill whirl into the mountain and an excavator load a thirty-five-ton block for transport. The tech wasn't always so elaborate, of course. She points out caves where workers once crouched watching crude explosions dislodge marble, all while eating tomatoes and lard and drinking a local red, called quarrymen's wine. "This mountain produces the best marble in the world," she concludes, then sighs. "We will finish with it in fifty years."

You can't use Carrara marble for everything; it's expensive and, as we've just learned, running out. Jefferson would use it only for special touches—like the columns of the UVA Rotunda, itself modeled on the Carrara-infused Pantheon—when he wanted to evoke the glory of Rome as a teaching moment for his students. But bumping up against limitations can itself spur beauty. When he couldn't find adequate building stone in America, Jefferson instead relied on deep red bricks, made from Virginia clay, set off with white trim: what became his buildings' signature look.

The marble of the gods.

As fine as Carrara marble is, Jefferson did not wish to be confined to Roman architecture; he still was searching for "modern" building alternatives. The Milan cathedral, some 150 miles north of the quarries, reinforced an important architectural lesson: what *not* to do.

Before Carrara, we had already visited the pitched roof of the cathedral, the famed Duomo. Since there's no prospect of falling (the roof slopes down to jagged crenellated walls with crosses), we could gaze around us and daydream in the summer sun for as long as we liked. Below us streets ran in all directions, trollies disgorged passengers, and shoppers entered smart fashion stores. Before us stood a 365-foot spire capped by a teetering bronze statue of the Madonna, and rows of pinnacles, so many the building looked like a porcupine. Carved into a series of fantastic shapes and statues, the very stone seemed to teem with life. A pleasant enough scene. For Jefferson, it was a living hell.

The Duomo was "a worthy object of philosophical contemplation, to be placed among the rarest instances of the misuse of money," he wrote in *Hints*. "On viewing the churches of Italy, it is evident without calculation that the same expense would have sufficed to throw the Apennines into the Adriatic and thereby render it terra firma from Leghorn to Constantinople." Not a quote you'll find on Milan's Office of Tourism website. "Jefferson only climbed Gothic cathedrals for the views," RGW said.

Built over six centuries, the Duomo is a mishmash of Gothic and rococo, two styles that Jefferson detested. He considered gargoyles and flying buttresses to be relics of the Dark Ages, signifying superstition and dogmatic religion. When Jefferson had observed the addition of Gothic windows to the Roman temple at Vienne in France, he fumed to a friend back in Paris that the change was barbaric. "I am glad you were not there," he wrote, "for you would have seen me more angry than I hope you will ever see me."

Rococo was hardly better in his eyes. This seventeenth-century style was far too extravagant for the restrained Jefferson, featuring buildings dripping with stylized seashells, cherubs, stucco foliage, and gilded bronze bling. As with Gothic, Jefferson thought the style dishonored the memory of Rome's clean harmony and geometry. Even if he wanted to put his own, modern touch on classical architecture, he didn't want to reject it completely. A better model for Jefferson came from the old friend he knew from the drunken cabinetmaker's book, Palladio.

The son of a stone mason, Andrea Palladio was born in Vicenza, in the Veneto region near Venice, in 1508 as Andrea della Gondola. When he was a young man, a prominent patron arranged for his architectural training and bestowed him with a new name from the goddess Pallas Athena, signifying wisdom. After roaming throughout Italy and Provence looking for Roman architecture, just as *Hints* encouraged American travelers to do two centuries later, Palladio began to build. Although he designed churches and public buildings, most of his commissions came from wealthy individuals who wanted country homes. He built these villas to look like temples, with pediments and sometimes domes. For those who didn't have the chance to view his creations in person, he wrote *The Four Books of Architecture*. Filled with drawings and measurements, it gave the aspiring architect more than enough ideas to get started.

As a young man, Jefferson followed Palladio religiously, copying the front facade of his own house from a drawing of Palladio's Villa Cornaro and the back from one of Palladio's Villa Pisani. Boxy and dome-less, this first Monticello was Georgian in style with a double portico (a porch with a roof supported by columns) and a flat roof. This was the version standing when Jefferson sailed for Europe. Even attempting to build a classical-style mansion in America at this early date should have gotten Jefferson a participation medal; a visiting Frenchman praised him in 1782 for being the only American who has "consulted the fine arts to know how he should shelter himself from the weather." But the guest still noted that the home, a mishmash of two designs from a centuries-old book, was "not however without some faults." No one today would judge it worthy of the back of a nickel.

"Palladio was the Bible," advised Jefferson later to a neighbor who was looking to build. "You should get it and stick close to it." When Jefferson reached Italy in 1787, he was only a three-day ride from three dozen of Palladio's influential villas. Naturally, you'd expect *Hints* to be filled with Jefferson's personal observations of his hero's buildings.

But Jefferson didn't go.

✦ ✦ ✦

The question tugs at me as we drive across the flatlands of the Veneto on the E70 after a few days in Venice: why didn't he visit the villas of his hero? Yes, he had time pressures; he had only justified his Italian detour on the need to bring back Piedmont rice. But his failure to visit the Veneto still strikes me as strange. The most famous Palladian in America already was playing hooky from work. Why not take a few days more for a pilgrimage, a chance he might never have again?

Getting to our Airbnb before nightfall will be tight. I pass by an exit for Vicenza, regret washing over me. What did *Hints* say? "When you are doubting whether a thing is worth the trouble of going to see, recollect that you will never again be so near it, that you may repent the not having seen it, but can never repent having seen it." When I see a second exit, I abruptly swerve on to the off-ramp and ask a surprised Liana to search for directions on her phone.

"Where are we going?" says Miranda, roused from her dozing by the screeching of the tires.

"It's a place called La Rotonda. But we're going to have to be really, really quick." The villa is on the outskirts of town and luckily isn't hard to find. I drive through a quiet residential neighborhood, then up a hill. Not just any hill—*The Four Books* describes the building as perching on top of a *monticello*, a small mountain, which likely gave Jefferson the name of his own home.

All's quiet except for the whine of cicadas, just like at Jefferson's estate. Naturally the building is closed for a long lunch break. I peer through the bars of a gate and a tangle of grapevines. There it is, set back from the road and past some formal gardens: a large, yellow building with a portico with five columns, crowned with a dome stretching to meet the sky, dominating what Palladio called the "theater" of hills around it.

After some moments of contemplation, we leave via a different route, turning onto an avenue running east, and spy the villa from that side and the modest houses below it. But something seems a little off. From this angle, it seems like I'm seeing the same thing I did before, because I am: Palladio's Rotonda has four symmetrical sides with a quartet of porticoes ringing the dome. The whole effect strikes me as a little severe, its angular geometry heavy. The domed buildings that Jefferson himself built on his return to America, Monticello and UVA's Rotunda, flow better, standing in perfect dialogue with their surroundings. He outdid his old master.

It dawns on me why Jefferson didn't make the time to visit these villas: he had outgrown them. His failure to make the trip was like Sherlock Holmes's famous dog that didn't bark, inaction that explains the key to a mystery. Palladio and ancient Rome would remain major influences on Jefferson, but not models to be copied unfailingly. He would no longer spend hours measuring and calculating the dimensions of a classical building as he had at the Arles amphitheater or attempt to replicate one wholesale as he had with the Maison Carrée.

Yes, Palladio was the Bible, he wrote—but that was advice for a neighbor dabbling in building, not for a seeker on a journey of architectural discovery. The freethinking Jefferson could never be confined to the strictures of others; after all, he even took a pair of scissors to a copy of the Bible, excising parts he didn't consider true. Back home, he'd tear down sections of his own Palladian copycat villa and make Monticello into something new. "Jefferson took Palladio and ran with it," RGW said. Did he ever.

Jefferson dreamed of capping his new version of his home with a dome. But not like the one on La Rotonda in Vicenza; as modern as it was for its time, Jefferson craved something even more contemporary— and buildable. Even as he enthused about the classical structure he saw on his travels, there was one domed building in Paris he couldn't get out of his mind, which he was "violently smitten" with: the most beautiful house in the most beautiful city in the world. He had built with his head. Now he would do so from his heart.

CHAPTER THIRTEEN

The Architecture of Dreams

CITY OF LOVE

Gazing at the construction of the Hôtel de Salm was one of Jefferson's favorite, albeit hazardous, pastimes. He would often walk the short distance from his Champs-Élysées house (itself stylishly modern) to the Jardin des Tuileries, where he would rent a chair to sit in. While the other garden visitors gabbed, he'd spend the afternoon staring a thousand feet across the Seine to the building emerging from the ground (which was not a hotel in the sense of a place where guests booked rooms; the word in French also meant a private residence). This small new mansion, commissioned by a German prince and executed by an avant-garde French architect, featured curving lines and a sense of coziness, capped by a dome. Jefferson stared at it so long, twisting his head to get a better view, that he'd invariably return home with a sore neck. And as we walk onto the Quai Anatole France, we're delighted to find him still in the act of staring.

"He looks pretty determined," Liana says. "Like he's plotting something." A little over a decade ago, Paris installed a nearly ten-foot bronze statue of Jefferson staring at the Hôtel de Salm. In his left hand, he holds his first plan for Monticello, the one with the double porticoes; in his right, a quill pen. He seems to be considering crumpling up his original building design and starting over.

Today, the Hôtel de Salm houses the Museum of the Legion of Honor and the Orders of Chivalry, displaying awards given to the French military over the years. The collections aren't a big interest of ours (do they give out a prize for Most Convincing Surrender?), but we tour the place anyway, tuning out the prattle about the military campaigns to study the building around us. We walk past a colonnade framing an interior courtyard. Inside we traverse a vestibule and pass cases of dangling medals, stern generals frowning from paintings, gilded chairs, and countless chandeliers. "It just seems to keep going on and on," Liana whispers. Even though the effect from the exterior was of a modest, compact whole, the house is surprisingly large inside.

All the "new and good houses," in Paris, Jefferson wrote, were of a single story—or if they weren't, like the Hôtel de Salm, they appeared to be. The new French architects turned away from the excesses of rococo to express a sense of humility, restraint, and balance, reflecting republican values of elegant simplicity. This new wave eventually gained its own name, neoclassicism, and Jefferson would become one of its biggest proponents in America.

We exit the museum and I hustle back to the statue to commune with it one last time. Jefferson's still staring at the Hôtel de Salm, still eternally contemplating whether he should junk the first Monticello and start designing *à la Parisienne*. "Do it," I whisper to him when no one is watching. "You've got to do it."

During the golden years he lived there, Paris was "every day enlarging and beautifying," Jefferson wrote, fast becoming the epicenter of neoclassical architecture. *Hints* doesn't bother chronicling the fast-changing innovations in the French capital. The guide ends simply with the word "Paris," which must have said it all. Perhaps the ambassador would give the Boys their own personal architectural tour when they finished their travels. Jefferson already had practice in this: he had spent three full weeks touring the buildings of the Parisian region in the company of a beautiful artist. A beautiful, married artist.

Jefferson standing guard over the Hôtel de Salm,
Derek standing guard over him.

Jefferson met Maria Cosway in August 1786 at a gathering of mutual friends in front of the gorgeous, domed Halle aux Blés, falling in love with both woman and building at the same time. Cosway was just twenty-six (to Jefferson's forty-three), Italian-born of English parents, a cultured painter. In the engraving Jefferson kept of her, she has soft features, dangling curls, and a coquettish look.

While he is rightfully castigated for his treatment of the enslaved Sally Hemings (who in 1786 was still living in Virginia), a woman unable to legally withhold her consent from sexual relations, biographers have mostly given him a pass for his affair with Cosway. He was a widower, and perhaps *liaisons dangereuses* were just what aristocrats did in the Paris of the 1780s; Cosway's husband, a painter and *bon vivant* himself, busied himself with his own amorous pursuits. Jefferson's first meeting with Maria left him thunderstruck, both by her charm and the stage set of their romance. The scene before him—the lovely woman in front of the lovely domed building—presented him with a solution both to his emotional emptiness and to an architectural conundrum.

The Halle aux Blés, the Parisian grain market, featured a soaring wooden dome with interlocking wooden ribs. Skylights, placed ingeniously between the ribs, flooded the building with brightness. It was "the most superb thing on earth," Jefferson gushed. He was concerned that workers at home would not be able to execute complicated technical building techniques for Roman or Palladian domes of heavy stone. Instead, Jefferson would bring the wooden rib pattern back home so that his carpenter, "who never heard of a dome," could follow it when rebuilding Monticello. Jefferson would have his "sky-room."

This encounter was just the start, though. While Jefferson's diplomatic contacts received hastily written excuses from him begging off appointments, the lovers spent three weeks strolling around Paris and the surrounding region. They flirted before the Pavilion of the Château of Louveciennes, an elegant building designed by one of the most audacious new French architects, Claude-Nicolas Ledoux. They strolled through the parks of the Désert de Retz and the Château de Marly, whose neoclassical ideas Jefferson would bring back to UVA. "How beautiful was every object!" gushed Jefferson in a letter to Cosway after that trip. "How grand the ideas excited by the remains of such a column!"

Paris revealed other wonders for them to discover. There was the Church of St. Geneviève, which would become the Panthéon during the French Revolution. There were the sixty toll gates ringing Paris (one just up the street from Jefferson's own house), serving a sinister purpose—enforcing a punitive internal customs duty that the populace hated—but stylishly designed. Each one of these "palaces," as Jefferson called them, was architecturally distinct, showing off domes or porticoes. Even paying customs duties could be classy.

And there was that place in the Latin Quarter where Jefferson bought graph paper. While it was initially intended for silk weavers, he repurposed the paper for his architectural drawings, allowing him to design with precision with the new drafting instruments he also ordered at this time. He purchased huge quantities of the French paper and, for the rest of his life, would dole it out like the last stores of a precious drug.

But the affair couldn't last. Showing off for Maria, Jefferson apparently leaped over a hedge, falling and breaking his right (writing) wrist. Shortly afterward, she returned as planned with her husband to London, leaving Jefferson "more dead than alive," he wrote to her, painfully using his left hand. He framed the letter as a dialogue between his head and his heart, debating what to do next.

His head, he wrote, had once pushed him to spend all his time on architecture; he'd even fall asleep surrounded by his designs. The day they met, his head had found the Halle aux Blés to be "worth all [he] had yet seen in Paris"—while his heart thought the same thing, but of her. He recounted the magical time they had spent touring in which his two pursuits, of architecture and Cosway, the desires of head and heart, fused in his mind. Without Maria, he concluded, he was "the most wretched of all earthly beings." Drawing "triangles and squares" on his graph paper was no longer enough. He would wait for her return in the spring, for "hope is sweeter than despair."

His heart seemed to have won the argument, but later, in her prolonged absence, Jefferson's rational head finally prevailed. Even if she divorced her husband, Jefferson could not bring this sexy Italian woman back with him to America if he clung to any kind of political ambition.

In the spring, as Maria prepared to return to Paris, Jefferson left to take the waters in the south of France, hoping they would heal his wrist. Afterward, he effectively ended the liaison.

Some years after returning home, Jefferson would dismantle his first version of Monticello, spending a summer sleeping under the "tent of heaven" as he rebuilt it with inspirations from France. Although the project took decades to complete, he didn't mind; "putting up and pulling down [is] one of my favorite amusements," he told a visitor. The house's new design harked back to the Hôtel de Salm: a building that stretched horizontally, with long windows everywhere, crowned with a dome. Jefferson cleverly placed second-story windows at floor level, making them appear to belong to the first story, and hid the upper story behind a balustrade. His home, lit internally by skylights, appeared to be all on the same level.

For over two centuries, visitors have admired Jefferson's
most personal architectural expression, Monticello.

His passion for what he called "modern" architecture always kept a place in his heart—as did Maria. He would keep her portrait for the rest of his life, although he didn't really need to. All he had to do was look around his redesigned home and he'd see reminders of their time together, echoes of the daring new buildings they had shared in Paris and that he embedded in the shape of Monticello. Reshaping his house would not only be an intellectual pursuit but his "delight": an act of love.

Jefferson had learned what Europe had to teach. He had once made his architectural designs in ink; back home he would use another innovation he came across in Paris, a pencil and eraser. It was both a practical and symbolic step forward. He would no longer be just copying ancient designs in immutable ink but dreaming, tinkering, and revising as he created something new. The buildings he'd design would no longer be Palladian or even French neoclassical copies. They would be Jeffersonian.

My own tour of European buildings concluded, it's time to visit my university again to test whether I finally understand the coded lessons he left for me.

FINAL EXAM

I'm sitting on a hulk of charred stone that emerges from the ground like a crashed Death Star. My perch is one of the original capitals of Jefferson's Rotunda, saved from the building when it partially burned down in 1895. It and some other survivors now live outside UVA's art museum. The marble is cool to the touch in the dusk. "I know where you come from," I whisper to it and its friends. These are Carrara boys.

At the nearby architecture school, I had gotten to meet RGW at a symposium after our trip. He had quite his own journey as well, I found out, literally born into modernism—the twentieth-century variety, not what Jefferson considered to be "modern"—yet carving out a distinguished career at the university most known for classical architecture in America. "My parents were modern art freaks," he told me, his mother an architect, his father a building contractor. The first house he lived in as a baby was a masterpiece built by renowned architect R. M. Schindler, whom his parents picked—after first interviewing and rejecting Frank Lloyd Wright.

"Why didn't they go with Wright?" I asked.

"I don't know. I never knew enough to ask," he replied. "You always need to ask."

"When I came here in 1976, I didn't have anything to do with Jefferson," he went on, explaining his more contemporary interests. But the old man grew on him.

"Now I'm the head of the Jefferson mafia," he told me. "I've written too damn much on him." And still he teaches on, converting students to become, in their self-describing words, "Jeffersonphiles and column-huggers."

We talked about how Europe widened Jefferson's horizons. He listened to my argument on Jefferson not visiting Palladian villas in Italy because the Virginian had moved, at least somewhat, beyond the strict teachings of the Venetian architect. He had heard this explanation from others as well but wasn't convinced.

"It might have just been a question of time; Jefferson couldn't spare it," he said.

My face dropped.

"Although I agree it's puzzling," he added, perhaps sensing my disappointment. "Jefferson can be a hard guy to figure out."

The Virginian's approach to architecture always remained eclectic. "He was a classicist who didn't mind breaking the rules," RGW told me. I decided that he approved of my fundamental thesis, if not the particular details: it was in Europe that Jefferson mastered the laws of architecture and also understood he could play with them to create something new. I'll take that as a passing grade.

Jefferson's most important work was the Virginia State Capitol, RGW told me, because of its effect on future public buildings. His most personal was Monticello. But his greatest was UVA. The Founder was intimately involved with its design and construction. RGW shared with me the remembrance of a nineteenth-century journalist who visited the university when it was a construction site and saw an old man—Jefferson, naturally—grabbing a chisel out of the hand of a sculptor to demonstrate how to turn the volute, the spiral scroll of a capital. "He specified the proportions on those damn buildings on the Lawn to one hundredth of an inch," he said. "That must have driven some of those workers crazy when they saw that."

"Why was UVA his greatest work?" I asked.

He paused and turned the question over. "It just is. There's nothing like it at that point in time. Or any time."

"Do you still notice new things when you walk on Grounds after all these years?"

"Sure," he replied and paused. "Walking up and down the Lawn as the sun comes through the columns...I've walked it a thousand times, and I still see new things at different times. A detail I hadn't paid much attention to."

I couldn't have asked for more inspiration for my own stroll from the art museum to the gardens in the heart of the university, announced by Jefferson's famous serpentine walls. "Some said he built the walls in this form to save bricks," RGW said. "But he's also saying this was a different sort of place. A special place."

The rippling walls lead to the Rotunda, looming against the dusky sky, with red brick, a white dome, and a small cap on top. My college friend Jon called it the Teat of Knowledge. RGW saw it, more professorially, as a perfect sphere. RGW explained how innovative it was for Jefferson to place this secular building—which also housed the library—at the center of the university rather than a chapel, the focus of every other institution of higher learning in the country at the time. Jefferson saw students as the metaphorical body of the university and the Rotunda, with its library, the mind.

I walk around to the front and gaze at the dome, built using the construction method Jefferson learned in Paris. The columns outside are Corinthian, recently restored (with marble from Carrara). Inside are Composite columns, the fanciest of the five orders, in the only place they're used on Grounds. I'm seeing the Rotunda like I never did before, back in the days when it was a convenient place to leave my clothes. Peering through its open doors, I can spot its unusual layout, a circular room bounded by three oval-shaped rooms, just like the Column of the Désert de Retz he had visited with Maria Cosway, a design that had "excited" ideas in Jefferson, now consummated.

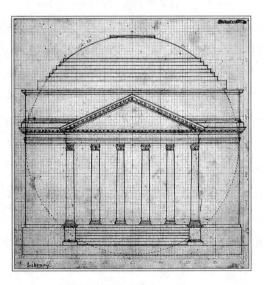

Jefferson's design of the Rotunda.

I notice how the building flows; it looks so much smoother than Palladio's La Rotonda, or the Pantheon, which it was modeled on (although drastically modified). When we saw the latter building in Rome, it looked cramped, hemmed in by structures on three sides of it. Jefferson's Rotunda sits snugly in the neoclassical tableau he created, his "academical village." To its south are the ten pavilions, five on each side, with student rooms between them.

The Lawn itself is shadowy, pricked by the occasional blue dot of a student on a cell phone. Some think its layout was inspired by the royal residence at Marly, which Jefferson and Maria visited. RGW thought the design was more likely a creature of constraints, as Jefferson had to squeeze his ideas into the dimensions between two ridges. Strong perfume comes off a gaggle of young women, their heels clip-clopping on the bricks as they head to a reception in the Rotunda. I set off to walk the Lawn (fully dressed, thankfully).

On my right, Pavilion I shows off a frieze of a dozen Apollo heads taken from a temple I saw in Rome. Nearby I come to Room Seven, reserved for a member of the Jefferson Literary and Debating Society, founded in 1825. Students stand outside it, sipping drinks, continuing what seems to be a nonstop party that started when I was there. Above them droop the Carrara acanthus leaves of Pavilion III, unheeded.

Even the student rooms, their brickwork nestled behind an arcade of simple Tuscan columns, display modest beauty. On his travels, Jefferson thrilled when he found French farmhouses ornamented even in a "small way...to show that the tenant's time is not [all] occupied in procuring physical necessaries." To be Jeffersonian, then, you don't have to build a villa or pavilion: just add whatever touch of class you can to your dwelling.

Each pavilion I encounter on the walk is different, as Jefferson intended, "no two alike so as to serve as specimens for the architectural lectures." Unlike when I was a student, now I can tell them apart. The architectural variety reminds me of assorted Lego pieces spilling out of a bag, building blocks for a student to store away in his or her mind. I spot elements I've seen on my travels: the three-bay front of a temple, a frieze from the Baths of Diocletian, nods to Rome, Palladio, and France. Jefferson scrambled the hierarchy of orders: Ionic was next to Doric; one pavilion would have a striking pediment, the next an unusual parapet. RGW talked of how European visitors he led on tours were sometimes shocked: you're not supposed to mix and match styles like that. Jefferson knew what he was doing, though. "You've got to know the rules to break them," RGW said. Jefferson liked both correctness, he told me, and being subversive. That's why you have to look at each damn building.

An idea springs to mind: what if the inspiration for this grab bag of styles is the 60 tollhouses ringing Paris, each one a "palace" with a different motif? I'll have to bounce that idea off the professor. Maybe he'll give me extra credit.

At the south end of the Lawn I come to the two most daring pavilions, the ones furthest from the source, the Rotunda, and closest to the future: an open vista, looking out on the possibility of a new nation. I gaze at Pavilion X on my left, its colossal columns bridging two stories but without a base—a possible nod to the Greek Revival style, trendy in the 1820s.

And on my right, Pavilion IX, the house of professor George Tucker, who looked out its lunette windows while writing the first science fiction novel in America, *Voyage to the Moon*, in 1827. Behind its Ionic columns is a niche with a graceful recessed alcove. Some considered this an unusual mark of French neoclassicism, inspired by a mansion Ledoux built in Paris. RGW instead thought it was an ancient Roman form that Jefferson might have seen elsewhere on his travels, like the Temple of Venus in Stowe. That Jefferson. I had a one-track mind in England, focusing on landscape gardens, but he used his trip there also to pick up architectural ideas and who knows what else, observing everything life presented to him.

I turn around and look at the Rotunda glimmering in the moonlight. Jefferson stares back at me: his statue visible through the building's open doors. I get what you're saying now, I think. When I look at the pavilions, I don't just see brick buildings with white columns; I see forms and shapes playing with each other. Now I can speak your language and read these symbols you left for us. All these pavilions are different, but none better than another. They're equal, and we members of this academic village are here to figure them out. And they're challenging anyone who views them: What are you going to do with this knowledge? What will you build?

"Thank you," I whisper. It all seems perfect. And it is, until I look to my left and see the small cottage behind Pavilion IX.

✦ ✦ ✦

Too often Jefferson lived in a dreamworld. But his idealized shapes, his flawless specimens of antiquity, had to exist in real life, with its messy consequences and terrible compromises. According to Jefferson's blueprints, the slave cottage behind Pavilion IX does not exist. Yet here it is.

Not only did Jefferson recognize that a system of bondage was unjust for the enslaved themselves, he wrote that owning other humans warped the personalities of slaveholders. A White child watching a parent "storm" against his enslaved workforce is "educated...in tyranny"—and will later repeat this same behavior himself. Jefferson didn't want to expose a new generation of students to this corrupting influence, ordering that students could not themselves bring slaves to school.

Yet UVA never would have survived without enslaved labor. Slaves not only did much of the construction work, they lived on Grounds, feeding students and professors, cleaning, stoking fires, and performing countless other tasks. Jefferson tried to keep the enslaved workforce out of sight, hiding their very existence. The graceful serpentine walls were once eight feet tall rather than today's reconstructed four, shielding the work of slaves doing laundry and slaughtering chickens in the pavilion gardens from view. Slaves lived in dark, damp cellars in the pavilions until professors demanded better accommodation for them—even at the expense of ruining Jefferson's pure architectural pattern. The humble building I'm looking at now was one such slave dwelling.

Slavery is an insistent, discordant note in this otherwise harmonious symphony of Jeffersonian architecture. The pavilions might symbolize the inherent value of different building styles, but the slave quarters behind them are clearly separate and not equal. Only recently have historians emphasized this other side of Jefferson's buildings. The very Rotunda steps were carved by an enslaved man whom Jefferson had owned, Thrimston Hern, later leased to UVA for this work. The quarry where enslaved workers dug out stone for the pavilions was just a few hundred yards from my dorm. At Monticello, there's a brick with a handprint left in it: the marker of an enslaved artisan's humanity, fingers splayed in the red clay, frozen in time.

I don't remember any of this being talked about while I was in school. But after years of pressure, from students and professors, the university is constructing a new Memorial to Enslaved Laborers, on the northeast side of the Rotunda, a monument that would have horrified Jefferson. The role of slaves working at UVA was not a topic he wanted his students to consider explicitly. Wasn't admiring classical buildings enough to fill young White students with strong republican values that would lead them eventually to reason their way out of a slave economy?

The answer, three and a half decades later, came back as an unequivocal "no." Jefferson's State Capitol, his beloved take on the Maison Carrée, turned into the capital of the Confederacy. UVA students left the Lawn to man the ranks of the rebel army. The Rotunda was requisitioned as an infirmary; wounded Confederate soldiers gazed up at the Carrara columns while, on the battlefields, their cause crumbled.

I suppose I shouldn't have been surprised at Jefferson's efforts to hide markers of slavery in his architecture, given, as I had already found out, that he also erased the role of enslaved gardeners from his Monticello landscape. Yet the Founder wanted his students to "follow truth wherever it may lead." And the truth I keep stumbling upon leads me inexorably back to Jefferson's massive failure on slavery.

Even though he didn't write about the subject in *Hints*, slavery permeated all of Jefferson's plans. He might discover exciting ideas on architecture, landscaping, or agriculture while on the road, but he wouldn't get far in executing them back home without relying on slave labor. By hewing so closely to the instructions in *Hints*, I've missed this story. It's not enough, I realize, to wait until the end of a thematic trip, as I look at how Jefferson put his plans into practice, to consider the role enslaved African Americans played in his life. I need to confront this issue as I travel. Otherwise I'm not truly understanding Jefferson—or the pain that he caused to the hundreds of people he owned.

When Liana and I travel to the French city of Nantes, once a major slaving port, we finally face this subject head-on. What I find there devastates me.

CHAPTER FOURTEEN

Those Who Labor for My Happiness

Enslaved persons sold at auction in Virginia by Thomas Jefferson while in Paris, 1785			
Stephen	Hanah	Philip	Nanny
Sall	Betty	Judy	Ambrose
John	Sal	Dinah	Abram
Aggy	George	Sue	Abby
Tomo	Cuffy	Gloster	Sally
Dilcey	Billy Warny	Sall	Sanco
Harry	Nat	Ambrose	Nanny
Peter	Daniel	Hanah	

Selected expenses of Thomas Jefferson in Paris, 1785			
Painting: *Herodias Bearing the Head of St. John*	Pianoforte (rented)	Chariot with green Moroccan upholstery	24 bottles of Haut Brion wine
Painting: *Holy Family*	Large candlesticks	Red and blue Damask curtains	Lease for new house, Count of Langeac's mansion
Porcelain statuettes of Venus with Cupid	Organ for teaching songs to birds	Opera, theater, and concert tickets	87 volumes of poetry
Queen-style armchairs with bronze leaves	*Code de l'humanité*	Monthly wages of *frotteur*, for waxing floors with his feet	3 dozen ivory-handled knives
Carpenter, for work on rented house	Stilton cheese	Travel expenses to the country estate of a nobleman to discuss the problem of slavery	Piece of silver to poor elderly White woman he encountered in the woods, as charity
Semicircular gilded mirror	Mahogany desk with adjustable top	Pedicure	Tickets to masquerade ball

The sky outside the hotel window is gunmetal gray, with dark clouds rolling in from the west Atlantic. Liana and I go down to the lobby, which is stuffed with nineteenth-century period furniture. We're in a small, stone boutique establishment, once a coaching inn, in the city center of Nantes, some 250 miles southwest of Paris. The proprietress gives us pastries and strong coffee. But something in this privileged setting feels off. Instead of the giddy anticipation normally brought by the beginning of a trip, apprehension builds within me, a sense that I'm wading into unfamiliar, treacherous waters. There will be no wine tastings or garden tours on this trip. We've come here to learn about slavery.

Thomas Jefferson enslaved more than six hundred people over his lifetime and freed only seven. That's a tragic fact, but not one that I've particularly dwelled on in my travels. Until now.

This was partially intentional on my part. I've been following in Jefferson's footsteps abroad. And in Europe, unlike back home, those footsteps were not accompanied by those of a slave behind him; he never took James Hemings with him on any of his long trips outside of Paris. Since Jefferson hated being seen as a slave owner, he journeyed "incognito," as he put it, as a private citizen. He relished that all his belongings were "contained in a single trunk," asking himself why he didn't "run away from his own crowded house and take refuge in the chamber of an inn." Traveling gave Jefferson an escape, a way of running from his true life and putting the "hideous" institution that he would soon return to out of mind. For his job might have been diplomat, but he couldn't have paid his bills without the tobacco grown by his slaves.

In Europe, he would have encountered few, if any, enslaved Africans along his route. France and England had effectively banned the institution within their own countries through judicial rulings (although they had not yet restricted the trade itself—French and English slavers still ran lucrative businesses). *Hints* never mentions the topic of slavery, and I accepted the omission at face value.

But I admit I was secretly relieved to do so.

I've always seen Jefferson as a humane, brilliant thinker who transcended his age. I embarked on this journey hoping just a touch of his genius would rub off on me. If I didn't believe that he still had something to say, that traveling on his trail would bring me insights about new places, even into the human condition itself, I would never have left home.

Of course, Jefferson's ownership of slaves is hardly a secret. The subject has always made me exceedingly uncomfortable, though. "All men are created equal," he wrote; slavery was a "moral depravity." So why did he free so few of the people he owned? He had eighty-three years to extricate himself from slavery and never did. That's a hell of a long time to wait for someone to do the right thing.

Although a few slave owners in Virginia did emancipate their slaves, most, like Jefferson, ignored the immorality of the institution. That the leaders of my state made such morally reprehensible choices has always disappointed me. Their descendants have never fully remedied the consequences of enslaving thousands of people for centuries: after abolition came Jim Crow and institutional racism, reflected today in everything from housing to employment to the criminal justice system, a scarred past not healed.

Or maybe I should say *we*, not *they*. These once legal crimes were committed by people who looked like me. Likely even by my own ancestors. Our family genealogists turned up records of my forebears farming in the eighteenth century within a few miles of some of the Jefferson landholdings. Who was picking our tobacco? What benefits did the color of our skin bring my family? Myself? The more I think about these questions, the more discomforting the answers become, and I'll find any excuse to cut the exercise short.

But for me, the root of the problem comes back to our country's founding, when the path was laid out for generations to follow. Should we consider Thomas Jefferson a freedom fighter or a slave trafficker? "If Jefferson was wrong, America is wrong," a nineteenth-century historian wrote. "If America is right, Jefferson was right." Which one is it? Accepting that he was wrong means many things were as well. Or are.

And so for a long time I rationalized. Jefferson's heart was in the right place, I told myself; his actions just lagged behind. He couldn't free his slaves because of restrictive laws and his own debts. Judging him too harshly smacks of presentism—applying current standards to people in the past. After all, many eighteenth-century Whites accepted the institution as a fact of life. In any case, he certainly held the right ideals on equality and expressed them stunningly. He just had the misfortune of being born in an age where he and so many others couldn't live up to them. It took our nation decades of struggle, including a bloody Civil War and a long civil rights movement—ongoing today—to make good on our nation's promise of freedom.

Do even the Sally Hemings allegations necessarily have to stain his character, I wondered at the beginning? For two centuries, many Americans, historians and members of the public alike, rejected the claim that Jefferson had fathered children by her. Recent scholarship, including a DNA test conducted on descendants of the Hemingses and Jeffersons, changed many minds on the question. Yet if true, might this even mean he was having a secret, loving biracial relationship? Could that redeem him?

So when I first embarked on this project, all I did was give the slavery issue a troubled, but slight, acknowledgment. It seemed relevant to any assessment of Jefferson's life and work, but not especially to his European journeys.

Then I actually embarked on the travels and things became clearer. The dreams Jefferson had while on the road would have remained imprisoned in his head had it not been for the unfree people who carried them out.

That rice he smuggled out of Italy? He sent it to South Carolina, where slaves would plant it in malaria-infested swamps. He would later order enslaved workers like George Granger to plant upland rice sent to him from the captain of a slaving ship.

Those English estates he yearned to emulate but make American? His sinuous paths and clever eye-catchers were constructed by the enslaved gardener Wormley Hughes and his crew. At Monticello, slaves lived in a sunken lane—which they dug, of course—shielding them from the view of sensitive White visitors to the mansion. Under his orders, Jefferson's slaves landscaped themselves out of sight.

That striking new architectural style Jefferson came up with, blending elements from France, Italy, and his own imagination? It would have existed only on blueprints without the work of skilled enslaved laborers like Thrimston Hern, who cut the stone steps of UVA's Rotunda. Or Jupiter Evans, who carved Monticello's limestone columns, or Lewis, who turned the elegant wooden balusters crowning the house's terrace. Or many, many others. Everywhere it's written that a structure was built "by Thomas Jefferson," it should read "by his slaves."

Reading his account books and analyses of his finances, I learned that without the enslaved, he never could have gotten on the road to begin with. Tobacco paid for his lifestyle, and it didn't pick itself. Jefferson avoided touching the plant. "I never saw a leaf of my tobacco packed [into barrels] in my life," he wrote in 1801, after four decades of living off the work of his slaves in the fields. For once, a subject bored the Renaissance Man.

What did interest him—a lavish European lifestyle—came at a steep cost. Jefferson instructed Nicholas Lewis, the caretaker of his plantations back home, to auction off slaves to keep his creditors at bay. In January 1785, Lewis sold thirty-one humans under his own name, keeping Jefferson's out of the paper. Over the next decade, Jefferson would authorize further auctions. His trips might have been an escape in his mind from his role as slave owner, which he seems to have genuinely detested. But they were only flights of fancy. His travels would have gone nowhere, his dreams died stillborn, without the work of people who had no say in the matter.

My admiration for Jefferson was slipping away into something else. What, I wasn't yet sure. But I now knew that while he might have pretended that slavery had nothing to do with his European journeys, he was wrong. It had everything to do with them.

I have to look harder at Jefferson and slavery. I need to make slavery a true Object of Attention, the most important one of all. The space between the lines in *Hints* holds a more powerful story than the written words themselves.

And so we've arrived in Nantes, to visit one of the few places in France that owns up to its role in the slave trade.

+ + +

The Chateau of the Dukes of Burgundy looks like the setting for a Disney movie, with jutting turrets and a broad walk over a dry moat. Not how I would have imagined one of the first institutions in France to grapple seriously with slavery, even if it does so only in some of its exhibits. The castle became a municipal museum a century ago, dedicated to telling the story of Nantes, mostly focusing on the city's golden age, the seventeenth and eighteenth centuries, the era when wealth poured in, elevating humble merchants to noble status. Rooms still show off frilly ladies' gowns, imported Chinese porcelain, and imposing mahogany desks, markers of the lives of the rich and famous. Other displays acknowledge the port's maritime heritage—figureheads from ships, boats in bottles, faded captain's logs. But the source of all this wealth and the purpose for many of these voyages were left unspoken for years, until local activists in the 1990s pushed museum directors to tell the true story of Nantes's rise to prominence.

Liana and I walk solemnly through these newer exhibits. Nantes, we learn, was one of four principal points of departure for slaving ships in France, along with Bordeaux, La Rochelle, and Le Havre, each of which Jefferson carefully explored. Over the span of two centuries,

French captains, funded by wealthy magnates, transported over a million African captives to North America, the majority to sugar plantations in their colony of Saint-Domingue (now Haiti and the Dominican Republic). We view portraits of the grand merchants, and their wives, who profited from the trade. In one frame, an elegant lady in an embroidered dress sips coffee, a half-smile on her lips, while a turbaned African slave holds a sugar bowl behind her—a Black woman added to the painting as a status symbol, a human accessory.

Around two hundred slave ships left Nantes during Jefferson's time abroad, we learn, carrying some fifty-five thousand humans. Signs tell about a handful of these voyages and the pain they spread in their wake. Typically, a slaving captain would buy hundreds of captured persons in West Africa to be sold in the Caribbean and sometimes in the United States. Even if the enslaved survived the passage (the death toll was ghastly), they would never again see their families or homeland. The engravings on display of African captives crammed together in the hulls, chained, unable to move, nauseate us. "They transported these people like animals," Liana whispers to me. "What a vicious commerce."

We see drawings of slaves hoeing under a stifling sun, a colonial overseer watching on horseback. The French sugar plantations in the Caribbean—many owned by slave-trading merchants—generated staggering profits, paying for some of the elegant neoclassical townhomes that caught Jefferson's eye as he visited French ports. We reach a case with sets of iron shackles. "This is almost unbearable," Liana says, exiting.

We leave, barely talking, following markers on the ground guiding us on a mile-long walk to another site on the banks of the Loire. This stretch of the river is quiet; long ago, the main port relocated forty miles away, where the river spills into the Atlantic. A briny smell wafts up from the water. Seagulls pick over a discarded carton of fries on the ground. When he poked around the docks that once stood here, Jefferson took notes on the size of vessels that could sail into Nantes rather than being obliged to moor at the deepwater port downriver. In his private travel journals he made a rare comment related to slavery—not one he would share with the Boys or anyone else who looked up to him. Slave traders in Nantes, he noted, preferred rice from the Carolinas to that from their Italian competitors, as it boiled faster.

We gaze at light blue plaques on the ground, each with the name of a slave vessel that departed from here. They surround the Memorial to the Abolition of Slavery, built of solid stone blocks. The exhibits are in the shadows below ground, a hidden world that must be sought out— symbolic of the fact that this subject was kept out of sight for so long.

Even now, this memorial is the only public building in Europe that honors slaves and their struggle for freedom. The four-hundred-yard-long esplanade along the river is open to all, free of charge. In 1998, on the 150th anniversary of the ending of slavery throughout the French Empire, the city of Nantes agreed to the demands of local Black activists to establish a place of remembrance. Following fourteen years of planning and consultation, the memorial opened in 2012. The curators made sure to include information about the struggle to free people from slave-like conditions today.

We descend as if into a galley, hanging on to beams of wood on either side of us. Light flickers in as through the timbers of a hold. We catch glimpses of the fast-moving current outside the building's pillars. Recordings play the sound of creaking planks, dripping water, and spiritual songs of hope. In front of us is a glass wall with the word "liberty" in forty-seven languages, from lands affected by the slave trade. *Liberté, Libertad, Uhuru, Fridɔm.* Liana whispers to me how moved she is. "I'm thinking of Cuba," she tells me, "of how I have both slave owners and slaves in my family tree."

We read quotes on the wall from people who fought to end bondage here and across the world. The words of Frederick Douglass, condemning the "corrupt, slaveholding, women-whipping, cradle-plundering, partial and hypocritical Christianity of this land." Passages from enslaved people who bore witness to horror. Of a girl who hugged and kissed her mother at the auction, then never saw her again. Of Olaudah Equiano, who wrote in 1789 of the "intolerably loathsome" stench of the hold of the slave ship he was transported in as a child. Of Jefferson's contemporary Adam Smith, noting the inefficiency of relying on the labor of man that was "squeezed out of him by violence only, and not by any interest of his own." Of Abraham Lincoln proclaiming that slaves "are, and henceforward shall be free." Of Martin Luther King, Jr., and his dream that "one day on the red hills of Georgia, the sons of former slaves and the sons of former slave owners will be able to sit down together at the table of brotherhood."

The interior of the Memorial to the
Abolition of Slavery.

I wonder if the wall includes Jefferson's words from the Declaration of Independence. It doesn't. He forfeited that right long ago. Although he arrived in Europe one of the prime American advocates for abolition, in Paris he mysteriously began beating a retreat from this stance.

In the Declaration of Independence, Jefferson had bitterly, if somewhat unfairly, placed blame for the slave trade on King George III. During the war, he pushed Virginia to ban the importation of enslaved persons and moved unsuccessfully for Congress to ban slavery in territories as a condition of statehood. In *Notes on Virginia* he called for abolition and compared White masters to despots.

No wonder the Parisian intellectuals who formed an abolition society invited him to join. But Jefferson begged off their requests. Never again would he publicly press for emancipation, even as others continued to do so. A few of his slaveholder contemporaries later matched their words with deeds. In 1799, George Washington provided in his will that the 123 slaves he owned would be free following the death of his wife (who emancipated them a year later in life). Jefferson's neighbor Edward Coles not only freed the 19 enslaved people he owned but bought them land in Illinois. Jefferson would not follow suit; the problem of slavery was one for "a younger generation" to solve, he wrote to Coles in 1814. By the time he was an old man, he supported the admission of Missouri to the Union as a slave state.

I walk back up to street level, to the plaques with names of slave vessels, and take out my journal. I fill pages with the names of ships that Jefferson might have tracked in French newspapers from the 1780s. *L'Aimable*, which means the Friendly One. *Le Bon Père*, the Good Father. *L'Espérance*, Hope.

Once I'm back home, after journeying into records and letters, the reasons for his backpedaling on abolition become clear to me. They had to do with ships in Jefferson's own past. Slave ships.

CHAPTER FIFTEEN

Hard Truths

In January 1772, The *Prince of Wales* sailed out of Bristol, England. A ten gunner, it had a previous life as a Spanish trading vessel before it was captured by the British. Now it was a slave ship—the first of three that marked, in a sense, Jefferson's life and destiny. It sailed to Calabar, in what is now Nigeria, where it forced 343 people on board. After close to nine excruciating months crossing the Atlantic, it landed on the James River, with only 280 disembarking. "The mortality amongst the slaves could not be prevented," wrote the London firm that commissioned the expedition to their agent in Virginia, John Wayles. Its job done, the ship began its return voyage to England on the date of Thomas Jefferson and Martha Wayles Skelton's first wedding anniversary.

Jefferson bought only around twenty enslaved people over the course of six decades. There was no need to purchase more; he inherited all the others, starting with fifty-two slaves from his father's estate in 1764 when he came of age. Four years later, as a twenty-five-year-old lawyer, Jefferson took on a client who would profoundly change his life, as well as those of hundreds of African Americans. Wayles, born in England to a family of modest means, had emigrated to Virginia decades earlier as a "Servant Boy." In the New World, he transformed himself into a member of high society, with a fortune built on debt collecting and slave trading. It was his daughter, Martha, a recent widow, whom Jefferson married in 1772.

NEW KENT, *Feb.* 3, 1769.

RUN away, on *Sunday* night laſt, from the ſubſcriber's plantation in *Cumberland* county, upon the branches of *Appamattox* river, near *Naſh's* bridge, three *Virginia* born Negro men, *viz.* PETER, about 27 years old; JEMBOY, about 20 years old; and HARRY, about 21 years old. They were all clothed in good white plains, good oſnabrugs ſhirts, and ſtockings made of the ſame ſort of cloth as their clothes, but carried away other clothes, and ſome ſtriped duffil blankets; their ſhoe heels were pegged and nailed with 3d nails, and 2d nails drove through the edges of the ſoles and clinched. Whoever brings the ſaid Negroes to me in *New Kent,* or delivers them to my overſeer, *Joſhua Blunckley,* at the place they went from, ſhall be paid 5 l. beſides the allowance by law; or, in caſe the ſaid Negroes are taken up ſeparate by different perſons, 35 s. for each. *Peter* has behaved badly about 7 or 8 years, but has not been much corrected; he by ſome means has learned to write a little, and has frequently wrote paſſes for himſelf and other Negroes to go a little diſtance, and I am apprehenſive he has now done the like again, or got ſome perſon to write for him.
WILLIAM MACON, jun.

A 1769 ad Jefferson placed in the Virginia Gazette, *offering a reward for the return of Sandy, an enslaved worker who had made a run for freedom. Sandy was recaptured.*

Wayles sold the souls who had survived the *Prince of Wales*'s passage to Virginia planters who bought on credit. But the year 1773 brought calamity for him and his family; the Virginia tobacco market collapsed. And John himself died at age fifty-eight.

After their mourning, Thomas and Martha found their own economic position had increased considerably. Or so it seemed at first. Wayles left the young couple eleven thousand acres of land and 135 enslaved people—including Elizabeth Hemings and her ten children. Hemings, the daughter of a slave and an English sea captain, was thirty-eight when she came to Monticello. The father of six of her children, including Robert, James, and Sally, a fact officially unacknowledged but widely known, was none other than John Wayles.

But the estate also included a time bomb: Wayles's debts, much of them from the *Prince of Wales*. Jefferson sold land to pay his share just as Virginian currency collapsed, making the sums he had just accumulated "not worth oak leaves," he wrote acidly. He'd have to come up with the money owed all over again. As the years passed, the Wayles obligation ballooned with interest, adding to the debt from Jefferson's own poor tobacco sales and profligate spending.

Paris provided no safety; insistent letters from creditors found him there. "The torment of mind I endure," Jefferson wrote to Nicholas Lewis, returning from his trip to the south of France to find grim news about his finances waiting for him, "is such really as to render life of little value." He took out loan after loan to stay afloat; the bankers he met in Amsterdam became an important new source of credit. He wrote to Lewis again, urging him to hire out enslaved workers temporarily to other plantations so as to make him more money.

Jefferson had once made plans for treating his enslaved workers more humanely, even sketching designs of Palladian-style cottages for them. He had devised a program in which slaves would be educated at public expense, then emancipated. But under his present circumstances in Paris, these were pipe dreams. Freeing his slaves, terminating his source of income while he was deeply in debt, would ruin his children's future, he had concluded. He was "haunted nightly" by the vision of a creditor stalking him, he wrote later. Instead, he brainstormed new projects in which he might employ his enslaved workforce, hoping to strike it rich.

In Paris, Jefferson also came to better appreciate the political risks he ran in championing abolition. Some Northern leaders applauded his efforts, but most Southern ones scorned them. Yet if he were ever to reenter elective politics, the South would be his base. Both the state of his personal finances and political future, then, counseled him to guard his silence on slavery. The Jefferson who had railed against the "moral evil" of slavery before sailing to Paris was never heard from again.

✦ ✦ ✦

A second slave ship in Jefferson's life, the *Robert*, sailed in May 1787, although its captain, Andrew Ramsey, would have instead described it as a run-of-the-mill transport vessel. Yet he brought on board someone whose surviving parent had no say in the matter: Sally Hemings.

Jefferson had asked for an older slave, Isabel, to accompany and safeguard his nine-year-old daughter, Polly, as she crossed the ocean to join him and her older sister, Patsy, in Paris. But Isabel became pregnant and Jefferson's relatives back home sent Hemings instead. Only fourteen, Sally looked much older. Observers remarked on her beauty; she might have resembled her half sister, Jefferson's late wife, Martha, who was also famous for her looks. Upon docking in London, Captain Ramsey— perhaps too eagerly—offered to take her back to Virginia with him.

Instead, Jefferson decided she should continue on with Polly to France. To bring her there he had to break the law. A complex series of French rulings prohibited slavery within the country's borders, but added a racist twist. Masters were supposed to report their slaves at ports of entry; they would then be refused admittance once declared. If they did arrive inside the country, though, an enslaved person could petition a court in Paris for freedom, and many, with free assistance from lawyers, did so.

When Jefferson met his daughter and slave at the port of Le Havre, he failed to register Sally as his property. He had similarly neglected to register her older brother James three years earlier. Deceiving customs officials, of course, was par for the course for Jefferson—he had smuggled rice out of Italy and later labeled costly Dutch porcelain as nondescript goods. With many free Black servants in Paris, he gambled that the authorities would not realize she was enslaved—and that she wouldn't later file a freedom suit.

Jefferson's conduct—illegally transporting a person for the purposes of forced labor—today would be considered human trafficking. He knew exactly what he was doing. When an acquaintance asked Jefferson whether he could bring an enslaved boy with him on a trip to Bordeaux, the ambassador counseled that French law prohibited it. However, "I have known an instance," he wrote, "where a person bringing in a slave, and saying nothing about it, has not been disturbed in his possession." He advised "to pursue the same plan, as the boy is so young that it is not probable he will think of claiming freedom."

In Paris, instead of staying with Patsy and Polly at their boarding school, Sally lived on the Champs-Élysées with Jefferson, her brother, and a few French servants. "During that time," her son Madison Hemings would tell a journalist in Ohio decades later, she became Jefferson's "concubine." In 1789, when she was sixteen, she became pregnant by the forty-six-year-old Jefferson, Madison stated, and later gave birth to six additional children (including himself) by her master back in Virginia.

The allegations of Jefferson's parentage of the Hemings children exploded in the press in 1802, when he was president; he stated he would not dignify them with a response. His White family vigorously denied them, though, later claiming that one or two of Jefferson's nephews must have fathered these children. For nearly two centuries, nearly all historians who considered the matter dismissed the statements of Madison Hemings and other Blacks with family stories about Jefferson's paternity. The president could not have done what was charged, scholars claimed; it would have been inconsistent with his high moral character. (See how far that excuse will get a politician facing scandal today.)

For a long time I, too, pinned the blame on the nephews. Even when a 1998 DNA study found that descendants of Sally's son Eston carry a Y-chromosome passed down by a male Jefferson—and thus not by the nephews, who were sons of Jefferson's sister—I still didn't want to believe what everything pointed to. The findings didn't provide definitive proof that Jefferson was the father, did they? Could the guilty party have been Jefferson's brother, who lived on his own plantation twenty miles away?

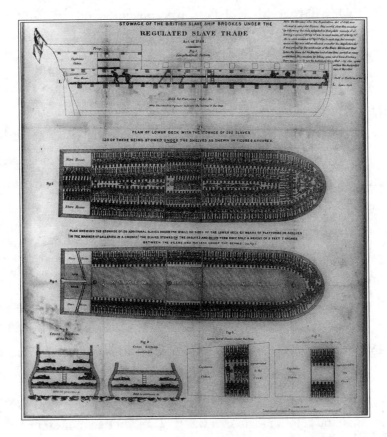

The Brookes, *which at the same time that Sally Hemings crossed the Atlantic in 1787 was engaged in an expedition enslaving hundreds of people in West Africa for transport to Jamaica.*

But much later I encountered a startling fact. Hemings's six children in Virginia were born in a period when Jefferson was frequently absent from Monticello, first serving as vice president, then president. Yet records prove he was home nine months before each of these births. The statistical chance that his occasional visits home would have matched up with all six of these points in time, experts concluded, was only 1 percent. How fitting that the smoking gun as to Jefferson's paternity, for me anyway, came from his own records of his travels.

Just what did serving as Jefferson's "concubine" signify? Although now somewhat archaic, the term describes a relationship between two people who are not married. Was there love between Jefferson and Hemings, as some have speculated? Or was this solely rape? Hemings could not withhold consent from her master, no matter how she felt. What actually transpired between them emotionally is, as noted historian Annette Gordon-Reed points out, unknowable. Hemings chose to return to America and Jefferson did ultimately free his children with her, as he had promised. What we do know is that he owned her for the rest of his life, depriving her of legal freedom. His step back from abolition, both in actions and words, led to Jefferson's enslaving his own children.

How Jefferson squared his interest in Hemings with his feelings toward Blacks is also hard to fathom. Since she was three-fourths White, he undoubtedly considered her superior to other slaves—mixing the races invariably resulted in an "improvement" of Blacks, he wrote in *Notes on Virginia*. In that book, he expressed his true feelings for African Americans: the color of their skin was dull, an "eternal monotony;" their kinky hair was inferior to the "flowing" locks of Caucasians; their bodies were asymmetrical. The griefs of African Americans were merely "transient," their love only "eager desire." They seemed "to require less sleep"; just like "[a]n animal whose body is at rest, and who does not reflect, must be disposed to sleep of course." He detested their "very strong and disagreeable odor." Blacks preferred the beauty of Whites to that of their own race, he surmised, similar to "the preference of the orangutan for the black women over those of his own species."

Jefferson suspected that Blacks were "inferior in the faculties of reason and imagination" to Whites. He dismissed examples of their achievement in science and literature; the thoughtful travel writings of Ignatius Sancho, who escaped slavery for a life in London, for example, were merely "plain narration." Due to these supposed differences, and the rancor that existed between the races, Blacks must be "removed beyond the reach of mixture." Emancipated slaves had to be deported. He drew up a scheme to send them to Africa.

+ + +

Jefferson considered that enslaved Blacks could perform some complex tasks if properly instructed. His investigations into Lighter Mechanical Arts and Manufactures in Europe, Object of Attention Three in *Hints*, gave him ideas he brought home. In 1785, Jefferson visited a gun manufactory outside Paris that used interchangeable musket parts and discovered that, even untrained, he could put them together without trouble as if assembling a jigsaw puzzle. Although he couldn't convince the inventor of the method, Honoré Blanc, to relocate to America, Jefferson promoted his concepts in America, and they were later taken up by Eli Whitney. After observing the beginnings of industrialization in Birmingham (and in 1791 in upstate New York), Jefferson established a small nail factory at Monticello, setting enslaved boys as young as ten to work.

He had also long pondered how to generate more money from his aged enslaved labor force. "The negroes too old to be hired," he wrote to Lewis three weeks after penning *Hints*, "could they not make a good profit by cultivating cotton?" Jefferson would later establish a small, short-lived textile operation, run by older slave women (with twelve-year-old girls helping with the spinning). While in the Washington administration he was the first to review Whitney's patent for a cotton gin, which mechanically separated cotton seeds from the plant far more efficiently than a human could by hand.

In the late eighteenth century, Jefferson and other thinkers dreamed that slavery would wane, that Americans would turn from tobacco, which required extensive human labor, to other pursuits. They expected Congress would ban the importation of slaves into the U.S. (although under a provision in the Constitution, it could not do so before January 1, 1808). These prospects, along with the spread of public education, gave hope that future, Enlightened generations would free people in bondage.

The opposite occurred. With cotton generating unheard-of profits thanks to technological advances, the institution of slavery only strengthened—especially in Mississippi and Alabama, where the crop grew best. With the halting of the legal importation of slaves from abroad, plantation owners in the Deep South instead bought thousands of slaves from Virginia, Maryland, and the Carolinas, sending them "down the river" to plant and harvest cotton, tearing families apart.

Slavery in eighteenth-century Virginia resembled, in a way, a light security prison. Cruel as the system was, it was looser than what would come later, and slaves seized on whatever flexibility they could find (or sometimes even bargain for) to shape the contours of their lives. Some enslaved men went hunting with guns at night or on Sundays; state law allowed for emancipation and for the education of slave children. But the new cotton plantations were as confining as Sing Sing. They brought more of the terror that comes to mind when today we think of slavery: gangs of laborers, vicious overseers, stifling laws, and horrifying violence.

These transformations benefited the bottom line of Virginia planters who sold people to cotton plantations. Some masters "bred" (their word) slaves for auction. Although Jefferson didn't engage in widespread slave trading, he did note the rising value of his human property. "A child raised every two years," he wrote, "is of more profit than the crop of the best laboring man."

Jefferson's yeoman farmer constituents praised his encouragement of agriculture and opening of the West, which displaced Native Americans. He, in turn, relied on these voters' political support. That so many followers were from states with widespread slaveholding made them even more useful to his cause. Jefferson would have lost the presidential election of 1800 to John Adams had it not been that, under the Constitution, each slave counted as three-fifths of a person, giving southern states extra weight in the Electoral College. (Instead, Jefferson tied with Aaron Burr, who was from his same party, and eventually was declared the victor by Congress.)

Jefferson ultimately expanded his base beyond the South, though, drawing support from working-class Northerners attracted to his republican values. Owners of northern textile factories, insurance firms, banks, and shipping companies welcomed the economic promise of increased cotton production as well, including in the newly purchased Louisiana Territory. In his reelection bid in 1804, Jefferson won fifteen out of seventeen states. The last legal years of the American transatlantic slave trade, under his presidency, saw a flotilla of slave vessels reaching our shores.

Toward the end of my journey into the historical records, I come across the last of a trio of slave ships that, to me, signify moments in Jefferson's life trajectory. In 1801, Rhode Island merchant Charles DeWolf outfitted a slaving vessel. Politically minded, he was appreciative of his president's encouragement of southern agriculture, which kept demand for enslaved labor high. His younger brother James was also interested in public affairs, serving as a state representative and senator from Rhode Island from Jefferson's party. James, too, was a slaver, once allegedly murdering an enslaved woman suspected of having smallpox to keep her from transmitting the disease. Charles DeWolf's expedition left to obtain a hundred captives in Africa, nearly half of them children.

He named his ship the *Thomas Jefferson*.

✦ ✦ ✦

What I've discovered leaves me feeling almost ill. So many things I once thought I knew about Jefferson I now question. A Renaissance man? Yet slaves carried out his projects. All men are created equal? In his own time, few Whites looked askance when a slaving ship was named for him.

The hardest pill to swallow is his racism. Yes, he was far from the only prejudiced thinker in the eighteenth century. But I thought he was different. I had convinced myself that although Jefferson truly believed in equality, his times didn't permit it. And that fortunately the nation later caught up in deeds to his prophetic words. But his own writings on Blacks tell a different story.

Jefferson's life work was building America into a free, prosperous society, "the world's best hope," as he put it. Yet he never dreamed that African Americans would live as citizens in this promised land and pursue happiness of their own. Jefferson would not have shared his travel advice with Blacks—much less with the slaves he forced to come work for him in Paris. The title for his guide might well have been *Hints to White Americans Traveling in Europe*.

How can I continue to seek inspiration from Thomas Jefferson? And to write about my journey in his footsteps? Does the world need more words about this man?

I suddenly have a gnawing feeling that my whole project has been a mistake. I picked the wrong man. The wrong dream. Jefferson wasn't who I thought he was.

And neither am I.

I've always looked at America as a meritocracy that slowly, if unevenly, has provided opportunity for all. Growing up in a well-to-do suburb of Washington, DC, I prided myself on how my family had gotten there—the hard way. My grandfathers carried lunch pails, not briefcases; one a union pipe fitter, the other a Teamster dispatcher. My grandmothers worked as a secretary and a sometime schoolteacher, respectively. Honest jobs, laying the groundwork for my parents to go to college, the twentieth-century version of Jefferson's yeoman farmers.

In small town Arkansas where I first grew up, my parents scratched their way upward. We lived in a Spartan trailer filled with books and plans. After a stint as a high school guidance counselor, Dad started in the army at a small base at a low civilian rank, retiring in the Pentagon decades later much closer to the top. Mom worked the cash register at a Toys"R"Us at night, earning money for her teaching certificate. If they achieved comfort, well, they earned it, didn't they? Passing the bar was my own contribution to our family success story: from hardscrabble lives to comfort in two generations.

Only now, as I'm starting to understand the history of race in our country, do I see how my family benefited from a thumb on the scale along the way. Blacks weren't getting the union pipe-fitting jobs in South Carolina or Louisiana and teaching posts in Oklahoma that my grandparents were offered in the 1950s. This was the era of Jim Crow, police dogs, and White-only water fountains, and it left a long shadow that continues to today. And would my parents have gotten work in a predominantly White town in Arkansas? Just as our distant Virginia ancestors were the owners, not the owned, I was born with a head start.

I'll never know when and how my skin color gave me a direct advantage over someone in a job interview or application. But it's clear that growing up in a wealthy, nearly all-White community positioned me for the achievements I previously considered solely my own. Including getting into Jefferson's university and spending an expensive year abroad to become fluent in French. And landing a job with a six-figure salary, allowing me to make these trips to Europe.

I've been poking fun at the Boys for blowing lots of cash on their pleasure trip through the Old World. But these three privileged White Southerners, each holding a prestigious degree as a doctor or lawyer paid for by their slaveholding families, have more in common with my own path than I've wanted to admit.

My paternal grandfather was a kind man, always smiling and sporting a gray cowboy hat. I'd swear that his eyes twinkled. A born raconteur, as soon as he saw his grandchildren he'd break out a story, told a hundred times, about the temperamental horse he rode as a boy or the idiocy of his commanding officers in the South Pacific during World War II. His stories nearly always ended with him doubling up in laughter. I thought the world of him.

In his eighties, in the grips of Alzheimer's, he retreated in his mind to his boyhood on a ranch. Names floated up from the past—his parents, schoolmates. And then he began using the n-word. We were shocked; none of us had heard him say anything like that before, nothing close. But once again he was a teenager in segregated Oklahoma. He had fallen through a tunnel to his past and brought us with him to a world long shielded from view. There were stories he had never told us.

Our past, our legacy of racism and centuries of privilege, can't be erased so quickly. I have no idea how to start addressing this legacy. But it can't be through another costly trip to Europe, chasing the trail of a man who talked of liberty but acted like a White supremacist.

And so I stop.

No more Saturdays poring through history texts in the library. No more midnight internet searches planning out my next adventure. I'm done. My notes and books go up in the attic. And I return to what I remember of normal life. The abandonment of my project is abrupt, unwanted. I've ended with more questions than when I began. But I don't think I'll find answers to them from someone whose own time on earth proved to be so disappointing.

Back to being a full-time father, husband, and bureaucrat. Whatever yearnings that led me to take these trips in the first place are stuffed back deep inside. Since I've ceased obsessing over them, my journeys stop being an omnipresent part of my days, and they naturally start to fade.

✦ ✦ ✦

Months pass. One day an email pops up in my inbox reminding me of an event I had signed up for earlier: the opening of Sally Hemings's room at Monticello. Archaeologists had determined where she likely lived—under the South Pavilion, in what in the twentieth century became a men's room—and museum staff had restored it. The Thomas Jefferson Foundation would now unveil her dwelling to the public, honoring her life and those of her enslaved compatriots in an opening they called Look Closer.

I thought I had put Jefferson behind. But declining to go to this ceremony I had committed to—about slavery, the very subject that drove me from my project—doesn't seem right.

If nothing else, this day might bring me closure. With mixed feelings, I wake up early on a Saturday morning and drive to Charlottesville one last time.

CHAPTER SIXTEEN

Look Closer: Stories of the Enslaved

The sound of a soaring violin coming from the large tent isn't itself unusual; Monticello has previously presented eighteenth-century music on its West Lawn. But as I approach, it's clear that this occasion is unlike any before: Karen Briggs, a noted African American violinist, playfully launches into "Gangsta's Paradise." Descendants of the plantation's enslaved community file in for a day in which their ancestors' stories rightfully take center stage. For once, the master of Monticello will not be the star. From a spot a few hundred yards away, I can almost hear another percussive sound keeping time with Briggs's drummer: the one made by Thomas Jefferson turning over in his grave.

Behind the band we have a perfect, nickel-worthy view of the main house. Two elevated walkways radiate from the mansion, one on the north side, one on the south, each terminating in a pavilion, with a plush lawn filling in the horseshoe-shaped design. Since the main event, called Look Closer, hasn't started yet, I walk to the South Pavilion. Below it is Sally Hemings's restored room.

I enter the small chamber, along with a handful of descendants, and view a remarkable musical and visual program. In one corner of the almost bare room is a mannequin-torso dress form of a plain brown frock, representing Hemings. Words appear on the wall, explaining how she sailed to France in 1787, while the sounds of waves echo in the chamber. Violin music plays as the words of her son by Jefferson, Madison Hemings, come into view, taken from an account he gave to an Ohio newspaperman in 1873. "He desired to bring my mother back with him," he said, "but she demurred. She was just beginning to understand the French language well and in France she was free." The music rises and a black-and-red pattern is projected on the dress form. White doves flutter on her dress, then fly from it onto the wall, flapping their wings. "While if she returned to Virginia, she would be re-enslaved. So she refused to return with him." We hear crowds murmuring, horses clopping, church bells chiming.

"To induce her to do so he promised her extraordinary privileges," Madison continues, "and made a solemn pledge that her children should be freed at the age of twenty-one years. In consequence of his promises, on which she implicitly relied, she returned with him to Virginia." The music hangs in the air and stops. The doves depart and the dress becomes plain brown again.

"Soon after their arrival, she gave birth to a child, of whom Thomas Jefferson was the father. It lived but a short time." We see the silhouette of a pregnant woman, then a mother holding a child. "She gave birth to four others, and Jefferson was the father of all of them." Two boys in silhouette play a folk air on the fiddle, and then five family members embrace. I realize with a start that some of them might have been born in this very room.

"Their names were Beverly, Harriet, Madison (myself), and Eston—three sons and one daughter." A quill pen makes scratching sounds. The names of the four children appear on the wall in Jefferson's handwriting. Then other names appear, from a page in Jefferson's *Farm Book* entitled "Roll of Negroes, 1810," right before his list of livestock.

"He was not in the habit of showing partiality or fatherly affection to us children." I feel a pit in my stomach. "We were the only children of his by a slave woman. My brothers, sister Harriet and myself, were used alike. When I was fourteen years old I was put to the carpenter trade... Harriet learned to spin and to weave in a little factory on the home plantation." We hear wheels whirring. This work happened just a stone's throw away from here, on Mulberry Row, the lane below the south dependencies.

"We were always permitted to be with our mother." Sally Hemings's dress turns black and red again. "It was her duty, all her life which I can remember, up to the time of father's death, to take care of his chamber and wardrobe, look after us children and do such light work as sewing, etc. We all became free agreeably to the treaty entered into by our parents before we were born. We all married and have raised families." Black birds fly free from the dress. The five-minute-long program ends with a statement that Jefferson freed only seven slaves, letting three others leave as well. These ten people were all from the Hemings family; four were his own children. Sally Hemings was "given her time" after his death— that is to say, she was allowed to depart the plantation without consequence, but also without formal freedom.

I step out, blinking in the bright sun, and hurry back to the tent to find a seat as the ceremony starts. Retired Monticello historian Cinder Stanton soon takes the microphone. She spent years poring over Jefferson's records, and she's unflinching in her assessment of him. "His voice has drowned out so many others," she says. "His plantation records are about work, not life, not talents, not values, not feelings, not about parents or husbands or wives."

Stanton refused to allow Jefferson to monopolize the story of the hundreds of people who lived at Monticello. In the early 1990s, she and others started the Getting Word project, tracing the genealogy of enslaved people from the plantation up to the present day. "We hoped by listening to the voices of the descendants we could hear the voices of their ancestors," she says. Over the course of a quarter century, researchers have connected with hundreds of people, many of whom are here today.

One of them now takes the stage and addresses the crowd in a soothing baritone voice. Bill Webb's "thirty-year-plus journey of discovery" began in the 1970s, he says, when he noticed a mysterious entry in a family Bible: "Brown Colbert, father of Melinda Colbert Edmundson, emigrated to Liberia and died soon after landing." Inspired by *Roots*, Webb began researching and years later connected with Getting Word. He learned that Colbert, a nephew of both Sally and James Hemings, was born at Monticello on Christmas Day, 1785 (a day Jefferson spent listening to a Mozart concerto in a Parisian museum). As a teenager, Colbert worked in the nailery, suffering a serious head injury when a fellow enslaved worker attacked him during a dispute. At the age of fifty, he became one of around fifteen thousand Blacks to sail to West Africa, his passage paid for by a colonization society. His new life in freedom lasted only a matter of weeks before he died from causes unknown.

Webb tells the audience about returning to Monticello with this knowledge of his forebears, working through complicated emotions. Upon learning that Webb was descended from Colbert, a reenactor at the nailery on Mulberry Row gave him a newly minted nail which he still holds close.

Many of the people sitting around in the tent must have similar stories; in their veins runs the blood of people who turned over red clay, who packed tobacco, who hauled water, who blasted limestone to create a canal, all on Jefferson's orders. People who lived and died, married and raised children, only to be tersely assessed as property in the plantation account books.

When Jefferson was young, he'd often tromp through the woods with an enslaved boy his own age, Jupiter Evans. Then the playing ceased. The teenaged Jupiter became Thomas's manservant and accompanied him to college. When Jefferson fell ill in 1774, the slave rode solo with copies of his master's essay *A Summary View of the Rights of British America*, to give to the Virginia House of Burgesses, meeting in rebellion. The document jump-started Jefferson's national political career. Evans became a coachman, manager of the stables, and stonecutter—the Doric columns on Monticello's main entrance are his work. By the year 1800, he must have spent more sustained time in Jefferson's presence than all but a few people.

That December, he fell ill while driving his master in a carriage in the cold. Evans sought out a healer at his own expense, who applied traditional African remedies, but even this couldn't save him. "I am sorry for him," Jefferson wrote, "as well as sensible he leaves a void in my domestic administration which I cannot fill up."

I wonder if a descendant of Evans's is here in the tent. Were stories passed down about him or his children? How do you resurrect a life when a slave owner collapses it down to a business expense? It's a tremendous challenge, given that state laws in many southern states, particularly in the nineteenth century, prohibited teaching enslaved children how to read and write. But it's not always impossible, as shown by those who are here today, who have begun their own difficult journeys. The process begins, as the next speaker reminds us, with African Americans' memories of their own past—for far too long dismissed by White historians.

"I wrote my first book...because of my impatience, my anger about the fact that Madison Hemings's words were not taken seriously in history," says author Annette Gordon-Reed from the stage. Madison was a victim of oppression. Yet as late as the 1990s, some White historians considered that the words of the enslaved had little to no intrinsic value and that their assertions had to be proven by other means, which struck

Gordon-Reed as perverse. Why automatically credit the words of the oppressors and ignore those of the victims?

Gordon-Reed's 1997 book, *Thomas Jefferson and Sally Hemings: An American Controversy*, presents evidence on Jefferson's paternity of Hemings's children from a variety of sources; she doesn't limit herself to Madison Hemings's statement. Yet she values it. "I wanted to give it the dignity of corroboration, the dignity of treating it as the testimony of the human being, particularly a human being who was a victim of a system that held millions in bondage," she tells the crowd. For a long time, I refused to believe that Jefferson was the father as well. Why hadn't I taken Madison Hemings's words seriously?

Gordon-Reed's first book wasn't really about Jefferson, she says—it was about listening to the stories of Blacks and making sure they are included in American history. "Telling a story and being believed is a powerful thing," she says. Her 2008 book, *The Hemingses of Monticello: An American Family*, was even more consequential than her first. After years of research, she presented a portrait of decades in the lives of an extended family of enslaved people. I think back to the first time I went to the library to check it out, after first confirming it was available. I spent a frustrating few minutes scanning the dozens of Jefferson biographies on the shelves and not finding it. Some of the books before me focused on his entire life, others just on an aspect of it—his architecture, wine, political career. Where is this book, specializing in his slaves? A return to the electronic catalogue solved the mystery: it was filed not under B-JEFFERSON, but B-HEMINGS FAMILY.

Thinking of this experience now, I feel my shame at my own blinders swell. I hadn't seen the Hemingses as existing in their own right. Everything was Jefferson; for me, nothing counted in this journey unless it was linked to the great man. When people of color did appear in this narrative, they were always in service to Jefferson and described by him.

Monticello is where Americans have been both at our best and at our worst, Gordon-Reed tells the crowd. It's all part of our shared story. All this must be remembered. The descendants who are here today had every right to want to turn away from this painful chapter, to willingly forget the hell that their ancestors lived through. Yet here they are, bearing witness.

Their journeys are surely more difficult, not to mention more important, than my own. But mine still means something to me. The willingness of these descendants to take a hard look at slavery encourages me to do the same. This history, our history, did not happen the way we the living would have wished it to, but we cannot pretend otherwise. The story of America includes Jefferson writing the Declaration of Independence and traveling through France, but also Brown Colbert venturing to Liberia and Jupiter Evans seeking succor in his dying hours with an African American healer.

As the ceremony concludes, Karen Briggs returns to the stage. The audience rises and begins singing "Lift Every Voice," sometimes called the Black national anthem. I stumble over the melody; there is much to learn.

No, I will not turn away from Jefferson's story. His is intertwined with the stories of hundreds of African Americans. My self-interrogations about my own views on Jefferson and White privilege have been halting, as stuttering as my singing is now. Yet I need to try to honestly learn about our past, a past that's still alive. To reach for an understanding of what must be clear to those who have seen their forebears' contributions erased from the history books. Of the long path African Americans have walked, out from bondage into a society that denied their equality and very humanity. Of the essential contributions they have made to the American experience along the way. Of the stories of their ancestors, truths passed down through generations. Of the undeniable fact that enslaved lives matter.

HIDDEN STRUGGLES

And so I do continue my travels, covering the remaining Objects of Attention in *Hints*. But none of my final trips are more meaningful than the one I take with my family on a bitterly cold winter's day where we join a small group on Monticello's Hemings Family tour. A guide announces he will highlight the lives of members of these enslaved people, raising difficult topics and providing time for visitors to ask questions, engage in dialogue, and contemplate what they've heard. Miranda, age twelve, and Nico, age nine, are in serious moods, ready to learn. When we started this journey, they were as enthusiastic as I was about Jefferson; I'm sure they're going to hear some hard truths today, though.

The tour leader starts by taking us to see the presentation in Sally Hemings's room. We exit a few minutes later, all of us shaken—including me, who had seen it before. "That was presented so beautifully," Liana says. "Sally Hemings could have been free. She chose to rely on that promise."

Nico looks particularly crestfallen. "Didn't that change your views of Jefferson, Miranda?" he asks. She nods her head and doesn't speak.

We cover the short distance to the kitchen, hidden from White visitors in the nineteenth century below the walkway that stretches from the main house to the South Pavilion. There we see a stew stove, a contraption that allowed cooks to regulate the temperature of sauces and stews by adjusting one of several charcoal burners; James Hemings made use of this technique when he returned from France. Jefferson came to the kitchen, the guide says, only to adjust the clock in the corner once a week, ensuring the food would be cooked on time.

"Does the layout here show poor planning?" he asks the group. "It was traditional to separate the kitchen from the house, because of the smells and the risk of fire. But this is extreme. The kitchen is about one hundred yards or so away from the dining room, on the north side of

Monticello. It clearly wasn't here for the convenience of his staff. Boys age ten or so would have to race with warm pots of food through this tunnel and up the stairs."

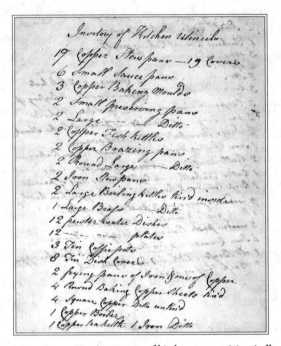

The inventory James Hemings wrote of kitchenware at Monticello, 1796.

"My views on Jefferson have changed severely," Nico whispers to me as we walk through the tunnel under the main house, following the paths of enslaved boys his own age.

We enter a room not part of regular house tours. "This space was part of the warming kitchen complex," the guide says. "Here enslaved boys handed the pots to others, who would put the food on fine china." They would then place the dishes on dumbwaiter self-service carts; White diners rarely glimpsed the enslaved kitchen staff. When a bottle of wine ran dry, all Jefferson had to do was place it in an empty slot near the fireplace, pull a cord, and wait a minute for a new one to appear. I remember touring Monticello as a child in the '80s, entranced by the magic of this tale. Until now, I hadn't thought of an enslaved boy spending his night in the wine cellar off the darkened tunnel, wondering when the yanking of the rope would stop so he could sleep.

For many years, Monticello mostly skipped over the issue of slavery, referring to "servants" and using the passive voice to refer to work on the plantation—tobacco "was planted," dinner "was served." Times have changed. The Thomas Jefferson Foundation now requires guides to state that Jefferson likely fathered Hemings's children. Monticello presents itself as a "site of conscience," where the story of those who lived in bondage shares space with that of their master.

"Was he considered a good slave owner?" an older African American visitor asks softly.

"A lot of people ask that," the guide replies. "He was an absentee owner for forty years and had a series of overseers during that time. Many had terrible reputations; some were abusive.

"There was one named Gabriel Lilly," he continues. "It was reported to Jefferson that he whipped a man three times a day when he was too sick to work. Jefferson said he knew that but knew of no one else who could serve his needs." The group falls silent.

We learn more about the Hemingses. The matriarch, an enslaved woman named Elizabeth, had six children by John Wayles and six by other men. Her progeny and their children mostly weren't subject to the overseer's lashes—they largely performed their work indoors, trading the cruelty of the fields for a loss of relative privacy and autonomy under the constant gaze of the Jeffersons. The guide fills in some of the blanks in the Sally Hemings narrative we already heard. She was only fourteen when she sailed to Europe, he tell us; Miranda's eyes bulge—Hemings was only a little over a year older than my daughter is now. He recounts how the *Pike County Republican* published her son Madison Hemings's life story in 1873 in an article entitled "Life Among the Lowly," which

Jefferson's White family attacked as false. "Just about all his claims have been substantiated," the guide says. African Americans in the group nod their head; I don't doubt they've heard a similar kind of story a thousand times.

After the tour, we step out to the East Portico. "I'm still processing this," Miranda says.

"I'm not," Nico announces. "I'm not enjoying the idea of your TJ book and such. I'm sad. I wouldn't say I hate him. But he's no longer my favorite Founding Father."

"The room felt heavy at times," Liana says. "I think so many people were looking to see if there was a glimpse of goodness in Jefferson. And we were all disappointed by that answer on the overseers. And he gave slaves as a gift to others. That's so cruel."

"Why?" Nico asks. "Why didn't he free his slaves? Didn't he believe in doing that? I'm so disappointed in this man. Do you think he was a good person?" he asks, turning to me.

"Saying someone is good or not is complicated," I say. "What do you think?"

"I don't know."

"He thought if he had sold his slaves, he would have had no income source. His career would have ended," I add, although I'm not sure why I'm playing devil's advocate.

"He could have used that big brain of his," Nico replies.

I suggest we walk and continue our reflections and learning. I've gone way off my once-clear itinerary—*Hints to Americans Traveling in Europe* does not detour to slave quarters in Virginia. But there's no doubt that enslaved families are always part of his story, whether he admitted it or not. The harmonious mansion expresses Jefferson's genius blend of Europe and America, but below it is where slaves brought tobacco in under the hot August sun, where they raised chickens to sell for pocket money, where they gathered by a bonfire at night to play the banjo.

Monticello was the lodestar of everyone's universe—both for the Whites who saw it as a Palladian paradise and for the Blacks who saw it as the world's most beautiful prison.

Although few enslaved people had the opportunity to reach destinations such as Europe, for them, travel was of the utmost importance, even a matter of life and death. Husbands reunited with their wives by visiting other plantations on day passes on Sundays or under the cover of night. Some slaves journeyed to other sites where they were hired out for work, sometimes permitted to keep a small amount of money. Some made a desperate gamble for freedom, striking out for the north.

My flaw, I realize, has been in only relating enslaved people to Jefferson—and, specifically, to his time abroad. The Hemings siblings were relevant to me because they went to Paris; other enslaved people were important because their work funded Jefferson's lifestyle. Yet of course the stories of their lives are valid in their own right, deserving to be heard. I need to expand my vision to take in these other travelers who left Monticello, whose journeys might have even more to teach me about the human condition than *Hints* does. The lives of the people who lived on the plantation are not chapters to add to the volumes filed under B-JEFFERSON; these narratives are B-HEMINGS, B-FOSSETT, B-HUBBARD, "powerful stories," as Annette-Gordon Reed put it, that every American should know.

I tell my family about a scene that transpired near here. On December 23, 1789, Jefferson, his daughters, and James and Sally Hemings came home after their years abroad. A great crowd of enslaved people gathered around the carriage that James was driving, lifting Jefferson out and hoisting him in the air to the sound of joyful shouting, as the enslaved man Wormley Hughes recalled later. Perhaps there was an element of genuine respect for him, as his White descendants claimed. But even stronger must have been the relief that he had returned at all. What if

Jefferson hadn't survived his long odyssey? The death of a plantation owner often resulted in the sale of slaves, breaking up families, ending marriages, and separating parents from children forever.

The homecoming was a rare occasion in which nearly everyone at the plantation gathered together. Here were the men who harvested tobacco, drove carriages, and hammered iron; women who hoed weeds, cooked stews, and sewed clothing. The people who fought for the time and space to carve out private lives away from the forced labor system that Whites had bound them to. Some were relatives of James and Sally Hemings—what did they think of their family members' return? Was word already spreading of Sally's pregnancy, of the "treaty" hammered out with the master? What paths to freedom might the African Americans in the assembled crowd dream for themselves?

I set out with my family on a walk around the Monticello grounds, with the stories of four enslaved people in my mind, who either were at this homecoming or heard about it soon afterward: two brothers of James and Sally, one nephew, and a young field hand from a different family. These men would each take different roads toward liberation. There was no obvious solution to the dilemma of escaping bondage. But one thing was clear: liberty required leaving the plantation.

Where to go? Each direction held its own promise and risks.

The oldest road out of Monticello runs east.

CHAPTER SEVENTEEN

The Long Walk to Freedom

TO THE EAST: BROKEN PROMISES

We descend a slope down to Mulberry Row and stop before a reconstructed one-story wooden house of an enslaved family. A sign inside reads "Not so Bad?" That's the reaction some visitors have when they see the cabin; although dwarfed by the mansion on the hill, it's not materially worse than the shacks of some poor White workers of the time. But the exhibit explains that there was much more to housing than a roof over one's head. Enslaved people could not own their dwelling; they could be taken away from it at any time and were subject to violence and family separation.

We walk a couple of hundred yards to the stables. A low, white stone structure still stands, once surrounded by wooden buildings. Here, Jupiter Evans cared for Thoroughbreds, workhorses, and mules. He and his successors worked on the carriages—the sleek racing phaeton, the sturdy landau fashioned by John Hemmings—and oiled up saddles, the aromas of leather, barnyard animals, and sweet clover and timothy filling the air.

Even as an old man, the enslaved Isaac Granger could remember when he was a boy impressed by the fine gilded springs and ironwork of the finest carriage on the premises, recalling the names of the horses. More darkly, Granger recollected when Archibald Cary, "as dry a looking a man as you ever saw in your life," visited. Granger would sprint through the woods, keeping ahead of Cary's carriage as it slowly ascended the mountain road, to be in place to open each of three gates, the last one here at the stable. If he missed opening a gate in time, Cary would "look about for him and whip him with his horsewhip."

Isaac Granger, working as a free blacksmith in
Petersburg, Virginia, around the year 1847.

On one wall of the stable today hangs a map of the Monticello grounds showing the ancient East Road, which ran straight through tobacco fields and down the mountain to the Rivanna River, where it connected with byways that led to the Three Notch'd Road to Richmond. Now it's just a path, crossing a meadow and plunging into a forest of pawpaws. I wonder how many times Robert Hemings came to these stables to saddle up a horse to take to this road.

Robert, the oldest child of Elizabeth Hemings by John Wayles, was one of the most well traveled people, Black or White, who lived at Monticello. As an enslaved valet, he lived at different times in both Annapolis and Philadelphia (where Dr. Shippen inoculated him against smallpox) and in 1784 once returned from Boston to Virginia by himself with his master's horses. When Jefferson was abroad, Hemings was able to hire himself out and keep his wages. In the course of his journeys, he met an enslaved woman in Fredericksburg, sixty-five miles from his home, and they married and had children. He must have been apprehensive when his master returned from Paris; would this result in a loss of his relative autonomy?

With Jefferson back, Robert again had to wait on him. When his master left with James Hemings to take his place as secretary of state in New York City in 1790, Robert traveled in advance of them, securing lodging along the route. Ultimately, James, the trained chef, stayed up north, while Robert was able to return to Virginia and again hire himself out. In 1794, he advocated for an arrangement by which a French émigré in Richmond would buy him and allow him to work off his purchase price. Although Jefferson was greatly displeased, he finally acquiesced. After several years of work for his new owner, Robert Hemings was finally free.

He would live with his wife and children for the next quarter century in the state capital, a hundred miles east of his humble cabin at Monticello. In the early 1800s, he and his family formed part of the small but thriving community of hundreds of free Blacks in Richmond, with tens of thousands of others scattered throughout the state. Some had purchased their freedom, as he had; others were liberated by landowners inspired by Revolutionary principles or the exhortations of Quakers and Methodists. By 1802, he had bought a half-acre lot in the city. Providing for his family was a struggle; he lost one of his hands in an incident involving firearms, the details of which are now lost to time. Despite his marketable skills as a valet, he refused to become a servant to Whites, even for pay, preferring to run a fruit stand. Although Hemings had been in the presence of presidents and generals, it was always as an unfree servant. Now he had charge of his own life.

On August 30, 1800, a storm of biblical proportions hit Richmond; when the clouds parted, things would never be the same for Hemings and other free Blacks in Virginia. That day, an enslaved blacksmith named Gabriel Prosser had planned a march on the capital to take the armory in the state's first major slave uprising. For years he had hired himself out, making contacts with other enslaved workers and preaching liberation. Once Gabriel and his conspirators seized arms and arrested Governor James Monroe, surely the Whites in power would live up to the ideals of the American Revolution—didn't they profess that all men are created equal?—and order emancipation.

But the severe summer storm prevented the slaves from marching; during the delay, two of them betrayed the plan to their owner. The state government lost no time in hanging Gabriel and other ringleaders, but the crackdown went beyond that, curtailing the few rights African Americans had. New laws made it illegal for enslaved workers to hire themselves out. Freed slaves had to leave the state within a year or be returned to bondage. Enslaved people could no longer congregate on Sundays without White supervision; more slave patrols roamed the state; and laws restricted the education of Blacks. The little toleration that Robert Hemings had found in Richmond, meager as it was, disappeared.

So did much of what was left of the idea of equality, talked so much of back in 1776. Following the Revolution, a number of White Virginians had admitted that slavery was evil, only questioning the timing and practicality of emancipation. Now, after Gabriel's Rebellion, White landowners increasingly promoted the myth that they, the benevolent masters, watched over grateful, loyal slaves who were incapable of living without their assistance, all part of God's plan.

Not only was the dream, however tenuous, of ending slavery in

Virginia dying, so was the way of life of the White planters. After two centuries of intensive tobacco farming, the soil was exhausted and the state's economy in a free fall. The Virginia gentry's most lucrative income source became selling enslaved people to slave drivers who took them to the burgeoning cotton plantations of the Deep South. Liberation never seemed further away.

In the midst of these dark times, in 1802, Robert Hemings's daughter got married. I wonder what he thought of the shrinking opportunities for her and his grandchildren to come. Had he put any hope in the uprisings? He might have known Gabriel, whose owner had a farm just outside of the city and a town house three blocks away from Robert's home. Did the rebel ever sound him out at his fruit stand, or in a secret meeting? Hemings wasn't a timid man—he had traveled alone all over the country and had demonstrated the force to stand up to his master. What did he think of the diminishing options left for Black Virginians after the rebellion failed?

We don't know; although he was literate, as many of his siblings were, nothing Robert wrote has survived. But we have clues that he aided runaway slaves in his own way. In 1799, Jefferson's cousin, who lived in Richmond, asked him for help in making inquiries about a runaway slave from Monticello; Robert refused, or at least stalled in doing so. Five years later, he likely helped a nephew of his who escaped to Richmond after a Monticello overseer whipped him on a day when the young man was too sick to work in the nailery.

Hemings lived for twenty-three years as his own master. In August 1819, Patsy Jefferson (who by then went as Martha Jefferson Randolph) wrote to her father, who was away at his second house at Poplar Forest, sending him the paperwork needed for his next wine order and informing him about the summer heat. In a postscript, she added, "poor old Robert Hemings is dead."

THE SOUTH: SOLD DOWN THE RIVER

We leave the stable and cut through a field to the garden below Mulberry Lane. "Imagine when the plants are in full force," Liana tells the kids on this winter's day. In fall, the thousand-foot-long enclosure shows off a medley of purple eggplants, yellow nasturtiums, and blue-violet Choux de Milan cabbage. And in the southeastern corner is tobacco, its light green leaves spread out—planted, the head gardener told me once, to give people an idea of what Monticello's cash crop looked like.

One person all too familiar with this crop was James Hubbard. His father was an enslaved boatman and shoemaker and, by the time the Jeffersons and Hemingses returned home in 1789, a foreman at the Poplar Forest plantation. Five years later, James, who had turned eleven, left his parents to work at Monticello's nailery, the building (reconstructed) that casts a shadow above us on the Row. At first among the least productive of the teenager workers, Hubbard gained strength and became one of the best.

We climb a set of stairs out of the garden and step into the nailery. The scenes that passed here are almost too painful to imagine: a "dozen little boys," as Jefferson put it, forced into this small, smoky room, pounding red-hot iron rod and shaping it into nails over twelve-hour workdays to meet their quota. "This is cruel," says Miranda softly. "It's just not right. Of course, none of this is right."

We walk west down Mulberry Row, the forest looming before us, to a field where Hubbard made charcoal. A sign indicates that the substance was used to heat the plantation house and fuel the stew stove and the nailery furnace. He would stack thirty cords of wood in the shape of a dome, with an opening in the middle, then cover it with sand or turf and light the base. Hubbard would watch over it for days, monitoring the slow heat and ensuring that the wood charred but didn't burn. Jefferson occasionally gave him small amounts of money to incentivize him to work efficiently and not waste wood. "He should have gotten paid for that," Nico says, frustrated. "Not just pocket change."

Not too far from here, in late August 1805, Hubbard made his bid for freedom. By then he lived alone in the woods at the southern base of the mountain—where, as Isaac Granger recalled later, "bears sometimes came" and "you could see the wolves in gangs running and howling." The nascent Underground Railroad did not stretch its network into these parts; running at night and seeking a safe house would be problematic. In his cabin, Hubbard devised his own plan: he would escape in broad daylight.

James had been carefully husbanding the meager bonuses he received from his charcoal work and possibly a little more money from selling pilfered nails. In exchange for a cash payment and an overcoat, Wilson Lilly, the White overseer's son, forged papers for him. With the rest of his savings, Hubbard bought nankeen britches, a dove-colored waistcoat, and a new hat and began his journey. But outside the nation's capital, a sheriff apprehended him. Hubbard presented his papers, claiming to be James Bolds—a fitting name for this undaunted man to assume. Unfortunately, Lilly had done a poor job forging the documents—the sheriff, who himself was barely literate, judged them "soe bad" and threw him in the Fairfax County jail.

I remember the start I had when I first came across that last detail. I was sitting in my local coffee shop, at my favorite table where I show up each weekend morning with my laptop and stacks of books, one of which, by Cinder Stanton, told of Hubbard's fate. The courthouse and adjoining jail where he was imprisoned (the latter having been rebuilt over time) are only two blocks from the café—I could almost see them from the nearest window.

As a schoolchild, I toured the historic complex of bricks and graceful white columns. Nobody mentioned that the prison had housed escaped slaves. My frustration at the half-truths I learned as a child mounted.

The site of much of my research for my journey with *Hints*, conducted over countless cups of coffee, overlooks a crime scene—for surely locking away a man on the verge of obtaining a lifetime of freedom constitutes a crime against humanity.

The Fairfax sheriff returned Hubbard to Monticello, after demanding a bonus on top of the legal reward he was due, on account of the "great Resk" he had run in capturing the "large fellow." Five years later, Hubbard escaped again with another forged pass. An ad for his return described him as "27 years of age, about six feet high, stout limbs and strong made, of daring demeanor, bold and harsh features, dark complexion." This time he headed west to the mountains, but, after a year, was again apprehended. Jefferson, who had sold him in absentia to a carpenter, demanded that he be "severely flogged in the presence of his old companions, and committed to jail." Hubbard was probably resold to a slave driver headed south. That was the punishment Jefferson recommended for a runaway, to send him "so distant as never more to be heard of among us. It would to the others be as if he were put out of the way by death."

Somewhere below us, not restored, is the South Road. Across Virginia, plantation owners sent apprehended escapees down south, in a line of other enslaved people chained together, intending to break their spirits. In the heat of Mississippi or Louisiana they picked cotton, monitored by vicious overseers, the prospect of seeing family again irrevocably gone. Now there were some five hundred miles of hostile terrain between them and northern freedom. Such was the fate of James Hubbard, whose boldness could not overcome the slave owner's guns and irons.

TO THE WEST: A LIFE OF QUIET STRUGGLE

From the site of the charcoal production, we tack back toward the kitchen, the setting of another powerful story. Like his sister Sally, James Hemings reached a deal with his master: he would obtain freedom once he had instructed another slave in the art of French cooking. And so, after first serving Secretary of State Jefferson in New York City and Philadelphia, he trained his younger brother Peter how to make sauces, fricassees, and *les oeufs à la neige,* or snow eggs, poached meringues in a sea of custard.

One year I heard Ashbell McElveen present at Monticello's annual Heritage Harvest Festival, a fall celebration of gardening, heritage plants, and the culinary traditions of people who lived on the mountain. Chef Ashbell, as he goes by, founded the James Hemings Society, promoting recognition of the first African American chef of continental cuisine.

"This was James's signature dish," he said, demonstrating an initial step in the preparation of snow eggs. He had a special guest to help him: Gayle Jessup White, a Hemings descendant, who stirred egg yolks in a large copper pot. "James could make astonishing dishes," he explained. "His food was so good, when he served it to politicians it put them in the mood to make deals. He was the man who established fine dining and service here in this country—Whites weren't in the kitchen."

Once James finished giving his lessons, it fell to the younger man to cook such delicacies. Peter didn't have the leverage or funds that his older brothers Robert and James had to negotiate or purchase his way out of slavery. And after Gabriel's Rebellion the legal path to freedom for Blacks in Virginia was closing. Nor would he try to escape; too many had tried that route and failed.

So Peter tried to make the best of the unfree life he found himself in. He married an enslaved domestic worker, Betsy, and helped raise their children. In 1809, the family moved to a cabin fashioned from chestnut logs on Mulberry Row. At Monticello at least he had a modicum of stability; other enslaved people were taken west by White planters who had had enough of the declining yields in Virginia and decided to try their luck elsewhere.

The Three Notch'd Road ran west to the mountains; any highway that headed to the newly formed states of Kentucky or Tennessee saw a lot of traffic. Beyond the Appalachians, ex-Virginia planters eagerly bought up land confiscated from Native Americans: rich, tobacco-growing earth. There, enslaved people worked and lived in arrangements similar to what they knew back home, an extension of the status quo, even as they missed their family in Virginia. Life in these states was marginally better for the enslaved than the cotton fields of the Deep South, but it remained harsh.

Wherever they found themselves, enslaved Blacks honored their traditions, incorporating elements of African culture in their music, dance, dress, speech, and food. Whites absorbed some of these cultural contributions unconsciously—and mostly without crediting Blacks when they did notice the source. (Even the southern accent was influenced in part by African American speaking cadences.) For his part, Peter Hemings helped spread culture through his cuisine, which blended his brother's French techniques with Black foodways. He and other enslaved cooks at Monticello worked with ingredients with African connections: sweet potatoes, okra, eggplants, and peanuts.

"There's so much African American influence on Southern cooking, we don't even realize it," Miranda notes as we reach the kitchen. She's been enthused about the origins and types of food ever since our trip to Italy.

"And rock-and-roll too," Nico adds. I'm proud that he knows something about our country's musical history. I point out the site of the smokehouse below us, where a jaw harp was found by Monticello archaeologists. At Christmas, African Americans gathered in front of that building; a fiddler would stand "with half-closed eyes and head thrown back, with one foot keeping time" before an appreciative crowd, an observer noted.

Notes on Virginia stated that Blacks were capable of playing and "imagining a small catch," particularly on "the instrument proper to them...

the Banjar, which they brought hither from Africa." Jefferson claimed that music was the "favorite passion of my soul"—but this love did not extend to music that *had* soul; he ignored Black rhythms. He scoffed at "nightwalkers," those who gathered in the dark, the only time that was theirs, to socialize, play songs, drink coffee, and eat fried meat and cakes with honey. Jefferson missed the cultural fusion going on right under his nose—African Americans were creating a new sound in the New World, one that Whites would someday copy and capitalize off.

Others couldn't get enough of the wild melodies of the banjo, the energetic call-and-response singing, and the syncopated percussion of Black music. Jefferson's younger brother would, Isaac Granger recalled, "come out among black people, play the fiddle and dance half the night." Sally's sons Madison and Eston made good money playing the violin. But the musicians who cashed in on songs like these in the nineteenth century were White minstrel players in blackface, who failed to share profits with the composers. Few Whites admitted the value of Black creations. This fundamental lack of respect was what led to James Hemings's downfall.

Earlier today, our guide told James's story. In 1801, Jefferson asked Hemings, who was living in Baltimore, to serve as the chef in the President's House. But he would only write to Hemings via a White intermediary, not deigning to communicate directly with his former slave. Having spent years working in close proximity to his owner, in Paris, New York, and Philadelphia, Hemings demanded the respect of a personal request. Jefferson hired a White chef instead. A year later, despondent, unable to find a proper chef's position, and drinking heavily, Hemings apparently committed suicide. He was thirty-six. "He found this a very difficult world to live in," the guide said. Many in the group murmured affirmation.

"James Hemings didn't want to be summoned like a slave," Chef Ashbell had said at the harvest festival. "That's why I'm here," the chef said, "to honor his legacy. Credit him as a Revolutionary Founding Father."

Ultimately, Peter Hemings moved from cooking to other tasks on the plantation. Several women, led by Edith Fossett, ultimately took over the kitchen; Senator Daniel Webster described her cuisine as "in half Virginian, half French style, in good taste and abundance." Hemings learned the art of making beer from an English brewer who was living in the area and produced a light ale each spring and fall. We stop before the beer cellar in the tunnel running under Monticello, a whitewashed room with oak casks and bottles. Hemings might have passed on his brewing skills to his nephew Daniel Farley, a free Black who grew hops for beer-making and played his violin at dances in Charlottesville.

We exit the tunnel and return to the West Lawn. July 4, 1826, was a dreadful day for the enslaved community at Monticello, for it portended a mass exodus of African Americans from the mountain to other planta-tions. The master's death that day set in motion a sale of nearly all of his estate and property—including his human property, the 130 people who lived in bondage. In January 1827, an auction block was set up on this lawn; 100 slaves were sold at that time, 30 more later. Some went to the work camps of the South; slightly more fortunate people remained in bondage in Virginia or were taken to points west. Mothers and sons, fathers and daughter, grandparents and grandchildren were all separated forever.

Peter Hemings, too, departed from Monticello, heading west. But he wasn't traveling to the tobacco lands beyond the mountains; in the midst of this suffering, Hemings finally got the break he deserved. Although at age fifty-seven he was nearing the end of his work life, given his considerable skills he had been appraised at the auction at $100. He likely assumed he would face additional years in bondage under a new owner—until his nephew, Farley, the musician, purchased him for a dollar, a sale at a symbolic price arranged to give him freedom in his last years. Hemings relocated only a few miles west to Charlottesville, where he supported himself as a tailor until his death.

THE NORTH: THE FLICKERING LIGHT OF FREEDOM

Of all the paths to freedom taken by enslaved people out of Monticello, none was more tortuous than that of the Fossetts.

Not long after his master returned from France, twelve-year-old Joseph Fossett had every expectation that he might obtain liberty at a young age. In the 1780s, his mother, Mary Hemings, had been hired out to a White merchant in Charlottesville, Thomas Bell. In 1792, Mary asked to be sold to him; after the purchase, Bell informally emancipated her and the couple lived together for years as partners. But Jefferson allowed the merchant to buy only the two children he had fathered with Hemings; her two children from previous relationships were not for sale. Instead of spending his teenage years free with his mother in town, Joe remained enslaved, working at the Monticello nailery.

The year after his fellow nail maker James Hubbard's flight north, Fossett, too, traveled clandestinely to Washington, DC, to visit his wife, Edith, a cook at the President's House, whom he had not seen in three years. Like Hubbard, he was apprehended—but his punishment was lighter, and he returned to his job as head enslaved blacksmith. He and Edith would subsequently have ten children, including, in 1815, Peter Fossett.

In 1826, Joe was one of the few slaves (all members of the Hemings family) freed in his master's will; they also received an exemption from the law requiring freed slaves to leave the state within a year. Yet there was a catch: his emancipation would only take effect the following Fourth of July, in 1827. While he remained in bondage, his wife and children were placed for sale at the West Lawn auction. Jefferson's caprices had denied him a childhood in freedom with his mother; now his own offspring were subject to a similar arbitrary decision that split them apart.

Joe Fossett did everything he could to preserve his family. A free Black relative in Charlottesville bought his wife and two youngest children, agreeing to remain their legal owner for the time being (for if they were formally freed, they would have to leave Virginia). But Joe and his relative couldn't afford to buy Peter, age eleven. The news came as a shock to the boy. As a member of the Hemings family, enjoying certain privileges, he often didn't even feel like a slave, he wrote years later in his memoir. With the death of the master, he was "suddenly...put upon an auction block and sold to strangers." The true nature of slavery was revealed; no matter how kind a White owner might seem in a given moment, an enslaved person was property to him, a disposable asset.

Desperate, Joe Fossett reached a handshake deal with Colonel John Jones, a presumed "friendly" White storeowner in Charlottesville, who agreed to buy Peter and sell him back to his father for the same purchase price he had paid once Joe had earned the money as a free blacksmith. A perfect plan. Except when Joe announced he had saved enough to buy his son, the slave owner reneged and refused to sell. Nor did Jones approve of the boy's habit of studying at night. "If I ever catch you with a book in your hands," Peter recalled his owner telling him, "thirty-and-nine lashes on your bare back."

In 1831, slaves in Virginia again rose up against their masters. Unlike Gabriel's aborted mission three decades earlier, the rebels went further this time, killing around sixty Whites. This uprising, too, failed and an even more oppressive backlash followed. A new state law criminalized teaching any people of color to read or write, which must have pleased Col. Jones. "No meetings, no night visits," wrote Martha Jefferson Randolph; now the state was crawling with slave patrols.

Some Black Virginians saw escape as the only option. Runaways did have an advantage that didn't exist when James Hubbard and Joe Fossett took to the road: the Underground Railroad, a shifting network of safe houses and "conductors," sympathetic Whites or free Blacks who helped transport and hide people. But the dangers were many. An escapee might need to run through the woods at night, guided by constellations while listening for mounted slave patrols and their snarling dogs, hoping to make it to a free state.

What lay in store for them there? "Under the flickering light of the North star," wrote Frederick Douglass, the great African American abolitionist, "stood a doubtful freedom." Life in the North was hard for ex-slaves, who faced severe racism and the lack of economic opportunities. Yet even a doubtful freedom was better than the living hell the South had become.

My family and I sit on a bench on the north side of Monticello, the last stop on our walk, near a recreated phaeton. In front of us was once the north orchard, full of cider apples; beyond that was, and is, what a nineteenth century visitor called a "savage" woods. Peter Fossett would have had different obstacles to contend with if he ran—he was no longer at Monticello. Still, the deep woods before us indicate the kind of physical hazards an escaping slave might have faced. The North Road ran through towering trees and "blasted" and "uprooted" trunks left to decay. It led to a ford across the Rivanna River, so dangerous that sometimes horses were injured and carriages broken in the rocky water; Jefferson's younger sister and her enslaved servant known as Little Sall both drowned attempting a crossing in 1774. Someone seeking freedom might have had to struggle through swamps and rushing rivers at night, or tried to trick White patrols in the light of day with a forged pass. In either case, the courage needed to make such an attempt is almost unfathomable, but Fossett tried.

"I...made an attempt to gain my own freedom," he wrote, but was caught. "My parents were here in Ohio, and I wanted to be with them and be free," he wrote, "so I resolved to get free or die in the attempt. I started the second time, was caught, handcuffed, and taken back and carried to Richmond and put in jail." After this latest transgression, Col. Jones put him on the auction block to be "sold like a horse." Finally, luck broke Fossett's way: a group of his relatives and friends of his late master purchased him so he could rejoin his family in the North.

In freedom, Fossett ran a successful catering business, drawing on the cooking skills he learned from his mother. He served as a conductor on the Underground Railroad. During the Civil War, he joined Cincinnati's Black Brigade, helping prepare the defense of the city against an expected Confederate invasion. A number of descendants of Monticello slaves fought for the Union in the Civil War; with victory came emancipation. Following the war, the former enslaved community of Monticello scattered farther, with many heading north.

In 1900, at the age of eighty-five, Peter Fossett, by then a prominent minister, came back to Monticello and was feted as one of the last survivors of an era. The house was by then owned by the Levys, a prominent Jewish family of philanthropists who had bought it decades earlier. His circle was complete: Fossett had departed a slave, restricted to the house's dark tunnels and hidden servant's entrance. When he returned a free man, he walked right through the front door.

Peter Fossett, later in life, as a pastor in
Ohio in the late nineteenth century.

WHAT WE CAN BE

Later (after I've been back to Europe, but worth recounting here), I speak with Gayle Jessup White. I knew her as the Hemings descendant who had helped Chef Ashbell at the festival. She's related to other enslaved people on the mountain as well: Jupiter Evans, whom the African American healer could not save, and James Hubbard, who ran for freedom.

And one other person I am well acquainted with. Thomas Jefferson.

As we talk, this past that I've been chasing has never seemed more real. All these bloodlines run in one person. Her genealogy is what the rest of us call American History.

"I didn't grow up knowing about my ties to Monticello," Jessup White tells me. "I've spent many years trying to find evidence to confirm it." She now works as a public relations and community engagement officer with the Thomas Jefferson Foundation and is writing a book about her journey of discovery. Her connection to the Jeffersons and Hemingses isn't what one might immediately assume—she descends directly from Peter (not his sister Sally) and, in a separate genealogical line, through one of Thomas Jefferson's great-great-grandsons, who had a child with his domestic servant. Her story adds a fresh chapter to the narratives told by her ancestors Madison Hemings and Peter Fossett, who both kept memories from the mountaintop alive. And her relative William Monroe Trotter, a Fossett descendant who cofounded both the African American newspaper the *Boston Guardian* and the prominent civil rights organization the Niagara Movement. Her family has never been afraid to speak truth to power.

"If we don't understand this history, then we will not as a nation succeed," she goes on. "The American experiment will fail. Since 1619, the Africans brought here were seen as less than human. It's imperative that White people see my ancestors as full humans—so they can see their descendants as fully equal, too."

Jessup White lives in Richmond, following a career as a broadcast journalist. No matter what her family achieves, though, she's left with a constant worry about their safety. White violence can affect any African American, across all genders, ages, and occupations. "My son went to MIT. But he's six feet tall with broad shoulders. He's a big, strong Black man. I know what can happen to him," she says, referencing the never-ending police killings of African Americans. "I want to be in a country where no mother gets a call in the middle of the night. Where no one does. I want to live in a country where this does not happen."

Despite the long road that still must be traveled, Jessup White is encouraged by changes at Monticello. The Look Closer event was an important step forward. "It's giving voice to people who had been wiped out," she says. These transformations "speak to American growth," she tells me. "They speak to what we can be. Think of that, something like that happening at a former plantation where my ancestors were enslaved."

It is a "paradox of liberty," she continues, referencing an exhibit on slave life at Monticello that she's helped put on, that "the man who wrote the Declaration of Independence also owned 607 slaves." Despite his major flaws—and no one can appreciate them more than members of her family—she still recognizes the importance of what Jefferson wrote in that document, although we remain far from achieving true equality.

Gayle Jessup White hasn't quit engaging with the past, even when the knowledge she uncovers—of family members whipped, sold, and treated like animals—brings pain. If she can find the strength to examine our troubled history, then the rest of have no excuse not to.

As for me, her example—and all the stories of her ancestors, who worked for freedom and family, who helped build a country and a culture—are a powerful reminder that the travels into the past I started out on years ago have more layers and contradictions than I ever expected.

I have miles to go before I truly understand the Hemingses, the Hubbards, or the Jeffersons, if ever I can. But I'll keep on the journey.

CHAPTER EIGHTEEN

The Last Days of the Ancien Régime

SMELLS LIKE OLD MONEY

Visiting Versailles makes me feel like a mere speck in the universe. As Liana and I approach it, the spring after my hard discoveries at Monticello, we stop hundreds of yards away to squeeze the entire palace in the frame of our camera. The amber-colored wings of the château stretch endlessly, with colonnade after colonnade and countless gilded balconies. You could fit sixty-one Monticellos inside it and still have room for a visitor's center.

As we saw when in Amsterdam on King's Day, Object of Attention Eight recommends learning about royal courts so as to contrast them with the "honest simplicity now prevailing in America." Of course, the monarchy is long gone in France, but I want to find traces of it—so we've come here to one of the places it was last spotted. I'm looking for glimpses of a vanished time: the days in which Louis XVI ruled France and the transformative year of 1789 when the French people forced their way into having a say in their country's government, with a small assist from the American ambassador.

For all Jefferson's faults—crimes even—as a slave owner, he was more than that. Paradoxically, while he kept hundreds of people in bondage, he fought for liberty for others. He helped establish America as a democratic society, a nation in which Blacks and women, at first excluded from the vision, would fight their way into joining on more equal terms. And he surreptitiously played the role of a revolutionary in France as well. But I'm getting ahead of my story—before the French Revolution came the *Ancien Régime*.

For most of the Virginian's time in Paris—the four and a half years he spent prior to the turning point in 1789—few dared to whisper of rebellion. King Louis XVI, ensconced in Versailles, remained too powerful. Jefferson, suffice to say, was not a fan of either the person or the palace.

Hints compares the royals in Versailles to the "lions, tigers, hyenas, and other beasts of prey" kept in the château's menagerie: dangerous predators, imposing and malevolent. Louis XVI's great-grandfather, the Sun King, had constructed much of the palace in the seventeenth century. But if Louis XIV were a lion, the king of kings and conqueror of foreign lands, his descendant was more akin to a housecat on a throne, with the attention span to match. Sixteen's heart might have been in the right place, Jefferson wrote, "but his mind was weakness itself, his constitution timid, his judgment null, and without sufficient firmness even to stand by the faith of his word." He was not the right man for the job, one he never applied for and never wanted, preferring to spend his days hunting.

If ever France needed a prescient leader, this was the time. The cost of living had skyrocketed, impoverishing common people. Meanwhile, the new class of merchants, manufacturers, and professionals resented how they were refused entry to the ranks of the elite despite their growing wealth. And, oh yes, the French state was nearly bankrupt, indebted from its expenditures during the American Revolution.

Yet at Versailles the party never stopped. All was still glitz and bling, lavish spreads in the gardens, fountains shooting water, gambling tables, masked balls, light shows to the sound of orchestras, flowing Champagne, furtive liaisons behind the shrubs, and revelers making love like it was going out of style (occasionally even with their own spouses). Liana and I tour the king's state apartments, with glittering chandeliers and frescoed ceilings, and his bedchamber, the room glowing warmly of gold. Here Louis ceremonially rose each morning before a crowd, as nobles vied for the honor of who would hand him his shirt and fasten his sword.

Each Tuesday, Ambassador's Day, Jefferson traveled to Versailles to converse with the royals and his fellow diplomats. Of course, the Virginian had a taste for the finer things, buying silver goblets and bottles of Haut Brion while in France and wearing lace ruffles. But compared to the beautiful people strutting around here, Jefferson looked almost rustic. Some admired him for it. Thomas Shippen noticed as much when he visited the palace in March of 1788. "When we were introduced to the King it was after waiting five minutes in his antechamber," Shippen wrote. Servants were still fixing Louis's hair, yet envoys and ministers "were prostrating themselves before him." Yet "although Mr. Jefferson was the plainest man in the room, and the most destitute of ribands, crosses and other insignia of rank, he was the most courted and most attended to (even by the Courtiers themselves) of the whole diplomatic corps."

We make our way to the Hall of Mirrors, the grandiose Baroque gallery. "What the heck is this?" Liana exclaims. "This strong smell. No, it can't be pee. But it's so old." She follows her nose to the corner of the room. "Yeah, that's pee. Did these people pee here or what? It's coming from the parquet floors. That smell is impregnated there forever." We had wanted to connect with the past, but the long-lost odor of drunk, lazy party-goers wasn't what we had in mind.

"What an odd thing, this place is so fancy, it's all Rococo and lacquered mirrors, and it *stinks*," Liana says in a Cuban whisper (a normal speaking voice for some cultures), attracting some attention from the other tourists. "What a contradiction. Those people held themselves up as so special." We could do worse with a metaphor for Versailles: beautiful on the outside, decadent and reeking at its core.

We exit and walk past fountains with carved stone gods and shrubs tortured into cubes and triangles. After a mile and a half, we reach the Petit Trianon, a small palace, whose architecture (neoclassical) and landscaping (English) Jefferson would have appreciated—if he had ever been let in. This was an exclusive section of the grounds, only admitting visitors upon the orders of its owner, Jefferson's least favorite person in the whole kingdom: Marie Antoinette.

"Haughty," Jefferson wrote, and "devoted to pleasure and expense," the queen "had an absolute ascendency" over her husband. She was so "detested," he wrote, that a social "explosion of some sort is not impossible." The magnetic Austrian princess had married Louis two decades earlier at the age of fourteen. By 1789, her subjects' love-hate relationship with her had turned mostly to hate. With her three-foot tall hairstyle and gowns dripping with diamonds, she was an easy mark for critics of royal wastefulness. Although it was unusual for a French aristocrat to *not* have a lover, misogynists singled out Marie Antoinette's suspected sexual encounters for disapproval. While finding fault, Jefferson still succumbed, like many others, to her fashion trendsetting, describing her style changes to Abigail Adams. Even haters had to know: what was the queen wearing?

We enter a place that might have driven Jefferson bananas: Marie Antoinette's Hameau, or Hamlet. In 1783, she commissioned a model agricultural operation on the land surrounding the Petit Trianon, gifted to her by the king. The farm was as spotless as if an ancestor of Walt Disney had designed it. A faux-peasant village consisted of a dozen thatched houses circling an artificial pond. These have now been reconstructed, as has the watermill with its own wheel (decorative) and dairy built over a stream (to keep milk products cool in the water). Fine breeds of livestock were shipped in from Switzerland, and a real farmer kept things running when the queen wasn't cosplaying as a peasant herself.

No one was fooled. As a visiting diplomat put it, "Royalty has here endeavored to conceal itself from its own Eye, but the Attempt is vain. A Dairy furnished with the Porcelain of Sèvres is a Semblance too splendid of rural Life." Many resented this unintentional mockery of rural customs. Construction of the Hamlet cost five hundred thousand livres at a time when an unskilled worker in Paris made about one livre a day. While Marie-Antoinette wanted an escape from the extravagances of court, even in her exclusive rural niche she remained the focus of attention. Her loose-fitting *chemise à la reine*—a light dress of white muslin with a high waistline—sparked a trend among other aristocratic women, who wanted to look equally fabulous as they, too, slummed it on farms.

Liana and I tour the restored Hameau, starting at the pond. "Oh look," an American tourist on a private tour says loudly, "rats!"

"Those are the water rats," her guide says in a thick French accent, and pulls out a bottle. "Would you like your glass of wine now?"

We check out the other animals on display: black rams munching in a field, chubby carp opening their mouths greedily, and a gaggle of white geese promenading. "I just think it's very interesting she chose to have this," Liana said. "She could have created something really exotic. But she did this. She must have had a longing for something. As fake as it was, it represented something to her. Simplicity. She wanted a taste of the simple life. Of peace and balance."

Jefferson didn't record his own thoughts about the Hameau; perhaps the feeling of dislike was mutual and the queen never invited him. He had his own antidote to this fakery: exploring the actual countryside, where you'd find less Sèvres porcelain and more misery, starvation, and cow shit. A year into Jefferson's time abroad, he finally discovered the real France.

THE HAPPINESS OF THE PEOPLE

Obsessed with hunting, the king spent each fall at one of his other palaces, Fontainebleau, thirty miles southeast of the capital, with an immense forest stocked with game. The court, along with ambassadors like Jefferson, dutifully followed. One day in the fall of 1785, the Virginian slipped away to hike in the woods. Seeing a "poor woman" walking, he asked her directions and strolled alongside her, asking about her life along the way. She was a day laborer, he learned, when she could get work. Paying rent and finding bread for her two children was nearly impossible. As they parted, Jefferson left her with twenty-four *sous*, three days' wages; "she burst into tears of a gratitude which I could perceive was unfeigned, because she was unable to utter a word."

In France's highly stratified society, gentlemen like Jefferson didn't chat with day laborers as equals. But those were precisely the kind of moments he sought out while traveling. Back home after his walk, he wrote a long letter to James Madison about his conversation with the woman; it "led me into a train of reflections," he wrote, on why France, with all its riches and power, tolerated such rampant poverty. The country needed a fairer distribution of property and a better taxation system—laborers paid taxes into the royal coffers while nobles skirted such financial obligations. The king had in fact tried to reform the system of revenues, but the aristocracy blocked his efforts, fearful of losing their privileges.

Jefferson dreamed of changing France and helping it down the road to democracy. This goal would be difficult to meet so long as so many peasants lived in abject poverty. In Jefferson's view, educated, empowered Frenchmen should be able to voice their concerns to representatives of their choosing—just like American yeoman farmers should do back home. For most of Jefferson's time in France, though, this vision seemed chimerical; the king, nobles, and clergy held tight to political and economic power in the country.

A contemporary cartoon showing the king, Church, and aristocracy riding on the back of the French people. "The mass of mankind has not been born with saddles on their backs," Jefferson wrote much later, "nor a favored few booted and spurred, ready to ride them legitimately, by the grace of god."

Nonetheless, Jefferson believed the place to begin was by diagnosing the country's social problems. To do so, as he traveled through France he "courted the society of gardeners, *vignerons*, coopers, farmers, etc.," he wrote, "and have devoted every moment of every day, almost, to the business of inquiry" into the "condition of the laboring poor." He urged Lafayette to make a similar trip "absolutely incognito" to learn about his countrymen. "You will feel a sublime pleasure," Jefferson wrote, "when you shall be able to apply your knowledge to the softening of their beds, or the throwing a morsel of meat into the kettle of vegetables."

His concerns weren't limited to France; most of Europe had authoritarian leaders whose subjects lived hand-to-mouth and had little say in politics. On his return trip from Amsterdam in 1788, Jefferson found even more varied political terrain to examine than he had in France. Since Germany was not unified, the ambassador passed through a patchwork of principalities, kingdoms, and Free Imperial Cities—the latter nominally connected to the dying Holy Roman Empire. Each small state featured a different political system and degree of freedom. Playing wandering proto-sociologist and political scientist, he observed that subjects of the Prussian king looked as fearful as slaves. He knew when he had crossed over into a feudal region when he spotted deer among the beech trees; the "little tyrants" in charge had prevented the people from hunting, reserving this sport for the nobles. He noted the number of beggars and ragged fields in more repressive regimes, their streets as quiet "as the mansions of the dead." In Frankfurt, however, a capitalistic city with more freedoms, "all is life, bustle, and motion."

Jefferson thought his insights might aid reform plans not just in Europe but back home. In 1787, American leaders met in Philadelphia to draft a constitution and debated its ratification the next year. Drawing on his European experiences, Jefferson advised James Madison from afar that "a bill of rights is what the people are entitled to against every government on earth." The Constitution required amending to make the new system more republican and less "kingly," he told another ally. Should anyone disagree, "send them to Europe to see something of the trappings of monarchy, and I will undertake that every man shall go back thoroughly cured."

So it comes as no surprise that *Hints* pairs Object of Attention Eight, Royal Courts (in all their perfidy), with Object Seven: Politics. Not political parties, which didn't truly exist yet in continental Europe (or America) at the time. Instead, the guide charges the traveler with examining how governmental policies "influence...the happiness of the people: take every possible occasion of entering into the hovels of the laborers, and especially at the moments of their repast, see what they eat, how they are clothed, whether they are obliged to labor too hard;

whether the government or their landlord takes from them an unjust proportion of their labor; on what footing stands the property they call their own, their personal liberty, etc." This empirical evidence would provide clues as to how well political systems served the governed.

When Jefferson wrote *Hints* in 1788, he also thought that making such observations would broaden the minds of the well-to-do travelers following his guide who might need some enlightening. John Rutledge, Jr., the son of a wealthy, conservative South Carolinian plantation owner, seemed to think it beneath his station to rub elbows with the poor. At the beginning of his travels, he "lamented" the sporadic uprisings occurring in France that year, judging the monarchical government as being "accommodated to the genius of the French people"—sentiments which shocked Jefferson.

Little did the ambassador realize how swiftly France would change in just a year and how prescient he had been in tasking the Boys with obtaining firsthand impressions of the lives of regular people. The winter of 1788–89 was exceptionally cruel and starvation was rampant. The price of bread rose by about 50 percent in the capital. Many Parisian workers spent most of their wages just on *le pain*; those who couldn't afford it sometimes resorted to looting bakeries. In some regions, hungry peasants rioted, some attacking châteaux and episcopal palaces.

With his government nearly bankrupt, and the nobles still effectively blocking his attempts at tax reform, Louis XVI reluctantly called for the Estates-General to assemble that May to "help us overcome all the difficulties we are facing with respect to the state of our finances," he announced in a royal letter. The ad hoc body consisted of representatives segregated by rank: the First Estate, the clergy; the Second Estate, the nobility; and the Third Estate, everyone else. More of a consultative group than a legislature, it had met throughout the Middle Ages and Renaissance but had not been summoned for 175 years.

Commoners gathered in the spring of 1789 to pick their representatives for the Third Estate. In a climate of severe economic distress, the
people drew up petitions of grievances to send to the king at his request,
complaining that the system of taxation was unfair, the Church needed
reform, and unjust laws prevented people from supplementing their
meager diet by hunting in the vast noble domains. Jefferson couldn't be
in the changing countryside in person, but Short and Rutledge—in effect
now his research assistants—were.

They reported back to him on dramatic uprisings. In Marseille, Short
recounted how citizen groups wrested control of the port city away from
its military governor. A new volunteer police force was now in charge;
"they patrol, they wear cockades, they assemble in great crowds, and
preserve perfect order," he wrote. Even the more conservative Rutledge
let himself be swept up in the moment. The protesters were only seeking equality, he wrote to Jefferson. The "disorder" he witnessed "is of
that sort which promises greater order than ever in the end"—a forecast
which would not entirely come true.

For his part, Jefferson tracked political transformations in Paris and
Versailles. He attended the Estates-General and conferred with Lafayette
and other liberal-minded aristocrats who favored the establishment of a
constitutional monarchy. The summer of 1789 turned increasingly chaotic as people took to the streets in Paris. No one—least of all the French
monarchy—knew what the outcome would be. "Is this a revolt?" Louis
XVI famously asked an adviser. "No, Sire, it's a revolution" came the reply.

The stakes were high. Jefferson was no longer leisurely chatting with
farmers about their lives but trying to make sense of convulsive political and economic changes in a climate rife with rumors and violence.
Accompanied by Short (who was back in Paris after his voyage ended),
he roamed the "tumults" in the streets "in order to be sure of what was
passing," he wrote, "for nothing can be believed but what one sees, or has

from an eyewitness." The ambassador's wanderings, through Paris and in and out of the debates at Versailles, gave him fodder for his detailed diplomatic reports chronicling the events, a sort of first draft of history. Jefferson's reviews of the changes were glowing: the deputies operated with "firmness and wisdom," he wrote, while the people marched with "spirit" towards the fulfillment of the natural rights of man.

Yet did he get the full story? It was difficult to understand a wrenching social movement—filled with street battles, beheadings, misinterpretations of the other side's motives, and an ever-present fear of counterattack—in the middle of what later would be called the "fog of war." And at times Jefferson blurred the lines between being an impartial observer and an interested participant. At the end of 1789, he left France for good, with preconceived notions of the French Revolution that he mostly stuck with for the rest of his life.

By returning home, what did he miss?

CHAPTER NINETEEN

French Revolutions

The day after our trip to Versailles, Liana and I arrive at a venerable establishment in Paris's Left Bank, the café Le Procope. This is the kind of place Jefferson liked, a spot for thinkers and philosophers. Voltaire guzzled dozens of cups of coffee and chocolate here while Benjamin Franklin hit the harder stuff. By the late 1780s, it had become a den of revolutionaries; today, the restaurant is one of the few places in Paris that prominently acknowledge the French Revolution. Maybe over lunch I can pick up a little knowledge about that strange event in history, in which a freedom-loving nation was founded in the midst of a bloodbath.

The waiter shows us to our table and we order a fine Bordeaux. "What would people eat during the times of the Revolution?" I ask.

"I recommend our historic dishes such as the *tête de veau*," he replies. The head of the calf. I shudder. "This was what the poor ate at that time. It later became a delicacy and still is today." Liana perks up—she loves strange cuts of meat, which horrify me. But she doesn't bite, opting for the braised beef cheeks instead.

Silence hangs over the table. "*Et monsieur?*"

"Oh, fine, the *tête de veau*."

I put the dubious dish out of mind and contemplate our surroundings. A reproduction of the Declaration of the Rights of Man and of the

Citizen covers much of one of the room's walls. The document was one of the great accomplishments of 1789. After much wrangling, the Third Estate, the grouping of the people's delegates, declared itself the true representative body of France, calling itself the National Assembly. Its leaders, Lafayette among them, wanted a list of fundamental rights to precede the country's first constitution. There was only one person in France who had already crafted a revolutionary mission statement—the author of the Declaration of Independence. Lafayette asked him for his help, although on the sly, for Jefferson's day job was serving as an ambassador to the king, not advising the rebels.

Jefferson spent long summer days making suggestions on a draft. "Men are born and remain free and equal in rights," the final Declaration would read; governments must protect the rights of "liberty, property, security, and resistance against oppression." Sovereignty ultimately rests in "the Nation"—not with a divinely appointed dictator. These statements of rights sound vaguely familiar to an American, as if our own founding document was given a French twist. Jefferson was pleased with the French Declaration's recognition that "no one may be disturbed on account of his opinions, even religious ones"—he had long championed religious freedom, both in Virginia and France. Although after my exploration of Jefferson and slavery I'm now seeking to understand the man rather than admire him, it's still gratifying to come across an instance where he did take a stand for liberty.

The waiter brings us our first course: *escargots*, oozing oil that we soak up with our bread, and a gooey French onion soup. Yet the restaurant's decorations are as much a highlight for me as the food. There's a striking painting of revolutionary soldiers planting a liberty tree before a crowd of women wearing sashes in blue, white, and red, symbolizing the new republic. Even the wallpaper features an array of liberty caps—the red bonnet, representing freedom, was first worn here in Le Procope.

Throughout the summer of 1789, Parisians filled cafés like this one, talking hopefully of rights and fearfully about how their new gains might be wrested away from them. The king, unhappy with the National Assembly's assertion of legislative power, had stationed German and Swiss mercenaries around the capital. With rumors flying that the foreign soldiers were there to shutter the assembly by force, some Parisians preemptively fought back.

Jefferson himself witnessed one of the first insurrections as a crowd of people in what is today the Place de la Concorde attacked the German cavalry with stones. He heard the firing of muskets; French troops, gone over to the people's side, pushed the mercenaries out of the plaza; the foreign troops soon evacuated the city center as well. The king had lost Paris.

Yet surely the monarchy would not give up that easily. Revolutionaries seized arms and ammunition from Parisian military depots to prepare against an inevitable counterattack. Now all they needed was gunpowder. And everyone knew where it was stored: in the old medieval fortress and prison, the Bastille. Crowds surrounded it on July 14—today celebrated as France's national day.

Jefferson heard the tale of what happened when he visited the house of one of the insurrection's leaders after the firing stopped. An unruly crowd assembled before the fortress until "a discharge from the Bastille killed four persons," Jefferson wrote. The mob then forced its way into the prison. "They took all the arms, discharged the prisoners, and such of the garrison as were not killed in the first moment of fury." As for the governor of the prison and his aide, the rebels "cut off their heads and sent them through the city in triumph to the Palais Royal." The violence didn't faze Jefferson. "We are not to expect to be translated from despotism to liberty in a featherbed," he wrote later to Lafayette.

The takers of the prison became heroes, feted in celebrations across the city—perhaps in the very room where Liana and I are dining.

Lafayette assumed command of the new citizen militias, leading a grand procession through Paris. He stopped the march when he spied Patsy Jefferson standing in the crowd, wearing revolutionary ribbons, so he could take his hat off to her. Just two years earlier, the ambassador had urged him to learn about the condition of the French laboring poor to try to better it. Now the thirty-one-year-old marquis was leading what he hoped to be a largely peaceful transformation of his country.

The governor of the Bastille, enjoying the use of his head for a few more minutes.

Lafayette sent the principal key of the Bastille back to his mentor in revolution, George Washington. The person who carried it back to America was none other than John Rutledge. The young man who had started his travels believing the monarchy was "accommodated to the genius of the French people" ended them by bringing the symbol of royal downfall to Mount Vernon—where it's still on display today.

Jefferson himself departed France in October 1789, taking with him a vision of a near-flawless revolution. When he left, reasonable, Enlightened aristocrats—the Jeffersons of France—were in charge and democracy was on the wing. The National Assembly served as a check on the absolute authority of the king, abolished feudal privileges, and outlawed the mandatory tithes the Church imposed on the population. The Declaration ensured that certain rights could never be infringed by the powerful. "I will agree to be stoned as a false prophet if all does not end well in this country," Jefferson wrote that summer. "Nor will it end with this country. Here is but the first chapter of the history of European liberty."

But he put the book down too early, missing a plot twist of gargantuan proportions. Some clues as to what happened next can be found in Le Procope today.

The waiter returns bearing *la pièce de résistance,* the long-awaited calf's head in sauce. I look down at it and force a smile. It doesn't smile back.

"I'll be back in a minute," I tell Liana abruptly, leaving her alone with the bovine. I'd rather use the W.C. as an excuse to delay the inevitable.

I'm pleased to see that the signs on the restroom read *citoyen* and *citoyenne,* the masculine and feminine versions of the word "citizen." One of the Revolution's triumphs was its transformation of French people from royal subjects to participating members of civic society. But emerging from the *citoyen* room I quickly find signs of the Revolution's darker side. One room features a portrait of a man named Jean-Paul Marat, his shirt rumpled, his gaze intense. Like Jefferson, he was a forty-six-year-old natural historian, politician, writer, and idealist in 1789—yet the comparisons end there. Over the years, Lafayette's Patriotic Society of 1789, a political club of moderates he formed with his allies, would come in for vicious attacks by the more radical Marat.

I enter the room, which once doubled as Marat's office. Today it features jumbles of old books and wooden printing press letters in recognition of how he would spend all day here working on his newspaper, *L'Ami du Peuple.* Le Procope still hangs a bell outside a window—when

Marat finished his copy, he'd ring it and a boy would come to bring it to the printing press down the street. But the paper's content could be disturbing. Even in 1789, the early stages of the Revolution, Marat harangued against the republic's "enemies" and threatened to expose traitors in his midst.

By 1793, a radical faction—egged on by Marat and led by Maximilien Robespierre, whose portrait also hangs in this restaurant—gained power in the assembly. Their favorite new toy was a machine designed by Dr. Joseph-Ignace Guillotin, built by a carpenter on the very block where we're dining: the guillotine. That year Robespierre began the Reign of Terror, ruthlessly executing some seventeen thousand political opponents after only the most summary of trials. Both the king and queen lost their heads.

France by that time was at war with a coalition of nations—including Austria, Prussia, Britain, Spain, and the Netherlands—that sought to restore the monarchy to power. After the government dissolved religious orders and conscripted men into the army, peasants in western France rose in rebellion against the revolutionaries as well, starting an unsuccessful civil war at great cost to both sides. The Reign of Terror finally came to a close in 1794 when Robespierre found himself on the wrong side of the guillotine. (Marat had earlier been assassinated in his house, only two blocks from Le Procope.) A more moderate government took over. The revolutionary's early idealism was extinguished. Five years later, Napoleon seized power in a coup and ended many of the reforms.

I return to the table to find Liana making good work of her beef cheeks. "Try these, honey. We ate them in Cuba whenever we could. It was so rare to have beefsteak." I sample them—they're surprisingly tender.

"We had to buy it on the black market, everything was so rationed," she continues. "Sometimes we we'd even get a knock in the middle of the night that someone had beef to sell. Then Mamí would fry it up quickly—we didn't want the authorities to come by the next day and find out."

"They're not bad," I reply. "Want to trade?"

"Derek. Enough talk. Eat your cow head," Liana says.

I stare at the animal below me, which looks as if it had its own run-in with the guillotine, and gingerly take a bite. What I've done for *Hints*, I think. Yet the meat is soft, the flavor rich. Of course, French traditional food would taste excellent; I never should have worried.

"Do these stories of the French Revolution make you think of Cuba?" I ask Liana.

"A little. We had some true believers, too. There was so much idealism at the beginning of our revolution, but most of it died off over time. The people who took control wound up creating their own inequalities. And they didn't believe in civil liberties. The rest of us just tried to survive."

Jefferson saw what he wanted to while he was in France; he captured the enthusiasm of the people when they first revolted but didn't dwell on the violence that occurred while he was there—which would grow exponentially after he left. He reminds me a little of Herbert Matthews, a *New York Times* correspondent who visited Fidel Castro and his rebels in the mountains of Cuba in 1956 when they were still a ragtag group of underdogs and had not openly declared their communist sympathies. Matthews enthusiastically praised their cause and never fully retreated from this view, even after they took power and began committing abuses.

Such are the hazards of this Object of Attention that Jefferson set out for us. Understanding the social problems and needs of a people not your own is a challenge. But truly evaluating a popular uprising while you're in the midst of it yourself—and when you're getting close to the subjects you're studying—can be nearly impossible. How can you step back and take a critical view when you're marching in the parade?

We end our meal with *îles flottantes*, meringue floating in a heavenly sea of caramel. I had always wanted to try it—it was James Hemings's signature dish, his "snow eggs." For all the good and bad the French

Revolution brought, it certainly shook up the social order. In the chaos and shifting power relations of 1789, the Hemings siblings had the courage to seize the opportunity of a lifetime.

SHACKLES HALF-OPENED

My dear friend
I Beg for liberty's sake You will Breack Every Engagement to Give us a dinner to Morrow Wenesday. We shall Be some Members of the National Assembly—eight of us whom I want to Coalize as Being the only Means to prevent a total dissolution and a civil war.

So wrote Lafayette, the fighter for freedom from tyranny (and from spelling) to Jefferson on August 25, 1789. The ambassador duly complied. After the feast, with "the cloth being removed and wine set on the table, after the American manner," the deputies talked deep into the night on how to reduce "the Aristocracy to insignificance and impotence," as Jefferson put it, in a debate "worthy of being placed in parallel with the finest dialogues of antiquity." Yet as the revolutionaries argued over how to achieve equality, who among them took notice of the only man in the house whose rights truly had been stolen from him?

At twenty-six, James Hemings had already broken barriers as the first African American to train as a French chef. Although enslaved, he and his sister, Sally, were paid wages by Jefferson while they worked in Paris, and James used some of his earnings to pay for private French lessons. He likely would have understood everything said at the table that night. What opportunities might he find for himself in this new France these leaders were constructing?

Hearing the revolutionaries' plans firsthand wasn't the only way

James Hemings learned about the whirlwind of changes taking place. "The frivolities of conversation have given way entirely to politics," Jefferson wrote, "men, women and children talk nothing else: and all you know talk a great deal." James probably went to the Palais Royal, a hotbed of agitation in the city, on errands or on his days off. Sally trained as a seamstress and boarded with a French family that ran a laundering business for six weeks in 1788, likely to avoid the typhus epidemic that had reached the doors of Jefferson's house. Both siblings, then, knew how to fend for themselves on the streets of Paris.

As Annette Gordon-Reed has observed, the pair interacted with the thriving community of Blacks in the capital, around a thousand strong. Free Blacks mostly worked as servants, concentrated in the neighborhood that Jefferson and James Hemings first lived in. Through them, both Hemingses undoubtedly learned about the possibility of a lawyer filing a freedom suit on their behalf. James knew at least casually the strongest advocates for abolition in France: they dined on his food.

How would they fare if they stayed? James Hemings had apprenticed under one of the most prominent chefs in France. And Paris in the 1780s was a welcoming climate for a cook. Before then, people looking for a meal outside the home had gone to taverns with communal tables or small places offering a bowl of simple soup. But the Palais Royal now featured elegant establishments with waiters and a menu. Hemings could have found work in one of these innovative new business models, *le restaurant*, or at the café Le Procope. As for his sister, she had trained as a servant and a seamstress. Given the sexism of the time, getting married would help allow her to remain in Paris, and as Gordon-Reed points out, there's no reason the "young and attractive" woman couldn't have found a husband.

What choice would they make? Defy their master and seek freedom? Or return home to a lifetime in bondage, where at least they would have their family?

Or was there a third way?

Liana and I take the metro to the Place du Général-Catroux, a mile north of where Jefferson lived on the Champs-Élysées. Here in this park is the only outdoor recognition of slavery on a large scale in Paris today, a sculpture called *Fers*, or *Irons*. Two gigantic bronze shackles rise from the ground, one closed, one half-open.

The artwork, installed a decade before our visit, commemorates the life of Thomas-Alexandre Dumas, the son of a French marquis and an enslaved woman. Born in what would later become Haiti, he came to France as a young man. Officer commissions in the army were reserved for noblemen, and given his race, one was denied to him. Refusing to give up on his dream, Dumas instead enlisted in 1786 as a regular cavalryman. The Revolution gave Black men opportunities—unlike women of any race, they were considered citizens. He rose spectacularly through the ranks to become one of Napoleon's greatest generals; his son would become one of France's most beloved novelists. One of the sculpture's shackles represents the unfree status of his mother; the other one, Dumas's trajectory—only half-open, representing his lifelong battles against racism.

Here was another potential option for James Hemings if he remained—joining the French army. A career as a soldier could be rewarding, although of course dangerous. But instead Hemings took a different tack, still reminiscent of Dumas's personal journey in a way: he and his sister would return home to fight for a better life for themselves and their family within the limits of the society they knew best. France was alluring, but despite the talk of freedom, there was a reason people were rioting and breaking down the doors of bakeries. The Revolution could take any number of perhaps bloody turns.

Yet they were going home on their own terms. James wrung a deal out of Jefferson (likely while they were both still in Paris) to free him after Hemings trained another enslaved person to cook French delicacies in his place. And, as we saw at Monticello, Sally reached what her son later called a "treaty" with Jefferson, by which he agreed to free his children by her when they reached the age of twenty-one. This act of standing up to their master might have been one of the quietest revolutions occurring in France of 1789, yet for Sally Hemings's descendants, the most important: she pried open their shackles.

SWEEP THEM ALL AWAY

"They're blocking Givors!" Mathieu enters the room almost breathless. "And chanting against Macron. It took me forever to get through. Givors! Who would have thought it?"

A few months after Liana and I went to Paris, I returned solo. I've come to a small village south of Lyon, France's second or third city (depending on how much you like Marseille), in central France, to visit our friends Mathieu and Rachel, the couple we met at the Airbnb near Naples. I've shown up to milk their hospitality and learn about the social movement sweeping France, that of the *gilets jaunes*, or yellow vests.

In the fall of 2018, in response to President Emmanuel Macron's new proposed gas tax, protesters took to the streets, blocking traffic and wearing the fluorescent vests that, under French law, all drivers must keep in their trunks, the better to be seen in case of an accident. As the months went on, demonstrators demanded that authorities address the high cost of living and lack of citizen participation in government as well. Mathieu is astonished that the yellow vest demonstrators have now even temporarily taken over Givors, down the road from his home deep in the countryside.

I've spent the last couple of days in their old farmhouse, sleeping on their guest bed and eating their bread (both were soft), just as Jefferson would have wanted me to. I want to experience Object Seven: Politics for myself in contemporary France and catch a glimpse of how regular people live. Instead of asking a peasant for a glass of water, though, I'll be asking an accountant for a glass of rosé. Our friends aren't the "laboring poor" with whom *Hints* is concerned; they're solidly middle class. So are 60 percent of French people, thanks to the gains made in the two centuries after the French Revolution. The social compact that lasted for much of the late twentieth century has now clearly frayed, though. The gas tax is just one challenge, as French workers face automation, skyrocketing costs of housing, and an ever more distant centralized government.

The *gilets jaunes* movement provides me an opportunity to see social change firsthand, too. Of course, these protests are far different from those that ushered in the French Revolution two centuries ago. But at a very basic level, they do share something in common: both began with people often overlooked by the dominant powers getting fed up and taking over the streets, disrupting the status quo and making their complaints known.

I've already gotten a peek at real French life. Yesterday, Mathieu, working from home for his job selling printers, kept muting an endless call to complain about how long his colleagues were blathering on. "On a Friday afternoon! Don't they have anything better to do!" Rachel, having finished up her day as a self-employed CPA, brought me to a small organic food store where we picked up luscious local peaches and grapes. That night, we went to a party at the local gymnastics club, celebrating the end of the season; both of their high-school-age kids are athletes. Count yourself lucky if you're invited to a French potluck—we dined on grilled merguez sausages, *pâté*, fresh salad, and lots of dry rosé. The other parents perked up when they realized I was from the States— they all had been there before and wanted to talk about it.

"We had a problem with our hotel in New York," Mathieu told me and an assembled crowd. "And the receptionist upgraded us for free.

That's the Americans for you—they solve problems. A French hotel worker wouldn't have cared less. And the English? They're assholes. No, we like the Americans." He paused and jabbed his finger in the air. "On a good day."

Many of my friends' doings—shepherding kids around, jumping on conference calls—seem familiar. But there are differences, too: The food was so good, the village so ancient. Rachel and Mathieu still hang out with their high school companions who never left the area. Americans can be so mobile; the French seem to cling tightly to their old friends, moving through life in a group. We stayed at the party until late, the *joie de vivre* increasing as the rosé flowed. By the end, Rachel was dancing on a table.

On Saturday, we head into Lyon where a large march will occur that day. Like any self-respecting Frenchman, Mathieu doesn't want to protest on an empty stomach, so we head to a small place in the heart of the old city. When Jefferson visited in 1787, Lyon was the epicenter of France's industrial production, with tens of thousands of workers laboring in silk and textile factories. Understand the workings of these factories was useless to Jefferson, though. Manufacturing was an Object of Attention in *Hints*—actually two Objects—but only of mild interest. "Lighter mechanical arts and manufacturing," Jefferson wrote, were worth a "superficial view." Since America had not yet industrialized, "it would be a waste of attention to examine these minutely." Items that were "inconvenient to be transported...ready-made" and had to be fabricated at home, like bridges, justified more study (and their own Object of Attention).

Jefferson famously prioritized agriculture over industry, but he was no Luddite. A tech geek at heart, he was fascinated by the innovations in Europe yet realized the U.S. couldn't compete with the mass-produced goods he saw in English factories. White Americans instead had a comparative advantage in agriculture, at least for the time being, given the land available and the laborers they had enslaved in the South.

Delaying industrialization also meant avoiding the dangerous over-crowding he saw in European cities—which he thought invariably led to political corruption. Jefferson mistrusted urban workers. Since they were dependent on others for pay and housing, they couldn't think for them-selves, he theorized; they added "just so much to the support of pure government as sores do to the strength of the human body." He strongly disapproved of workers' attacks on factories in Paris in 1789 following rumors that a prominent employer planned to reduce wages. His preferred agitators were farmers with pitchforks, not proles with sledgehammers.

This dismissal of the urban laboring poor was a blind spot that prevented him from fully understanding the French Revolution. He didn't comprehend the suffering of the *sans-culottes* (those "without silk breeches" worn by the wealthy) in cities, nor their thirst for revenge, sus-ceptibility to rumors, or desire to defend their Revolution at all costs—no matter how much blood flowed.

We settle into our seats at a *bouchon*, a small inn once frequented by silk workers. The old factories have all closed, although a nearby store still sells chic scarves. We're joined by Fabien, a friend of the couple who works as an engineer for Michelin. Over a lunch of blood sausage and a cheese spread called *cervelle de canut* ("silk worker's brains"—don't ask), we talk about the *gilets jaunes*.

"The interesting thing about this movement is that it involves 'normal' people, middle-class people," Fabien offers. "It's not just from the Left or the Right. It's the silent majority speaking up.

"In our culture we have the idea of *ras-le-bol*; that means 'sweep them all away!'" he says, gesturing with his arm and nearly taking out the bottle of wine. "That's what they want here, to get rid of all the people in power and start over.

"But they have many demands," he reflects. "I'm not really sure what they're doing."

"That's why they have so many demands, so politicians can't take them over!" says Rachel. The three of them, like many French people, are sympathetic with some of the movement's aims yet haven't considered joining it themselves. Rachel expresses concern about the violent turn that some of the demonstrations have taken. That doesn't seem to faze Mathieu, who has the heart of a rebel.

"We the French like to shit on everyone! We even cut off our king's head! That's what the French Revolution means: we're capable of killing them. When there's one strike in Germany, here we have a hundred. Here we cut off heads!"

The executions of Louis XVI and Marie-Antoinette shocked much of the Western world at the time—and can still embarrass the French today (although not Mathieu). Their deaths dismayed Jefferson, as did the many others that occurred, but he remained a fervent supporter of the Revolution, even as Short, who had stayed behind in Paris, warned him of how the leaders had become "fanatic." "[R]ather than [the French Revolution] should have failed, I would have seen half the earth desolated," he responded to Short in 1793. "Were there but an Adam and an Eve left in every country, and left free, it would be better than as it now is."

How could Jefferson support the regime that executed some of his own friends? I think back to the subject I explored before this trip: slavery. Jefferson's fervor for freedom in France grew even as he retrenched on the cause of liberty for African Americans. As I had learned, the late 1780s and early 1790s were a time in which his debts worsened, hampering him from freeing the people he had enslaved. It was also when he retreated from publicly advocating for emancipation. I wonder whether playing the role of one of the French Revolution's greatest American champions assuaged Jefferson's conscience. Even if some people questioned the morality of his role as a slave owner—Jefferson himself certainly did—no one could doubt the intensity he brought to the fight to save the French Revolution. He remained the Apostle of Liberty, at least in his own mind.

What does seem clear is that, with respect to France, he abandoned his own advice. Although he normally prized firsthand, objective observations of social change, he ignored Short's reports on the atrocities committed in Paris. In one part of his brain, he recalled the friendship he had for some of the moderate leaders; in another, he rationalized their executions as a necessary byproduct of the march from despotism to liberty. Whether he did so for complicated psychological reasons or not, Jefferson's unquestioned support for the revolutionaries, even during the Reign of Terror, doesn't wear well today. Yet it turned out to be one of the primary issues that propelled his national political career back home.

In the 1790s, the American public split fiercely on what stance to take toward France when it declared war on the United Kingdom and other European countries. Support their revolutionary efforts and honor U.S. treaty obligations? Remain neutral? Trade again with the enemy, Britain? Jefferson, of course, was one of the strongest defenders of the new order in France, but Alexander Hamilton and other Federalists, who favored closer ties to England, carried the day in the Cabinet. In response to this and other differences, Jefferson and Madison covertly organized the first political party in America, the Democratic-Republicans.

Jefferson kept in mind the efforts taken by Lafayette's Patriotic Society of 1789 and its heirs. He observed how Lafayette's "extensive and zealous party" brought in "all the honest [people] of the kingdom sufficiently at [their] leisure to think," a broad coalition of "men of letters" and the bourgeoisie. Common people never joined Lafayette's Society, though. Jefferson and Madison would go even further, assembling their own party with a wide base, including farmers, urban artisans, and reformers from all backgrounds. Jefferson was confident that, once mobilized, his supporters would put a definitive end to the projects of the "little party" of Federalists, who were "hostile to France."

Democratic-Republican societies sprang up in American cities, celebrating Bastille Day and advocating for workers' rights. As Washington retired in 1796, the Democratic-Republicans entered the electoral fray against the Federalists, with relations toward revolutionary France one of the most hotly debated issues. Jefferson was elected vice president that year.

After lunch, we unexpectedly come across a couple of dozen people chanting in yellow vests in the heart of the old city, a splinter group from the main protest a mile away. Police in riot gear with large shields encircle them, ordering their dispersal and then moving in. In the commotion, a young protester falls to the ground and cries out, clutching her head.

Police in the foreground, an injured protester behind them.

Rachel begs off from continuing on, worried about safety, and Mathieu is late for his garage rock band's weekend practice. But Fabien gamely volunteers to walk with me to the main protest. We find the agitators, broken into smaller groups by the police. On a quiet side street, three people in yellow vests sit down at an outdoor café, and after Fabien introduces us, they invite us to join them. The most talkative is named Serge, an architectural designer in his mid-fifties, with graying hair and an earnest expression. He's been demonstrating since the beginning and continues now, even, after some seven months, fewer *gilets jaunes* are taking to the streets.

"It's not a system," he tells us. "People just show up. It started with the gas tax, but it's moved beyond that. We have a number of demands now. At first the extreme Right had a large presence in our movement, but less so now," he says. Critics have pointed out the anti-Semitism of some of the protesters, however. "We've even made connections with the environmental movement. The end of the month is a problem for workers, but the end of the world is a problem for all of us."

Earlier in 2019, President Macron asked towns to prepare lists of their grievances and send them to him—somewhat oddly, since the previous time a French head of state tried that tactic, in 1789, it didn't end so well for him. Citizens, especially those from rural areas, spoke up about the high salaries of elected elites, the low minimum wage, the problems caused by the recent reduction in the national speed limit, and the disappearance of public services from the countryside. The idea of increased citizen participation in government in some form is popular; Serge and many other *gilets jaunes* support a proposal by which important decisions would be put to the people by referendum.

I ask him about the dangers of protesting. "Sometimes, violent people have mixed in with us," he tells us. "At the beginning, they broke a lot of shop windows. But the police response has gone way too far. They've used gas against us, hit us in the back with their shields for no reason, clubbed people on the head. Once we were leaving and they threw tear-gas grenades at us, one grenade hit me. It's scandalous.

"But still we keep going. There are sometime eruptions, but they're healthy; it's relieving stress. In a given moment in society, it's necessary that people move, that they breathe."

Serge seems so knowledgeable that I ask him if he's one of the local organizers. "No, we have no leaders. We're like 'good children'; most of us are well behaved. Unions tried to become involved, but no one controls our movement. That's both its weakness and force.

"We don't believe politicians," he concludes, pulling down one of his eyelids, a French gesture indicating disbelief. "They say one thing, do another. If one was in front of me, he wouldn't say what he really believed." More eyelid pulls.

President Macron's election in 2017 was a repudiation of traditional politics; he had formed his own party only a year earlier as an alternative to the status quo. But the *gilets jaunes* now see him as a sellout, arrogant and distant from the people. Theirs is a decentralized movement, beyond the control of formal organizations. While parties from both the far Left and far Right have supported the demonstrators, mainstream politicians have mostly watched these organic protests warily.

It makes me think back to the early uprisings that Jefferson, Short, and Rutledge witnessed, before the French had even established formal political parties. That was also when the Industrial Revolution was just beginning; it has since come and gone, leaving dislocated, frustrated workers not knowing what to do next. I wonder if traditional party politics are on a similar way out, or at least subject to their own wrenching changes in the future.

As Fabien and I return to the city center we hear a roar. A rowdy group of yellow vests emerge from a side street, chanting, banging pans, and walking briskly down a route they don't seem to have a permit for. A phalanx of grim-faced police officers approaches; a confrontation might be imminent. Where should my sympathies lie? Serge had made his cause sound compelling, a democratic revolution by the common man. Yet some in the nationwide demonstrations have taken advantage of the chaos to engage in baser instincts—looting stores, vandalizing monuments. What will the *gilets jaunes* do to achieve their goals? Where will all this end?

I don't know. Nor does anyone, really; the protests might move in any number of directions. As a traveler, I've found my role, to observe and learn. I've done my best to do so here, trying to understand a leaderless movement that expresses itself through righteous anger. Jefferson once advised that it is better not to believe anything than to jump to an unfounded conclusion, yet he himself stuck to a rosy view of the French Revolution in the face of all evidence to the contrary. I won't make his mistake.

Still, I'm glad I've made this trip to Lyon and seen the demonstrations with my own eyes. Whether they sweep away the old order or wind up as a minor footnote to history—perhaps even an ugly one—the *gilets jaunes* refuse to remain ignored. They insist that their fellow citizens and leaders bear witness to their pain and hear their struggles. A people must always have a "spirit of resistance," Jefferson wrote, and the yellow vests have taken up this mantle today, blocking streets, shouting demands, dreaming of a French revolution.

CHAPTER TWENTY

À la Recherche du Moose Perdu

Even after scouring the building, I still haven't found my moose.

I'm in the creepiest place I've visited yet on my tour of *Hints*, the Fragonard Museum, a veterinary school that has operated in the Parisian suburbs since 1766. Today, a Saturday, the grounds are deserted. I walk past souvenirs from two centuries of dissection: a jar of cow ovaries, the towering skeleton of a giraffe, and, finally, a preserved calf with two heads (what the café Le Procope might have called a family meal).

A gallery at the back is particularly spooky. It displays the work of Honoré Fragonard, a man born two centuries ahead of his time—his true calling would have been directing horror movies. Here's his display of a horse skeleton, preserved by a technique akin to mummification, with a similarly embalmed human rider perched on top. And a display of monkeys made to seem as if they are dancing. Finally, *la pièce de résistance*: the Four Horsemen of the Apocalypse, with a flayed human mounting a horse, accompanied by human fetuses riding sheep and horse fetuses.

After leaving this gallery, I notice a stuffed llama, observed in life by Georges-Louis Leclerc, the famed Count de Buffon, the director of the King's Garden in Paris in the late eighteenth century. Buffon, arguably the greatest naturalist of his day, described this animal (or its offspring) in the pages of his groundbreaking work, *Natural History*. Jefferson had no quarrel with the llama, but he was infuriated by a conclusion Buffon drew in his writings: that American mammals were inferior in size and capabilities when compared to their Old World equivalents. After this particular animal died in 1772, Buffon sent it to the veterinary school to be stuffed in a tasteful manner. Thankfully, Fragonard had just been dismissed from the school (on the grounds that he was a madman), so the llama doesn't have a fetus jockey on its back.

Comme c'est bizarre! But who am I to judge; my own quest is odd enough. I've been prowling through these displays because I'm looking for a moose skeleton, and a very specific one at that—the one Jefferson brought to Paris in 1787 in his quest to convince the count of the error of his ways. A moose that has since gone AWOL.

Clearly, I need professional help.

I walk back to the young man at the entrance desk. "*Pardonnez-moi, monsieur,*" I begin, then switch to English for this delicate ask. "You wouldn't have, say, a moose here by chance?"

"Ah yes, we have one of those things. It is behind you," he says cheerfully, in a *très fort* French accent. He points to a furry head with protruding flat horns mounted above me, high on the wall. I had walked right past him. I'm possibly the world's worst moose-hunter.

My spirits rise, but there's no indication of the animal's provenance. I return to the desk and tried to sound nonchalant. "How old do you think it is?"

"Ah, it must be the nineteenth century."

My face falls. If it's not Jefferson's moose, it's dead to me.

"You wouldn't have any other moose, would you? One that's older? Maybe in the back?"

He clicks through the computerized records. "*Non,* I am very sorry;

this is our only, how you say, moose. Perhaps you try the Natural History Museum?"

Unfortunately, I already had. And the Museum of Hunting and Nature. Even Deyrolle, the taxidermy store that dates from the nineteenth century. To be sure, I found specimens on display: an Alaskan moose in one, a Canadian in another, gazing down benevolently from their perches at generations of visiting Parisian schoolchildren. But none were that selfless creature who gave his life for Jefferson and science, only to become a furry pawn in a geopolitical battle.

Buffon and other French natural historians claimed that North America was a degenerate continent with a miserable climate: cold, damp, and filled with noxious vapors, stunting the growth of plants and animals. Mammals in the Americas, Buffon asserted, were all smaller than their European or African equivalents. The New World was fit only for frogs and snakes.

Some of Buffon's acolytes argued that people, too, grew puny and feeble in North America's climate. Native Americans, they asserted, were primitives; the men were lazy, their sexual desire was weak and their genitalia small. It was no wonder, the haughty Frenchmen concluded, that even European colonists who came to this cold continent hadn't amounted to much.

Jefferson was furious. Was Buffon as crazy as Fragonard with his flayed fetuses? The damning claims not only insulted Native Americans, they reduced American standing in the world and discouraged immigration and investment. Jefferson was convinced that Buffon had gotten the science flat wrong. He devoted the largest section of *Notes on Virginia* to extolling Native American culture, praising the achievements of colonists, and tabulating the impressive size of New World mammals. Of course, America's climate was not inferior to that of Europe: "as if both sides [of the Atlantic] were not warmed by the same genial sun."

But reasoning got him nowhere. In Paris, Jefferson wrangled a dinner invitation to meet the count, presenting him with a copy of *Notes* and a panther skin he had bought in Philadelphia, proving the size of American great cats. Jefferson expounded on his theory of the equivalence of the two continents' climate, using the moose as his poster animal. The European reindeer was not equivalent to the moose, Jefferson argued; the former was so small it could walk upright beneath the belly of our American quadruped. Buffon, as the Virginian recounted later, just smiled infuriatingly and handed him one of the thirty-six volumes he had authored. "When Mr. Jefferson shall have read this," he said, "he will be perfectly satisfied that I am right."

*A 1796 drawing of a moose, looking cheerful but
not much bigger than a reindeer.*

The ambassador realized he needed to move from talk to action. From his mansion on the Champs-Élysées, he commissioned backwoods hunters to find him the biggest four-legged animal in New Hampshire, stuff it, and send it to him. A large moose is worth a thousand words.

The odyssey took months. Even once they had killed it, hunters had to cut a path through the forest to drag its hulking body through the snow. Then the unfortunate beast was left behind on the dock at Portsmouth, decomposing while waiting for another transport across the Atlantic. After it finally arrived in the fall of 1787, Jefferson was disappointed to find that "a great deal of [the skin] has come off, and the rest is ready to drop off." Nonetheless, he presented it to the stunned Buffon. His moose was about seven feet high, Jefferson noted, although he had good information that they often reached ten feet. In any case, the European elk could not compare—it was only two-thirds of the height of this animal. Recognizing his error, the Frenchman promised to correct his study, although before he could do so, he inconveniently died. Some forty years later, though, the proud Jefferson was still boasting about how he had turned around the views of the great naturalist.

But what of the true hero in this story, the intrepid moose? It has never been heard from since. Jefferson wrote to a famed Parisian naturalist in 1803, inquiring after it, hoping beyond hope that Buffon's successors still kept his old hairy friend on display. During the French Revolution, the count's collection turned into one of the first natural history museums in the world—but the directors later deaccessioned thousands of specimens due to lack of space. Although Jefferson's correspondent responded to the rest of his letter, he passed over the fate of the misplaced moose in silence. No doubt the bones were lost, boxed up in the basement of an obscure museum or forgotten in the attic of an eccentric collector.

With time to kill, and Liana incomprehensibly abandoning me to shop in Paris, I had convinced myself I just might find a trace of the martyred animal. And so I poked around every museum I could find that had collections dating back to the eighteenth century. *Rien.*

Yet when the disappointment of my failed hunt wears off, I realize something about Jefferson's campaign to change Buffon's mind. It was never just about the moose. As a history geek, obsessed with tangible objects, I thought searching for the bones might be an amusing way to connect with Jefferson's experiences, just as I had tasted wine from his favorite vineyards and strolled through the same gardens and buildings he admired. But maybe it's time to consider his natural history investigations less as an amateur historian and more as a scientist—even if science is the one subject I always dreaded in school.

The skeleton was certainly an impressive prop in his argument, but more important were the years Jefferson spent collecting empirical data on natural history, a labor of love. "Nature intended me for the tranquil pursuits of science," he wrote, "by rendering them my supreme delight." His methods were revolutionary: he commissioned people to obtain information for him, leading Americans to incorporate science into their daily lives. Among the many scientific topics that interested him, climatology was at the top of the list—important not just in battling Buffon but for understanding how the planet worked. Analyzing the evidence, Jefferson concluded that temperatures were on the rise.

So I take to the road, seeking to understand what a Jeffersonian approach to natural history might look like today. My hypothesis: as we face the unprecedented crisis of global warming caused by human activities, Jefferson still has something to teach us today.

On my first stop, however, I discover that even on this revised mission, the story of Buffon and the quadruped has a little more to give. And if it can inspire this history lover to learn about science for a change, then the moose did not die in vain.

THE MOUSE TO THE MAMMOTH

After several months on the road, John Rutledge and Thomas Shippen reached Geneva, Switzerland, in 1788 with work to do. *Hints* tasked them with observing natural history and climate. In Germany, they were to note the presence of native walnut trees, goats, and wild boar. As they crossed the Alps into Italy, they were to record the limits of the zone in which olive trees grew. Requiring relatively little care, olives might replace other crops more dependent on slave labor in the American South. Jefferson asked the South Carolinian to determine the tree's northern range, its hardiness, and whether "it exists by the help of shelter from mountains." If the young man failed to do so, he would "hereafter much repent it."

None of these asks were particularly challenging; Jefferson did not make natural history a full-fledged Object of Attention but rather only a secondary line of inquiry in *Hints*. Just as well—neither of the Boys had shown much inclination toward science. Living up to Jefferson's example would not be easy. He traveled through France with a portable thermometer taking daily temperature readings and making other meteorological observations. He discovered how climate affected people, recording how peasants whose farms were shielded from harsh northern winds by mountain spurs were more prosperous than those on the exposed plains. He took notes on technology, on everything from how steam engines powered gristmills to how canal gates operated (and how he might improve their design).

The most important scientific riddle in *Hints* came at the end of the journey and had stumped Jefferson himself. Near the city of Tours in western France, the travelers were to investigate the curious case of shells found in some hills. They looked remarkably like seashells but had been discovered some 170 miles from the ocean. Had a flood covered the earth and deposited them there? Or had "the bed of the ocean, the principal residence of the shelled tribe...by some great convulsion of nature, been heaved to the heights at which we now find shells?" Traveling to Tours in 1787, Jefferson heard a local natural historian offer a third theory: the objects were rocks, "spontaneously produced" out of the earth with a kind of special fluid inside them.

After making calculations, Jefferson discounted the claim that a deluge once covered these hills. As for the second supposition—could ocean beds really have transformed into mountains, particularly if the earth was only six thousand years old, as religious scholars maintained? Wouldn't that imply that God's original design wasn't perfect? Yet wouldn't it also be too coincidental for rocks to perfectly resemble seashells? "There is a wonder [here] somewhere," he wrote; better to withhold judgment altogether than reach a conclusion unsupported by evidence. "Ignorance is preferable to error," he went on, "and he is less remote from the truth who believes nothing, than he who believes what is wrong."

For the Boys to solve the mystery of the shells in the mountains, they'd have to up their game considerably. Perhaps sensing that beginning their trip with a weeks-long spa binge had not been the way to win Jefferson's approval, the Boys dabbled in natural history as they headed south through Germany. Shippen met with a local naturalist, who handed him a treatise on inoculating cattle from smallpox and another on manure—neither of which the young American could read, since they were in German. A start, but no one was ready to compare the Boys to Isaac Newton quite yet.

Geneva, though, presented opportunities. Although modest in size, the city was the capital of a republic (of the same name) and a haven for humanistic scholars, including the greatest natural historian this side of Buffon, the forty-eight-year-old Swiss thinker and action hero, Horace Bénédict de Saussure. Like Jefferson, Saussure was a Renaissance Man, contributing to the new field of geology, building the first solar oven, and categorizing the animals of Switzerland. Jefferson considered him to be "one of the best philosophers of the present age." He might have added one of the most daring as well. A pioneering climber and only the third man ever to summit Mont Blanc, Saussure called mountain peaks "nature's laboratory," the ideal setting for conducting experiments on atmospheric pressure, humidity, and the transparency of the sky. Just two months before the Boys' arrival, he spent a harrowing night on top of Mont Blanc during a lightning storm, dashing out of his tent to check readings on his electrometer during its climax.

A print from Saussure's Voyage dans les Alpes, *which Jefferson bought in 1788 as the Boys made their way toward Geneva.*

Among other inventions, the Swiss thinker developed a hygrometer, an instrument that measures humidity in the atmosphere. Knowing that human hair shortens in length in dry air, he took one of his wife's blond strands and stretched it tight, monitoring whether it contracted or lengthened as weather conditions varied. Jefferson bought one of Saussure's models, along with another based on a design by Benjamin Franklin, and asked a London manufacturer to produce a modified hygrometer incorporating his own suggestions. He planned to distribute these instruments to observers in Europe and North America in order to build a true climatic database. "I verily believe," Jefferson wrote to an English contact as the Boys were approaching Geneva, that this experiment would prove "that the atmosphere of our part of America is less humid than that of this part of Europe: and that this furnishes an instance more wherein philosophers [i.e., Buffon and his gang]...hasten to general conclusions from too few observations, and on false testimony of these observations."

Saussure welcomed the rambling Americans when they arrived, giving them a personal tour of his cabinet of curiosities. His cabinet—a French word that here meant "room," rather than "cupboard"—was "filled with rare and curious animals," as Rutledge put it, as well as minerals, scientific instruments, and experiments in progress. Jefferson would later create his own impressive display of natural curiosities in the entrance hall of Monticello, but he always regretted that he had been unable to dedicate his life to his "passion," science. He would have done so, he claimed, had he not been "drawn by the history of the times" to toil in "politics and government, towards which I had naturally no inclination."

This was the age of gentlemen naturalists, amateurs who contributed to the fields of botany, geology, climatology, chemistry, physics, astronomy, and paleontology. The self-taught natural historians were men of means—Buffon a nobleman, Saussure a patrician, and Jefferson, of course, a slave-owning aristocrat. Women were not admitted into scientific societies.

Some of these men's private collections later turned into public museums. Several decades after *Hints* was written, the term "scientist" was coined and professionals began working in ever more specialized branches of science for a salary. Technical advances occurred so rapidly that it became impossible to keep up with the latest in all scientific disciplines—men like Jefferson and Saussure were among the last who were experts in a wide array of fields.

Eager to contribute to the conversation in Saussure's cabinet, the Boys wracked their brains for what scientific knowledge they had to share—expertise on the spas of Belgium wouldn't cut it. What about that "skin of a very large animal...from the northern part of America" Rutledge had seen in Jefferson's house back in Paris? He vaguely recalled that it was a specimen unknown to Buffon but couldn't remember its name. And what of the "very large and huge bones" found by the Ohio River, some of which Jefferson owned? If only he had paid more attention when Jefferson was dispensing knowledge. Rutledge gamely tried to describe the specimens but gave only an "imperfect" account. And so the young man sheepishly penned a letter to his mentor, asking for help.

Thanks to the efficient French and Swiss postal systems, Jefferson received it just five days later and replied right away. The towering horned creature was a moose; the strange bones discovered on the Ohio were from a mammoth. Buffon had taken the latter for an elephant, but the Virginian determined that they were from a different species—with the elephant a "native only of the torrid zone," while the much larger mammoth lived north of 36½° latitude. Of course, Jefferson dryly wrote, all this was covered in *Notes on Virginia*; had the Boys bothered to bring a copy with them on their trip they would have known this already. Jefferson was confident, though, that Saussure would not fall for the count's fanciful theories. "Cautious in not letting his assent run before his evidence," Jefferson wrote to Rutledge, Saussure "possesses the wisdom which so few possess of preferring ignorance to error. The contrary disposition in those who call themselves philosophers in this country classes them in fact with the writers of romance."

He also shared a little of the backstory on how he acquired these bones, a teachable moment for the Boys. His approach—to the moose, the mammoth, and the scientific method in general—stood as an example to generations of natural historians. Long before he obtained his moose,

Jefferson sought out hard data to refute Buffon's claims of the inferiority of North American mammals. Having grown up in the woods of Virginia's Southwest Mountains, Jefferson had his own observations to draw from, but he needed more. In late 1783 and early 1784, before sailing for Paris, he wrote to acquaintances asking about animals "from the mouse to the mammoth as far as you have known them actually weighed; and where not weighed, you can probably conjecture pretty nearly."

One of his correspondents sent him the thigh bone of what he called a "big buffalo," which complemented the large tooth of an unknown animal sent to him by another informant. Jefferson identified both as mammoth specimens. The Virginian included the mammoth on his table of mammals, since he had found no case of Nature "having permitted any one race of her animals to become extinct; of her having formed any link in her great work so weak as to be broken." The mammoth might still wander some frozen land of the north, he surmised.

The most colorful of his sources, the Virginia planter Archibald Cary, informed Jefferson that he once "Killd a bear, not fat which waighed 410 pounds after he was Quartered, and have seen much larger but had no oppartunaty of Trying their Waight." He listed the approximate weight of a dozen other animals, adding that "Ratts" in the New World "are full as large as Ever I saw in England." Cary concluded—brimming with more national pride than mastery of spelling—that "it proceeds from Vanaty in the European Gentlemen who not only think our anamals Less than theirs but assume as Great a superiority to their Minds as they do to the sise of their anamals." But even though the quality of the data Jefferson received varied, when appropriate he incorporated it into tables contrasting the weight of North American and European mammals.

Even James Madison got in on the action, volunteering to dissect a weasel. The future Father of the Constitution examined the membrane of a female specimen's bladder and measured the distance between the vulva and anus, reassuring Jefferson that the American weasel was more impressively built than its European counterpart.

But a big-assed weasel would never impress Buffon. Either a moose or mammoth would do the trick, though, and there seemed to be considerably more moose roaming around North America than mammoths. In 1784, Jefferson developed a survey of seventeen questions on his new favorite beast. How far south does the moose range? How does it differ from the caribou and elk? Are its horns pointed or palmated? Does it sweat when it runs, or only drip from the tongue like a dog? Do its feet make a rattling sound? Contacts in New England responded, one enclosing moose hair.

A year later, when Buffon rejected the Virginian's arguments on the equality of the two climate's continents, all this preparation paid off: Jefferson wrote to his most trusted moose informants to commission a hunt, telling them the skeleton "would be an acquisition here more precious than you could imagine." He knew what time of year the animal could be bagged and gave precise instructions on how to stuff it. He understood its moosey nature and how to distinguish it from other species. To clear up any lingering confusion as to its identification, he also asked for elk and caribou horns to be collected—all of which he presented to the Frenchman in Paris.

His victory over the count wouldn't have been possible without the contributions of these non-professionals who had volunteered their time and knowledge to him. Seeking such help was completely in character for him—if "the people" had great capacity for democracy, why not also for natural history?

Jefferson just wanted the data. He didn't realize he was starting a movement.

THE FOUNDING CITIZEN SCIENTIST

Throughout his long life, Jefferson sought to "promote useful science," in all its branches "in every part of the earth." For nearly five decades, beginning on July 1, 1776, wherever he found himself, Jefferson took a temperature reading at dawn and at the hottest point of the afternoon. (One of the few personal notes he recorded of the Fourth of July that year was that it was seventy-six degrees in Philadelphia—a counterpoint to the legend passed down that the entire summer was sweltering.) He asked others to do the same, allowing him to monitor the weather from sites across Virginia, New York, Pennsylvania, Quebec, France, and elsewhere.

He also sought to enlist the government to deploy resources monitoring climate, proposing that a deputy in each county of Virginia receive a thermometer and take readings twice a day, along with measuring wind direction. When in 1803 he commissioned the Lewis and Clark expedition to go west, he explained to the adventurers how to record climate, not only using a thermometer but by observing when plants flowered and when birds arrived. As president, he established the first physical science agency within the federal government, tasked with studying and measuring the country's coast—an entity that, after various reorganizations, still exists today.

Unfortunately, although unsurprisingly, a certain group was not included in his efforts to expand the collection of scientific data: African Americans. This despite the fact that a free Black polymath who rivaled Jefferson in his love of learning, Benjamin Banneker, wrote to him. An accomplished astronomer, Banneker also reveled in describing the nature he found near his Maryland home, from the behavior of bees to the emergence of cicadas from the ground. He authored a series of almanacs containing weather predictions and his calculations on sunrises and tides. As a surveyor, he helped lay out the boundaries of Washington, DC, in 1791, while Jefferson was secretary of state.

That same year, Banneker forwarded him one of his almanacs—and included a damning observation in his letter. "[H]ow pitiable is it to reflect," he wrote, that "by fraud and violence," Jefferson held "so numerous a part of my brethren under groaning captivity and cruel oppression." His fellow natural historian was "guilty of that most criminal act" he professed to detest in others.

Passing over the charge, Jefferson replied to Banneker that he sent his almanac on to the Academy of Sciences in Paris, to serve as a response to the "doubts which have been entertained" about Blacks. But even though Jefferson asked seemingly any White man with a pulse to gather weather and share scientific data with him, he didn't request that Banneker do the same. (Banneker, who understood spherical trigonometry, was light-years beyond the Jefferson favorite Archibald Cary, he of the Ratts and Bears.) The Virginian later wrote a letter to a friend, claiming a White naturalist had been "puffing" up the astronomer's abilities. Of course, Banneker didn't need Jefferson's (or anyone's) permission to continue making advances in science, but his work would not be in collaboration with the sage of Monticello—who once again placed his faith only in White men.

Despite this major flaw, Jefferson nonetheless passionately "encourag[ed] the progress of science in all its branches," as he put it, involving White men, at least, in ways that most other elite practitioners wouldn't have thought to. But, over time, science became more specialized and common folk banished from the process. Scientists wanted firmer control over the data—no amateurs allowed.

Yet in recent decades has the pendulum begun to swing back. The practice of regular people collecting information has now become trendy and has its own name: citizen science. As environmental challenges mount—from global warming to pollution to species extinction—scientists have again turned to the public for help collecting information, a solution that would have pleased Jefferson to no end.

To learn more about this phenomenon, I visit one of the leading French government officials charged with promoting citizen science in his country. Christophe ushers me into his office, with a view of the Eiffel Tower to die for, and hands me a report he coauthored, filled with confusing terms: the interactive annotation of data sets, synchronization, algorithms that automate statistical data validation.

My anxiety rises; I'm reminded of my recurring nightmare of taking a test I failed to study for. Science class always seemed tedious to me as a student, a time for daydreaming rather than taking useful notes. In eighth grade, many of my friends worried whether they would get into the Thomas Jefferson High School for Science and Technology, one of the leading schools in the country and only a few miles from my house. None of my teachers encouraged me to apply—which left me not disappointed but relieved.

Fortunately, Christophe, an unassuming soft-spoken agronomist with a graying beard, puts me at ease. "Citizen science really took off in the early 2000s," he says. "Although that doesn't take into account astrophysics. There is a tradition of amateurs making observations about the stars long before that," he adds.

"One of the keys is the smartphone," he goes on. "We ask people to make observations—say about ticks, which are a big problem in France. We need more data to study them. Or about ash trees, which are fighting a fungal pathogen. We want to know which trees have developed a genetic resistance to it. It's so easy for people to take pictures and put information in their phone. If they had to write us a letter, they'd never do it." Although there was resistance to this movement from some scientists in his agency, who worried about the quality of the data, most have gotten behind his work, he tells me. "Researchers could never get such great information on their own."

Christophe describes more of his projects, including one with a very

French focus: measuring how planting native pilosella stops erosion in vineyards. "Citizen science differs by country," he explains. "Americans have a lot of interest in community-based research on health issues. The English have a long tradition of gathering data on birds. Countries in the Global South have more participation in agriculture." This puts me more at ease; I like the example of different people focusing on the topics that are meaningful to them. In my case, that would include nature. And so I find a group with an activity scheduled in Geneva and arrange to spend a Saturday in the city getting schooled.

I begin my morning at the History of Science Museum, housed in a small nineteenth-century pavilion in a public park overlooking Lake Geneva, which is flecked with sails. Outside on a lawn sloping down to the water comes the pungent smell of barbecued meat and the pounding of reggaeton. Families kick around soccer balls, and young women soak in the mild sun, ignoring the full-scale reconstructions of scientific instruments near the museum's entrance: parabolic mirrors, sundials, and the like. Inside I find collections of Saussure's tools, including his hygrometer and the telescope his wife used to watch him slowly ascend Mont Blanc. If he had been here with me, Jefferson wouldn't have been able to contain his excitement; I could see him grabbing the instruments and passing them out to the people outside, urging them to put more clothes on and start collecting data.

It's time for the small, informal event to start. I hop on a tram and then a local train. Although still within city limits, as ordered houses give way to vineyards and farms, it feels like the deep countryside. I disembark and walk down a long dirt road to a park entrance. There, a volunteer points me to an app to download on my smartphone and gives instructions on how to send photos and information to a nonprofit, which will add the data to a database tracking threatened fauna. "Here we have a *centaurea*," she tells our group, pointing to a thistly plant. "Take a picture and send it in. Now we determine if it's a local or invasive variety." She warns us to look out for the Asian long-horned beetle, which has been attacking trees across Switzerland—which makes me think back to Jefferson's search for the hated Hessian fly.

We painstakingly crouch and zero in on plant after plant. I fumble with the app—on technological matters, I'm like a seventy-five-year-old trapped in a forty-five-year-old's body. For a change of pace, the volunteer demonstrates a different project she helps run—collecting and pressing leaves and flowers, which will be sent to a site that will determine the plant's DNA. After that burst of excitement, we're back to photographing weeds.

The real citizen scientists can't get enough of this. Jefferson would have been equally enthralled; "there is not a sprig of grass that shoots uninteresting to me," he once wrote. I can only imagine him poring over online maps and databases and setting up a similar system at Monticello. But after two hours in which we've only advanced about five hundred feet, I'm itching to move faster. "A patient pursuit of facts, and cautious combination and comparison of them, is the drudgery to which man is subjected by his Maker, if he wishes to attain sure knowledge," Jefferson wrote in *Notes on Virginia*. As it turns out, I'm not a big fan of drudgery; plenty of sprigs shoot uninteresting to me. I feel a pang of unexpected sympathy with the Boys, who were looking forward to a nice European vacation until their mentor guilted them into studying sheep dung and olive tree roots.

As I thank the volunteer and make my getaway down the trail, I realize that you can't turn into a citizen scientist overnight. The practice involves commitment, knowledge, focus, and a willingness to grasp the big picture. Yet every effort helps. Although my few photos might seem inconsequential, when multiplied by thousands taken by more dedicated volunteers over years, they all add up to a useful sum of knowledge of local botany and the threats it faces.

And the benefits go beyond the data collected. "Through citizen sci-ence," Christophe had told me, "people understand more about the work scientists are doing. This way the youth understand the challenges our world is facing"—including climate change. That most daunting of prob-lems is never far from our minds as Liana and I travel to a place that, due to global warming, likely won't exist by the close of this century in its current form: France's Atlantic shore.

As If Both Sides of the Atlantic Were Not Warmed by the Same Genial Sun

"A CHANGE IN OUR CLIMATE IS TAKING PLACE HOWEVER"

In our rental, Liana and I tool along the rocky Breton coast in the northwest corner of France, one of the last stops in *Hints*. Although he didn't make it quite as far north as we are—the peninsula of Finistère, or land's end, which juts into the ocean like the head of a mastiff—Jefferson, too, spent several days exploring tidal Brittany.

Rutledge and Short arrived there as well, tracking west from Italy through Provence and then north up the French Atlantic coast. Short did his best to make natural history observations throughout his journey—although he regretted not having bought a portable thermometer and barometer in Paris, not finding them for sale elsewhere. Nonetheless, he charted the weather, tracked the olive tree's range, and collected seeds, doing it all except solve the puzzle of the shells in the Loire. He also noted when Burgundy wine grapes came ripe, a data point useful not only for oenological purposes but as a clue to when the region's seasons changed.

Jefferson encouraged such observations of what he called "indexes of climate" and often took them himself. Even after his thermometer broke in Nice on his own trip across France, Jefferson was undeterred, studying the changing flora and fauna as he traveled. An "estimate of climate may be otherwise made from the advance of the spring, as manifested by animal and vegetable subjects," he wrote later; everything from when the first whippoorwill is heard to when "the first brood of house flies" appear might be a helpful indicator. On his French journey, he recorded where he first saw swallows, listened to nightingales, and tasted cherries. Observing that strawberries and peas were ripe in May on both the eastern end of the Canal du Languedoc (near the Mediterranean) and the western (near the Atlantic), but not along the canal itself, he theorized that the sea moderated the area's temperature.

One of the most useful indices of climate variation was apple trees—they were planted across France, allowing Jefferson to note when they bloomed in different places that spring. He knew what he was looking at; Jefferson experimented with such varieties as Hewe's Crab and Golden Wildings in his Monticello orchards, expertly tended to during this time by the enslaved George Granger. Each fall, Granger supervised apple picking and each spring bottled cider, the table drink of the day in Virginia, safer than bacteria-filled water. Jefferson sampled many a *pomme* in France but concluded "they have no apple here to compare to our Newtown Pippin."

In the last week of March 1787, he recorded apple blossoms in the south of France. As late as June of that year, cider-producing trees were still blooming in the chilly clime of Brittany. Given global warming, I hypothesized that Breton apple trees flower much earlier today than in the late eighteenth century. Indeed, a French citizen science group reported that some now bloom in late March—the same time they blossomed in Provence in Jefferson's day, although these two regions have climates as different as New England's and coastal California's.

To investigate this ourselves, Liana and I pull up on a mid-April day, after detouring past roads closed by flooding, to an apple orchard in Finistère that still grows varieties from Jefferson's time.

In front of a warehouse, I meet Mark, a sturdy man with graying hair pulled back in a ponytail, who's volunteered to show me around. A writer and artist, Mark now works to conserve Breton pomological culture, which he sees as a "link to another world," that of his Celtic forebears. In Brittany, he tells me, the names of apples grown for eating are in French, while those cultivated to make powerful hard cider, magical blends tasting of honeysuckle and cut grass, are in Breton. No mystery as to which kind of apples the Celts preferred.

We stroll through the orchard, owned by Mark's quiet friend Claude, who shambles along with us in an old cardigan. "My family has had this cidery since 1872," he tells us. "I learned from my grandfather and great-uncles." The pair points out the different varieties of trees, with ancient Breton names: C'hwerv-brizh, Troajenn-Hir, Boutailh-bihan, their tiny green buds coming out. The trees used to blossom here only in mid- to late May, but now, warm Aprils often speed up the process, putting the fragile blossoms at the mercy of frosts.

Apple trees don't just indicate a changing climate through their blossoming time—sometimes the trees themselves become victims of global warming. Plants once selected and cultivated to mesh perfectly with a local climate now were struggling to survive. I had heard similar stories from an orchardist during our earlier trip to Italy. A late April frost had killed her cherry trees, and an unforgiving summer drought damaged her ox-snout apples and drunken pears, varieties that have been part of Umbrian life since the Middle Ages—but might not be for much longer. Concerned agronomists are working on new hybrids that can withstand the earlier blooms and erratic spring weather. Will all these transformations spell the death knell for heirlooms?

"Does global warming present a challenge for you?" I ask as we return to the warehouse and Claude brings out some bottles to taste.

"Yes, a real problem," Mark tells me. "Some trees are blooming early as a result," as much as by three weeks. He shows me a Kermerian apple, small, red, and tart, the base of much Breton cider production. "This variety does not handle cold winters well."

Another problem—also related to climate change, as it turns out—is even more pressing. "The sea has been encroaching," Claude says; we saw the Atlantic in the distance as we walked with him. "My orchard was all under water recently. We've had severe storms in recent years." Flooding can lead to fungus attacking the tree roots, he tells me.

Mark recounts the great storm of 1987, which destroyed some 80 percent of cider trees in Brittany. "Some people got out of the business at that time," he says, "but it also inspired others to try and preserve what was left before it's gone." Orchards don't have to be victims of global warming—they can be part of the solution, too. Leaves produce oxygen, Mark reminds me, important in combating rising carbon dioxide levels. And the trees provide biodiversity, sheltering insects and birds, like the orchard owl. Even as they preserve the past, Breton pomologists are searching for which of the old varieties will survive, in a world where much—but not all—has been lost.

"We like our apples bittersweet here," Mark tells me, handing me a glass of dry cider along with, quite unintentionally, a metaphor for this tale.

Our discussions on climate would have intensely interested Jefferson. He worried that the field of meteorology was not advancing as rapidly as other scientific disciplines—although he certainly was doing his part to move it forward. He published an extensive study of how temperature, humidity, and wind direction varied within his state from the coastal plain to the mountains, relying on readings from thermometers and barometers, as well as "indexes of climate," such as where catalpa trees grew and parakeets lived. After living in Paris for some years, he compared the "cheerful" climate of America with that of Europe and its "perpetual bank of clouds."

Most scientists today recognize that Jefferson lived in what is called the Little Ice Age, a period from roughly 1550 (if not earlier) to 1850 in which the earth was moderately cooler than in prior centuries (although with irregular intervals of warming interspersed). They're still debating the different natural causes of this cooling, with everything from levels of solar radiation to the tilt of the earth's orbit to volcanic activity identified as possible factors. In December 1788, Jefferson wrote to Short that it was only 8 degrees Fahrenheit in Paris; Short responded detailing the "excessive" cold blanketing Rome and the widespread suffering that it caused. In both countries, heating costs rose and rivers froze (preventing merchants from shipping goods). The following spring, the great snows melted, causing severe flooding. The discontent stemming from that bitterly cold winter helped lead to the French Revolution of 1789.

But that frigid season was an outlier; Jefferson noticed that temperatures in general trended up. "A change in our climate however is taking place very sensibly," he wrote, contrasting the deep snows and frozen rivers from his childhood with the generally more moderate climate of his adult years—leading to an "unfortunate fluctuation between heat and cold, in the spring of the year, which is very fatal to fruits." He was not observing the global warming crisis we face today, fueled by human activity, but rather the tail end of the Little Ice Age—a period little enough understood today and not at all in Jefferson's day. "May we not hope that the methods invented in latter times," he wrote, "will at length ascertain this curious fact in physical history."

Jefferson was particularly concerned about the potential for man to influence climate. In *Notes on Virginia*, he concluded that sea breezes traveled farther inland in his state than they did in years past due to coastal deforestation. Trees helped block the wind; Benjamin Franklin had earlier conjectured that the sun acted more strongly on a country "cleared of woods." Jefferson lamented that the Gloucester hickory, its habitat "now almost entirely cleared," had nearly vanished. "I wish I was a despot that I might save the noble, beautiful trees that are daily falling sacrifice to the cupidity of their owners, or the necessity of the poor," he once told a guest at the President's House. "The unnecessary felling of a tree, perhaps the growth of centuries, seems to me a crime little short of murder." As a result, he instructed his overseer to use "economy" in taking wood from Monticello Mountain.

He hoped *Notes on Virginia* would create a baseline of meteorological data for his state that later observers could consult. He encouraged other such studies across America, advising observers to pay "steady attention to the thermometer, to the plants growing there, the times of their leafing and flowering, its animal inhabitants, beasts, birds, reptiles and insects, its prevalent winds, quantities of rain and snow, temperature of fountains and other indexes of climate." Over much time, this would "show the effect of clearing and culture towards changes of climate."

After leaving the orchard, Liana and I drive to a nearby beach, deserted off-season. We hop from rock to rock over brackish tidal pools. "This is so calming," she says. "It feels so clean, it's like a shot of medicine." But as we stroll on, it's clear that not all is well. "You can see the erosion that's occurring on those cliffs," Liana says. "Those houses can't be here for long." I try to imagine the ocean's violent assaults in winter, seawater surging toward Claude's apple trees, and the magnitude of the problem sinks in. Generations from now, this shore itself might become a distant memory.

When Jefferson traveled the coast of France, he remarked on channels near the mouths of river filled with silt and sand. "The land gains there on the sea," he wrote; some ancient ports were now, in the eighteenth century, located inland. At Aigues-Mortes, some five miles from the Mediterranean, he observed "iron rings to which vessels were formerly moored," although now the town was surrounded only by "ponds which cannot be navigated."

Walking on the coast of Brittany.

Today, the opposite holds true: the sea inexorably gains on the land. Rather being cut off from the Mediterranean, Aigues-Mortes risks being overrun by it.

Since the Industrial Revolution, and especially in recent decades, global temperatures have been steadily climbing upward. Of course, I've long had a general (if tenuous) understanding of this problem, but only now have I focused on it for real. Belatedly, I've learned how certain gases in our lower atmosphere—gases that have been increasing at alarming rates in recent years—trap and absorb infrared radiation emanating from the earth, heating the planet as if it were a greenhouse. The primary culprit is carbon dioxide produced by burning fossil fuels, but many other human activities contribute to the effect as well, such as agricultural operations, which release methane, and deforestation, which deprives the planet of trees that absorb carbon. The last three decades have been the warmest such period in the northern hemisphere in the last fourteen hundred years. Much worse is yet to come.

Climate change also leads to extreme weather patterns. More precipitation falls in a concentrated period of time than in decades past. Due to higher sea levels, ocean storm surges cause a greater toll than ever before—as seen by the intensified tempests that batter the Breton coast. Higher temperatures cause the polar ice caps to melt and sea levels to rise, robbing the land. Researchers project that much of this coast—including this beach and Claude's orchard—will be underwater before the end of the twenty-first century. So will many places that Jefferson visited: Nantes, the city that has begun to face up to its slave-owning past; Bordeaux, the center of the wine trade; Arles, where we saw the bullfight, all projected to vanish under the ascendant ocean. For future travelers, *Hints* might be a moot point—the places described in it won't exist.

The problems are worldwide; Jefferson's rejoinder to Buffon—"as if both sides [of the Atlantic] were not warmed by the same genial sun"—has never seemed more prescient. Littoral regions are at risk of submersion, while severe weather jeopardizes the lives, livelihoods, food security, and water supplies of people across the planet, particularly communities of the poor and minorities with less access to safety nets. Although the effects on humans differ from what Jefferson and Short observed during the winter of 1788–89, unless climate change is checked, they will be just as real—and will certainly lead to social unrest.

A few subjects of special interest to Jefferson illustrate the massive changes occurring. Rice, which Jefferson smuggled out of Italy, is often grown in coastal zones, with harvests increasingly destroyed by flooding. The plant itself might be losing much of its nutritional content as it draws in a higher proportion of carbon dioxide rather than nutrients from the soil. Wine is also going through transformations. Since grapes are highly sensitive to climate, some producers in Bordeaux are experimenting with heat-resistant varieties, at the risk of changing their wine's storied taste. Even the beloved moose of New Hampshire are dying off at an unprecedented rate due to diseases carried by ticks, whose population has exploded in a now warmer climate. The Objects of Attention I've spent the last years exploring might look radically different, then, to someone who journeys, *Hints* in hand, decades from now.

Given all this, it's easy to feel down, even when walking hand in hand with your partner on a stunning windswept beach. The following morning, we drive to the Breton port of Guilvinec, to see how local fishermen are adapting to global warming, hoping for a little good news for a change.

❖   ❖   ❖

"I [am not]...acquainted with the fishy tribe," Jefferson wrote once, but as the ambassador from a country reliant on maritime industries, he had to learn fast. Before leaving America for France in 1784, he conducted "actual inspection and inquiry" on the range of codfish and whales in different seasons. He spent his Atlantic crossing on the *Ceres* learning from the captain and watching for whale spouts. The ship "becalmed" for several windless days over the Grand Banks, where the mixture of the warm Gulf Stream and cold Labrador currents sparked the growth of plankton, eaten by mackerel and herring that were in turn prey for millions of cod. The crew effortlessly pulled up so many fish that the passengers ate only cod tongues and sounds (swim bladders), throwing the rest away. Why worry about conservation when you live in a world of such abundance? Jefferson later fretted, though, that climate change spurred by human activities might have "problematical" effects on this fishing.

Through his investigations, he discovered comparative advantages for both American fishermen and whalers. The best grade of cod, called dun fish, could be taken in coastal New England waters in winter, when British and French fleets off North America had returned home. "This is what foreign fishermen can never supply," he wrote. And although right whales were no longer sighted off the New England coast—Jefferson assumed they had just "retired" to other areas, fleeing hunters—he learned how American whalers were exploiting sperm whales "in the warmer latitudes" off of Brazil. Traveling to seaports in France, he carefully studied the vessels docked and the types of oil burned locally. Armed with this knowledge, he successfully fought to open French markets to American whale and codfish oil, his greatest commercial diplomatic achievement. "Science never appears so beautiful," he wrote, "as when applied to the uses of human life."

Yet centuries of whaling, aided by sonar and mechanized harpoons, took their toll. By the late twentieth century, sperm whale populations were only a third of what they had been in Jefferson's day, while just a few hundred right whales survived. An international treaty finally banned commercial whaling in 1982. Meanwhile, overfishing by massive trawlers led to an almost total collapse in the stock of northern cod in the early 1990s.

Today, fisheries managers must also confront the challenges of climate change, as rising temperatures lead to changes in fish distribution. Ocean acidification—global warming's "evil twin," as some call it—compounds matters. Seas absorb carbon dioxide, which turns their waters more acidic, killing some species of plankton and slowing the growth of fish. This is the dark side of technological progress, never dreamed of by the sunny Jefferson, who, while supporting conservation measures, never comprehended that plants and animals could go extinct.

Liana and I pull up in Guilvinec, the once thriving capital of the

French sardine processing industry before the factories closed. In 2000, the town reinvented itself, opening a cultural center and museum called La Cité de la Pêche, centered on its active fish auction market, which still sells the catches of a thousand or so local fishermen.

I meet a man by the docks who introduces himself as Philippe. Stocky, with a shockingly white beard and a jaunty white sweater with horizontal blue stripes, he looks every bit the ex-fisherman. He now works at the cultural center, where he "helps people understand where fish come from and its true cost," he tells me. I ask about cod, the species that once fueled economies and inspired French cooking. "Codfish have left our region because of global warming," he replies. "You can still fish them off the northwest coast of Ireland, but the French import most of their cod now. Greenland is now the biggest producer."

Philippe shows the way to the auction floor, where a guide, Rachel, points out the rows of fish in plastic containers. "There's no frozen fish here," she says; everything has just been caught. As if on cue, a boat pulls into the docks and a small crew begins unloading, along with an old man in a beret. "He's an ex-fisherman; he just comes here to volunteer because he misses it," she tells us. "And they give him some rock lobsters as a gesture of appreciation."

A small group of buyers hold devices that look like walkie-talkies, pressing a button when they want to bid. La Cité de la Pêche guarantees a minimum price, providing the stability that small, artisanal fishermen need. The port works with coastal fishermen, who bring in fine, restaurant-quality fish, rather than industrial trawlers, which catch much greater quantities but also burn tremendous amounts of greenhouse gases.

Afterward we attend a workshop put on by a woman named Scarlette, whose hair color, now graying, clearly once matched her first name. After a decade of fishing, she's turned to harvesting seaweed. "We have eight hundred and fifty varieties here in Finistère," she says. "It's like our great

American forest." Bretons used to collect it for fertilizer; now Scarlette and others are trying to popularize it as food, emphasizing that this renewable resource doesn't require the clear-cutting of forests for farmland.

Two fishy characters in the auction house.

Even global warming can provide opportunity if you look in the right places. "The temperature of the sea has gone up one degree Celsius in the last fifty years," she says. "Now we have a seaweed variety growing here that used to only be found in Spain." She demonstrates methods of cooking it. "My generation thought that chemicals made everything better," she says. "We were wrong. This seaweed is completely natural. I eat it every morning at four a.m. and I feel like Popeye."

"Scarlette is an inspiration," Liana enthuses as we leave, clutching bags of algae. "She brought back a tradition that most people had forgotten about. And she doesn't just use seaweed for pills and vitamins, she eats it. Who would have thought of putting seaweed in your guacamole? She's like Claude with his apples—she's going back to the old ways but making them new."

We'll have a lot to think about when we return home. Even if not all of us turn into citizen scientists, we still need to act. Otherwise the future—soon to be the present—will be a chaotic one of submerged coasts, scarcer drinking water, and impoverished communities.

I'm used to turning to Jefferson for answers on everything. Could he have any for this crisis?

He passionately regarded climate as a key to understanding much of how the world worked. And he encouraged citizens to make regular weather observations and to observe the natural history of their region and how humans affected it—helpful actions to take today. After learning about his failings on slavery, I'm glad to reacquaint myself with Jefferson the visionary. That's the person I liked in the first place.

Yet, although he foresaw that humans might induce climate change, Jefferson simply wasn't equipped to understand the phenomenon of global warming caused by industrialization and other human activities—a problem that, according to data currently available, only began after his death. He was confined to the limits of the science of his era; he didn't believe species extinction was possible. He normally (although not always) opposed strong governmental responses to national or global problems, preferring to rely on private initiative.

While some of Jefferson's views—say, on free speech—might seem relevant today, he's ultimately a creature of his times, I conclude. The contours of the present crisis would seem alien to him. His principles might point us in the right direction, but he can't provide specific solutions today. It's fitting that I'm nearly at the end of my journey, then. I'll have to leave him behind and figure out my own path soon enough, in a world fundamentally different from his own.

But there is one answer Jefferson can provide.

+ + +

"Dig a hole like this, big enough for the roots to spread," Dad tells us. I couldn't think of anyone better to guide me on this project. "Now you need to put it in some soil that's friable—topsoil, mulch." It's tough to keep fruit trees alive here, because of the pests, he says, so we'll need patience and a long-view. In our backyard, not far from Nico's garden, we're putting in saplings I got from Monticello's Center for Historic Plants. We plant a Marseille fig tree, a Heath's cling peach, a persimmon, and Jefferson's favorite apple trees. Dad points out the best location for each.

No, Jefferson can't show us the way out of this crisis. But I'm not ready to throw him out yet, either. "I like the dreams of the future better than the history of the past," he wrote. We need some of his forward thinking.

A constant in Jefferson's life was his love of trees—he loved to describe them, worried about their loss, and brought countless seeds to France to be distributed. A French nonprofit has taken to planting pecan trees across its country in his name, symbolizing his work. And, I'm heartened to learn, Brittany plans to plant 25 million trees in its region, pumping more oxygen into the atmosphere. Such actions can't counter global warming alone, but they can form a part of the solution.

"We have to do this now," Liana says, happily dirty. "We need to begin." Along with our nascent orchard, we donated to a nonprofit to help offset our carbon footprint from our travels. Not that this gesture is sufficient, or that it justifies other lifestyle choices—there's certainly much more for us to do. But it's time to start somewhere.

The program we chose to support works to replant some of the New England forest: home to the long-tailed weasel, the deer mouse, and that large quadruped that makes a rattling noise when it runs, the American moose.

CHAPTER TWENTY-TWO

We'll Always Have Paris

We're rolling down a highway past fields and vineyards. Liana, Miranda, and Nico chat and watch the scenery while I negotiate the curves of the route. I'm the only one among us who knows we're headed to Paris.

Although, as they will find out, there's a catch.

It's nearly eight years to the day since Liana and I ran our wine marathon in Bordeaux, which makes this early September...2020. The year the novel coronavirus pandemic swept the planet, taking hundreds of thousands of lives, disrupting many others, and putting countless travel plans on hold.

Despite all the trips we had already taken, earlier in the year I still had places on *Hints'* itinerary left to explore (boating down the Canal du Midi!) and Objects of Attention to which I had given a nod (Manufacturing) but wanted to learn more about. Most of all, I dreamed of ending our journey in the same place *Hints* does, Paris. I had visions of our finishing with a long Jeffersonian-themed walk in the City of Lights, as proud as cyclists peddling ceremonial laps down the Champs-Élysées on the final leg of the Tour de France. Maybe one last trip would teach me whatever I still needed to discover about Jefferson and myself, whatever has stayed just out of reach.

When COVID-19 hit, like many I struggled to adapt to the new reality, searching first for how to stay safe. We were fortunate; Liana and I were able to telework, and the kids gamely slogged through their online classes. I still clung to the hope that the virus would be checked and we could follow through on our travel plans this year. But as weeks turned into months and things only got worse, I accepted this would not be the case.

Which left me with a decision to make: Should I wait for the pandemic to recede and then return to France, perhaps next summer? Find somewhere else to go? Or declare our journey over? Naturally I looked to the person I always turned to for advice. What would Jefferson do?

Epidemics were a constant feature of life in his time. His first trip outside of Virginia, in 1766, was to Philadelphia to get inoculated against smallpox. Jefferson survived a series of outbreaks of deadly diseases, none worse than the yellow fever epidemic of 1793, which broke out when he was secretary of state—again in Philadelphia, then the nation's capital. Americans back then were confused and fearful, with only a poor understanding of the disease, as we were in the early days of COVID-19. Neither Jefferson nor other scientifically minded people in the city ever learned how it spread (by mosquitoes). Some five thousand people, 10 percent of Philadelphia's population at the time, lost their lives that summer.

Although most government officials departed the capital, "all flying who can," Jefferson stayed. There was some "danger" in remaining, he wrote, but he had the advantage of living in a house on the Schuylkill River away from the crowded city center where infections were prevalent. There he cloistered himself in his home office, surrounded by nature and calm. "I never before knew the value of trees," he wrote that year—he took his meals, worked, and received visitors under the plane trees that "embosomed" his house. Finally, when he could not keep conducting business (only one of his clerks was still at his post), he returned to Monticello in the fall, earlier than originally planned, to wait out the epidemic.

The incident constituted one of many instances of Jefferson's adapting his plans to events beyond his control and making the best of the situation. The same occurred with his dreams of travel. When he left France in October 1789, he had requested only a six-month sabbatical from his post to check on his plantations and financial affairs. Even though he brought an enormous number of essentials home with him (including Bordeaux wine, a pear tree, a harpsichord, and many books), he left even more items behind in the Champs-Élysées house that he was still renting. He had big plans for when he'd return: a longer trip through Italy, a tour of Greece. But when he disembarked from the *Clermont* in Norfolk, Virginia, he discovered he had been both nominated and confirmed as the first U.S. secretary of state. He would never return to the Old World.

Jefferson's political career monopolized his time for most of the two decades that followed: four years at State (followed by a three-year sulk at home, unhappy with the Federalists' domination of government), four years as vice president, and eight years as president.

But that didn't mean he quit traveling. In 1791, he made his last great trip, the two-month-long trek to New England with James Madison and James Hemings, searching for both the Hessian fly and for allies to build an opposition party. Aside from that expedition, his travel was mostly work-related; he made twenty-six round-trips from Monticello to the national capital (which was first in New York City, then Philadelphia, and finally, in 1800, Washington, DC). Jefferson still kept his eyes open while on the road, though, always observing and making the most of wherever he found himself. In 1790, returning home from New York with James Madison, he spent several days on the road with Thomas Shippen, who was also en route to Virginia. The old companions found themselves stuck for a day in a sleepy town on the Eastern Shore of Maryland while waiting for a ferry to cross the Chesapeake. Boredom did not ensue. "We

talked and dined and strolled and rowed ourselves in boats," Shippen
wrote, "and feasted on delicious crabs."

As vice president, Jefferson sometimes took the public stagecoach
to Philadelphia (rather than his own carriage with an enslaved driver)
in order to chat with Americans of modest means and learn about their
concerns—similar to the conversations he had had in France a decade
earlier. Even while president, Jefferson would take a long, daily horseback ride, alone with his thoughts, taking note of changes in the new
capital. The end of his term, in March 1809, came as a relief; "never did a
prisoner, released from his chains, feel such relief as I shall on shaking off
the shackles of power," he wrote during his last week in office. Finally, he
could return to his own pursuits full-time. After the sixty-five-year-old
Jefferson crossed the Potomac River into Virginia, he would never again
leave his home state in the nearly eighteen years he had left of life.

Yet in retirement he rarely stayed still. From breakfast to noon, he
was "mostly on horseback," he wrote, riding to his satellite plantation
at Tufton Farm and elsewhere. At lunch, he would regale guests with
stories of the French Revolution, of the buildings of Italy and gardens of
England, of the wines he kept importing and the unusual plant seeds his
European friends kept sending him. He showed visitors animal bones in
the entrance hall and told them about the moose that got away.

And he kept journeying around his own state. In 1818, Jefferson traveled to a ramshackle tavern in the Blue Ridge Mountains for a meeting with state leaders to decide where to locate the future University of
Virginia (Jefferson won out with his proposal for Charlottesville). Most
impressively of all, he hiked the Peaks of Otter, one of whose three summits was then considered the highest in Virginia, loaded down with scientific instruments, at the age of seventy-one.

Taking his experience into account, I accepted the new reality before
me. It was time to move on and let go of my dreams of more European

travel, for now. Going abroad so many times was a privilege, one for which both I and my credit card companies were immensely grateful. Like Jefferson, I had stockpiled enough memories of our trips in the Old World to last a lifetime; I had learned what I could from this improbable journey across western Europe. After all, *Hints* was never meant to last forever—Jefferson intended Americans to return to the States with treasured finds and cautionary tales alike to apply this knowledge to projects at home. I always knew I'd have to leave Jefferson someday, and now that day was knocking insistently on my door.

But if I could at all help it, I was never going to end this eight-year odyssey on my couch. Even if we couldn't go to France for a big finish on the Champs-Élysées, just like Jefferson we could make some memories close to home.

Which brings us to our Honda Pilot bouncing along the road. As we round a bend and a certain highway exit comes into view, it's time to announce our surprise destination.

"Everyone! Exciting news! We're going to Paris!"

Quizzical faces peer back at me.

"Paris, Virginia."

* * *

Nestled in the foothills of the Blue Ridge Mountains, Paris, Virginia, is a speck of a place, with some sixty-seven residents, fewer even than in Jefferson's day. As we drive up, I feel that sense of delicious anticipation you often get when arriving in an unfamiliar locale—just like Liana and I had when we arrived in France's version of Paris. What will we find?

We walk into the Ashby Inn, a restaurant in an old stone building, and take seats on the garden patio on a gorgeous day. And like so many times before, we bond over food. We had done the same last night at home. Dad and Mom came over and brought the last of the Vacqueyras wine. Its taste transported the adults back to that week we shared in the farmhouse in Provence years ago. Since that trip, Dad's memory has worsened, yet he never complains about his fate. He seems to genuinely appreciate each moment he's given, always smiling and cracking jokes. I now know I never had to look to Jefferson to find a guide to life. He's right here.

Yesterday, we ate outside, near Nico's garden. And we had a new chef in charge: Miranda. She's soaked in the food lessons of France and Italy, more than I would have expected from a thirteen-year-old. She cooked steak with a fig reduction sauce, an homage to that homemade fig-and-grape sauce Dad served at our farewell dinner in Vacqueyras. We couldn't get enough of it.

Here in Paris, our entrées arrive. Nico has a burger, which he pronounces "pretty delicious." Liana enjoys her duck confit salad with wild mushrooms and tiny edible flowers.

"Mmm, this is so rich and creamy," Miranda says of her braised beef short ribs with polenta. "I need to make it myself."

"This place is so awesome," she continues. "It reminds me of Europe. They have dishes I've never tried before. And it's in such a great setting; the waiters are so nice."

"I like it when a meal is the event of the day," Nico says. "Dad, is your food book-worthy?" Although just ten, he knows how to bring the snark (no idea where he got that from). And yes, my lobster with white beans is memorable.

"I can't wait to read what you've written, Dad!" Miranda adds. She's been asking to do so for some time now. Stuck at home during the coronavirus lockdowns, I've spent nights and weekends typing up my experiences, reliving them along the way. Shaping our trips into stories on the page has given me a sense of purpose during the pandemic. Although we struggled on our Jeffersonian journey at times, we nearly always discovered wonder. Recalling those challenges overcome has brought me both solace and a determination to see things through to the end.

"Not yet," I respond. "We're still traveling. Let's wait for this trip to finish."

That won't be long. We're ending our journey in three days with a bona fide Jefferson-approved adventure. But first we're going to retrace a few of the trips he made as an old man in his and my home state. Although Jefferson never returned to Europe, he spent plenty of time applying lessons from his journeys on his Virginia estates. I'm looking forward to discovering lasting ripple effects of the ideas he brought home with him—and seeing how the Boys fared after their travels, too. It's time then for our updated 2020 version of his guide: *Hints to Americans Traveling When They Can't Go to Europe.*

A LEGACY OF *HINTS*

The next day we pull up at Monticello—not for a house tour, which we've done countless times, but for a bite to eat. Last year, Monticello launched the Farm Table café. It was inspired in part by Alice Waters, the famed restaurateur and author, who when she visited was shocked by the dichotomy between the thousand-foot kitchen garden and the sad-sack eatery serving chicken fingers. "Jefferson would have been very, very frightened by that café," she said at last fall's Monticello Heritage Harvest Festival, which I attended. After her initial, disappointing visit here years ago, Waters worked with the Thomas Jefferson Foundation to change their mindset about food for visitors. Most of the fruits and vegetables used at the revamped café come from Tufton Farm, a sprawling expanse two miles away that was once a plantation owned by Jefferson.

At Farm Table we order tomato bisque, corn soup, pattypan squash salad, and sandwiches of squash and greens. I notice a wine advertised as from Monticello and ask about it. "It's actually from a place nearby that makes it for us," the woman at the counter says, "Barboursville Vineyards."

"Oh yes, we know it," I say and smile, thinking back to the epic tasting Fernando hosted for us in his cottage. Once I order a glass of chardonnay, he's with us in spirit on these last miles.

"This is actually pretty good," Nico says while munching his sandwich. "I'm enjoying this book-cation."

We head to Tufton Farm to see what we just ate. Peggy shows us around; she's the Curator of Plants, she tells us, and is accompanied by her Director of Wildlife: her dog Esther, famed for scaring off rabbits, groundhogs, and other furry marauders. Peggy points out boxes of bees, which produce honey sent to Farm Table, and buckets of freshly picked red peppers (Jefferson considered them a "valuable addition" to his garden). We tour the crops growing in the red clay: tomatoes, gourds, zucchini, and pumpkins, surrounded by an electric fence—"We get black bears here in spring," Peggy tells us.

Agriculture was Object of Attention One and deservingly so. As I had learned earlier, Jefferson returned home with new crops, exotic foods (with recipes by James Hemings), and farming innovations, including the design for the plow he drew from the back of his carriage in France. He put many of these ideas into practice at Tufton Farm, riding there several times a week in retirement to check on progress.

Later, after our visit, I catch up with the farm manager, Keith, who's tall, in his late thirties with sandy brown hair. He started here in 2017 as part of an effort to bring full-fledged agriculture (in addition to gardening) back to Monticello. That was the year I toured Italy, exploring what would captivate Jefferson today, the flavors of Slow Food heirlooms or high-tech solutions to food production (or perhaps both principles at the same time). Keith, too, was wrestling with Jefferson's agricultural ideas and how to translate them into this age.

"I'm forced to ask the question: what kind of farmer would Jefferson be today?" he tells me. "My personal view is that he practiced good husbandry, crop rotation, and manuring. He didn't get everything right, but he had a scientific approach toward growing. I see him as still relevant today."

Keith's originally from British Columbia, so he speaks calmly and doesn't wave his hands as much as Alessandre did at Il Monticello. But he, too, wants to experiment, engage with the community, and serve as a good steward of the land. Keith tests what grows best in given soil and other conditions—trying out both heirlooms, like Louisiana Red okra, and modern varieties. "We have a snapshot of what worked for Jefferson two hundred years ago, and that's valuable," he says. Now he wants to discover the best solutions for today, whether old or new.

He also is trying to make his farming sustainable. Tufton is deficient in phosphorus; the history of growing tobacco there helped deplete the earth of that key mineral. To remedy this, he's planted buckwheat, which enhances soil structure and helps make phosphorous available for the next crop. "There's been a lot of erosion here; you can see topsoil deposited into the watershed," he says. He recounts how a survey Jefferson made of the property in the 1790s didn't show any rock outcroppings. Now there are several prominent ones, the earth that once covered those stones having washed away. Just like Jefferson's weather observations have proven useful today, so too, then, has his cartography. Keith also has to deal with the effects of climate change on his crops; he plants cover crops to fight erosion caused by severe storms.

Of course, agriculture has never occurred in a social vacuum. Jefferson enslaved hundreds of people to work his land. Throughout history, growing and distributing food has raised issues of power, money, and freedom, and still does so today. "Our country is so polarized," Keith says sadly. "There's a gulf; sometimes it seems like it's rural America

versus the rest of the country. Foodies, people who really appreciate their food, can be seen as liberals," and dismissed by some, he tells
me. "But civic engagement can occur around food. Everyone eats. We
all can appreciate farming and its importance to society. I want to help
raise the profile of farmers, to encourage them to diversify, to keep land
from getting paved over and developed." He dreams of creating a public
garden where visitors can learn about agriculture. "I want this place to be
enriching, healing," he says.

None of this will be easy, particularly during a pandemic; it may take
better times to put some of his ideas in place. Yet Keith's plans remind
me in a way of Jefferson's promotion of citizen science—an attempt to
engage people in issues and teach that even small efforts can make a
difference. "I believe that people can come together over food," he says
fervently. Nothing could be more Jeffersonian.

✦ ✦ ✦

The next day we follow Jefferson's footsteps to his second house at
Poplar Forest near Lynchburg, where he went to escape the crowds of
houseguests that clung to Monticello like barnacles. We approach via a
long entranceway lined with tulip poplars. I think back to our tour of
those nineteen gardens in England, a trip that we all remember vividly,
Nico with fondness and Miranda with horror. Growing American plants
was all the craze in eighteenth-century England; we saw centuries-old
tulip poplars over there, too. Inspired, Jefferson made sure to highlight
native plants and trees in his own landscape designs.

We walk behind the house, smaller than Monticello, and examine a
curious redbrick octagonal structure standing on a small rise. It's the size
of a closet, with a lunette window and a small dome. There's another one
just like it on the other side of the house, tiny symmetrical architectural

masterpieces. A sign points out their purpose: they're privies. "Even his pooping places were fancy," Miranda says, admiringly. This serious-minded man of the Enlightenment could never wholly give himself over to romanticism—these follies fulfill the most basic of human functions.

It's never a good sign, though, when the bathroom is the highlight of the landscape design today. Jefferson once had used plantings to give a sense of wildness and mystery here, but that's long gone. Later owners covered the land fronting the mansion with boxwoods (since removed); the back reverted to a humdrum grass lawn. Archaeologists continue to study the estate, trying to decode the layout of Jefferson's intricate planting scheme.

As I had learned, Jefferson's ideal landscape not only featured eye-catchers and follies, it told visitors an American story, emphasizing native plants and the promise of the West. He included sweeping lawns to symbolize agricultural prosperity—but grassy vistas were merely one element among many, serving to set off the wildness of the woods. In that respect, he presaged Frederick Law Olmsted, the great nineteenth-century designer of New York's Central Park and other public gardens that juxtaposed pastoral meadows with wooded thickets and rocky precipices.

Behind the house at Poplar Forest, though, the lawn is the only design feature left from his day. It's similar to the grassy plots we passed by on our drive, to the homogeneous suburban lawnscape of my childhood. This is understandable; Poplar Forest is still studying Jefferson's layout (and surely doesn't have a huge landscaping budget in any case.) Yet having seen the genius of Capability Brown on display in England and of Jefferson at Monticello, I am struck by how monotonous endless expanses of grass can seem. In our yard, Nico's started on a small scale with his whimsical garden—this trip reminds me that I, too, should try harder to turn the rest of our property into a landscape, not just a lawn.

As at Monticello and UVA, there was a tragic side to the Poplar Forest estate, too. Around one hundred enslaved people lived here over the years that Jefferson owned the plantation. He arranged work stations and housing to keep the enslaved mostly out of sight of Whites in the mansion. Jefferson concealed the kitchen below the main house (later it was moved to an outdoor terrace due to the smoke it generated). There the enslaved cook Hannah prepared meals, unseen by the White diners above her.

Enslaved people lived in cabins far from the main house. We walk to the site of one of the dwellings. Today there stands a "ghost structure," timber frames indicating only its outline, since not enough is known to faithfully recreate it. And we visit an actual house that lodged enslaved people; built in the 1850s, it postdates Jefferson. Inside, a guide talks about the Black workers. We hear of James Hubbard, whose story I learned earlier; he spent his youth here before running from Monticello and being sold and sent down south. Of John Hemmings, the gifted woodworker, who did the paneling at Poplar Forest (one of his mahogany doors is still on display inside). He spent months here exercising his craft, longing to return home to his wife at Monticello, he wrote to Jefferson, a plea that went unheeded until the master deemed his work complete.

We hear of Billy, who attacked an overseer and two other enslaved workers in disputes. He was thrown in the Bedford jail and sentenced to thirty lashes and the burning of his hand and later sent to Louisiana. Of Hannah, who was not only a cook but a healer—and Billy's mother. She attended to the men whom he injured, working desperately to cure them. If any of them had died, her son's fate would have been worse. Hannah was literate; a letter she wrote to Jefferson has been preserved, where she mentions her Christian faith, which she surely leaned strongly on during this time. The trials she endured—like those of the other unfree people here—are unfathomable.

Unlike Monticello, Poplar Forest is mostly bare inside, with few furnishings. That's fine by us; the unadorned interior allows us to better appreciate the structure itself. As we learned on our travels, architecture was one of Jefferson's greatest passions. Without the ideas he picked up on the road he never would have come up with his own signature style.

Looking out a window inside Poplar Forest.

As we tour the house, I look for elements he brought back. From Rome came the Tuscan order outside (seen in its plain columns) and fancier Ionic designs in the parlor. The dining room, shaped in the form of a perfect cube and placed in the center of the house, once featured an entablature of human faces (now represented by drawings) inspired by the Roman Diocletian baths. Nico pipes up: this central room with its skylight, he says, reminds him of a Roman courtyard. Palladio gave Jefferson the idea for the service wings elongating out in each direction from the house. France inspired the long, triple-sash windows, the alcove bed, and the illusion that the house is only one story. The bricks, of course, were Virginian, the wood handiwork that of John Hemmings.

We study the house's unusual octagon shape, with some windows facing eight directions, allowing light to spill in. This was Jefferson at his finest: deploying math to illuminate his life. I only wish my now favorite UVA professor, Richard Guy Wilson, was here to grade our efforts at evaluating Poplar Forest—so, afterward, I ring him up.

"In some ways, it was the ideal home," he tells me. "It displayed perfect geometry—everywhere except for the damn staircases: he had to add them later to make things more practical. But it was really ideal. Here he had the chance to start fresh. Monticello was an evolution of another time," RGW explains, "Jefferson had already built a house before he went to France. His initial scheme for it was not ideal. He changed it as he could. But at Poplar Forest, he had the chance to create *the* ideal."

I bounce an idea off him. "Professor, Jefferson wanted his buildings to be models; he wanted people to look at them and understand architecture. But here he was trying to get away from it all. So, would you say he was more building for himself? Was this him more doing what he liked?"

"Yes, that makes sense," RGW replies. "Poplar Forest wasn't a public display. It was personal." I beam on my end of the phone. Sounds like I got extra credit for that one.

But one thing about Jefferson's building design ideas nags at me. Unlike at the beginning of my journey, I now actually like architecture and notice the buildings I pass by. Neoclassical buildings today tend toward stodginess: government offices, banks, and the like. The style speaks of power and tradition, not the avant-garde. Yet when Jefferson promoted his revival of classical architecture in America, it was a break from what came before. He meant it to challenge the viewer, to inspire civic virtue and remind him or her of the importance of the democratic experiment.

So, what happened? I ask RGW whether this style now represents the past, not the future.

"I know what you're saying," he replies. "Classical architecture doesn't have the same meaning today as it used to. People aren't thinking of Greece and Rome necessarily when they see it today," he continues—because we're so used to seeing it. "The style fell out of favor for a long time, then there was a revival. And a reaction against it, which I understand—I'm a modernist, too."

Even if Jeffersonian architecture is not the most current today, there's no denying that our only architect-president left a towering legacy, translating European concepts onto American sites and giving those who followed new ideas to play with. "I see him as renewing an important variety of architecture," RGW says, "instead of building the same damn thing over and over again."

+   +   +

We've all enjoyed these few days on the road. Travel close to home can be as rewarding as far-off trips. And the effortlessness with which I was able to engage with the topics in *Hints* has gratified me—so unlike that early trip to Amsterdam, where I struggled to master three different Objects of Attention at once. Now, moving from one subject to the next feels as familiar as greeting old friends. Here at the end, I consider myself a mature traveler, ready for anything that comes my way (so long as it's Jefferson-themed in some way and I've spent eight years studying it).

Before taking stock of what effect these travels had on Jefferson—and me—there's one other cast of characters I need to check in on. Whatever happened to the Boys? Did each return "charged like a bee with the honey of wisdom," as Jefferson predicted, and lead a fulfilling life? Or was their European journey the highlight of an existence that turned tragic or mundane?

After ending his journey early and returning home to Philadelphia, Thomas Lee Shippen traveled south to Virginia in 1790 (the trip in which he ate blue crabs with Jefferson along the way), where he met and later married a fabulously wealthy heiress. He dropped his legal career— which he had never warmed to anyway—and lived the life of a country-gentleman intellectual in Pennsylvania, surrounded by a vast library. But throughout the 1790s, he suffered from a disease (which one is unknown today) that left him coughing and fighting for breath; even the laudanum he took didn't dull the pain. Jefferson stayed in touch and tried to cheer him up, but in 1798, Shippen contracted tuberculosis and died at age thirty-two.

Although John Rutledge returned home with the key from the Bastille, his political ideals would shift. He was elected to the U.S. House of Representatives as a Federalist, the party that took an increasingly hostile stance to both revolutionary France and Jefferson's Democratic-Republicans. When Jefferson and Aaron Burr, both Democratic-Republicans, found themselves tied in the Electoral College in the winter of 1800–01 (since electors didn't then distinguish between voting for president or vice president), Rutledge supported Burr's candidacy, likely seeing him as more supportive of the Federalists. Rutledge had turned on his mentor.

Two years later, Rutledge wrote a letter under an assumed name to attack some members of Jefferson's government. When the deceit was discovered, Rutledge assured the president that he still respected him. Yet he had forgotten one of *Hints'* lessons: avoid the duplicity common in European leaders and act with "honest simplicity." Jefferson never responded to his last letter. Like Shippen, Rutledge, too, predeceased Jefferson, dying in 1819.

The Boy who never wanted the travels to end was William Short. He remained in Paris running the small U.S. diplomatic mission as the *chargé d'affaires* for three years after Jefferson left, then performed similar tasks in Amsterdam and Madrid, bouncing from country to country in an "unsettled vagabond kind of life" for nearly two decades as America's first career diplomat. He had another reason to linger in Europe: his torrid affair with the wife of a French nobleman, Rosalie, the Duchesse de la Rochefoucauld. After her husband (a close friend of Jefferson's) was executed in the French Revolution in 1792, William and Rosalie lived as a couple for some seven years.

In 1795, Jefferson bought land for Short only five miles from Monticello in the hopes that his "adoptive son" would move there. We stop by—the property is now owned by UVA—and glimpse terrain similar to that of Jefferson's, with rolling hills, stone walls and wood fences, and thickets of pine trees. But Jefferson and Short wouldn't become lifelong neighbors; when Short finally returned home in 1809, he based himself in Philadelphia, selling his Virginia property.

Yet he remained close friends with Jefferson and visited him when he could. "Come and see the finest portion of your country which, if you have not forgotten, you still do not know, because it is no longer the same as when you knew it," Jefferson wrote to him in 1819, beckoning him to Virginia one more time. Never stop traveling—even places you've seen before change.

Although Short had his disappointments in life (Rosalie left him for a Frenchman), he achieved financial success in America investing in real estate. He became far wealthier than Jefferson ever was, lending him thousands of dollars and contributing to a fund that (unsuccessfully) sought to settle the ex-president's debts so he could keep Monticello in his family.

Far more so than Jefferson did late in life, Short took action to try to help Black Americans. He became interested in travel accounts of great African cities and civilizations, holding these up as proof that Blacks were equal to Whites. Short had no problem with racial mixture (unlike Jefferson, who objected to interracial coupling even as he secretly fathered children with Sally Hemings). He practically begged his mentor to speak out "in some public way" against the "infamous traffic in human flesh." Short freed two enslaved men he inherited after the death of his brother and supported their efforts to emigrate to Liberia. *Hints* advises travelers to consider how a person's degree of liberty affected his happiness. More so than its writer, William Short took that command seriously.

With the Objects of Attention acknowledged and the Boys' fates reckoned with, I'm left with a farewell that won't be easy: to the man who sparked this odyssey, Thomas Jefferson.

CHAPTER TWENTY-THREE

The Never-Ending Pursuit of Happiness

ONE FOOT OFF THE PEDESTAL, ONE FOOT ON

The three-story brick building on the downtown pedestrian mall displays bas-relief sculptures of Jefferson flanked by James Madison and James Monroe, towering like Roman gods over the mortals below. Jefferson holds our founding document in his left hand and clasps his greatcoat with his right with a satisfied expression, as if to say, what more do you want from me?

A plaque lists his accomplishments—although few visitors in the 1960s, when it was placed at Charlottesville's City Hall, needed reminders of what he had wrought. It includes the trio of deeds he asked to be put on his memorial obelisk at Monticello after his death: "Author of the Declaration of American Independence, of the Virginia Statute of Religious Freedom, and Father of the University of Virginia." And three more for good measure: president of the United States, governor of Virginia, and, in a fit of parochial pride, member of the local bar (the most doable of his feats).

A few paces away stands the Freedom of Speech Wall, a fifty-four-foot-long granite slate on which passersby can write whatever they want in chalk. It was put up by the Thomas Jefferson Center for the Protection of Free Expression in 2006 in homage to the First Amendment and also honoring Jefferson as the apostle of liberty. Today, the messages on the wall support the Black Lives Matter movement.

When I started my trip in 2012, this Jefferson of the City Hall sculpture was the one I had in mind—the Renaissance man, civilized and kind, champion of freedom and, I hoped, giver of life-changing travel advice. This was the man I had lionized since I was a boy. Many people I met on my travels had similar unabashedly positive views of him—starting with the British racer at the Marathon du Médoc who ran up to me to tell me how much she admired him. That same year of 2012, when I dressed as Jefferson to begin my journey, a new eight-hundred-pound bronze statue of him went up in the Virginia State Capitol. It depicts him as a diplomat in Paris in 1788 holding plans for the capitol modeled on the Maison Carrée at Nîmes. An inscription praises him as the Architect of Liberty. There's no mention of slavery anywhere.

The Jefferson of 1788 was of great interest to me, as well to that sculptor—that's when he wrote *Hints* and completed his journey to Amsterdam. If it hadn't been for his travels, there would be far fewer statues of him today. Jefferson left for Europe a grief-stricken widower, disillusioned with politics. He returned not only with groundbreaking ideas on architecture, agriculture, landscaping, and science but with a renewed commitment to fighting for the liberty he saw in the balance in the early days of the French Revolution. Back home he founded a political party and helped enshrine ideals—republicanism and democracy, freedom of religion and press, a government by and for the people—we cherish today. With the Louisiana Purchase, he nearly doubled the size of America, allowing liberty to spread across the continent.

But only for some. Occupying these western lands meant ousting the Native Americans who lived there. And Jefferson permitted the expansion of slavery in the new territories. As I discovered earlier, his backtracking on public support for emancipation traces back to his time in Paris, too. His debts worsened while he was abroad, stymieing any plans to free the people he enslaved. That fateful year of 1788 was when Sally Hemings sailed to Paris. Not long after, Jefferson would father the first of at least six children by her. This side of his complicated, troubling life was never included in the inscriptions on his memorials.

We walk down West Main Street to UVA while I reflect on my one-time hero. I've covered the mile connecting the Downtown Mall to the grounds of the school so many times, first as a student and then as a young lawyer in Charlottesville; each block holds memories for me. We pass by the old brick train station and, catty-corner to it, the apartment Liana and I shared after she arrived from Cuba, back when she was learning English at the nearby Jefferson School.

But knowing what I now know, this promenade takes on a different meaning, revealing a hidden history. Downtown was the center of African American life in Charlottesville for well over a century until urban planners demolished many of their houses in the 1960s, moving Blacks out of sight. By the site of a small carousel today is where Joe Fossett, freed by Jefferson's will, kept his blacksmith shop, desperately trying to earn enough money to buy his son Peter out of bondage. Near an intersection now featuring a hotel and a brewery, Sally Hemings lived with two of her sons after Jefferson's death.

We arrive at UVA's new Memorial to Enslaved Laborers, a circle of granite rising from the earth. On the walls are names of 578 slaves forced to build and maintain the university, like Sam, who constructed roofing for Pavilion VII. Thousands of identities are unknown. Some are signified on the wall by the work they did: servant, gardener, daughter, cook, seamstress, pianist, janitor, brickmason, stonecutter. Other spots are left blank, waiting for future researchers to uncover the names of workers which Jefferson's university never bothered to record.

"This reminds me of the Vietnam Veterans Memorial in D.C.," Liana says. Around us are students of all races and their parents—many are moving their kids in on this early September day, with in-person instruction having been delayed due to the pandemic. The interior of the circles features a water table and timeline of slavery in the U.S., which includes the inscription "1776: Jefferson writes the Declaration of Independence proclaiming that 'all men are created equal.' In his life-time he owned over 600 African Americans in bondage."

We walk the short distance past the serpentine walls to the north side of UVA's Rotunda and spy several original Carrara capitals. They once topped off columns but now rest as historical curiosities in the grass, saved from the building when it burned in 1895. "Do you know where the marble for these things came from, kids?" I ask.

"Yes, we risked our lives going up to that quarry," says Nico. "All for the book." He narrows his eyes. "It better be a good one."

Finally, we reach UVA's Jefferson statue. He's perched on a small platform resting on top of a plinth that resembles the Liberty Bell (who knew he had such a sense of balance), holding the Declaration of Independence determinedly, looking ready to take on the world. The inscription, from 1910, states that the sculpture aims "to perpetuate the teachings and examples of the Founder of the Republic." Angel-like female spirits surround the bell; one holds a tablet with the names of deities carved on it, from Allah to Zeus, signifying religious freedom.

The statue has served as a landmark at the university for genera-tions. I remember once leading fellow members of our student Amnesty International group in a candlelight vigil for political prisoners on a raw night here, warm wax from my candle dripping onto my skin. Jefferson looked down at me like the patron saint of liberty I took him to be, the irony of him holding people captive lost on me.

Object of Attention Six concludes that painting and statuary "are worth seeing but not studying." Now that directive strikes me as part of the problem. Jefferson and his statues and myths have been in back-drop to our lives forever, seen but not studied. Yet if he's up on a pedes-tal, his life deserves critical scrutiny.

In 2020, America engaged in a national debate over how to remember our past. Crowds focused righteous anger on Confederate monuments in particular, toppling many of them, arguing that people who took up arms against our nation in defense of a cruel institution should not be honored. Critics also started a dialogue over how to commemorate Founding Fathers who had owned humans—a sea change from when I started this project, the very year a new statue of Jefferson was going up, his legacy still accepted unquestionably by many. Some today support providing context to such memorials, reminding us that the people who forged our nation also deprived Blacks of their most fundamental rights.

"If Jefferson was wrong, America is wrong," a nineteenth-century historian famously wrote. "If America is right, Jefferson was right." Previous generations had swept Jefferson's failings—crimes even—aside, convinced that undermining his status as a hero would taint views toward the American experiment itself. But what if he's right and wrong? Can he be both? Ultimately, Jefferson is nothing more than a reflection of ourselves, capable both of fighting for freedom and engaging in cruelty, of lifting people up and shutting his mind to the fate of others.

On August 11, 2017, the spot where we're now standing drew national attention. Hundreds of neo-Nazis descended on Charlottesville, pro-testing the planned removal of a statue of Robert E. Lee from a munic-ipal park downtown. (The following day, one in their number would kill a peaceful counterprotester.) That night they marched to the uni-versity and encircled this Jefferson statue, their torches held high, to the same place where my fellow students had clutched our candles for human rights years earlier. They chanted "White lives matter!" and "You will not replace us!" united in fury.

They never reached the statue. Standing in the breach was a small group of UVA students. Although the neo-Nazis far outnumbered them, they didn't yield, locking arms and chanting a message of equality. Their backs were to the sculpture, clinging to it as if rallying around a flag, reclaiming it from these forces of hatred. Surely the students weren't endorsing everything Jefferson did in life, but they nevertheless felt compelled to counter the horde of screaming racists and anti-Semites by symbolically protecting the statue. Despite all his many failings, Jefferson forever believed in the human capacity to improve the world. And that's something worth saving.

Through my trips I see him in a new light: not as a demigod but a fellow traveler who put his boots on one at a time, got lost, had vehicle breakdowns, and searched for places to eat and sleep in strange lands. He discovered palaces and hovels, rivers and mountains, distant horizons far from home. Just like I did.

As I journeyed on, I lost my faith in him, bitterly disappointed by the gap between his high-minded words and duplicitous deeds on slavery. I wouldn't dress up like him for something so lighthearted as a race today. But I ultimately conclude he needs to be remembered, not forgotten, as a complete person with triumphs and failures. Doing so helps keep alive the memory of the African Americans he held in bondage. And despite his grave shortcomings, Jefferson still inspires positive action today: by citizen scientists and stewards of the land, by architects and winemakers and college students facing down a violent mob.

I'll always treasure the *Hints* he gave us. No, he didn't have all the answers. But if a guide at least asks you some good questions—then we can take it from there.

Miranda sidles up to me as I linger at the statue. "Are we done now? Now can I read what you've written, Dad?"

"Not yet, sweetie. Not until we have our last adventure," I respond.

THE FINISH LINE

At the age of seventy-one, Jefferson explored what he took to be the highest mountaintop in Virginia, the loftiest of the three summits called the Peaks of Otter. If you know anything about him by now, you'll know the trek wasn't just for sport. In the company of a Portuguese naturalist and a young Virginian lawyer-botanist, he planned to spend days taking their elevation "and then exploring the sides of them for subjects botanical." He aimed to add the height data to a projected revised version of *Notes on Virginia*. As for what he'd do with any botanical discoveries—well, that depended on what he found.

We drive up to a parking lot at the base of these mountains on a pleasantly warm day. One of the summits, Sharp Top, rises up to our right like a jagged tooth. Naturally, that's the one that caught Jefferson's eye. No one else is there, but rangers had left free maps to the different trails on a table—something you-know-who would have approved of ("some preparation seems necessary"). No doubt he also would have given his blessing to our plans to climb to a high point and look down on the land below, that staple technique he used throughout his travels.

"Should we tackle Sharp Top?" I query the rest of the traveling party. "Hey, Jefferson did it when he was a senior citizen." By a 3–1 vote, a decision is rendered: we'll take on the gentlest of the three peaks, Harkening Hill. I've always been a poor man's Jefferson. Why stop now?

First, though, I fish out a bottle I had been saving, Schloss Johannisberg, a riesling we got in Germany. At that winery in a château, I had felt dejected when a guided tour and tasting didn't work out—but we rallied to assemble a DIY tasting, fending for ourselves, an essential lesson for the then-aspiring traveler.

"Drinking before we hike? I'm only going to have a little," Liana says prudently.

"It'll be just like the wine marathon," I promise. "You'll forget about the alcohol when we get going." The race that kicked off this crazy journey is on my mind, too: today's September 8, the eighth anniversary of our run, which brought us tastes of fabled wines and hints of a world of promise that awaited should we take this challenge on. Today we reach the finish line.

We both take a swig straight from the bottle. "It's sweet—then I taste a rush of flowers and honey," Liana reports. While the parents drink, the kids rush the trail, eager to start. Even though we picked the lowest of the peaks, the trail still shoots steeply uphill. Trees soar over a sea of delicate ferns and decaying bracken giving off a pungent smell. All we hear is the whine of cicadas. I spy an interpretive sign on another trail paralleling ours and bushwhack down an incline to read it. Suddenly I'm falling, tumbling down the hill until I roll to a stop.

"Are you OK?" Liana calls out.

"Yeah, I stepped on that log and it gave way under me." I look down. My hand is cut; I'm perspiring, my shirt damp. "A little blood but I'm fine," I report to Liana. Only fitting. It's been a journey of blood, sweat, and tears to get to this point. (No, check that—just blood and sweat. Just like there's no crying in baseball, there will be none in *Hints*. I hope.)

We keep hiking, up, up, the kids singing ahead of us on the trail. I think back to that hike we all did at Harpers Ferry seven years ago—Miranda and Nico are so much bigger now, eager and able to tackle this hill. We see some bear scat and from then on walk in a tighter group, yelling out "Hey, bear!" from time to time. But my family remains in good spirits. I try to look as happy as they do. The clock's ticking on a journey I don't want to end, although I know it needs to.

We pass the time performing a little citizen science. Earlier we downloaded an app called iNaturalist, which allows users to post pictures of plants and animals and identify species while generating crowdsourced data for researchers. As we hike, we snap photos of yellow crownbeard, snowberries, invasive knotweed, pale purple self-heals, and dancing swallowtail butterflies. (I scientifically confirm there are no moose to be found on the mountain.)

The trail flattens out. We rest a little on top of a pile of boulders, then steel ourselves for a last push up to the top of a ridge. Nico, the smallest of all of us, announces he's tired. We all have heavy legs, but we push on. A sign on the last kilometer of the wine marathon read "*Terminer en Beauté*," End in Beauty. And when we round a bend and see the summit, a vista of blue-green mountains in the distance and a valley dotted with farms below, that's exactly what we've done.

We find a flat rock and spread out a picnic blanket; we have the whole mountain to ourselves. It's time for our farewell lunch, and we bring out some special food for the occasion. At our Airbnb, Liana and Miranda had fried up crunchy *arancini*, balls made from the Piedmont rice I brought home (purchased, not smuggled) from Elisa's farm near Milan. We munch on teatime sandwiches, refined enough to eat in an English garden pavilion (a prospect that would make Miranda shudder). Liana unwraps cod croquettes, which call up memories of the fishing boats coming into Guilvinec in the twilight. And herring rolls, as tangy and juicy as the ones we had in Amsterdam; the kids take a pass on those. I bring out a wine from my backpack that I had ordered online as a surprise, a 2012 Château Montrose.

"Do you know the significance of this?" I ask Liana eagerly. "Do you recognize it, honey?"

"Not exactly."

"This is the vineyard you did your business in during the race. These grapes were harvested not too long after that."

If you think this would faze Liana, you don't know her by now. "Mmm, it's powerful, yet smooth and balanced," she says. "I think it's even silky. And it's really matured now."

"It had the best fertilizer," I respond.

A picnic eight years in the making.

Contented and stuffed, we lie back and watch the hawks gliding over the valley below. Finally, I break the silence and ask everyone for their favorite moment on our journey.

"For some reason I really remember our nighttime meals," says Miranda. "We were always out doing things and arriving super late for dinner. We'd be so hungry. And we learned about culture through the food. I love to cook now." During the pandemic, with time on her hands, she's been fixing dinner and dessert for us several times a week. "I remember the *spaghetti carbonara* we had late at night in Rome," she continues. "It was so creamy and delicious. We'd never had it before. And

I loved it in Provence when Grandma would wake me up and say, 'It's time to go get the bread.' And we'd walk and get those flaky croissants, fresh out of the baker's oven. That was my favorite breakfast," she says and pauses. "It still is."

"I loved Provence so much too," says Nico, "going there with the grandparents. It was my first trip outside of the country. And I love all the gardens I saw. I love it when there's orderly chaos. That's what Jefferson liked and I do, too. He didn't want to line up his plants like soldiers in an army. Gardens are supposed to be magical."

"I loved everything," says Liana. "The little trips and the big fancy trips. The whole journey has been something that's defined our family and gave it a purpose. This was our thing."

"I hate to hear you say 'was,'" I say. "It's still going on. For a few more minutes," I pause. "And then we'll find something else."

"This has been something our kids will talk to their kids about," Liana replies. "This is part of our history."

From my backpack, I pull out my last trick: a thin bottle of dessert wine from Il Monticello, where Alessandre gave us his hand-waving explanation of how he made it. We all think back to that day three years ago, the manic ascent of Carrara, a meal shared among the olive trees. The wine goes down easy, sweet and unctuous like nectar, tasting of honey and apricots.

It was moments like that at Il Monticello that made the journey so worthwhile. Walking through the stone streets of Saorge high in the Alps late at night. Watching an old man in a beret haul fish off a boat. Stirring warm curds to make *primo sale Derek* cheese. I learned about so many subjects, and more than I ever dreamed I would about Jefferson, but it was the thousands of scenes of tiny human drama I experienced along the way that will stick with me.

I'm proud I could share these moments with my children in their age of wonder. And with Dad, still vigorous when we set out together on the road. He might not remember all our trips together, but I do. And when someday I can't either, they'll be down on paper. Someone might read about them and get to know him a little bit, too, and smile.

I'm proud that Liana ran her race. She was with me nearly every step of the way, appreciating architecture and painting and wine, slipping me the answers about the aesthetics of these subjects. She sacrificed much to give me the time I needed to research, accepting a Founding Father into the family. I'm proud that Miranda discovered the flavors of Italy and a new interest in cooking foods from other lands. That Nico started his garden and absorbed so much about other cultures. And that I discovered this passion I never knew I had, of sharing my story on the page. Maybe I'll even try to write something again someday. (Did John Adams travel anywhere?)

Ultimately, my quest was not in search of Jefferson but of myself. I began worried that life was passing me by, that soon it would be too late to fulfill my dreams. Now I'm squarely in middle age but not afraid of it. I found a world to explore, with questions to answer and adventures to be had. I'll never be a Jefferson, a true Renaissance Man, but I'm happy with who I've become: an eternal work in progress, ready for the next stop on this never-ending pursuit of happiness.

"All right, I guess it's time to go back down," I say.

"Wait, come in, let's hug first," says Liana. We squeeze together in a tight circle, soaking up these last seconds.

"This changed my life," says Nico.

"Thank you for gifting this to us," says Liana.

"It was such an awesome journey," Miranda says. "And now it's complete." It's my turn, but it's hard to find the words. I look at the cut on my hand, feel the sweat drenching my shirt. Blood, sweat—and now that third fluid unexpectedly flows down my cheeks.

It's time.

"We all did it," I begin, my voice cracking. I'll have to talk fast if I want to get any words out while still appearing reasonably fatherlike.

"Well kids, you wanted to read what I've written. And when we're down off this mountain you can. But I know the beginning by heart. It goes like this: Napoleon loosens up to my left."

Nico gives a soft laugh and squeezes my arm. "Napoleon?"

"Yes. Napoleon loosens up to my left and Roman legionaries stretch in front of me. But I am the only Thomas Jefferson at the starting line."

Acknowledgments

First, thanks to all the people we met along the way (a few names were changed for privacy) who kindly shared their stories. And especially Mathieu, Rachel, and *famille: on se voit l'année prochaine!*

Thanks to all the members of the Arlington Creative Nonfiction Group, especially Tim Grove for showing me the path, Michael Lasher for walking it with me, and Mathina Calliope for sharing the trail magic I needed to become a writer. I could not have finished without you three.

Thanks to Fernando Franco—these Acknowledgments pair perfectly with an Octagon. Thanks to Richard Guy Wilson for helping teach me how to see a building. And I have to give a yell, as the song says, to all my UVA friends who helped and encouraged me, you know who you are!

Thanks to Monticello, including Endrina Tay, Anna Berkes, Fraser Nieman, Peggy Cornett, Keith Nevison, Bill Barker, Pat Brodowski, Gayle Jessup White, and Mary Blair Zakaib. I also owe a debt to Lucia "Cinder" Stanton and her colleagues for their decades of work uncovering Jefferson's past and those of the enslaved. Additionally, I first met Tom Burford, aka Professor Apple, at Monticello; he passed away in 2020 and is remembered with fondness.

Thanks to Thomas Jefferson for being so obsessive that he took notes on everything and kept them.

Thanks to my wonderful agent, Amanda Jain, for advocating for this project. Much thanks to my fantastic editors, Anna Michels and Jenna Jankowski, for their creative input and for pushing me to find the deeper meanings of my story. And to Sara Walker and Sarah Otterness for wordsmithing that was always spot on (or was it spot-on?).

Most of all, thanks to my family. To Dad for teaching me how to be funny and to Mom for teaching me how to be organized. For once I've done both at the same time.

Thanks to Nicolas, for bringing his nonstop energy and enthusiasm to our travels, and to Miranda, for sharing her grace and optimism. Someday, let's check in on those English gardens again!

Most of all, thank you to Liana, for traveling down this road with me with love.

Reading Group Guide

1. What do you think of the itinerary Jefferson drew up? If you could add another location to his itinerary, where would it be and why?

2. Discuss the key points of interest in Jefferson's *Hints*. Which did you find most interesting? Did you find ways of exploring his points of interest in your own life?

3. Derek finds himself stuck in place at the beginning of his journey. Have you ever found yourself in a similar situation? If so, what did you do to get out of the rut?

4. Jefferson is most widely known as the author of the Declaration of Independence and as the third president of the United States, but what was the most surprising thing you learned about him from this book?

5. Of all the trips Derek and his family took in pursuit of Jefferson, which one would you most like to go on?

6. It's difficult to reconcile Jefferson as an influential Founding Father as well as a slave owner. Did your vision of him change by the end of the book?

7. How did enslaved people at Monticello find paths to freedom? For those who could not escape, how did they preserve their culture in the context of a cruel institution?

8. Sharing his experiences with family and friends makes Derek's travels more meaningful. What do you think are the benefits of traveling with others?

9. When facing adversity—in the form of a global pandemic—Derek finds a way to celebrate Jefferson's lessons with his family while staying safe at home. What are ways you can apply these principles to your everyday life?

10. In what ways has travel changed since Jefferson wrote *Hints*? In what ways has it stayed the same?

A Conversation with the Author

We know you've been a Jefferson fanatic your whole life—can you remember the first moment you realized your fascination with the Founding Father?

There's a photo of me standing by the fishpond at Monticello in corduroys when I was about six. My interest in him comes from around that time, or at a visit to Colonial Williamsburg around the same age. When I was young, I used to devour books about our early history, and Jefferson—our brainy, can-do Founder—always stood above the rest.

This project is such a massive undertaking—the writing, the travel, the research—it's been years in the making. How did you keep everything straight when finally putting the book together?

The lawyer's curse: we have a high threshold for painstaking research and a mania for organization. Liana can begrudgingly attest that an entire room of our house, what we call the Jefferson Room, is full of wooden cabinets stuffed with folders of notes and documents and bookcases stocked with volumes on you-know-who. Now that I'm done, much of this space will likely be reclaimed by the powers that be. I only can hope the Jefferson bobblehead who presides over the room will escape deportation to the basement.

I've spent a lot of quality time in our Jefferson Room, especially when it came time to prepare the endnotes. The writing of the book went down nicely with a smooth glass of wine; preparing the seemingly endless endnotes required whiskey, straight up. Actually, enough talk about the endnotes; it's too soon.

What's the most absurd fact or anecdote you uncovered in your research that didn't make it into the book?

There are so many. My favorite is the scholarly treatise I came across about Jefferson's latrines. (It was actually a good read, perfect for leafing through when…oh, never mind.)

You mention in the book that your whole family was supportive of the project, but how did they initially take the idea?

Liana was 100 percent on board from the beginning and remained so throughout. I couldn't have asked for a more supportive partner; she made many sacrifices to give me the time to work on this. The kids were very young at the start but rolled with it. They loved every trip we went on. Luckily for them, it wasn't all Jefferson; I built in some side trips to various kid-friendly places that I didn't include in the book. Also, we stopped off for a few days in Iceland when we flew Icelandair on one trip and did the same in Turkey, flying on Turkish Airlines—those countries amazed us all. If only Jefferson had visited either place, we might have stayed longer.

Having to cloister myself away to do the writing was tough on all of us, but it helped that we have such a strong family support network, with Liana's parents living with us and mine just a few miles away.

How about any trips or experiences that didn't make it into the book?

Thanks to the Google alert I had for "Thomas Jefferson," in 2014 I learned of an unusual-sounding play featuring a rapping Jefferson that was going to open Off-Broadway in a few months and purchased a pair of tickets that very minute. After I told Liana about my impulse buy, however, I began to get cold feet, fretting about the expense. "Do you think I could go on StubHub and get our money back?" I asked her. "Would anyone else pay $90 for a ticket to go see—what's it called—*Hamilton*?"

Thankfully, sanity (that is to say, Liana) prevailed.

Do you find that you're able to apply what you've learned from your travels to normal life? If so, in what ways?

Discovering so much about the Objects of Attention was fun. I knew hardly anything about most of these subjects before I started, and it felt like going back to college again. Which might have been the point. Now it feels good to walk around with a newfound appreciation for things I used to ignore.

I'm no expert, but I now see architecture and landscape gardens in a different way. Neither one meant anything to me before; now I notice buildings and gardens and want to try to understand them. And I think my adventures with the bottle came through loud and clear. Wine-tasting seemed incredibly snobbish and esoteric to me before; now I appreciate the work that goes into producing wine and the connection it can give you to a time and place.

The greatest thing I learned from Jefferson was to read voraciously and then get out there and explore. Take your time to study what's around you, and when you can, reflect on your journey. Even now as I embark on my post-*Hints* life, I don't plan to forget that lesson.

Can you talk a little bit about the conflict most people feel toward Jefferson as a slave owner and a Founding Father? Do you think we should apply contemporary ethics to historical figures?

For centuries, Americans have placed Jefferson at the center of our national Founding myth. But many of us rationalized and minimized the gap between his words "all men are created equal" and his legacy of slaveholding. It's true that he was far from the only slaveholder. But most of us expected more from him; he was so forward-thinking. He wrote that the institution was "evil"—so it seems vastly disappointing (or worse) to many that he persisted as a slaveholder.

Some would say that criticizing Jefferson for his failing is "presentism," holding him up to current sensibilities, not those of the eighteenth century. Yet I included the example of George Washington and Edward Coles, two Virginians who did free their slaves. And I referenced the work of people who did keep pushing for abolition, or taking some action, even on a small scale, like William Short. In Jefferson's time, some Southern landowners who shared his Enlightenment values actually acted on them.

I will say that writing the chapters on slavery was by far the most painful part of this journey. It's sickening to read about that time in American history and remember how millions of our countrymen suffered. And discovering all the things Jefferson did, or did not do, as a slave owner felt like receiving one gut punch after another.

I'm glad that researchers at Monticello have uncovered the histories of some enslaved people and we can now all learn about how they lived—not only recognizing the importance of the power their master held over them but also considering the value of their lives in their own right, apart from their effect on his.

Jefferson is obviously an influential figure in your life, but what other authors—or books—have helped you along the way?

Reading Annie Dillard's *Pilgrim at Tinker Creek* first made me want to write. I went on to draw inspiration from other writers who blend history, travel, and humor, like Bill Bryson, the late Tony Horwitz, Sarah Vowell, and my patron saint, the English author Tim Moore. Also Michael Pollan, Ta-Nehisi Coates, Mark Kurlansky, and many others. Not the least of whom is John McPhee, the Joe DiMaggio of creative nonfiction. Although his writing looks effortless, he's confessed that he labors over every word—a tremendous example for a rookie writer. And of course I owe a tremendous debt to the many scholars who have written about Jefferson's life and times, many of whom I mention in the endnotes.

As a father, what do you hope your two children take away from this journey?

They already have taken away so much, especially a love of the world and travel. By now they've turned into co-planners of our journeys. I can't wait to see where we go next.

Of all Jefferson's teachings, which do you think is most beneficial to us today?

The theme of religious liberty wasn't prominent in *Hints* itself and I only mention it a few times in the book. But Jefferson did as much as anyone to establish religious freedom in our country and he deserves much credit for that.

Most of all, I love his quote, "I like the dreams of the future better than the history of the past." That's perhaps an odd one to highlight for a book focused on history so much. Yet there could be nothing more Jeffersonian than not just understanding the world but changing it.

Illustration Credits

Page 112. Miranda appreciating gardens, courtesy of Liana Miranda

Page 125. Liana in the olives, author photo

Page 134. The author and kids in Gragnano, courtesy of Liana Miranda

Page 142. The author making cheese, author photo

Page 156. Bullfighting in Arles, courtesy of Liana Miranda

Page 160. Nîmes, courtesy of Liana Miranda

Page 160. Model of the Virginia State Capitol by Jean-Pierre Fouquet, courtesy of the Library of Virginia

Page 164. Carrara, courtesy of Liana Miranda

Page 172. The author by the TJ statue in Paris, author photo

Page 175. Monticello, by the Historic American Buildings Survey, courtesy of the Library of Congress, Prints and Photographs Division

Page 179. Drawing of the Rotunda, courtesy of Thomas Jefferson Architectural Drawings, University Archives, Special Collections, University of Virginia

Page 194. Nantes, courtesy of Liana Miranda

Page 197. Runaway advertisement for Sandy, courtesy of the Virginia Museum of History & Culture (*Virginia Gazette*, February 9, 1769)

Page 201. Stowage of the British slave ship "Brookes" under the Regulated Slave Trade Act of 1788, courtesy of the Library of Congress, Rare Book and Special Collections Division

Page 218 Inventory by James Hemings, Feb. 20, 1796, courtesy of the Library of Congress, Manuscript Division

Page 224. Isaac Granger, courtesy of the Tracy W. McGregor Library of American History, Albert and Shirley Small Special Collections Department, University of Virginia Library

Page 238 Peter Fossett, from Wendell P. Dabney, *Cincinnati's Colored Citizens* (Cincinnati: Dabney Publishing Co., 1926)

Page 247. *Le Peuple sous l'ancien Régime*, courtesy of the Library of Congress, Prints and Photograph Division

Page 255. *Arrestation de Mr. de Launay, gouverneur de la Bastille, le 14 Juillet 1789* by Pierre Gabriel Berthault and François Louis Prieur in *Collection complète des tableaux historiques de la révolution française* (Paris: chez Auber, 1804), courtesy of the Library of Congress, Prints and Photograph Division

Page 268. *Gilets jaunes*, author photo

Page 275. Moose or Elk from George Shaw and John Frederick Miller, *Cimelia physica: Figures of rare and curious quadrupeds, birds, &c. together with several of the most elegant plants* (London: printed by T. Bensley for Benjamin and John White and John Sewell, 1796)

Page 280. *Voyage Autour du Mont-Blanc* from Horace-Bénédict Saussure, *Voyages dans les Alpes* (Geneva: S. Fauche Neuchatel, 1779), courtesy of the Library of Congress, Rare Books and Special Collections Division

Page 297. The author and Liana on the Brittany coast, courtesy of Liana Miranda

Page 302. The author with an exceedingly large fish, courtesy of Liana Miranda

Page 317. Poplar Forest window, courtesy of Liana Miranda and by permission of the Corporation for Jefferson's Poplar Forest

Page 332. Picnic, courtesy of Liana Miranda

Page 406. Author bio pic, courtesy of Liana Miranda

Abbreviations

DAM Damien Lee Fowler, *Dining at Monticello: In Good Taste and Abundance* (Chapel Hill: UNC Press, 2005).

FB Edwin Morris Betts, *Thomas Jefferson's Farm Book* (Charlottesville: UVA Press, 1987).

FO Founders Online, a project of the National Archives that makes documents of the American Founders publicly available, in cooperation with UVA Press; https://founders.archives.gov. FO includes the Jefferson Papers published by Princeton University Press as well as the Jefferson Retirement Series, edited by the Thomas Jefferson Foundation.

JTV Dumas Malone, *Jefferson the Virginian* (Boston: Little, Brown and Co., 1948).

MB Memorandum Books, the detailed account books kept by TJ for most of his life, edited by James Bear, Jr., and Lucia Stanton, Princeton University Press, available online via FO.

NSV Thomas Jefferson, *Notes on the State of Virginia*, William Peden, ed. (Chapel Hill: UNC Press, 1954).

RSE Peter Hatch, *"A Rich Spot of Earth": Thomas Jefferson's Revolutionary Garden* (New Haven: Yale University Press, 2012).

ROM Dumas Malone, *Thomas Jefferson and the Rights of Man* (New York: Little, Brown and Co., 1951).

TDLTJ Sarah Randolph, *The Domestic Life of Thomas Jefferson* (NY: Harper and Brothers, 1871).

THM Annette Gordon-Reed, *The Hemingses of Monticello: An American Family* (New York: W. W. Norton and Co., 2008).

TJ If you don't know who this is by now, read the book again (more slowly this time).

TJA TJ Autobiography, 6 Jan.–29 Jan., 1821, FO "early access" document.

TJE Thomas Jefferson Encyclopedia, a collection of over a thousand articles mostly prepared by researchers at the Thomas Jefferson Foundation.

TJP Howard C. Rice, Jr., *Thomas Jefferson's Paris* (Princeton: Princeton University Press, 1976).

TWL Lucia Stanton, *Those Who Labor for My Happiness: Slavery at Thomas Jefferson's Monticello* (Charlottesville: UVA Press, 2012).

WTJ Susan Stein, *The Worlds of Thomas Jefferson at Monticello* (New York: Abrams, 1993).

Notes

Note: In this book, I changed TJ's spelling and grammar at times to reflect modern usage. I mostly did the same for other eighteenth- and nineteenth-century writers, although I occasionally left the writing "as is" for effect (as with Archibald Cary). I accessed the websites listed in the sources below in December 2020.

CHAPTER ONE: THE STARTING LINE

built like a fine horse—Edmund Bacon in James A. Bear, Jr., *Jefferson at Monticello* (Charlottesville: UVA Press, 1967), 71. "Physical Descriptions of Jefferson," TJE, https://monticello.org/site/research-and-collections /physical-descriptions-jefferson.

small notebook with ivory pages—TJ to Thomas Mann Randolph, Apr. 18, 1790; WTJ, 103. You can view it in Monticello's museum today.

his greatest accomplishment was known only to a few—Robert McDonald, "Thomas Jefferson's Changing Reputation as Author of the Declaration of Independence: The First Fifty Years," *Journal of the Early Republic* 19 (Summer 1999), 170, 178–181; Pauline Maier, *American Scripture: Making the Declaration of Independence* (New York: Alfred A. Knopf, 1997), 162. His authorship of the Declaration was not widely known until the 1790s, when his political allies began promoting it.

a two-month sojourn in England—MB, 1786, FO.

ostensibly to take mineral waters—TJ to John Jay, Jan. 9, 1787, FO.

tasted wines and made contacts with producers—The two best books on Jefferson and his favorite liquid, each featuring lengthy discussions of Jefferson's Bordeaux habit, are James Gabler's *Passions, The Wines and Travels of Thomas Jefferson* (Baltimore: Bacchus Press, 1995) and John Hailman's *Thomas Jefferson on Wine* (Jackson: University Press of Mississippi, 2006). Just thinking of these books makes me want to read them again by the fireside with a glass of claret. (Better yet, two glasses, one for each book.)

a work trip to Amsterdam—Notes on a Tour through Holland and the Rhine Valley, 3 March 1788–23 April 1788, FO.

"I am constantly roving about"—TJ to Lafayette, Apr. 11, 1787, FO.

Hints to Americans Traveling in Europe—June 19, 1788, FO. Although TJ never published it, the five-thousand-page letter is comprehensive enough to resemble a guide book. The Library of Congress has made public photos of the original *Hints*: https://www.loc.gov/resource/mtj1.010_0680_0688/?st=gallery.

"voluptuary dress and arts of European women"—TJ to John Banister, Jr., Oct. 15, 1785, FO.

The fledgling republic was teetering financially—Drew R. McCoy, *Elusive Republic: Political Economy in Jeffersonian America* (Chapel Hill: UNC Press, 1980), 103–105.

sitting at the feet of my mentor's statue—I liked to study near the statue of a seated Jefferson at the end of the Lawn, near Pavilion IX (not the more well-known statue north of the Rotunda).

covering a mile in a brisk fourteen and a half minutes—undated memorandum now appended to TJ to James Madison, June 20, 1787, FO.

he'd find time to explore his world—TJ to Madame de Corny, June 30, 1787, FO (describing daily walks through the Bois de Boulogne); TJ to Thomas Mann Randolph, Nov. 16, 1801 (riding as president). For inspiring quotes to motivate you on your next workout, check out "Exercise," TJE, https://monticello.org/site/research-and-collections/exercise, which details TJ's love of regular walks and rides.

a "walking encyclopedia"—TDLTJ, 37.

"calculate an eclipse"—James Parton, *Life of Thomas* Jefferson (Boston: James R. Osgood and Company, 1874), 165. I'm not sure he ever tied an artery, but he did the rest of the activities claimed and then some.

Château Lafite Rothschild—Notes of a Tour into Southern Parts of France etc., 3 March–10 June, 1787, FO. In 1985, Malcolm Forbes purchased the most expensive bottle of wine in history, $156,000 for a Lafite supposedly bought by Jefferson on his trip.

CHAPTER TWO: SOMETHING NEW UNDER THE SUN

rough, overly sweet Madeira—TJ to Stephen Cathalan, before June 6, 1817, FO; Alex Liddell, *Madeira: The Mid-Atlantic Wine* (London: Hurst and Co., 1998) 33–43. Although if you offer me a glass of vintage Madeira today, I won't turn it down.

"rambled"—TJ to William Short, Mar. 15, 1787.

plucked snails, grafted vines—Notes of a Tour into Southern Parts of France, etc., 3 March–10 June, 1787, FO.

bought vine cuttings and bottles—TJ to Geismar, July 13, 1788 FO; MB 1788, 1789, FO.

the happiest days of his life—TJ to John Banister, Jr., June 19, 1787 (TJ wrote that he "never passed three months and a half more delightfully").

Jefferson's rankings, the Napoleonic hierarchy—Gabler, *Passions*, 118, 120, 122.

Only the producer provided the "genuine" article—TJ to Alexander Donald, May 13, 1791, FO.

He would travel home from France with 363 bottles in tow—Hailman, *Thomas Jefferson on Wine*, 197.

most châteaux in Bordeaux date from the nineteenth century—Hugh Johnson, *Vintage: The Story of Wine* (New York: Simon and Schuster, 1989), 375–377.

Thomas Shippen—Paul C. Nigel, *The Lees of Virginia: Seven Generations of an American Family* (New York: Oxford University Press, 1990), 116; ROM, 145. William Shippen, Jr., Thomas's father, was the physician for the Continental Army and treated TJ on several occasions. Like TJ, he was a member of the American Philosophical Society. William married Alice Lee of the famous Virginia dynasty—hence Thomas's middle name, Lee.

John Rutledge, Jr.—Biographical Directory of the U.S. Congress, "Rutledge, John Jr., 1766-1819," https://bioguideretro.congress.gov/Home/MemberDetails?memIndex=R000553; ROM, 145. Rutledge's father had been a delegate to the Continental Congress when TJ was there and served as governor of South Carolina when Jefferson was governor of Virginia. The young man's uncle Edward was the youngest signer of the Declaration of Independence.

William Short—George Green Shackelford, *Jefferson's Adoptive Son* (Lexington: University Press of Kentucky,

1993); "William Short," TJE, https://monticello.org/site/research-and-collections/william-short. Of the Boys, William Short by far had the longest relationship with TJ. Short was a somewhat distant relation of TJ's late wife, Martha. He accompanied the Jefferson family in their flight from the British at Monticello to safety at Poplar Forest; MB 1781, FO. A contemporary of James Madison (eight years younger) and James Monroe (one year younger), like them he was a Virginia lawyer and TJ protégé—but he never achieved their same political success, which bothered him. In his portrait by Rembrandt Peale he has thin brown hair and an unassuming, slightly haunted look, a doppelganger for the singer Paul Simon.

"We can no longer say"—TJ to Joseph Priestly, Mar. 21, 1801, FO.

Shippen dropped out; the other two skipped the Médoc—William Short to TJ, Oct. 28, 1788, FO; Short to TJ, Apr. 28, 1789, FO.

"the land of corn"—TJ to Short, Mar. 27, 1787, FO.

"They dung a little"—Notes of a Tour into Southern Parts of France etc., 3 March–10 June, 1787, FO.

bottles to George Washington—TJ to John Jay, Sept. 17, 1789, FO; TJ to Short, Sept. 6, 1790, FO.

"The sooner the race is begun"—Short to TJ, Mar. 2, 1789, FO; TJ to Short, Mar. 27, 1789, FO; Short to TJ, Apr. 3, 1789, FO.

CHAPTER THREE: TRAVELING LIKE JEFFERSON

"trudge on"—TJ to John Page, Jan. 20, 1763, FO.

living at home with his mother and six siblings—TJ had nine siblings in total. Two died as infants and one, Mary, married and left home in 1760.

"Thrown into the society"—TJ to Thomas Jefferson Randolph, Nov. 24, 1808, FO "early access" document.

"evil" institution—NSV, 87.

Talked "the most nonsense"—TJ to John Page, Dec. 25, 1762.

surveyor and cartographer—TJA.

"remarkable powers of endurance"—TDLTJ, 19–20.

traveled Indian trails to prepare the definitive map of the colony—TJA; NSV, 18; TDLTJ n, 19–20; William C. Wooldridge, *Mapping Virginia: From the Age of Exploration to the Civil War* (Charlottesville: UVA Press, 2012), 111–114.

hosted Cherokee leaders at his house—TJ to John Adams, June 11, 1812.

his surveying equipment and books—TJA; JTV, 32; Susan Kern, *The Jeffersons at Shadwell* (New Haven: Yale University Press, 2010), 33–34, 180.

"When young, I was passionately fond of reading"—TJ to the editor of the *Journal de Paris*, 29 Aug. 1787, FO.

Voyage Around the World and *Description of America*—Kern, *The Jeffersons at Shadwell*, 35–37.

loved the outdoors and became an exceptional horseman—Bear, *Jefferson at Monticello*, 5, 17, 21, 60; Henry Randall, *The Life of Thomas Jefferson* (Philadelphia: J. B. Lippincott, 1858), Vol. I, 68; TJ to John de Barth, Mar. 17, 1792, FO; TJE, "Exercise."

yearned for culture and learning—TJ to John Harvie, Jan. 14, 1760, FO.

ambassadors of the Enlightenment—TJA; TJ to Louis H. Girardin, Jan. 15, 1815; JTV, 98–105; Jonathan Israel, *Democratic Enlightenment* (New York: Oxford University Press, 2012), 1–7.

England, France, Holland, and Italy—TJ to John Page, Jan. 20, 1763, FO.

barrels over poorly maintained roads—T. H. Breen, *Tobacco Culture: The Mentality of Great Tidewater Planters on the Eve of Revolution* (Princeton: Princeton University Press, 1985), 51–53; Arthur Pierce Middleton, *Tobacco Coast: A Maritime History of Chesapeake Bay in the Colonial Era* (Johns Hopkins: Baltimore, 1984), 113; Barbara McEwan, *Thomas Jefferson: Farmer* (Jefferson, NC: McFarland and Co., 1991), 48–49; TWL, 27; TJE, "Road to Monticello," https://monticello.org/site/research-and-collections/road-monticello.

the Dutch pottery Thomas's mother prized—Kern, *The Jeffersons at Shadwell*, 82.

canals—FB, 341–411; TJ to Thomas Mann Randolph, Feb. 3, 1793, FO.

"the great rivers"—John Adams to Benjamin Rush, Jan. 25, 1806, FO "early access" document.

authorize the removal of boulders—Project for Making the Rivanna River Navigable, 1771, FO.

a seat in the House of Burgesses—JTV, 121.

recorded his life accomplishments—Summary of Public Service [after 2 September 1800], FO (note that this was a private memorandum; he didn't publish it).

traveled often to Williamsburg—MB, 1769, 1770, FO.

a "lithe and exquisitely formed figure"—"Martha Wayles Skelton Jefferson," TJE, https://monticello.org/site/research-and-collections/martha-wayles-skelton-jefferson#:~:text=Martha%20Wayles%20Skelton%20Jefferson%20(October,after%20her%20daughter%20was%20born. The quote is from her granddaughter, Ellen Randolph Coolidge. See also William G. Hyland, Jr., *Martha Jefferson: An Intimate Life with Thomas Jefferson* (New York: Rowman and Littlefield, 2015), 5–7.

a lanky, awkward, mild-mannered redhead—JTV 48. Earlier, as a twenty-year-old, when he attempted to woo a young woman, Jefferson had prepared a speech "in as moving language as I knew how," yet "only a few broken sentences, uttered in great disorder, and interrupted with pauses of uncommon length" came out. The twenty-year-old me would have sympathized. TJ to John Page, Oct. 7, 1763.

"love of music and the world"—TDLTJ, 44. The only surviving book with Martha's signature in it (indicating she had owned it before their marriage in 1772) was *The Adventures of Telemachus*, which featured, as its author stated, an intriguing map of the Mediterranean "curiously Engraved by very good Hands."

adored the books of Laurence Sterne—Virginia Scharff, *The Women Jefferson Loved* (New York: HarperCollins, 2010), 78, 148; Andrew Burstein, *The Inner Jefferson: Portrait of a Grieving Optimist* (Charlottesville: UVA Press, 1995), 42-56, 60-62.

"uncheckered happiness"—TJA.

She fell ill each time she gave birth—THM 141.

Only two of her six children would survive—TJE, "Martha Wayles Skelton Jefferson."

Traveled to the Continental Congress—MBM, 1775, FO.

so he could return to tend to Martha—TJ to Richard Henry Lee, July 16, 1776, FO.

requested he join Franklin but he declined—John Hancock to TJ, Sept. 30, 1776; and TJ to John Hancock, Oct. 11, 1776.

elected governor; projects for reform—JTV, 261–285.

enemy forces landed; the British overran much of the state—John Selby, *The Revolution in Virginia, 1775–83* (Williamsburg: Colonial Williamsburg Foundation, 1988), 221–224, 265–281; Michael Kranish, *Flight from Monticello: Thomas Jefferson at War* (New York: Oxford University Press, 2010), 163–199; "Diary of Arnold's Invasion and Notes on Subsequent Events in 1781," FO.

dragoons charged—Kranish, *Flight from Monticello*, 283. "Diary of Arnold's Invasion and Notes on Subsequent Events in 1781," FO provides Jefferson's view; THM, 138–140, and THL, 101, 133–134, explores the event from the perspective of enslaved people. At the TJ Foundation's annual recreation of this event, my children drilled in formation with sticks as part of a volunteer militia. Not a single dragoon entered Monticello during their watch.

Jefferson escaped—Kranish, *Flight from Monticello*, 283–285; MB 1782, FO.

charged him with weakness—JTV, 361–362; Archibald Cary to TJ, June 19, 1781, FO; TJ to Isaac Zane, Dec. 24, 1781, FO (blaming Patrick Henry).

"I have retired to my farm"—TJ to Edmund Randolph, Sept. 16, 1781, FO.

"combining public service with private gratification"—TJ to Lafayette, Aug. 4, 1781, FO; TJA, FO.

"Folded...in the arms of retirement"—TJ to Chastellux, Nov. 26, 1782.

his plantings and a geography—MB, 1782, FO; Edwin Betts, ed., *Thomas Jefferson's Garden Book* (Redmond: Thomas Jefferson Foundation, 2008), 94–95; NSV, xiii–xv.

Martha died—TDLTJ 63; Bear, *Jefferson at Monticello*, 99–100. TJ recorded in his Memorandum Book for September 6 "my dear wife died today at 11:45 a.m."

spent the summer fighting fever—TJ to James Monroe, May 20, 1782, FO (TJ revealed that his wife continued "dangerously ill").

"Time wastes too fast"—Lines copied from *Tristram Shandy* by Martha and Thomas Jefferson [Before 6 September 1782], FO.

"dead to the world"—TJ to Chastellux, Nov. 26, 1782, FO.

stayed in his library—Randall, vol. I, 382.

"melancholy rambles"—TDLTJ, 63.

"accepted a post"—TJA; Robert R. Livingston to TJ, Enclosing Jefferson's Appointment as a Peace Commissioner, Nov. 13, 1782, FO. Before learning that the treaty was signed, TJ made an attempt to sail out of Baltimore in January 1783, but was unable to rejoin the French frigate waiting for him out in the Chesapeake Bay due to the ice present. Dad and I recreated TJ's trip in our canoe once on a mild December day. We, too, turned back after a while—after Dad noticed water seeping into our Grumman.

He won a seat in Congress—Edmund Randolph to James Madison, June 28, 1783, FO. The Virginia General Assembly selected him; there was no direct popular election for Congressmen in the state at the time.

Jefferson set out to the west—MB 1783, FO.

a simple questionnaire—Marbois' Queries Concerning Virginia [Before 30 November 1780], FO; NSV, xi–xii.

"on loose papers"—TJA.

"vaunted scene of Europe"—TJ to Charles Bellini, Sept. 30, 1785, FO.

we've been exploring Jefferson-related sites on the East Coast—During that summer and those that followed, we filled weekends exploring TJ places and meeting people with a connection to his life and interests: beekeepers, fisherwomen, historians, TJ interpreters, the state legislator who represents TJ's old district, banjo makers, recreators of *batteaux*, archivists, and many others. This background paid off when I hit the road in Europe, seeking to make connections.

wriggled into a different cave—MB 1783, FO; NSV, 21–23; Jim McConkey, "The Story of Cave Hill" (Grottoes: 2010).

one of his greatest traveling insights—NSV, 19–20; MB 1783, FO.

over time—In *Jefferson's Shadow: The Story of His Science* (New Haven: Yale University Press, 2012), 79–80, Keith Thomson brilliantly analyzes this passage, noting that it got Jefferson "into trouble with Biblical literalists" later.

Harper House—The National Park Service confirmed that all documentation indicates that Jefferson likely stopped at Harper House (in a 1973 letter responsive to a Monticello researcher's inquiries).

"height back of the tavern"—TJ to Horatio G. Spafford, May 14, 1809, FO.

decamped to Princeton—MB 1783; JTV, 403–404; Madison to TJ, July 17, 1783, FO.

a weak national government—Gordon Wood, *The Creation of the American Republic, 1776–1789* (Chapel Hill: UNC Press, 1969), 356–357.

a president with little power and a secretary of foreign affairs—Richard B. Morris, *The Forging of the Union, 1781–1789* (New York: Harper and Row, 1987), 100–106, 194–198. John Jay served as secretary of foreign affairs for most of Jefferson's time abroad, working out of an office in Fraunces Tavern in New York.

"Our body was little numerous"—TJA.

"Heaven was silent"—TJ's Observations on Démeunier's Manuscript, June 22, 1786, FO. TJ explained the vote in more detail in his letter to Madison, Apr. 25, 1784.

receive training as a barber—THM 155–156; MB 1784, FO.

hundreds of other enslaved people—TWL, 106.

assist Benjamin Franklin—TJ to Madison, May 8, 1784, FO.

traveled to Boston—MB 1784, FO. Before departing, Jefferson investigated the state of New England's maritime industries (see Ch. 21).

sailed on July 5—MB 1784, FO.

questions for the ship's captain—"V. Replies to Queries: Massachusetts, July 1784," FO.

a thermometer and pocket telescope—MB 1784, FO.

a copy of *Don Quixote*—TJ to George Cabot, July 24, 1784, FO.

CHAPTER FOUR: PARIS, SPRINGTIME

the Atlantic had been placid, the English Channel choppy, Patsy ill—Martha Jefferson to Eliza House Trist, after Aug. 24, 1785, FO; TJ to Monroe, Nov. 11, 1784, FO.

they ripped him off—Martha Jefferson to Trist, after Aug. 24, 1785, FO. MB 1784, FO.

sent James Hemings to ride ahead—MB 1784, FO; THM, 160–161.

the Hôtel d'Orléans—MB 1784, FO; TJP, 13–14.

the "seasoning" all new residents went—TJ to James Monroe, Mar. 18, 1785, FO.

"to all the brilliant pleasures"—TJ to Baron von Geismar, Sept. 6, 1785, FO.

"make you adore your own country"—TJ to Monroe, June 17, 1785, FO.

"makes men wiser, but less happy"—TJ to Peter Carr, Aug. 10, 1787, FO.

roaming the city on foot—TJ to Monroe, Mar. 18 and Apr. 15, 1785, FO.

"The object of walking"—TJ to Peter Carr, Aug. 19, 1785, FO.

he felt "perfectly reestablished"—TJ to Monroe, Apr. 15, 1785, FO.

the Palais Royal—TJP, 14–15; Eric Hazan, *The Invention of Paris: A History in Footsteps* (New York: Verso, 2010), 19–26; Claude Fohlen, *Jefferson à Paris* (Paris: Perrin, 1995), 128–130; William Howard Adams, *The Paris Years of Thomas Jefferson* (New Haven: Yale University Press, 1997), 56–59; Jeremy D. Popkin, *Panorama of Paris* (University Park: Pennsylvania State University Press, 1999), 202–209; M.B. Raymond, *Les Mimes du Palais-Royal* (Paris: Chez Hardouin et Gattey, 1787).

the *Salons des Échecs*—TJP, 16; MB 1786, FO.

absorbing staggering costs—Herbert Sloan, *Principle and Interest: Thomas Jefferson and the Problem of Debt* (Charlottesville: UVA Press, 2001), 18–19, 22–23, 26 (on debt in Parisian years); MB 1784–89, FO. TJ complained to Madison that Congress paid the expenses in full of the ambassadors to France who had preceded him—TJ to Madison, May 25, 1788, FO.

he kept going back there—TJP, 15–18; MB 1785–1789, FO. Rice notes that the Café Mécanique there had dumbwaiters (tiered food-delivery shelves that avoided the need for hovering servers); this might have given TJ the idea for the same at Monticello.

"highly advantageous to the proprietors"—TJ to James Currie, Jan. 14, 1785, FO.

pioneered both the French fry and the dollar—While in Congress in 1784, TJ promoted a decimal-based currency system, reviewing the advantages of the Spanish *dolár* as a model and concluding that "I question if a common measure of more convenient size than the Dollar could be proposed." "Notes on Coinage, March–May, 1784," FO; Malone, Jefferson the Virginian, 416–417. Congress adopted the dollar as the national currency the following year. Later, President Jefferson handwrote a list of menus served at the President's

House, which included "raw potatoes, deep-fried in small slices," likely taken from a French recipe, thereby supersizing his contributions to American culinary history. RSE, 180-181; Fowler, Dining at Monticello, 148.

a bookseller he liked in the Palais Royal—MB 1787, FO.

"every afternoon I was disengaged"—TJ to Samuel H. Smith, Sept. 21, 1814, FO.

salon culture in Paris—Kevin J. Hayes, *The Road to Monticello: The Life and Mind of Thomas Jefferson* (New York: Oxford University Press, 2008), 294–298.

in Paris in 1785 and London two years later—NSV, xvi–xx.

Franklin having returned home—Benjamin Franklin to George Washington, Sept. 20, 1785, FO.

the neoclassical mansion he moved into—TJ to Abigail Adams, Sept. 4, 1785, FO; TJP, 8–9. Jefferson lived at the Hôtel de Langeac from 1785–89. It was torn down in the nineteenth century; today there is a historic plaque marking its site.

he wanted to extend his stay—George Ticknor's Account of a Visit to Monticello [4–7 Feb. 1815], FO.

the financiers of Amsterdam—ROM, 189–190.

His country was facing "something like a bankruptcy," he wrote—TJ to GW, May 2, 1788, FO.

"press[ed] on my mind like a mountain"—TJ to John Adams, Mar. 2, 1788, FO.

Adams was on his way to this ceremony—Abigail Adams to TJ, Feb. 26, 1788.

a "very few hours' warning" of his trip, he wrote—TJ to Stephen Cathalan, Jr., Mar. 3, 1788, FO.

everything he needed at the ready—WTJ, 103, 363, 366–367; Silvio Bedini, *Thomas Jefferson: Statesman of Science* (New York: Macmillan, 1990), 152–153. *Hints* recommends four guidebooks that Jefferson acquired abroad. He also bought practical guides to Paris, London, and Amsterdam. https://tjlibraries.monticello.org /transcripts/sowerby/sowerby.html.

"Some preparation seems necessary"—TJ to Joseph Priestly, Nov. 29, 1802.

strolled the mile from his Champs-Élysées home—undated memorandum now appended to TJ to Madison, June 20, 1787, FO.

CHAPTER FIVE: THE EARTH BELONGS ALWAYS TO THE LIVING

Amsterdam in 1788—Two excellent books dealing with Amsterdam in the eighteenth century—as well as its glory years of the 1600s—are Russell Shorto's *Amsterdam: A History of the World's Most Liberal City* (New York: Random House, 2013) and Simon Schama's *The Embarrassment of Riches: An Interpretation of Dutch Culture in the Golden Age* (New York: Knopf, 1987).

He noted how—TJ, Notes of a Tour through Holland and the Rhine Valley, March 3–April 23, 1788, FO.

"the roar of joy the most universal I had ever heard"—TJ to William Short, Mar. 10, 1788, FO.

the Patriots, the Prince—Shorto, *Amsterdam*, 227–228; Schama, *The Embarrassment of Riches*, 248–253; ROM, 184–186; E. H. Kossman, *The Low Countries, 1780-1940* (Oxford: The Clarendon Press, 1963), 34–47; Peter Nicolaisen, "Thomas Jefferson, John Adams, and the Dutch Patriots," in *Old World, New World: American and Europe in the Age of Jefferson*, Sadsoky et al., eds. (Charlottesville: UVA Press, 2012), 105–130.

"legitimate authorities"—TJA.

fretted that the resurgent Orangeists might retaliate—TJ to John Adams, Sept. 28, 1787, FO.

"immeasurable avarice"—Adams to TJ, Feb. 12, 1788; TJ to John Jay, Mar. 13, 1788, FO; ROM, 190–191.

"[B]y this journey"—TJA.

experience Amsterdam as a traveler—and shopper—Shackelford, *Thomas Jefferson's Travels in Europe, 1784–89* (Baltimore: The Johns Hopkins University Press, 1995), 134–135; MB 1788, FO. In WTJ, 23, Monticello curator Susan Stein characterized Jefferson's stay in Europe as "shopping for a lifetime."

"The earth belongs always to the living"—TJ to Madison, Sept. 6, 1789, FO; Herbert Sloan, "The Earth Belongs in Usufruct to the Living," in Peter Onuf, ed., *Jeffersonian Legacies* (Charlottesville: UVA Press, 1993), 281–315.

In his private letter to Madison, Jefferson employed both the phrase I used and the one that Professor Sloan quotes in his article. By using the term "usufruct," TJ meant that living people hold rights to use and enjoy the earth, but only temporarily, for ownership must later pass to a new generation. TJ proposed canceling debt each generation, calculating that a new generation came forth each nineteen years. He went on to claim that laws should expire after nineteen years as well, providing the next generation with a clean slate. James Madison shredded this argument in his response. Madison to TJ, Feb. 4, 1790, FO.

the Grand Tour—Geoffrey Trease, *The Grand Tour* (London: Heinemann, 1967), 1–15, 185–186, 194; Jeremy Black, *Italy and the Grand Tour* (New Haven: Yale University Press, 2003), 15, 75–80, 101, 110–111; Joseph Addison, *Remarks on Several Parts of Italy in the Years 1701, 1702, 1703* (London: J. and R. Tonson, 1767).

"gulp it all down in a day"—TJ to Lafayette, Apr. 11, 1787, FO.

a "foreign traveler"—TJ to Chastellux, Apr. 4, 1787, FO.

wore an orange ribbon in public—MB 1788, FO.

porcelain cups (which he smuggled back to Paris)—MB 1788, FO; TJ to Andre Limozin, Mar. 27, 1788, May 4, 1788, and May 17, 1788, FO.

The waffle iron—MB, 1788, FO.

"I am miserable until I owe not a shilling"—TJ to Nicholas Lewis, Dec. 19, 1786, FO. I modernized the "till" to "until."

Rutledge, Jr., and Shippen, planning a grand tour—ROM, 145, 149–151; Shackleton, *Jefferson's Adoptive Son*, 32–34.

"charged, like a bee, with the honey of wisdom"—TJ to William Shippen, May 8, 1788, FO and TJ to John Rutledge, Sr., July 12, 1788, FO.

"scribble[d] very hastily and undigested" TJ to Rutledge, Jr. June 19, 1788; also see TJ to Shippen, June 19, 1788.

travel in military uniform; almost threw them in jail—Shackelford, *Jefferson's Adoptive Son*, 34; TL Shippen to TJ, July 31, 1788 (editorial note), FO.

"unoranged."—Shippen to TJ, May 29, 1788, FO.

"Temptations...seduced us"—Shippen to TJ, May 29, 1788, FO.

"glare of pomp and pleasure"—TJ to Peter Carr, Aug. 10, 1787, FO.

"fondness for European luxury"—TJ to John Bannister, Jr., Oct. 15, 1785, FO.

"a spirit for female intrigue"—TJ to John Bannister, Jr., Oct. 15, 1785, FO.

catching venereal disease—Shackelford, *Jefferson's Adoptive Son*, 38, 198 n. 63.

"leave this heavenly place"—Rutledge, Jr., to TJ, July 8, 1788, FO.

"it must be very extraordinary"—Shippen to TJ, July 6, 1788, FO.

still luxuriating in the baths—Shippen to TJ, July 12, 1788, FO.

"You shall hear from me on the road"—TJ to Short, Mar. 29, 1788, FO.

Jefferson sailed south—MB 1788, FO; Shackelford, *Thomas Jefferson's Travels*, 136–137.

"all his effects contained in a single trunk"—TJ to Madame de Tott, Apr. 5, 1787, FO.

"I am become an Italian"—Shippen to TJ, July 31, 1788, FO.

"different shades of perfection"—Short to TJ, Jan. 14, 1789, FO.

a canvas by Goltzius, commissioned others—WTJ, 143–144. I won't attempt to follow *Hints*' itinerary from start to finish—For that reason, I chose not to go to Vienna and Trieste, two places Jefferson included in *Hints*, since the Boys had initially intended to travel to Italy via that route (they didn't in the end). As Jefferson didn't go to either place himself, he didn't have much to say about them. Similarly, I skipped a few other locations along the way. I ultimately focused my time on the road on places that held significance for Jefferson's Objects of Attention and the questions he had about them.

"The earth belongs always to the living"—TJ to Madison, Sept. 6, 1789, FO. In an earlier note, I explained what TJ meant by this statement—that debts and laws should expire after nineteen years. Here, I'm engaging in the time-honored tradition of reinterpreting TJ's words and applying them to the present. What I took from the phrase when in Amsterdam was Jefferson's sense of carpe diem and of the need to live in the present, unafraid to shape a new future. (I also wouldn't mind having a few debts canceled, though.)

CHAPTER SIX: RAMBLES THROUGH THE VINEYARDS

the château of Clos Vougeot—Johnson, *Vintage*, 130, 271, 274.

made direct contacts with producers—TJ to Alexander Donald, Sept. 17, 1787, FO.

"We could...make as great a variety of wines"—TJ to C. J. Lasteyrie, July 15, 1808, FO "early access" document.

brandy, beer or cider—Tom Burford, *Apples of North America* (Portland: Timber Press, 2013), 12; Peter Hatch, *The Fruit and Fruit Trees of Monticello* (Charlottesville: UVA Press, 1998), 81; Richard J. Hooker, *Food and Drink in America: A History* (New York: The Bobbs-Merrille Co., 1981), 81–88; Michael Pollan, *The Botany of Desire: A Plant's-Eye View of the World* (New York: Random House, 2001), 21–22.

sweet, fortified Madeira—TJ to Stephen Cathalan, before June 6, 1817, FO; Liddell, *Madeira*, 33–43.

"The delicacy and innocence"—TJ to Stephen Cathalan, before June 6, 1817, FO. TJ was discussing French wines when he wrote to Cathalan; he also praised light Montepulciano wines from Italy when advising newly elected President Monroe on how to stock the President's House cellar. TJ to Monroe, April 8, 1817, FO.

"do not terminate the most sociable meals"—TJ to Charles Bellini, Sept. 30, 1785, FO.

President's House—People only began calling the president's residence in Washington, DC, the "White House" during the first term of James Madison, TJ's successor. Ralph Ketcham, *James Madison: A Biography* (Charlottesville: UVA Press, 1990), 477.

promote lighter European wines—TJ to Albert Gallatin, June 1 and 2, 1807, FO, "early access" documents; TJ to William H. Crawford, Nov. 10, 1818, FO; TJ to Jean Guillaume Hyde de Neville, Dec. 13, 1818, FO; Gabler, *Passions*, 197–202, 212–215.

"No nation is drunken"—TJ to Jean Guillaume Hyde de Neville, Dec. 13, 1818, FO.

"poison of whisky"—TJ to William H. Crawford, Nov. 10, 1818.

Jefferson developed his own classification—TJ to Victor Adolphus Sasserno and to Stephen Cathalan, both on May 26, 1819, FO. Jefferson referred to wines as "rough" or "astringent" interchangeably.

Jefferson's Tasting Notes: Red Burgundy—I compiled these and subsequent "tasting notes" loosely from Jefferson's writings; they're meant to be fun. The quotes are his—in the case of these Burgundies, in Notes of a Tour to the Southern Parts of France etc. [3 Mar.–10 June, 1787], FO. I added the pairings and places, inspired by Jefferson's travel notes and my own experiences. There might have been a glass or two of wine involved as I did so. The Jefferson family passed down a recipe for roast duck with onion sauce. DAM, 124.

The Cistercian monks of Burgundy—Johnson, *Vintage*, 130–133.

a "vile and disloyal" plant—Johnson, *Vintage*, 130–133. Gamay is the principal grape in Beaujolais—perhaps why you drink the Beaujolais Nouveau so quickly after it's made (although some Beaujolais producers have now upped their game).

the monks' estate was nationalized during the French Revolution and sold off to locals—Johnson, *Vintage*, 274–275.

hundreds of different proprietors—Jean-Robert Pitte, *Bordeaux/Burgundy: A Vintage Rivalry* (Berkeley: University of CA Press, 2008), 118–120.

"rambled through their most celebrated vineyards"—TJ to Short, Mar. 15, 1787. In Notes of a Tour to the Southern Parts of France etc. [3 Mar.–10 June, 1787], FO, TJ made a diagram showing Burgundian villages and the kind of wine each specialized in. Although Rutledge and Shippen didn't come here, William Short did in September 1788. So Short could catch up with the others, who were heading south through Germany to

Switzerland, Jefferson drew up a route that plunged him through Burgundy. Short repaid his mentor with detailed observations on the local grapes, comparing them to native varieties in Virginia.

"now planting, pruning, and sticking their vines"— Notes of a Tour into Southern Parts of France etc. [3 Ma.–10 June, 1787], FO.

"On such slight circumstances"—Notes of a Tour to the Southern Parts of France etc. [3 Mar.–10 June, 1787], FO.

Jefferson's Tasting Notes: Rieslings of Schloss Johanissberg—Notes of a Tour through Holland and the Rhine Valley, March 3–April 23, 1788, FO.

the site of a Roman battle—Shackelford, *Thomas Jefferson's Travels*, 140; TJ, Notes of a Tour through Holland and the Rhine Valley, March 3–April 23, 1788, FO.

"Here the vines begin"—TJ, Notes of a Tour through Holland and the Rhine Valley, March 3–April 23, 1788, FO. We also later visited Heidelberg castle, which Jefferson found "the most imposing ruin of the modern age," a half hour before it closed. We just had time to scramble around the Great Tun, a massive, communal wine cask. Jefferson reported that he had been told it could hold the equivalent of 283,200 bottles; he measured its dimensions to verify.

The riesling story—Stuart Pigott, *The Riesling Story: Best White Wine on Earth* (New York: Stewart, Tabori and Chang, 2014), 18–20; Hugh Johnson and Jancis Robinson, *The World Atlas of Wine* (London: Mitchell Beazley, 2013, 7th ed.), 218; Jay McIneney, *Bacchus and Me: Adventures in the Wine Cellar* (New York: Vintage Books, 2002), 11–12.

"Its fine wines are made on the hills"—TJ, Notes of a Tour through Holland and the Rhine Valley, March 3–April 23, 1788, FO.

"a small but dull kind of batteau"—TJ, Notes of a Tour through Holland and the Rhine Valley, March 3–April 23, 1788, FO.

cuttings of riesling vines—TJ to Geismar, July 13, 1788.

"a species of gambling," he wrote to friends; "either way you are ruined"—TJ to William Drayton, July 30, 1787, FO.

"the parent of misery"—TJ to George Wythe, Sept. 16, 1787, FO.

employed in "barren spots"—TJ to William Drayton, July 30, 1787, FO.

Schloss Johannisberg and its sweet wine—TJ, Notes of a Tour through Holland and the Rhine Valley, March 3–April 23, 1788, FO; Johnson, *Vintage*, 290–291.

"comparing an olive and a pineapple"—memorandum to Henry Scheaff [after 20 Feb., 1793], FO.

a glass of his own Monticello riesling—TJ to Geismar, July 13, 1788, FO.

CHAPTER SEVEN: JEFFERSON'S DREAM

Jefferson's Tasting Notes: American Scuppernong—TJ to William Johnson, May 10, 1817, FO; pepper-and-okra soup from DAM, 106. The pairing I suggest is one of strong American flavors.

the mansion Jefferson sketched for James Barbour—Beltramini, *Jefferson and Palladio*, 164–165; James Barbour to TJ, Mar. 29, 1817, FO.

Jefferson's dream came crashing down—Hatch, *The Fruit and Fruit Trees of Monticello*, 131, 134, 137–139, 146; Hailman, *Thomas Jefferson on Wine*, 371–372. Fernando also recounted that Jefferson did not select the right grapes for Virginia; pinot noir is too "finicky," for this climate and riesling also presents challenges. The signature grapes of Virginia, after decades of experimentation, some of it by Fernando himself, are now flowery Viognier and peppery Cabernet Franc.

an "exquisite wine"—TJ to William Johnson, May 10, 1817, FO; TJ to Samuel Maverick, May 12, 1822, FO, "early access" document.

"sunk a good deal of money" into his elusive project of "introducing the culture of the vine"—TJ to Louis H. Girardin, Dec. 25, 1815, FO.

"bewitching poison"—TJ to William H. Crawford, Nov. 10, 1818, FO.

a thriving wine industry in Virginia—See generally Todd Kliman, *The Wild Vine: A Forgotten Grape and the Untold Story of American Wine* (New York: Broadway Paperbacks, 2010); Richard Leahy, *Beyond Jefferson's Vines: The Evolution of Quality Wine in Virginia* (New York: CreateSpace, 2014).

cut his wine with water—TJ to Joseph Fenwick, Sept. 6, 1790, FO; Randall, *Life of Thomas Jefferson*, Vol. 3, 344.

Jefferson's Tasting Notes: White Hermitage—TJ to Stephen Cathalan, June 29, 1807, FO. John Hailman translated *doux et liquoureux* as "sweet and luscious." White Hermitage, smooth and floral, goes well with garlic (which TJ loved)—so why not try it with a garlicky Provençal aioli sauce over fish?

Hermitage—Raymond Doumay, "*Le flueve qui fit déborder le vin*," in *Les Vins du Rhone et de la Mediterranée* (Editions Montalba, 1978), 47–48.

White Hermitage was Jefferson's go-to—TJ to James Monroe, Apr. 8, 1817, FO; TJ to William Alston, Oct. 6, 1818, FO. Similarly, Jefferson might have been the only person in the world to prefer still wine from Champagne rather than its more famous bubbly.

formed part of his broader campaign—TJ to Stephen Cathalan, before June 6, 1817, FO. TJ wrote, referring to the White Hermitage and several wines from the south of France, "I am anxious to introduce here these fine wines in place of the [highly] alcoholic wines of Spain and Portugal; and the universal approbation of all who taste them at my table will, I am persuaded, turn by degrees the current of demand from this part of our country."

a series of toasts—Hooker, *Food and Drink in America*, 89.

Jefferson's gatherings—Hailman, 258–260, 290–299, 318, 322; Stein, "The 'Feast of Reason'" in *Dining at Monticello*, 74–78; John B. Boles, *Jefferson: Architect of American Liberty* (New York: Basic Books, 2017), 333–334.

"the first wine in the world," the "most elegant *everyday*" wines—TJ, Memorandum on Wine [after 23 Apr. 1788]; TJ to James Monroe, Apr. 8, 1817, FO (the emphasis is his).

Trying one Provençal wine—TJ to Stephen Cathalan, before June 6, 1817, FO.

the market in Aix-en-Provence—We also all had an epic long lunch at the centuries-old Les Deux Garçons (which later burned down), where I tackled a tower of seafood, washing it down with a white Coteaux d'Aix while watching the kids dart out to splash in the nearby medieval fountains. It was a scene I only could have dreamed of when I wandered the streets of Aix alone as a student, *Evocations of Old Aix-en-Provence* in hand.

In the hills of the Lubéron—The restaurant is l'Auberge de la Loube, which Peter Mayle loved (but did not name) in *A Year in Provence*. After one of my French professors in Aix tipped me off to it, Mom and I went and had what at the time was the most memorable meal of our lives. *Merci, maman!*

Hungarian Tokays, Italian Chiantis, Sicilian Marsala—Hailman, *Thomas Jefferson on Wine*, 256, 305–306. Thomas Appleton to TJ, Mar. 15, 1804.

Zinfandel's origins lie with Italian Primitivo grapes—Johnson and Robinson, *The World Atlas of Wine*, 177.

"I find friendship to be like wine"—TJ to Dr. Benjamin Rush, Aug. 17, 1811.

CHAPTER EIGHT: SITTING IN AN ENGLISH GARDEN

the neighborhood in London where his mother spent her childhood—Jane Randolph was born in Shadwell in London's docklands. Her father, a wealthy ship's captain and planter, relocated from Virginia to London for several years before returning home. After marrying her in 1739, Peter Jefferson named their plantation house Shadwell in homage. JTV, 4, 14–17. Liana and I had pints in the creaky Prospect of Whitby, which dates from the sixteenth century, once a famed smugglers' hangout. Surely the genteel Randolphs never drank in such a sketchy place...did they?

Golden Square—MB, 1786, FO. The site where Jefferson stayed (the best I could figure out) was a Nordic pastry shop when we went there. I informed the cashier of that fact as I ordered raisin Danishes; he took it in stride.

Jefferson's diplomatic duties—TJ to Jay, Mar. 12, 1786, FO.

"It was impossible" TJA.

pioneered the very concept of liberty—Jefferson set these ideas out in his *A Summary View of the Rights of British America*. See Draft of Instructions to Virginia Delegates in the Continental Congress, July, 1774, FO; Joseph Ellis, *American Sphinx: The Character of Thomas Jefferson* (New York: Vintage Books, 1998), 36–38.

what Adams called an "ominous" cloud of smoke—Adams to TJ, June 7, 1785, FO.

"wretched" architecture—TJ to John Page, May 4, 1786.

let back into an arrangement with the mother country—Jon Meacham, *Thomas Jefferson: The Art of Power* (New York: Random House, 2012), 194. A British general told TJ that Parliament would not let America rejoin the empire even if it wanted to.

ranked it as an art form—*Hints to Americans*, FO.

French versus English gardens—Frederick Doveton Nichols and Ralph E. Griswold, *Thomas Jefferson, Landscape Architect* (Charlottesville: UVA Press, 1978), 76–79; Charles Quest-Rinon, *The English Garden: A Social History* (New York: Penguin Books, 2001), 79–80, 121–123; Andrea Wulf, *Brothers Gardeners: A Generation of Gentleman Naturalists and the Birth of an Obsession* (New York: Vintage, 2010), 93–95. As Professors Annette Gordon-Reed and Peter Onuf make clear in *Most Blessed of the Patriarchs: Thomas Jefferson and the Empire of the Imagination* (New York: Liveright Publishing, 2016), 140, nature held a special meaning in Jefferson's thought; he saw it as the source of "all value."

In his rented carriage—MB, 1786, FO. In the *Founding Gardeners: The Revolutionary Generation, Nature, and the Shaping of the American Nation* (New York: Alfred A. Knopf, 2011), Andrea Wulf includes an excellent chapter on the garden tour and its influence on Jefferson's landscaping, noting the prevalence of American plants in England (35–57).

Thomas Whately's *Observations on Modern Gardening*—(London: T. Payne, 1770); *Notes on a Tour of English Gardens* [2–14 Apr. 1786], FO.

"such practical things"—*Notes on a Tour of English Gardens* [2–14 Apr. 1786], FO.

calling it *Notes*—*Notes on a Tour of English Gardens* [2–14 Apr. 1786], FO.

more water and a stronger sense of unity—*Notes on a Tour of English Gardens* [2–14 Apr. 1786], FO.

The next two landscapes—The humble park was Enfield Chase, the cluster of trees Forty Hall. The latter did provide an interesting house tour. Afterward, the kids enjoyed dressing up in Elizabethan-era clothes.

specimens at Kew—Richard Mabey, *The Flowers of Kew: 350 Years of Flower Paintings from the Royal Botanic Gardens* (New York: Atheneum, 1989) 3–8; Quest-Rinon, *The English Garden*, 158–159; "Kew Gardens," https://www.kew.org/kew-gardens.

a "furious maniac"—TJ to Short, Dec. 8, 1788, FO.

'A Repetition of winding Walks'—Diary of John Adams, Apr. 20, 1786, FO.

plant-loving Europeans willing to make trades—Lucia Stanton, "Rice," TJE, https://monticello.org/site/research-and-collections/rice; "Madame de Tessé," TJE, https://monticello.org/site/research-and-collections/madame-de-tessé.

stocked up on American specimens—Wulf, *Founding Gardeners*, 55–56; MB 1786, FO.

Hampton's gardens were "old fashioned"—*Notes on a Tour of English Gardens* [2–14 Apr. 1786], FO.

Patsy, books, and peas in a pint jar—TJ to Martha Jefferson, Nov. 28, 1783; WTJ; Betts, *Garden Book*, 4.

Jefferson would design many such structures for Monticello—Jack McLaughlin, *Jefferson and Monticello: Biography of a Builder* (New York: Henry Holt and Co., 1988), 341–342, 353–355; Nichols and Griswold, *Thomas Jefferson*, 107–111.

"leaped the fence"—Quest-Rinon, *The English Garden*, 124.

"useless," showing "too much of art"—*Notes on a Tour of English Gardens* [2–14 Apr. 1786], FO.

"consult the genius of the place"—Quest-Rinon, *The English Garden*, 123.

"so cleverly that nature itself"—Christopher Maycock, *A Passionate Poet: Susanna Blamire, 1747–94: A Biography* (Penzance: Pattern Press, 2003), 65.

a staggering 7,000 pounds—*Notes on a Tour of English Gardens* [2–14 Apr. 1786], FO.

fog, mountains "looming," the "workhouse of nature"—NSV, 80–81; TJ to Maria Cosway, Oct. 12, 1786, FO.

blast and level the top of the mountain, hauling everything—Betts, *Garden Book*, 17; TJE, "Water Supply," https://monticello.org/site/research-and-collections/water-supply.

a draft of the commercial treaty—American Commissioners to Carmarthen, Apr. 4, 1786; Wulf, *Founding Gardeners*, 42–43.

CHAPTER NINE: BEHIND THE FENCE

Staying in the Talbot Hotel—MB, 1786, FO.

one of two *fermes ornées*—Wulf, *Founding Gardeners*, 51–53.

"Ostentations of Vanity"—Diary of John Adams, Apr. 20, 1786, FO (referring to Osterley Park).

"But I am not an Englishman"—Abigail Adams Smith to John Quincy Adams, July 27, 1786, FO. The garden was Wooburn Farms. The Protestant vandals didn't kill this garden, but time and development did; a school and housing have taken over the space it once occupied. After walking around for an hour or two, we pronounced it an ex-garden.

Landscape garden tours became the trend—Quest-Rinon, *The English Garden*, 147–149.

Lancelot "Capability" Brown—Quest-Rinon, *The English Garden*, 131–136.

In Shenstone's day—Quest-Rinon, *The English Garden*, 129–131; Wulf, *Founding Gardeners*, 51–53.

a "grazing farm"—*Notes on a Tour of English Gardens* [2–14 Apr. 1786], FO.

the one on a BBC Intelligence Services compound—This was Caversham Park, the first place in Britain to broadcast the news of Hitler's surrender. It's not normally open to the public. A radio host I contacted who worked there kindly escorted me through the security and across the grounds—and was pleasantly surprised to learn from me that Capability Brown designed them. The BBC sold the facility off two years after my visit.

Tony Blair—This was Wotton House, in Buckinghamshire.

Lord Cobham and his paths—Andrea Wulf and Emma Gieben-Gamal, *This Other Eden: Seven Great Gardens and 300 Years of English History* (London: Little, Brown and Co., 2005), 106–120.

"Mysterious Orgies"—Wulf, *Founding Gardeners*, 47.

the "country Whigs"—Ellis, *American Sphinx*, 36–38.

"unassisted by the wealth"—Jefferson's "Original Rough Draught" of the Declaration of Independence [11 June–4 July, 1776], FO.

"keep alive that sacred fire"—NSV, 164–165.

his "trinity" of British heroes—TJ to Benjamin Rush, Jan. 6, 1811, FO.

"American worthies"—TJ to William Short, Apr. 6, 1790, FO.

the "capital stroke" in the realm of landscapes—Quest-Rinon, *The English Garden*, 128.

claimed the land of poorer farmers—Quest-Rinon, *The English Garden*, 137–139.

Lord Cobham and the poachers—George Monbiot, "Why You'll Never See Executions or Evictions on a National Trust Tea Towel," *The Guardian*, Feb. 23, 2009.

Stowe was "superb"—Adams, Notes of a Tour of English County Seats etc., with Thomas Jefferson, Apr. 4-10, 1786, FO.

"the article in which it surpasses all the earth"—TJ to John Page, May 4, 1786, FO.

the garden in the back of his mansion—McLaughlin, *Jefferson and Monticello*, 345. It's unclear how many of these changes he actually carried out.

"far beyond my ideas"—TJ to John Page, May 4, 1786, FO.

"the leaves of the trees"—TJ to Homastubbee and Puckshunubbee, Dec. 17, 1803, FO.

"empire of liberty"—TJ to George Rogers Clark, Dec. 25, 1780, FO.

"roundabout" roads—Jefferson had enslaved workers create two roundabout roads before going to Europe; on his return, he expanded the network and incorporated them into his landscaping narrative. He recorded this work in his Garden Book.

"scarcely a speck of cultivation"—Margaret Bayard Smith, Account of a Visit to Monticello [29 July–2 Aug. 1809], FO.

"rich profusion" of views and "[S]hade is our Elysium;" TJ to William Hamilton, July 31, 1806, FO "early access" document..

pruned the lower branches—*id.*; Margaret Bayard-Smith, Account of a Visit to Monticello [29 July–2 Aug., 1809], FO.

the Juno and Jove of our forest—TJ to Adrienne-Catherine de Noialles, Comtesse de Tessé, Oct. 26, 1805, FO "early access" document.

four tulip poplar timbers—Sir Augustus John Foster: *Jeffersonian America: Notes on the United States of America Collected in the Years 1805–6–7 and 11–12* (San Marino, CA: The Huntington Library, 1954), 144.

American elk, springs—MB 1771, FO; Betts, *Garden Book*, 292–294; Margaret Bayard-Smith, Account of a Visit to Monticello [29 July–2 Aug., 1809], FO.

"the dreams of the future"—TJ to John Adams, Aug. 1, 1816.

"I do not (while in public life)"—TJ to James Bowling, Sept. 21, 1792, FO.

a ten-foot-high wooden paling—RSE, 28, 33. Monticello has now restored some of the wooden fencing.

okra, eggplant, sesame, watermelon—RSE, 21, 137, 145, 150; TJ to Nicholas Lewis, Sept. 17, 1787, FO.

French figs and Mandan corn and Arikara beans—RSE, 27, 129, 165–166.

Enslaved gardeners grew these staples—RSE, 63–69; TLH, 21, 68, 113–126; Dianne Swann-Wright, "African Americans and Monticello's Food Culture," in DAM, 38–41.

CHAPTER TEN: A CONTINUED FEAST THROUGH ITALY

a "continued feast"—TJ to William Short, Apr. 7, 1787, FO.

macaroni, capers, garlicky dishes, and tomatoes—RSE, 179–180; DAM, 102; Hailman, *Thomas Jefferson on Wine*, 340–342.

seeking "curious and enchanting objects"—MB 1787, FO; *Hints to Americans Traveling in Europe*, FO.

"hanging to a cloud"—Jefferson, Notes of a Tour to the Southern Parts of France etc. [3 Mar.–10 June], 1787, FO.

"dark-colored" fields "sometimes tinged with red"—Jefferson, Notes of a Tour to the Southern Parts of France etc. [3 Mar.–10 June, 1787], FO.

inspired Hannibal—Jefferson tried to find Hannibal's trail but was unsuccessful. TJ to George Wythe, Sept. 16, 1787, FO. He, too, liked to follow in the footsteps of famous men—so even my Jefferson-following itself was Jeffersonian.

"black and rich" soil, "abundance" of figs, ribbed bumps "not unlike the jaw-teeth of the mammoth"—Jefferson, Notes of a Tour to the Southern Parts of France etc. [3 Mar.–10 June, 1787], FO.

"a field where the inhabitants"—TJ to John Rutledge Sr., Aug. 6, 1787, FO.

"traveling through the night"—TJ to Martha Jefferson, May 5, 1787.

"gurgling stream"—Jefferson, Notes of a Tour to the Southern Parts of France etc. [3 Mar.–10 June, 1787], FO.

His excuse for leaving his diplomatic post—TJ to John Jay, Jan. 9, 1787, FO.

Raised on classical literature—Peter Onuf and Nicholas P. Cole, *Thomas Jefferson, the Classical World, and Early America* (Charlottesville: UVA Press, 2011), 2–5 (noting how even though Jefferson grew up with the Classics, he didn't want to literally model American government on the Roman example); Thomas Ricks, *First Principles: What America's Founders Learned from the Greeks and Romans and How that Shaped Our Country* (New York: Harper, 2020), 113; Louis B. Wright, "Thomas Jefferson and the Classics," *Proceedings of the American Philosophical Society* 87, no. 3 (1943), 223–233.

the young Jefferson and Italy—"Italy," TJE, https://monticello.org/site/research-and-collections/italy; Betts, *Garden Book*, 6, 47; Helen Cripe, *Jefferson and Music* (Charlottesville: UVA Press, 1979), 17, 20; Randall, *Life of Thomas Jefferson*, Vol. I, 131–132.

he had discussed with John Rutledge's uncle—Edward Rutledge to TJ, Oct. 14, 1786, FO; TJ to Edward Rutledge, July 14, 1787, FO.

"sift the matter to the bottom"—TJ to Edward Rutledge, July 14, 1787, FO.

informing Jay of his detour—TJ to Jay, May 4, 1787, FO.

the consequence for smuggling—*Id.*; TJ, Notes of a Tour to the Southern Parts of France etc. [3 Mar.–10 June, 1787], FO.

a "peep…into Elysium," as he put it—TJ to Maria Cosway, July 1, 1787, FO.

"What a number of vegetables"—TJ to Rutledge, Jr., June 19, 1788, FO.

"superlatively fine"—TJ to Thomas Appleton, Oct. 26, 1806, FO "early access" document.

"the favorite beverage"—TJ to Edmund Rogers, Feb. 14, 1824, FO "early access" document (referring to coffee—not necessarily espresso, though—and thanking Rogers for sending him Colombian beans).

Carlo Petrini—Peter Popham, "Carlo Petrini: The Slow Food Gourmet Who Started a Revolution," *The Independent*, Dec. 10, 2009.

Parmalat in dairy, Monini and Carapelli in olive oil—M. Bonetti, N. Hadjidimitriou, M. Peroni, and A. Zanoli, "The Food Industry in Italy," 265, 275, www.ip.aua.gr/studies/italian%20team_final.pdf.

some allies of this network established Eataly—Corby Kummer, "The Supermarket of the Future," *The Atlantic*, May 2007.

asparagus, anchovies, gumbo, and Creole stews—RSE, 199–200; DAM, 23, 106, 123. Back in Virginia, TJ often ordered anchovies from Europe—see TJ to Stephen Cathalan, Jan. 18, 1818, FO (just one example of several requests).

Whites in Virginia should receive fifty acres—He did so in his proposed constitution for Virginia. See First Draft by Jefferson [before June 1776], FO.

Problems with tobacco, "impoverished the soil"—NSV, 166; McEwan, *Thomas Jefferson*, 40–52. His Farm Book is replete with letters complaining about low prices for his tobacco crop.

added meat as a "condiment"—TJ to Vine Utley, Mar. 21, 1819, FO.

peas, lettuce, tomatoes—RSE, 154–157, 167–173, 213–219.

the venison his cooks prepared—RSE, 179.

He grew Italian peaches—Hatch, *Fruit and Fruit Trees*, 89–91.

olives, thing that "contributes the most"—TJ to William Drayton, May 7, 1789, FO; TJ to George Wythe, Sept. 16, 1787, FO. See also Lucia Stanton's excellent article "Mediterranean Journey," TJE, https://monticello.org/site/research-and-collections/mediterranean-journey-1787#footnote4_lkqfky3.

"richest gift of heaven"—TJ to George Wythe, Sept. 16, 1787, FO.

Sesame oil—RSE, 150; DAM, 137.

"The failure of one thing"—TJ to Charles Willson Peale, Aug. 20, 1811, FO.

crop rotation and fertilizers—McEwan, *Thomas Jefferson*, 25–32, FB, 310–321; RSE, 86, 94. TJ once thanked a friend for sending him a "charming treatise on manures," TJ to William Strickland, Mar. 23, 1798, FO.

the Arikara bean—TJ to Benjamin Smith Barton, Oct. 6, 1810, FO.

"only one or two of the *best* species"—TJ to Bernard McMahon, Jan. 13, 1810, FO.

"turn the greatest quantity of this useful action"—TJ to Charles Willson Peale, Apr. 17, 1813, FO.

"ill clad dirty"—Short to TJ, Feb. 17, 1789, FO.

"most famous for the excellence of that article"—Short to TJ, Feb. 11, 1789, FO.

"perforated with holes"—TJ, Notes on Macaroni Machine [after 11 Feb. 1789], FO.

"mathematically perfect" plow—TJ to John Taylor, Dec. 29, 1794, FO; Lucia Stanton, "Better Tools for a New and Better World: Jefferson Perfects the Plow," in *Old World, New World: America and Europe in the Age of Jefferson* (Charlottesville, VA: UVA Press, 2012), 200–222.

"diffuses plenty and happiness"—NSV, 168.

"this single commodity"—TJ to John Harvie, July 25, 1790, FO.

"olives, figs, oranges, mulberries, corn, and garden stuff"—Jefferson, Notes of a Tour to the Southern Parts of France etc. [3 Mar.–10 June, 1787], FO.

"pernicious Insect"—William Hay to TJ, Apr. 26, 1787, FO; Madison to TJ, July 24, 1788, FO; Lucia Stanton, "Hessian Fly," TJE, https://monticello.org/site/research-and-collections/hessian-fly.

on the trail of this wheat-fly—Jefferson, Notes on the Hessian Fly, 24 May–18 June, 1791, FO.

planting in the late fall—FB, 84.

culture of "infinite wretchedness"—NSV, 166.

"the best kind" of wheat—TJ to Thomas Mann Randolph, Nov. 12, 1790, FO.

Sicilian wheat—TJ to John F. Mercer, Sept. 5, 1797, FO.

Growing wheat; a perfect "machine"—FB 46; TWL, 73–74; 142–145; McEwan, *Thomas Jefferson*, 53–58.

James Hemings was training—THM, 168.

Mazzei wrote to him—Philip Mazzei to TJ, Apr. 17, 1787, FO.

the ambassador's "grumblings"—TJ to Mazzei, May 6, 1787, FO.

macaroni—DAM, 102; "Macaroni," TJE, https://monticello.org/site/research-and-collections/macaroni #footnote5_wyzwgbr.

Scientific breeding of animals and selection of plants—McEwan, *Thomas Jefferson*, 67, 118, 126. Jefferson once wrote that he was "always desirous of trying the merits of new races of animals, and of adding them, if worthy, to our national stock." TJ to Mayer and Branz, Jan. 18, 1808, FO "early access" document.

CHAPTER ELEVEN: THE RICE SMUGGLER

"but none is made there now," and "poor cheese"—Jefferson, Notes of a Tour to the Southern Parts of France etc. [3 Mar.–10 June, 1787], FO. Rutledge also took detailed notes on the making of Parmesan cheese—see Elizabeth Cometti, "Mr. Jefferson Prepares an Itinerary," *Journal of Southern History*, Vol. 12, No. 1, 1946, 103 n. 46. TJ ordered an eighty-pound block of the cheese when he was president; MB, 1807, FO.

a different, better variety—Notes of a Tour to the Southern Parts of France etc. [3 Mar.–10 June, 1787], FO TJ to Edward Rutledge, July 14, 1787, FO.

"Poggio, a muleteer"—Jefferson, Notes of a Tour to the Southern Parts of France etc. [3 Mar.–10 June, 1787], FO.

a network of amateurs—RSE, 19–21. Jefferson's correspondence with Madame de Tessé, André Thoüin, and Malesherbes reveals a lot of friendly plant-trading.

corn and riesling grapes—RSE, 21; Hailman, *Thomas Jefferson on Wine*, 81.

apples and opossums—TJ to Madison, Sept. 17, 1787, and Feb. 6, 1788, FO.

vials—Margaret Bayard Smith, Account of a Visit to Monticello [29 July–2 Aug. 1809], FO (she spelled them "phials").

"annually with pestilential fevers," Jefferson wrote—TJ to Malesherbes, Mar. 11, 1789.

Jefferson's rice quest "succeeded...perfectly"—Benjamin Vaughn to TJ, Mar. 17, 1790, FO; Nathaniel Cutting to TJ, July 6, 1790, FO; TJ to Benjamin Waterhouse, Dec. 1, 1808; Lucia Stanton, "Rice," TJE, https://monticello.org/site/research-and-collections/rice.

"The greatest service"—TJ, Summary of Public Service [after 2 Sept. 1800], FO.

layers of interior defenses—Ellis, *American Sphinx*, 81, 105–106, 146, 177.

"If any person wished to retire"—Jefferson, Notes of a Tour to the Southern Parts of France etc. [3 Mar.–10 June, 1787], FO.

CHAPTER TWELVE: REMEDIAL EDUCATION

The Rotunda, harmony and function—Richard Guy Wilson, ed., *Thomas Jefferson's Academical Village* (Charlottesville: UVA Press, 2009) 85, 106–110; Richard Guy Wilson, David Neumann, and Sara A. Butler, *The Campus Guide: University of Virginia* (New York: Princeton Architectural Press, 1999), 65; Garry Wills, *Mr. Jefferson's University* (National Geographic Directions, Washington, DC), 53, 79, 107.

"essay in architecture"—TJ to Benjamin Henry Latrobe, Oct. 10, 1809, FO.

designing the university, scattering buildings—TJ to William Thornton, May 9, 1817, FO; TJ to James Dinsmore, Apr. 13, 1817, FO.

"from an old drunken cabinetmaker"—George Green Shackelford, "William Short and Albemarle," *The Magazine of Albemarle County History*, XV, 1957, 23.

"models in architecture" for students, "no two alike"—TJ to Wilson Cary Nichols, Apr. 2, 1816; TJ to William Thornton, May 9, 1817; Wills, *Mr. Jefferson's University*, 52–54.

student rooms—Wills, *Mr. Jefferson's University*, 11, 13.

"rude, misshapen piles"—NSV, 152–153.

few trained architects, the "first principles"—NSV, 153; William Howard Adams, *Jefferson's Monticello* (New York: Abbeville Press, 1983), 4–6. Adams notes that Peter Harrison was a trained architect but not a professional.

high hopes for UVA—Wills, *Mr. Jefferson's University*, 25; TJ to Joseph Priestley, Jan. 18, 1800, FO.

give out merit scholarships—TJ to José Corrêa da Serra, Nov. 25, 1817, FO. TJ proposed that Virginia should arrange for young men "of the most promising genius whose parents are too poor to give them further education" to attend university, although he admitted that this might be a "utopian dream."

"here we are not afraid to follow truth"—TJ to William Roscoe, Dec. 27, 1820, FO "early access" document.

"exhibiting models of architecture"—Shackelford, "William Short and Albemarle," 23.

Inebriated students—Maurie D. McInnis, "Violence," in McInnis and Louis P. Nelson, eds., *Educated in Tyranny: Slavery at Thomas Jefferson's University* (Charlottesville: UVA Press, 2019), 110; Alan Taylor, *Thomas Jefferson's Education* (New York: W.W. Norton, 2019), 264–290.

UVA expelled three students; Jefferson was left speechless—Wills, *Mr. Jefferson's University*, 127–128; Wilson, *Academical Village*, 103; Ellis, *American Sphinx*, 343. The student was Wilson Miles Cary, the great-grandson of TJ's childhood friend Dabney Carr, who married TJ's sister Martha. Taylor, *Thomas Jefferson's Education*, 243; TJ to Joseph Coolidge, Oct. 13, 1825, FO "early access" document.

what he called "cubic" architecture—TJA.

He visited many on his 1787 trip—Jefferson, Notes of a Tour to the Southern Parts of France etc. [3 Mar.–10 June, 1787], FO; Lloyd DeWitt, "What He Saw: Thomas Jefferson's Grand Tour," in DeWitt and Corey Piper, *Thomas Jefferson Architect* (New Haven: Yale University Press, 2019), 51–60.

"stories a thousand years old" —TJ to Madame de Tessé, Mar. 20, 1787, FO.

Palladio traveled there as well—Manfred Wundram, *Palladio, 1508–1580: The Rules of Harmony* (Köln: Taschen, 2016), 8–9.

He recorded that it was surrounded by buildings—Jefferson, Notes of a Tour to the Southern Parts of France etc. [3 Mar.–10 June, 178], FO.

Jefferson added a similar arcade at UVA—Wills, *Mr. Jefferson's University*, 55; Wilson, *Academical Village*, 18–19.

"antiquities from morning to night"—TJ to Madame de Tessé, Mar. 20, 1787, FO.

Jefferson, Washington and the rest—WTJ, 219–220; Giovanna Capitelli, "Jefferson and the First Public Statues in the United States" and Mario Guderzo, "Canova and the Monument to George Washington," both in Guido Beltramini and Fulvio Lenzo, eds., *Jefferson and Palladio: Constructing a New World* (Milan: Officina Libraria, 2015), 117–129.

an example of civic virtue—Onuf and Cole, *Thomas Jefferson, the Classical World*, 2–5 (although, as previously noted, Jefferson didn't want to literally model American government on the Roman example). Richard Guy Wilson has an excellent essay in this book entitled "Thomas Jefferson's Classical Architecture: An American Agenda." See also Ricks, *First Principles*.

The Romans' architectural contributions—Ian Sutton, *Western Architecture* (New York: Thames and Hudson, 1999), 18–23.

devoured books, copied them into his own designs—McLaughlin, *Jefferson and Monticello*, 53–59.

"all the judges of architecture"—TJ to Madison, Sept. 20, 1785, FO.

the Maison Carrée, "the most perfect"—TJ to James Buchanan and William Hay, Jan. 26, 1786, FO; TJ to Madison, Sept. 20, 1785, FO; Mabel Wilson, "Race, Reason, and the Architecture of Jefferson's Virginia Statehouse," in Dewitt and Piper, *Thomas Jefferson Architect*, 87–88.

didn't create a carbon copy of the Maison Carrée—Hugh Howard, *Thomas Jefferson: Architect* (New York: Rizzoli, 2003), 68, 70, 73; TJA; Fiske Kimball, *The Capitol of Virginia: A Landmark of American Architecture* (Richmond: Library of Virginia, 2002), 3–13.

building contractors constructed based on sight—Adams, *Jefferson's Monticello*, 4–6.

Jefferson developed detailed work plans—Hugh Howard, *Dr. Kimball and Mr. Jefferson: Rediscovering the Founding Fathers of American Architecture* (New York: Bloomsbury, 2006), 64.

"most perfect example"— Wilson, "Thomas Jefferson's Classical Architecture: An American Agenda" in Onuf and Cole, Thomas Jefferson, the Classical World, 112.

"like a lover at this mistress"—TJ to Madame de Tessé, Mar. 20, 1787, FO.

the statue of Washington, carved out of Carrara—Howard, *Thomas Jefferson*, 70.

The Boys spent months touring; "passion" for buildings—Short to TJ, Nov. 29, Dec. 23, and Dec. 31, 1788; Jan. 14, Feb. 11, Feb. 17, Feb. 25, and Mar. 2, 1789, FO. Short bought a book of Palladio prints after touring the architect's hometown of Vicenza.

a "little commission"—TJ to Short, Feb. 28, 1789, FO.

a design he had made—TJ to Short, Feb. 28, 1789, FO.

bricks—McLaughlin, *Jefferson and Monticello*, 80–83; Richard Guy Wilson, "Jefferson's Creation of American Classical Architecture" and 109, 112; and Travis MacDonald, "Jefferson Builder"; both essays are found in Beltramini and Lenzo, eds., *Jefferson and Palladio*, 109, 112, 140–141.

"modern" alternatives—TJ to Pierre-Charles L'Enfant, Apr. 10, 1791, FO.

"seen me more angry"—TJ to Madame de Tessé, Mar. 20, 1787, FO.

Andrea Palladio's youth—Guido Beltramini, *The Private Palladio* (Zurich: Lars Müller Publishers, 2012), 16, 23; Witold Rybczynski, *The Perfect House: A Journey with the Renaissance Master Andrea Palladio* (New York: Scribner, 2002), 22–23.

Palladio, roaming and building—Rybczynski, *The Perfect House*, 38–45, 83–84.

Palladio's villas—Rybczynski, *The Perfect House*: so many cites on this point I won't even begin to list them. Read the whole thing; I think you'll like it.

he wrote *The Four Books of Architecture*—Andrea Palladio, *The Four Books of Architecture* (New York: Dover Publications, 1968).

Jefferson followed Palladio religiously—Howard, *Thomas Jefferson*, 42; Adams, *Jefferson's Monticello*, 47, 49, 55, 60; Rybczynski, *The Perfect House*, 127.

this first Monticello—Howard, *Thomas Jefferson*, 41–42.

"consulted the fine arts"—Marquis de Chastellux, *Travels in North America in the Years 1780, 1781, and 1782* (New York: 1828), 227.

"Palladio was the Bible"—Isaac A. Coles's Account of a Conversation with Thomas Jefferson [before 23 Feb. 1816], FO.

on top of a *monticello*—Beltramini, *Jefferson and Palladio*, 23.

took a pair of scissors to a copy of the Bible—Peter Manseau, *The Jefferson Bible: A Biography* (Princeton: Princeton University Press, 2020), 4–5. It might not literally have been "scissors"; Manseau refers to TJ using a blade.

"violently smitten" with—TJ to Madame de Tessé, Mar. 20, 1787, FO.

CHAPTER THIRTEEN: THE ARCHITECTURE OF DREAMS

Gazing at the Hôtel de Salm—MB, 1785, FO.

This small new mansion—Howard, *Thomas Jefferson*, 42–43; Adams, *Jefferson's Monticello*, 93.

return home with a sore neck—TJ to Madame de Tessé, Mar. 20, 1787, FO.

"new and good houses"—TJ to John Brown, Apr. 5, 1797, FO; McLaughlin, *Jefferson and Monticello*, 209–210.

neoclassicism—TJ to Pierre-Charles L'Enfant, Apr. 10, 1791, FO; Adams, *The Paris Years*, 48–52, 60–65; Wilson in *Jefferson and Palladio* 109, 114. RGW notes that Jefferson included Palladio in his definition of "modern" architecture. He also sees Jefferson as having just as much (or more) influence from the British inheritors of the Palladian tradition than the French—see this essay as well as his "Jefferson and England," in Dewitt and Piper, *Thomas Jefferson Architect*.

"every day enlarging"; neoclassical architecture—TJ to Madame de Bréhan, Mar. 14, 1789, FO; TJ to David Humphries, Aug. 14, 1787, FO; TJ to Charles Bellini, Sept. 30, 1785, FO.

Jefferson met Maria Cosway—TJ to Maria Cosway, Oct. 12, 1786, FO; MB 1786, FO.

the coquettish Maria Cosway Scharff, *The Women Jefferson Loved*, 204–205; Jon Kukla, *Mr. Jefferson's Women* (New York: Alfred A. Knopf, 2007), 86–91; WTJ, 176.

Cosway's husband—Scharff, *The Women Jefferson Loved*, 205. Richard Cosway also painted and sold pornographic snuff boxes. I thought you should know.

The Halle aux Blés, "the most superb thing on earth"—Adams, *Jefferson's Monticello*, 114–115; TJ to Maria Cosway, Oct. 12, 1786, FO.

"never heard of a dome," "sky-room"—Adams, *Jefferson's Monticello*, 98–99.

strolling around Paris—TJ to Maria Cosway, Oct. 12, 1786, FO; TJP, 109.

"How grand the ideas excited by the remains of such a column!"—TJ to Maria Cosway, Oct. 12, 1786, FO. What TJ possibly could have meant by reminding his lover of an exciting erect column has mystified scholars for centuries.

the Church of St. Geneviève—TJP, 6. Although TJ didn't name-check it in his "head and heart letter," this building in the heart of the Latin Quarter was a TJ fave; he owned and displayed two prints of it; WTJ, 180.

toll gate "palaces"—TJ to David Humphries, Aug. 14, 1787; TJP, 3–4, 51.

that place in the Latin Quarter—WTJ, 372–373; TJ to David Rittenhouse, Mar. 19, 1791, FO. The excellent exhibit "Thomas Jefferson, Architect: Palladian Models, Democratic Principles, and the Conflict of Ideals" at the

Chrysler Museum of Art in 2019-2020 had some of the paper on display—with the address of the printer still visible.

Jefferson leaped over a hedge—TJ to Cosway, Oct. 12, 1786, FO; Kukla, *Mr. Jefferson's Women*, 96–98. It's unclear exactly what TJ's mishap consisted of—some stories have him falling off a horse.

head and heart letter—TJ to Cosway, Oct. 12, 1786, FO.

could not bring this woman back with him—Scharff, *The Women Jefferson Loved*, 213.

he effectively ended the liaison—Burstein, *The Inner Jefferson*, 106–107.

the "tent of heaven"—TJ to Benjamin Hawkins, Mar. 22, 1796, FO; Adams, *Jefferson's Monticello*, 91–92, 95; Howard, *Thomas Jefferson*, 47.

"putting up and pulling down"—"Architecture is my delight…(Quotation)," TJE, https://monticello.org/site/research-and-collections/architecture-my-delightquotation.

The house's new design—McLaughlin, *Jefferson and Monticello*, 209–210, 249–255.

placed second-story windows at floor level—Howard, *Thomas Jefferson*, 49; Mills Lane, *Architecture of the Old South: Virginia* (Beehive, 1987), 97.

lit internally by skylights, appeared to be one story—Adams, *Jefferson's Monticello*, 100, 115; Howard, *Thomas Jefferson*, 61.

"modern" architecture—TJ to Pierre-Charles L'Enfant, Apr. 10, 1791, FO.

his "delight" and "putting up and pulling down"—"Architecture is my delight…(Quotation)," TJE, https://monticello.org/site/research-and-collections/architecture-my-delightquotation.

a pencil and eraser—WTJ, 372–373; TJ to David Rittenhouse, Mar. 19, 1791, FO.

the Rotunda, with its library, the mind—Wilson, *Academical Village*, 108.

the dome, built using the construction method—Wilson et al., *Campus Guide*, 65.

Inside are Composite columns—*Thomas Jefferson's Academical Village*, 107.

like the Column of the Désert de Retz—Frederick Doveton Nichols, *Thomas Jefferson's Architectural Drawings* (Charlottesville: UVA Press, 1961), 9; Wills, *Mr. Jefferson's University*, 103–105.

his "academical village"—TJ to William Short, Nov. 10, 1818. TJ used this term in several letters—naturally, I'm going with the one to Short.

The Lawn and the royal residence at Marly—Wilson, *Academical Village*, 85.

Pavilion I—Howard, *Thomas Jefferson*, 160; Wilson et al., *Campus Guide*, 45.

Pavilion III—Wilson et al., *Campus Guide*, 51–52.

"to show that the tenant's time"—Jefferson, Notes of a Tour to the Southern Parts of France etc. [3 Mar.–10 June, 1787], FO; Wilson et al., *Campus Guide*, 40.

"no two alike" —TJ to William Thornton, May 9, 1817, FO.

Pavilion X—Wilson, *Academical Village*, 106; Howard, *Thomas Jefferson*, 164; Wilson et al., *Campus Guide*, 61. Or perhaps it was a nod to ancient Greek architecture, not the 1820s Revival style.

Pavilion IX—Wilson, *Academical Village*, 83–84; Howard, *Thomas Jefferson*, 163; Wilson et al., *Campus Guide*, 59–61.

dreamworld—Andrew Burstein memorably characterized Jefferson as moving through a "well-ordered dreamworld" in his The Inner Jefferson, 21.

the slave cottage behind Pavilion IX—Louis P. Nelson and Maurie D. McInnis, "Landscape of Slavery," in *Educated in Tyranny*, 65, 71–73.

"educated…in tyranny"—NSV, 162. McInnis and Nelson, of course, brilliantly took this quote for the title of their book.

students could not bring slaves to school—Maurie D. McInnis in *Educated in Tyranny*, 12.

Jefferson tried to keep the enslaved workforce out of sight—Nelson and McInnis in *Educated in Tyranny*, 48–51, 54, 57, 59, 62, 63, 65, 68, 71.

one of the first slave dwellings, built in 1825—Louis P. Nelson and Maurie D. McInnis, "Landscape of Slavery," in *Educated in Tyranny*, 72.

Thrimston Hern—THL, 140.

the capital of the Confederacy—Howard, *Thomas Jefferson*, 68.

Rotunda requisitioned—Wilson, et al., *Campus Guide*, 20, 124.

CHAPTER FOURTEEN: THOSE WHO LABOR FOR MY HAPPINESS

"Those Who Labor for My Happiness"—The full quote by TJ is "I have my house to build, my fields to form, and to watch for the happiness of those who labor for mine." TJ to Angelica Schuyler Church, Nov. 27, 1793, FO. Lucinda Stanton, paraphrasing, shortened it to six words and used it as the title for her book *Those Who Labor for My Happiness: Slavery at Thomas Jefferson's Monticello*. I relied on her book and Annette Gordon-Reed's *The Hemingses of Monticello* extensively in this chapter and the three that follow. I'm indebted to their research, as well as that of the late Dianne Swann-Wright and all who worked on Monticello's Getting Word project.

Enslaved persons sold, 1785—FB, 25. Additionally see B. Bernetiae Reed's compelling *The Slave Families of Thomas Jefferson: A Pictorial Study Book with an Interpretation of His Farm Book in Genealogy Charts* (Greensboro: Sylvest-Sarah, 2007).

Selected expenses of Thomas Jefferson in Paris, 1785—MB, 1785; WTJ, 144, 146, 237, 304, 308, 310.

enslaved over six hundred people and freed only seven—"Slavery FAQ's," https://monticello.org/slavery /slavery-faqs/property/#free.

unlike back home—TJ was constantly attended to by enslaved persons on his travels back home—Jupiter Evans from 1764 to 1774, then Robert Hemings, and later others. TWL, 107–108. In fact, his earliest memory was of being brought on a pillow by an enslaved rider on horseback to a relative's house at Tuckahoe, near Richmond. Randall, *Life of Thomas Jefferson*, Vol. I, 11.

not accompanied by those of a slave behind him—TJ traveled in 1786 to England with his French valet Adrien Petit and William Stephens Smith, the American legation's secretary in London. Shackelford, *Thomas Jefferson's Travels*, 43; MB 1786. When he traveled through the south of France and Italy in 1787, TJ hired a valet named Petit Jean in Dijon; MB 1787, FO; TJ to Short, Mar. 15, 1787, FO. In 1788, he brought his French servant Lespagnol with him; MB 1788, FO.

he journeyed "incognito"—TJ to Lafayette, Apr. 11, 1787, FO; TJ to John Banister, Jr., June 19, 1787, FO.

"contained in a single trunk"—TJ to Madame de Tott, Apr. 5, 1787, FO.

the "hideous" institution—TJ to William Short, Sept. 8, 1823, FO "early access" document.

slavery was a "moral depravity"—TJ to Thomas Cooper, Sept. 10, 1814, FO.

"If Jefferson was wrong, America is wrong"—James Parton, *Life of Thomas Jefferson* (Boston: James R. Osgood and Company, 1874), iii, 165.

historians rejected the claim—Francis D. Cogliano, *Thomas Jefferson: Reputation and Legacy* (Charlottesville: UVA Press, 2008), 183–184.

a DNA test conducted—E. A. Foster, "Jefferson Fathered Slave's Last Child," *Nature*, Nov. 1998.

Planting rice—Lucia Stanton, "Rice," TJE, https://monticello.org/site/research-and-collections/rice.

Wormley Hughes, the sunken lane—TJ to Edmund Bacon, Nov. 24, 1807, FO "early access" document; TJ to Martha Jefferson Randolph, June 6, 1814, FO.

skilled enslaved laborers like Thrimston Hern—THL, 140. He also cut the bases and capitals of the columns of

Monticello's West Portico: John Gorman to TJ, July 1, 1820, FO "early access" document; John Gorman to TJ, Aug. 30, 1823, FO "early access" document.

Jupiter Evans carved Monticello's limestone columns—TWL, 109.

Lewis turned the balusters—TJ to James Dinsmore, Dec. 15, 1807, FO "early access" document.

"I never saw a leaf of tobacco"—TJ to Thomas Leiper, Feb. 23, 1801, FO.

Lewis sold thirty-one humans under his own name—FB, 25. To be clear, Jefferson did not directly sell people to pay for any particular trip. He inherited the lion's share of his debt from his late father-in-law, John Wayles. Nonetheless, his expensive Parisian lifestyle contributed to his debt and perceived need to auction off slaves. For more on the issue of Jefferson's debt, which worsened while abroad, see https://monticello.org/site/research-and-collections/debt. His travels resulted in additional expenses. (He charged his expenses on his travels to the U.S. government only when they were in the course of his public duties; see TJ to William Short, July 28, 1791, FO. He thus did not charge the government for his 1787 trip; he decided to pay half his expenses for his return trip from Amsterdam himself since he engaged in exploration en route. MB 1788, FO.)

authorize further auctions—FB, 25.

municipal museum, telling the true story—Charles Becker, "L'exposition Les Anneaux de la Mémoire," *La Politique Africaine*, 1993; Krystel Gauldé, *Nantes et la Traite Négrière Atlantique* (Chateau des Ducs de Bretagne, 2017).

Slave traders in Nantes—Jefferson, Notes of a Tour to the Southern Parts of France etc. [3 Mar.–10 June 1787], FO.

the memorial—Francoise Vergès, ed., *Liberté! Le Mémorial de l'abolition de l'esclavage* (Chateau des Ducs de Bretagne, 2015), 13; https://memorial.nantes.fr.

In the Declaration of Independence—Jefferson's "Original Rough Draught" of the Declaration of Independence [11 June–4 July 1776], FO. TJ wrote that the king's supposed support of the slave trade was a "cruel war against human nature itself, violating its most sacred rights and liberties in the persons of a distant people who never offended him." Congress deleted the passage from his draft.

ban the importation of enslaved persons, ban slavery in territories—A Bill Concerning Slaves, 18 June 1779; TJA; Report of the Committee, 1 Mar. 1784, FO; TJ's Observations on Démeunier's Manuscript, June 22, 1786, FO.

In *Notes on Virginia*—NSV, 87, 137–138, 162–163.

invited him to join—TJ to Brissot de Warville, Feb. 11, 1788, FO.

George Washington provided in his will—"Last Will and Testament, 9 July, 1799, FO." Additionally, the will freed his enslaved valet, William Lee, upon Washington's death.

Edward Coles, "a younger generation"—Kurt E. Leichtel and Bruce Carveth, *Crusade Against Slavery: Edward Coles, Pioneer of Freedom* (Carbondale: Southern Illinois University Press, 2018), 54–70; TJ to Edward Coles, Aug. 25, 1814, FO.

he supported the admission of Missouri—TJ to John Holmes, Apr. 22, 1820, FO "early access" document.

CHAPTER FIFTEEN: HARD TRUTHS

The *Prince of Wales*—Trans-Atlantic Slave Trade Database, "Prince of Wales," #17812, https://www.slavevoyages.org/voyage/database#.

"The mortality amongst the slaves"—Farell and Jones to Wayles and Randolph, Apr. 23, 1773, FO.

return voyage to England, first wedding anniversary—Trans-Atlantic Slave Trade Database, "Prince of Wales;" Hyland, Jr., *Martha Jefferson*, 86–89.

TJ's purchase of and inheritance of enslaved persons—TWL, 106.

John Wayles's life trajectory—THM, 59–61, 68–72.

It was his daughter Martha—TJA.

Wayles sold the souls—THM, 6.

the Virginia tobacco market collapsed—Douglas Irwin, *Clashing Over Commerce: A History of U.S. Trade Policy* (Chicago: University of Chicago Press, 2017), 43.

John died—MB 1773; FO.

The unacknowledged father—Madison Hemings, "Life Among the Lowly"; THM, 37, 49, 77–80, 88–90.

Wayles's debts, sums "not worth oak leaves"—JTV, 441–444; ROM, 203–204; THM, 316–317; TJ to Alexander McCaul, Apr. 19, 1786, FO. Ellis provides a good summary of TJ's problems with debt in *American Sphinx*, 162–166.

"The torment of mind I endure"—TJ to Nicholas Lewis, July 29, 1787, FO.

the bankers he met in Amsterdam—MB, 1788.

He wrote to Lewis again—TJ to Nicholas Lewis, July 11, 1788, FO.

sketching designs of Palladian-style cottages for them—Henry Wiencek, *Master of the Mountain: Thomas Jefferson and His Slaves* (New York: Farrar, Straus and Giroux, 2012), 34–35.

Freeing his slaves would ruin his children's future—TJ to Nicholas Lewis, July 29, 1787, FO. By this point, TJ wasn't even seriously considering freeing his slaves—he was internally debating whether selling some of them or keeping them to engage in more labor for him would be more profitable.

"haunted nightly"—TJ to D. L. Hylton, Mar. 17, 1792, FO.

brainstormed new projects—TJ to Nicholas Lewis, July 29, 1787, FO; TJ to Nicholas Lewis, July 11, 1788, FO.

the political risks he ran—TJ to Madison, May 11, 1785; Richard Price to TJ, July 2, 1785; Madison to TJ, Nov. 15, 1785 (wishing for enlightened students to read about Jefferson's emancipation plans in *Notes*, but worrying that it might offend the "narrow-minded").

"moral evil"—NSV, 87.

Jefferson's relatives sent Hemings instead—TJ to Francis Eppes, Aug. 30, 1785, FO; Eppes to TJ, Apr. 14, 1787, FO; TWL, 135–136. "Isabel" was Isabel Hern, an enslaved domestic worker, and wife of David Hern, an enslaved carpenter who also blasted through the rock to construct TJ's canal on the Rivanna.

Sally Hemings's age, appearance—THM 192–193, 284–285.

Captain Ramsey offered; she continued on to France—THM, 198–203.

A complex series of French rulings; filing suit—THM, 172–177.

failed to register Sally—THM, 202.

neglected to register James—THM, 174–175, 185–186.

Deceiving customs officials—Jefferson, Notes of a Tour to the Southern Parts of France etc. [3 Mar.–10 June, 1787], FO; Andre Limozin to TJ, Aug. 6, 1788, FO.

Trafficking—Jefferson himself characterized the importation of slaves as "violations of human rights" in his Sixth State of the Union Address.

"I have known an instance"—TJ to Paul Bentalou, Aug. 25, 1786, FO.

Sally lived on the Champs-Élysées—THM, 211.

"During that time"—Madison Hemings, "Life Among the Lowly, No. 1," *The Pike County Republican*, Mar. 17, 1873 (L. F. Harlow, ed.), found at https://www.encyclopediavirginia.org/_Life_Among_the_Lowly_No _1_by_Madison_Hemings_March_13_1873.

Allegations; no response by Jefferson; the nephews—Joshua D. Rothman, "James Callender and Social Knowledge of Interracial Sex in Antebellum Virginia," in Lewis and Onuf, eds., *Sally Hemings and Thomas Jefferson*, 88–90, 95–96, 104–106.

nearly all historians dismissed the statements—Scot A. French and Edward L. Ayers, "The Strange Career of Thomas Jefferson; Race and Slavery in American Memory, 1943–1993," in Onuf, *Jeffersonian Legacies*.

a 1998 DNA study—E. A. Foster, "Jefferson Fathered Slave's Last Child," *Nature*, Nov. 1998. The DNA study indicated that Eston Hemings, one of Sally's sons, was a Jefferson male—but not conclusively a descendant of TJ, since the testing subjects were descendants of TJ's grandfather. It did rule out the nephews, Peter and Samuel Carr, who were sons of Jefferson's sister.

The statistical chance—"Monticello Affirms Thomas Jefferson Fathered Children with Sally Hemings," Thomas Jefferson Foundation, https://monticello.org/thomas-jefferson/jefferson-slavery/thomas-jefferson-and -sally-hemings-a-brief-account/monticello-affirms-thomas-jefferson-fathered-children-with-sally -hemings/.

Jefferson's "concubine"—Gordon-Reed defines it as "a woman who lived with a man without being married to him," THM, 107.

Was there love?—In THM, Gordon-Reed devotes a chapter, "'The Treaty' and 'Did They Love Each Other?'" to the subject of each of their motivations. In particular, see 365.

Description of Blacks—NSV, 138–139, 141, 143.

Emancipated slaves had to be deported—NSV, 139; TJ to Jared Sparks, Feb. 4, 1824, FO "early access" document. In 1820, in a private letter, he proposed that emancipated slaves be sent to Santo Domingo, although he no longer publicly advocated for such a scheme. TJ to Albert Gallatin, Dec. 26, 1820, FO "early access" document.

MB, 1789, FO (note on TJ's purchase of muskets).

Honoré Blanc and his methods, later taken up by Eli Whitney—TJ to John Jay, Aug. 30, 1785, FO; TJ to James Monroe, Nov. 14, 1801, FO; Thomson, *Jefferson's Shadow*, 162–164; Bedini, *Thomas Jefferson*, 248, 292–293. TJ found Blanc's methods so "advantageous" that he bought half a dozen arms and sent them to Henry Knox, the secretary at war. TJ to Knox, Sept. 12, 1789, FO. Whitney later established an arms manufactory claiming to use interchangeable parts, although some questioned whether he actually employed this technology.

Birmingham, New York, nail factory—MB 1786, FO; "Jefferson's Journal of the Tour, 20 May–10 June 1791," FO; "Nailery," TJE, https://monticello.org/site/research-and-collections/nailery.

"The negroes too old to be hired"—TJ to Nicholas Lewis, July 11, 1788, FO.

a small, short-lived textile operation—TJ to Tadeusz Kosciuszko, June 28, 1812, FO; "Textile Shop," TJE, https:// monticello.org/site/research-and-collections/textile-shop.

Whitney's patent for a cotton gin—Bedini, *Thomas Jefferson*, 141–143.

dreamed that slavery would wane—Andrew Delbanco, *The War Before the War: Fugitive Slaves and the Struggle for America's Soul from the Revolution to the Civil War* (New York: Penguin Press, 2018), 25–26.

it could not do so before January 1, 1808—Article 1, Section 9 of the U.S. Constitution.

sending them "down the river" to plant and harvest cotton—Delbanco, *The War Before the War*, 26–33; Sven Becket, *Empire of Cotton: A Global History* (New York: Alfred A. Knopf, 2015), 102–104; Ira Berlin, *Generations of Captivity: A History of African-American Slaves* (Cambridge: Belknap Press, 2003), 168–173.

Hunting, emancipation, education—TWL, 6, 21–22, 114–116, 164–66.

"A child raised every two years"—TJ to Joel Yancey, Jan. 17, 1819, FO. TJ used the term "breeding" woman in this letter, although he did not mention selling children at auction.

Jefferson's yeoman farmer constituents—Dumas Malone, *Jefferson the President: First Term, 1801–1805* (Boston: Little, Brown and Co., 1970), 338–339 (on celebrations of the Louisiana Purchase); Garry Wills, *"Negro President": Jefferson and the Slave Power* (New York: Houghton Mifflin, 2003), 115–116.

would have lost—Wills, *"Negro President": Jefferson and the Slave Power*, 1–5.

Expanded his base, won fifteen out of seventeen states—Malone, *Jefferson the President*, 433; Meacham, *Thomas*

Jefferson, 392–393, 406; Edward J. Lawson, *A Magnificent Catastrophe: The Tumultuous Election of 1800, America's First Presidential Campaign* (New York: Free Press, 2007), 274–275.

The DeWolfs—Paul Davis, "Living Off the Trade," *Providence Journal*, Mar. 17, 2006; James DeWolf, Biographical Directory of the U.S. Congress, https://bioguideretro.congress.gov/Home/MemberDetails ?memIndex=D000295; Trans-Atlantic Slave Trade Database, "Thomas Jefferson," #3657.

"the world's best hope"—First Inaugural Address, Mar. 4,1801, FO.

CHAPTER SIXTEEN: LOOK CLOSER: STORIES OF THE ENSLAVED

"Gangsta's Paradise"—Annette Gordon-Reed, the coolest professor I never had, name-checked the song from the stage.

"He desired to bring my mother back with him"—This and the other quotes from Madison Hemings used in the presentation come from the account he published in "Life Among the Lowly, No. 1," *The Pike County Republican* (previously cited). You can see the stunning Monticello presentation at https://monticello.org /sallyhemings/, which contains a wealth of information about her and interviews with descendant Diana Redman, Professor Gordon-Reed, and Lucia Stanton.

researchers have connected with hundreds of people—Lucia Stanton and Dianne Swann-Wright, "Bonds of Memory: Identity and the Hemings Family," in Jan Ellen Lewis and Peter S. Onuf, *Sally Hemings and Thomas Jefferson: History, Memory, and Civic Culture* (Charlottesville: UVA Press, 1999), 161–183.

a day Jefferson spent listening to a Mozart concerto—MB 1785, FO.

worked in the nailery, suffering a serious head injury—TWL, 86; THM, 509, 579–580.

his passage paid for; died from causes unknown—TWL, 288–289 (discussing Bill Webb's contributions to the research on Colbert); THM, 580.

Jupiter Evans—TWL, 107–113.

"I am sorry for him"—TJ to Thomas Mann Randolph, Jr., Feb. 4, 1800. Lucia Stanton ends her thoroughly researched recounting of Evans's life with this damning phrase as well. In his letter, Jefferson doesn't even get around to mentioning the death of Evans (whom Randolph knew well, too) until after discussing the details of which fields a prospective tenant was to rent.

little to no intrinsic value—Gordon-Reed expanded on this point in her essay "'The Memories of a Few Negroes': Rescuing America's Future at Monticello," in Lewis and Onuf, *Sally Hemings and Thomas Jefferson*, 237–241.

Gordon-Reed's 1997 book—Annette Gordon-Reed, *Thomas Jefferson and Sally Hemings: An American Controversy* (Charlottesville: UVA Press, 1997).

a stew stove—Fraser Nieman, "Monticello's First Kitchen: Archaeologists Discover Evidence of Equipment Needed for French Cuisine," *Monticello Magazine*, Summer, 2019; Justin Sarafin, "Like Clockwork: French Influence in Monticello's Kitchen" in DAM, 24; Justin Sarafin, 25.

For many years, Monticello mostly skipped over the issue of slavery—TWL, viii; Eric Gable, *Anthropology and Egalitarianism: Ethnographic Encounters from Monticello to Guinea-Bissau* (Bloomington: Indiana University Press, 2011), 52; Justin Sarafin, 53; French and Ayers, "The Strange Career of TJ," in Onuf, *Jeffersonian Legacies*, 434, 444; Justin Sarafin, 446.

a "site of conscience"—Monticello belongs to the International Coalition of Sites of Conscience; see https:// monticello.org/thomas-jefferson-foundation/site-of-conscience/.

Tobacco, chickens, banjo—TJ, "On Tobacco Culture," May 4, 1784, FO; TWL, 21; NSV, 288, n. 10.

The return of the Jeffersons and Hemingses on Dec. 23, 1789—THM, 397–401.

CHAPTER SEVENTEEN: THE LONG WALK TO FREEDOM

cared for Thoroughbreds—FB 87–88, 109–111; TWL 108, 112; "F. stable," TJE, https://monticello.org
/mulberry-row/places/f-stable.

worked on the carriages—Isaac Jefferson, "Life of Isaac Jefferson of Petersburg, Blacksmith, 1847" *Encyclopedia
Virginia,* https://www.encyclopediavirginia.org/_Life_of_Isaac_Jefferson_of_Petersburg_Virginia_Blacksmith
_by_Isaac_Jefferson_1847. He went by the surname "Granger" but in his reminiscences was identified by
the writer as "Jefferson"—whether this was his choice or not is not known.

Isaac Granger could remember—Isaac Jefferson, "Life of Isaac Jefferson."

lived in both Annapolis and Philadelphia—MB, 1775, 1776, 1784, FO.

returned from Boston to Virginia—MB, 1784.

Hemings was able to hire himself out—TJ to Nicholas Lewis, July 1, 1784, FO; THL, 170.

they married and had children—THM, 450.

Robert traveled in advance, returned to Virginia—THM, 437–438.

Robert Hemings was finally free—"Deed of Manumission of Robert Hemings, 24 Dec., 1794," FO; TJ to Thomas
Mann Randolph, Dec. 26, 1794, FO.

He would live with his wife—Martha Randolph to TJ, Jan. 15, 1795, FO; TJ to George Jefferson, June 21, 1799,
FO; THM, 522–527.

the small but thriving community—Douglas R. Egerton, *Gabriel's Rebellion: The Virginia Slave Conspiracies of 1800
and 1802* (Chapel Hill: UNC Press, 1993), 11, 19, 49.

By 1802, he had bought a half-acre lot in the city—"Robert Hemings," TJE, https://monticello.org/site
/research-and-collections/robert-hemings.

he lost one of his hands—Isaac Jefferson, "Life of Isaac Jefferson."

preferring to run a fruit stand—THM, 522–523.

planned a march—Egerton, *Gabriel's Rebellion,* 24, 49–69.

during the delay—*Id.,* 69–70.

hanging Gabriel and other ringleaders—James Sidbury, *Ploughshares into Swords: Race, Rebellion, and Identity in
Gabriel's Virginia, 1730–1810* (Cambridge: Cambridge University Press, 1997), 125–127.

New laws—Egerton, *Gabriel's Rebellion,* 148, 164–167.

Following the Revolution—Nicolas Guyatt, *Bind Us Apart: How Enlightened Americans Invented Racial Segregation*
(New York: Basic Books, 2016), 79; Ira Berlin, *Many Thousands Gone: The First Two Centuries of Slavery in
North America* (Cambridge: Belknap Press, 1998), 361–363.

the dream of ending slavery in Virginia dying; so was the way of life of the White planters—Delbanco, *The War
Before the War,* 26–27; Susan Dunn, *Dominion of Memories: Jefferson, Madison, and the Decline of Virginia*
(New York: Basic Books, 2007), 7–10.

most lucrative income source—Dunn, *Dominion of Memories,* 45; Egerton, *Gabriel's Rebellion,* 161.

Robert Hemings's daughter got married—THM, 522.

a farm and a town house three blocks away—Egerton, *Gabriel's Rebellion,* 19, 23; "Robert Hemings," TJE.

he was literate—THM, 402.

making inquiries about a runaway slave—TJ to George Jefferson, May 18, 1799, FO; George Jefferson to TJ, June
3, 1799, FO.

he likely helped a nephew of his—THM, 578.

"poor old Robert Hemings is dead"—Martha Jefferson Randolph to TJ, Aug. 7, 1819, FO.

James Hubbard's early years—THL, 145–147; Wiencek, *Master of the Mountain,* 143–144. TJ bought squirrel skins
from James Hubbard, the father; MB 1780, FO.

a "dozen little boys"—TJ to Nicolas Demenunier, Apr. 29, 1795, FO. Incredibly, this quote follows a passage in which TJ praises the liberties brought on by the French Revolution. See also "Nailery," TJE, https://monticello.org/site/research-and-collections/nailery.

money to incentivize him—MB 1799 and MB 1802 (Hubbard), FO; TWL, 80–81.

"bears sometimes came"—Isaac Jefferson, "Life of Isaac Jefferson."

forged papers; began his journey—TWL, 148; Wiencek, *Master of the Mountain*, 145–146.

capturing the "large fellow"—Daniel Bradley to TJ, Sept. 7, 1805, FO "early access" document.

"severely flogged"—TJ to Reuben Perry, Apr. 16, 1812, FO; Hubbard's escape and capture—TWL, 150–152; Wiencek, *Master of the Mountain*, 147–148.

"so distant"—TJ to Thomas Mann Randolph, June 8, 1803, FO.

the South Road—Note that the South Road was not a major throughway at Monticello; Hubbard just as easily might have left via the main East Road. I mention it for its symbolism.

In Mississippi or Louisiana—Berlin, *Many Thousands Gone*, 345–346.

James Hemings would obtain freedom—THM, 452–453; "Agreement with James Hemings," Sept. 15, 1793, FO.

he trained his younger brother Peter how to make sauces, fricassees, and snow eggs—THM, 504–505; DAM, 25, 167, 178.

Chef Ashbell—Check out his website at https://jameshemingssociety.org/ashbell-mcelveen/. I got to talk to him some time after the festival, and we discovered that we both had spent a year in college studying at the same school in Aix-en-Provence—that's where he became a Francophile and took steps on the road to becoming a chef, he told me.

married Betsy, moved to a cabin—TJ to Edmund Bacon, Feb. 27, 1809, FO "early access document"; "Peter Hemings," TJE, https://monticello.org/site/research-and-collections/peter-hemings.

ex-Virginia planters eagerly bought up land—Berlin, *Many Thousands Gone*, 265; Dunn, *Dominion of Memories*, 8, 42; TJ to Albert Gallatin, Nov. 24, 1818, FO. Kentucky originally even formed part of the Old Dominion, becoming a state in its own right only in 1792 (as Tennessee did in 1796, splitting from North Carolina).

Even the southern accent—Erik R. Thomas, "Rural White Southern Accents," in Bernd Kormann and Edgar Werner, eds., *A Handbook of Varieties of English: A Multimedia Reference Tool* (New York: Mouton de Gruyter, 2004), 300–301, 319–320; Eugene D. Genovese, *Roll, Jordan, Roll: The World the Slaves Made* (New York: Pantheon Books, 1975), 433.

blended French techniques with Black foodways—RSE, 135–137, 143–144, 186–188, 192–194. Peter came up with his own recipe for muffins, a "great luxury," that, Jefferson noted, his cooks in Washington couldn't replicate. TJ to Martha Randolph, Nov. 2, 1802, FO.

a jaw's harp was found—"Brass Jaw Harp," accessed via Monticello Explorer; for a link, navigate to https://monticello.org/research-education/for-educators/jefferson-quotes-and-documents/.

"with half-closed eyes"—THL, 22.

"imagining a small catch," "the Banjar"—NSV, 140, 288, n. 10.

"the favorite passion of my soul"—TJ to Giovanni Fabbroni, June 8, 1778, FO.

"nightwalkers," those who gathered in the dark—THL 21, 116; TJ to Richard Richardson, Feb. 10, 1800, FO; NSV, 139.

Black music—Martha Jefferson Randolph noted the words to African American songs she heard. Many referenced travel, including a rowing tune with a chorus of "oh yo! oh yo! oh yo!" Another boasted about avoiding Captain Shields, the notorious police officer who harassed African Americans in Richmond: "I was an old hare, I was born in the snow, I was pursued by the black horse of Shields." Elizabeth Langhorne, "Black Music and Tales from Jefferson's Monticello," *Journal of the Virginia Folklore Society*, 1979, 60–67.

"come out among black people"—Isaac Jefferson, "Life of Isaac Jefferson."

Sally's sons Madison and Eston—TWL, 166, 200, 224, 234.

But the musicians who cashed in—Laurent Dubois, *The Banjo: America's African Instrument* (Cambridge: Belknap Press, 2016), 194–202; Eric Lott, *Love and Theft: Blackface Minstrelsy and the American Working Class* (New York: Oxford University Press, 1993), 15 (noting that Frederick Douglass called Whites who profited off black music "filthy scum").

apparently committed suicide—William Evans to TJ, Nov. 5, 1801, FO. The record is unclear, though, just how he lost his life; some (including Ashbell McElveen) maintain that it was not a suicide.

Edith Fossett, her cuisine—TWL, 187–188; DAM, 42, 74.

the art of making beer—THM, 729, n. 4; "Beer," TJE, https://monticello.org/site/research-and-collections /beer.

his nephew Daniel Farley—THL, 222.

1827 slave auction—"Slave Auction," https://monticello.org/slaveauction/.

Peter Hemings's freedom—TWL, 222.

Mary Hemings, Thomas Bell, and Joe Fossett—TWL, 216–218.

Fossett, too, traveled clandestinely to Washington, DC—TWL, 188–189.

Ten children including, in 1815, Peter Fossett—"Recollections of Peter Fossett," *New York World*, Jan. 30, 1898, https://monticello.org/slavery/slave-memoirs-oral-histories/recollections-of-peter-fossett/; "Fossett-Hemings Family," TJE, https:///getting-word/families/fossett-hemings-family.

freed in his master's will—"Last Will and Testament," https://monticello.org/site/research-and-collections /last-will-and-testament.

couldn't afford to buy Peter, age eleven—TWL, 202.

"suddenly...put upon an auction block"—"Recollections of Peter Fossett," *New York World*, Jan. 30, 1898, https:// monticello.org/slavery/slave-memoirs-oral-histories/recollections-of-peter-fossett/.

"If I ever catch you with a book"—*Id.*

In 1831, slaves in Virginia again rose up—Berlin, *Generations of Captivity*, 203–204.

"No meetings, no night visiting"—TWL, 200.

the Underground Railroad—Eric Foner, *Gateway to Freedom: The Hidden History of the Underground Railroad* (New York: W. W. Norton and Co., 2015), 13–19.

"Under the flickering light of the North star;" northern racism—Delblanco, *The War Before the War*, 35, 128–132.

the north orchard—Hatch, *The Fruit and Fruit Trees of Monticello*, 7–8.

"blasted" and "uprooted" trunks—Francis C. Gray, "Account of a Visit to Monticello" [4–7 Feb. 1815], FO.

Jefferson's younger sister and her enslaved servant—MB 1774, FO.

"an attempt to gain my own freedom"—"Recollections of Peter Fossett."

rejoin his family; in freedom—TWL, 204–205.

fought for the Union—TWL, 251–280.

right through the front door—TWL, 205–206. Stanton tells this story beautifully.

William Monroe Trotter—TWL, 297–299; Kerri Greenidge, *Black Radical: The Lives and Times of William Monroe Trotter* (New York: Liveright, 2019).

CHAPTER EIGHTEEN: THE LAST DAYS OF THE ANCIEN RÉGIME

the Sun King constructed much—Simon Schama, *Citizens: A Chronicle of the French Revolution* (New York, Alfred A. Knopf, 1989), 369–370.

"his mind was weakness itself"—TJA.

preferring to spend his days hunting—John Hardman, *Louis XVI* (New Haven: Yale University Press, 1993), 126.

impoverishing common people—William Doyle, *The Oxford History of the French Revolution* (New York: Oxford University Press, 1989), 14–23.

the new class—Georges Lefebvre, *The Coming of the French Revolution* (Princeton: Princeton University Press, 1937), 42–50.

the French state was nearly bankrupt—Doyle, *Oxford History*, 66, 84–85.

at Versailles the party never stopped—Colin Jones, *Versailles* (New York: Basic Books, 2018), 86–96; Evelyne Lever, *Marie Antoinette: The Last Queen of France* (New York: St. Martin Griffin's, 2000), 28–29. The Palais Royal became a trendier place to be seen, however.

Jefferson traveled to Versailles—MB 1784, FO.

Goblets, Haut Brion, lace ruffles—WTJ, 327; Hailman, *Thomas Jefferson on Wine*, 81–83, 131, 149–151; G. S. Wilson, *Jefferson on Display* (Charlottesville: UVA Press 2018), 26–27; MB 1784, FO.

"the plainest man in the room"—TJP, 99–100.

the Petit Trianon and its owner—Lever, *Marie Antoinette*, 34, 59.

"an absolute ascendency"—TJA; TJ to Madison, June 20, 1787.

a social "explosion of some sort"—TJ to Madison, Aug. 2, 1787.

married Louis—Antonia Fraser, *Marie Antoinette: The Journey* (New York: Nan A. Talese, 2001), 70.

Criticisms of Marie Antoinette—Lever, *Marie Antoinette*, 143, 164–168, 182, 191; Fraser, *Marie Antoinette*, 225–226, 240–242, 252, 254.

describing her style changes—TJ to Abigail Adams, Sept. 4, 1785, FO.

commissioned a model agricultural operation—Lever, *Marie Antoinette*, 157–159; Fraser, *Marie Antoinette*, 206–208.

"endeavored to conceal itself"—TJP, 101. The diplomat was Gouverneur Morris.

Her loose-fitting *chemise à la reine*—Lever, *Marie Antoinette*, 134–135.

the king spent each fall at Fontainebleau—MB 1785, FO; Hardman, *Louis XVI*, 33.

a "poor woman" walking—TJ to Madison, Oct. 28, 1785.

"led me into a train of reflections"—*Id*. In his autobiography, TJ spilled much ink detailing "the monstrous abuses of power under which this people were ground to powder," listing unfair taxes, the system of forced labor obliging peasants to build roads without pay, the royal monopoly on selling salt and other products, and the grossly unequal system of land distribution, the "shackles...on freedom of conscience, of thought, and of speech; on the press by the censure...the enormous expenses of the Queen, the princes and the court...and the riches, luxury, indolence and immorality of the clergy," TJA.

The king's reform attempts—Mike Rapport, *The Unruly City: Paris, London, and New York in the Age of Revolution* (New York: Basic Books, 2017), 126–127; Doyle, *Oxford History*, 68–73.

so long as so many peasants lived in abject poverty—ROM, 180–183.

"mass of mankind" (photo caption)—TJ to Roger Chew Weightman, June 24, 1826, FO "early access" document.

"courted the society of gardeners"—TJ to Chastellux, Apr. 4, 1787. Chastellux himself had written a travel account of his time in the U.S. with a glowing review of Jefferson and Monticello.

the "condition of the laboring poor"—TJ to Short, Mar. 15, 1787, FO (*vignerons* are wine producers).

"absolutely incognito"—TJ to Lafayette, Apr. 11, 1787. TJ advised Lafayette to "look into their kettles, eat their bread, loll on their beds under pretense of resting yourself, but in fact to find if they are soft."

a patchwork of principalities—James J. Sheehan, *German History, 1770–1866* (Oxford: Clarendon Press, 1989).

the "little tyrants"—Notes on a Tour through Holland and the Rhine Valley, 3 March 1788–23 April 1788, FO. Impressed by the industriousness of German farmers, TJ devised a plan (which he never pursued) to encourage some to come to Monticello and work as tenant farmers on his land. TJ to Edward Bancroft, Jan. 26, 1788, FO.

"a bill of rights"—TJ to Madison, Dec. 20, 1787, FO.

"send them to Europe"—TJ to Benjamin Hawkins, Aug. 4, 1787, FO.

"accommodated to the genius"—John Rutledge, Jr., to TJ, June 22, 1788, FO; TJ to John Rutledge, Jr., July 13, 1788, FO.

Social problems, 1788–89—Schama, *Citizens*, 305–326; Lefebvre, *The Coming of the French Revolution*, 101–107; Richard Cobb, *Voices of the French Revolution* (Topsfield: Salem House Publishers, 1988) (inset on "hunger").

"help us overcome all the difficulties"—*Lettre du Roi Louis XVI pour la convocation des Etats-généraux, à Versailles*, Apr. 27, 1789, https://archive.org/details/lettreduroipourl_4/page/n3/mode/2up.

The ad hoc body—Doyle, *Oxford History*, 59, 88.

Representatives, petitions of grievances—Lefebvre, *The Coming of the French Revolution*, 71–74; Schama, *Citizens*, 308–319.

"they patrol, they wear cockades"—Short to TJ, Apr. 3, 1789; Schama, *Citizens*, 343–345.

The "disorder"—Rutledge, Jr., to TJ, Apr. 3, 1789.

tracked developments, attended the Estates General, conferred—ROM, 214–231.

"Is this a revolt?"—Christopher Prendergast, *The Fourteenth of July and the Taking of the Bastille* (London: Profile Books, 2008), 30. The adviser was the Duc de La Rochefoucauld-Liancourt, the cousin of Jefferson's good friend Louis-Alexandre de la Rochefoucauld. Although TJ's friend would not survive the French Revolution, his friend's cousin did and later visited TJ at Monticello.

roamed the "tumults"—TJ to Jay, July 19, 1789, FO.

"firmness and wisdom"—TJ to Diaditi, Aug. 3, 1789, FO.

CHAPTER NINETEEN: FRENCH REVOLUTIONS

Le Procope—Rapport, *The Unruly City*, 187; Christopher Hibbert, *The Days of the French Revolution* (New York: Quill William Morrow, 1999), 166; Schama, *Citizens*, 441.

the National Assembly—Hibbert, *Days of the French Revolution*, 58–59.

a list of fundamental rights—Lafayette to TJ, July 6, 1789.

making suggestions on a draft—TJ to Lafayette, July 6, 1789, FO; ROM, 223–225. During the early days of the Revolution, TJ advised the French moderate leaders that it would be acceptable to settle for a constitutional monarchy with a bicameral legislature, so long as they had a strong Declaration of Rights.

These statements of rights sound vaguely familiar—Maier, *American Scripture*, 167–168. John Ferling notes how TJ wished that the Declaration of Rights had gone further than it did; see his *Apostles of Revolution: Jefferson, Paine, Monroe and the Struggle Against the Old Order in America and Europe* (New York: Bloomsbury, 2018), 161–162.

long championed religious freedom—John Ragosta details how the Virginia Statute for Religious Freedom, which TJ had introduced and fought for years, passed in 1786 in his *Religious Freedom: Jefferson's Legacy, America's Creed* (Charlottesville, UVA Press: 2013), 66–100. The statute disestablished the Church of England in Virginia and guaranteed the free exercise of religion for those of all faiths. TJ sent a copy of it to the Count de Mirabeau (who would become one of the leaders of the early years of the French Revolution), asking him to "avail mankind of this example of emancipating human reason"; TJ to Mirabeau, Aug. 20, 1786. Another moderate leader of the Revolution, Condorcet, effusively praised the law in print—as well as the statement TJ had made *Notes on Virginia* that "it does me no injury for my neighbor to say there are twenty gods, or no god"; ROM, 110. From Paris, TJ pushed Madison to support what became the First Amendment to the U.S. Constitution. 99–100. In a famous 1802 letter, TJ wrote that the First Amendment built "a wall of separation between the Church and State." *Id.*, at 37–38, 232.

Jefferson witnessed one of the first insurrections—TJA; *Citizens*, 383–385. TJ provided a blow-by-blow account of how the crowd repelled the mercenaries. Afterward, he wrote, "[t]he people now armed themselves with such weapons as they could find in armorer's shops and private houses, and with bludgeons, and were roaming all night through all parts of the city, without any decided object."

July 14—today celebrated as France's national day. In *The Fourteenth of July,* Prendergast brilliantly describes how the assault on the Bastille entered into French folk memory and became a national holiday a century later.

"a discharge from the Bastille"—TJA. TJ "joined the crowds to watch the razing of the Bastille stone by stone," Adams, *The Paris Years,* 291, for after the assault, crews went to work taking it down. There was no military need to do so, but enterprising men realized the prison was worth more in death than in life. It was a propaganda gold mine. They constructed nearly a hundred model Bastilles from its stone and sent them around the kingdom, along with paperweights and medals made from the rubble, to popularize their cause.

"from despotism to liberty"—TJ to Lafayette, Apr. 2, 1790, FO.

heroes, feted in celebrations—Prendergast, *The Fourteenth of July,* 87; Hibbert, *Days of the French Revolution,* 82–83.

leading a grand procession, spied Patsy Jefferson—"Marquis de Lafayette," TJE, https://monticello.org/site /research-and-collections/marquis-de-lafayette; TJ to Richard Price, July 17, 1789, FO. Lafayette brought the king (under duress) from Versailles to Paris, where he put a revolutionary cockade on his hat and effectively accepted the participation of the National Assembly in Government. Lefebvre, *The Coming of the French Revolution,* 116–117.

Rutledge carried the key—Sara Georgini, "How the Key to the Bastille Ended Up in George Washington's Possession," *Smithsonian Magazine,* July 14, 2016; "The Bastille Key," https://www.mountvernon.org /library/digitalhistory/digital-encyclopedia/article/bastille-key.

reforms by October 1789—Doyle, *Oxford History,* 117–119, 132–133.

"stoned as a false prophet"—TJ to Diodati, Aug. 3, 1789.

calf's head—thankfully, the *tête de veau* didn't have eyes or other facial features, just glistening, quivering slabs of meat. Which was bad enough to look at.

Marat in the early years of the Revolution—Rapport, *The Unruly City,* 187–188; Doyle, *Oxford History,* 120, 134, 154; Schama, *Citizens,* 445, 449.

a radical faction gained power—Doyle, *Oxford History,* 228, 234–237, 246–248; Rapport, *The Unruly City,* 223– 234. Robespierre served as a leader in the Committee of Public Safety, which effectively constituted France's provisional government for around a year.

designed by Dr. Guillotin—Schama, *Citizens,* 619–623.

the Reign of Terror—Schama, *Citizens,* 754–760, 766–768; Hibbert, *Days of the French Revolution,* 219–248.

the king and queen lost their heads—Hibbert, *Days of the French Revolution,* 185–189, 221–222. Louis was executed in 1793 but before what many historians consider to be the beginning of the Reign of Terror.

France was at war—Doyle, *Oxford History,* 197–219.

an unsuccessful civil war—Schama, *Citizens,* 690–704; Doyle, *Oxford History,* 220–246.

Robespierre's end—Schama, *Citizens,* 839–846.

Marat had earlier been assassinated—Schama, *Citizens,* 735–739, 741–742.

A more moderate government took over—Doyle, *Oxford History,* 281–282, 287–288, 318–320.

Napoleon seized power, ended reforms—Doyle, *Oxford History,* 374–390.

"I Beg for liberty's sake"—Lafayette to TJ, Aug. 25, 1789, FO.

"the cloth being removed"—TJA.

paid wages, French lessons—MB 1788, FO; THM, 178, 180, 209, 236–241.

"frivolities of conversation" —TJ to David Humphreys, Mar. 18, 1789, FO.

James probably went to the Palais Royal—This is my supposition, given that the wildly popular Palais Royal attracted many visitors. Hemings did have both free time and spending money—see THM, 171. Sally surely went there at some point as well. Twentieth-century Monticello archaeologists found a white porcelain ointment jar on Mulberry Row, with the name of the apothecary shop printed on it and the inscription "next to the Café Foy," the place where the orator whipped up the crowd to storm the Bastille. She might have acquired the jar and kept it later as a relic (although this, like so much of the lives of enslaved people, can't be known for sure).

trained as a seamstress and boarded—THM, 238–241, 244–247.

the thriving community of Blacks, a freedom suit—THM, 175–182.

welcoming climate—Jonathan Conlin, *Tales of Two Cities: Paris, London, and the Birth of the Modern City* (Berkley: Counterpoint, 2013), 96–102; Popkin, *Panorama of Paris*, 193–196.

the "young and attractive" woman—THM, 350.

Thomas-Alexandre Dumas—THM, 189; Tom Reiss, *The Black Count: Glory, Revolution, Betrayal, and the Real Count of Monte Cristo* (New York: Broadway Paperbacks, 2012).

protestors took to the streets—Sophie Amsili, "*Qui sont les gilets jaunes?*," *Les Echos*, Nov. 18, 2018.

the French middle class—Grégoire Normand, "French Middle Class under Pressure, According to OECD," *La Tribune*, Apr. 12, 2019, https://www.euractiv.com/section/middle-ground-politics/news/french-middle -class-under-pressure-according-to-oecd/.

silk and textile factories—Doyle, *Oxford History*, 87.

a comparative advantage in agriculture—NSV, 164–165. Later, ignoring his own observations, he started the nail- ery with enslaved teenage workers at Monticello, which failed in the face of cheaper British imports.

"as sores do to the strength of the human body"—NSV, 164–165; TJ to Madison, Dec. 20, 1787. TJ later changed his tune, finding that "experience has taught me that manufactures are now as necessary to our indepen- dence as to our comfort." TJ to Benjamin Austin, Jan. 9, 1816, FO.

disapproved of workers' attacks on factories—TJA. Schama details the assaults in *Citizens*, 326–330.

"fanatic" and "Were there but an Adam and an Eve"—Short to TJ, Dec. 8, 1792, FO; TJ to Short, Jan. 3, 1793, FO.

executed some of his own friends—Among Jefferson's friends who lost their lives during the French Revolution were the mathematician and social reformer the Marquis de Condorcet (who died in prison in 1794), the pro-American natural historian Duc de la Rochefoucauld (killed while escaping in 1792), and the statesman Malesherbes (guillotined in 1794), who had traded plants with TJ. See TJP, 74–75.

split fiercely on the stance toward France—ROM, 486–487; Dumas Malone, *Thomas Jefferson and the Ordeal of Liberty* (Boston: Little, Brown and Co., 1962), 39–89.

the Democratic-Republicans—Todd Estes, "Jefferson as Party Leader" in *A Companion to Thomas Jefferson*, Francis D. Cogliano, ed. (Malden, MA: Blackwell Publishing, 2012), 128–139; ROM, 420–428, 457–465, 477 (while noting the difference between the Jeffersonian grouping and modern-day political parties); Malone, *The Ordeal of Liberty*, 264–267; Noble E. Cunningham, Jr., *The Jeffersonian Republicans: The Formation of Party Organization, 1789–1801* (Chapel Hill: UNC Press, 1957), 20–21. Note that political scientists often call the party the Democratic-Republicans (which flags that they spawned the Democratic party), but histo- rians normally prefer the term "Republicans," what the group mostly called itself at the time. The preferred usage in rap musicals is "Democratic-Republicans," sometimes preceded by an f-bomb.

"extensive and zealous party"—TJA.

the "little party" of Federalists—TJ to Short, Jan. 3, 1793.

Democratic-Republican societies sprang up—Sean Wilentz, *Chants Democratic: New York City and the Rise of the American Working Class, 1788–1850* (New York: Oxford University Press, 2004), 68–74; François Furstenberg, *When the United States Spoke French: Five Refugees Who Shaped a Nation* (New York: Penguin Press), 2014, 42–43, 50, 136; Rapport, *The Unruly City*, 292–305; Ferling, *Apostles of Revolution*, 303–305; Cunningham, *The Jeffersonian Republicans*, 62–65.

entered the electoral fray—Malone, *The Ordeal of Liberty*, 273–288; Cunningham, *The Jeffersonian Republicans*, 100–101.

lists of their grievances—Marcelo Wesfried, "*Fiscalité, immigration, élites...découvrez les premières doléances du 'grand débat,*" *Le Figaro*, Jan. 10, 2019.

a decentralized movement—Vincent Glad, "'*Gilets jaunes*': *arrêtons avec la théorie du complot de l'extrême droite*," *La Libération*, Nov. 9, 2018 ; Loris Boichot, "*Wauquiez, Le Pen, Mélenchon...Qui sera (ou pas) aux côtés des 'gilets jaunes' samedi?*," *Le Figaro*, Nov. 14, 2018; Quentin Laurent, "*Gilets jaunes: la mobilisation du 17 novembre divise la gauche,* " *Le Parisien*, Nov. 13, 2018.

"spirit of resistance"—TJ to William Stephens Smith, Nov. 13, 1787. TJ was referring to Shays's Rebellion, an uprising of debtors in western Massachusetts, but his letter made the more universal point that a people must periodically rise up to protect its rights: "[a]nd what country can preserve its liberties if their rulers are not warned from time to time that their people preserve the spirit of resistance?" This letter also includes one of TJ's most incendiary statements, that "[t]he tree of liberty must be refreshed from time to time with the blood of patriots and tyrants."

CHAPTER TWENTY: A LA RECHERCHE DU MOOSE PERDU

Note on the chapter title: the French do not actually say "*le moose*" but "*l'élan*." That might have been useful to know when I was over there. However, there was plenty of confusion over the name of the animal in TJ's time, too, and just what species it was—see NSV, 271 n. 65. Our future president's quest has spawned a rich mini-genre of Jefferson-and-the-moose literature, including Keith Thomson's *Jefferson's Shadow*, 9–11, 13, 68–69 (which holds out the tantalizing possibility that the remains of the beast might still exist somewhere in the City of Lights), and Lee Allan Dugatkin's *Mr. Jefferson and the Giant Moose: Natural History in Early America* (Chicago: University of Chicago Press, 2009), 89–100, which sports an unforgettable cover of Jefferson riding a moose. These books probably cover other scientific issues, but they had me at "moose."

Buffon and his acolytes—Thomson, *Jefferson's Shadow*, 62–73, 101, 107–109, 111–115; Dugatkin, *Mr. Jefferson*, 20–44, 69–70.

the largest section of *Notes on Virginia*—Much of TJ's response to Query VI, Productions Mineral, Vegetable, and Animal, addresses these subjects.

"as if both sides" —NSV, 47.

"When Mr. Jefferson shall have read this"—Thomson, *Jefferson's Shadow*, 13, 68; Hayes, *Road to Monticello*, 303.

he commissioned backwoods hunters—TJ to John Sullivan, Jan. 7, 1786, FO; TJ to William Whipple, Jan. 7, 1786, FO.

the unfortunate beast, killed, left behind—John Sullivan to TJ, Apr. 16, 1787, FO; Sullivan to TJ, May 9, 1787, FO.

"a great deal of [the skin] has come off"—TJ to Buffon, Oct. 1, 1787.

Nonetheless, he presented it to Buffon—John Sullivan to TJ, June 22, 1784, with enclosure, FO; TJ to Buffon, Oct. 1, 1787, FO; L. J. M. Daubenton to TJ, Oct. 2, 1787; TJ to Lacépède, Feb. 24, 1803.

turned around the views—Dugatkin, *Mr. Jefferson*, 100.

wrote to a famed Parisian naturalist—TJ to Lacépède, Feb. 24, 1803, FO. Bernard Germain de Lacépède, who had worked under Buffon, developed a theory of the transmutation of species.

one of the first natural history museums—John McKay, *Discovering the Mammoth: A Tale of Giants, Unicorns, Ivory, and the Birth of a New Science* (New York: Pegasus Books, 2017), 171.

Jefferson's correspondent responded—Lacépède to TJ, July 25, 1803, FO.

"Nature intended me"—TJ to Pierre Samuel du Pont de Nemours, Mar. 2, 1809, FO "early access" document.

"it exists by the help of shelter"—TJ to John Rutledge, Jr., June 19, 1788, FO.

a portable thermometer—Lucia Stanton, "Mediterranean Journey (1787)", TJE, https://monticello.org/site /research-and-collections/mediterranean-journey-1787#footnote4_lkqfky3.

farms shielded by mountain spurs—TJ to Lafayette, Apr. 11, 1787, FO.

steam engines and canal gates—Notes of a Tour into Southern Parts of France etc., 3 Mar.–10 June, 1787, FO.

"the principal residence of the shelled tribe"—NSV, 32. TJ was aware of the phenomenon of the shells even before he reached Tours and noted similar finds at the foot of North Mountain in Virginia.

"spontaneously produced"—Notes of a Tour into Southern Parts of France etc., 3 Mar.–10 June, 1787, FO.

"a wonder [here] somewhere"—NSV, 31–33.

Shippen met with a local naturalist—TL Shippen to TJ, July 31, 1788, FO.

Saussure was a Renaissance Man—Anne Fauche and Stéphane Fischer, "The Skies of Mont Blanc: Following the Traces of Horace-Bénédict de Saussure" (Geneva: Musée d'histoire des sciences, 2011).

"one of the best philosophers"—TJ to John Rutledge, Jr., Sept. 9, 1788. TJ bought Saussure's *Voyages dans les Alpes* a week after writing *Hints* and directing the Boys to Geneva.

"nature's laboratory"—Fauche and Fischer, "The Skies of Mont Blanc."

the Swiss thinker developed a hygrometer—Margarida Archinard, "*Les instruments scientifiques d' Horace-Bénédict de Saussure*," *Le monde alpin et rhodanien*, Vol. 1/2, 1988, 152–155; Fauche and Fischer, "The Skies of Mont Blanc."

"I verily believe"—TJ to Benjamin Vaughn, July 23, 1788, FO; Bedini, *Thomas Jefferson*, 163–164, 185–186.

His cabinet "filled with rare and curious animals"—Rutledge, Jr., to TJ, Sept. 4, 1788, FO.

the entrance hall—TJE, "Entrance hall," https://monticello.org/house-gardens/the-house/room-furnishings /entrance-hall/; Thomson, *Jefferson's Shadow*, 166–167.

"drawn by the history of the times"—TJ to Caspar Wistar, June 10, 1817, FO.

the age of gentlemen naturalists—Tom Shactman, *Gentleman Scientists and Revolutionaries: The Founding Fathers in the Age of Enlightenment* (New York: Macmillan, 2014).

the term "scientist" was coined—Shactman, *Gentleman Scientists and Revolutionaries*, xii; Andrea Wulf, *The Invention of Nature: Alexander Von Humboldt's New World* (New York: Vintage Books, 2015), 278–279.

"skin of a very large animal"—Rutledge, Jr., to TJ, Sept. 4, 1788, FO.

"native only of the torrid zone"—NSV, 45.

"Cautious in not letting his assent"—TJ to Rutledge, Jr., Sept. 9, 1788, FO.

"from the mouse to the mammoth"—TJ to Thomas Walker, Sept. 25, 1783; Archibald Cary to TJ, Oct. 12, 1783, FO.

"big buffalo," which complemented the large tooth—George Rogers Clark to TJ, Feb. 20, 1782, FO; TJ to Clark, Jan. 6, 1783, FO; Arthur Campbell to TJ, Nov. 7, 1782, FO. Later research—aided by specimens that Jefferson sent to Parisian natural historian Georges Cuvier—established that these and other bones came from what Cuvier named the mastodon, a distinct species from the mammoth. Thomson, *Jefferson's Shadow*, 53–59.

"having permitted any one race"—NSV, 53–54.

"Killd a bear"—Archibald Cary to TJ, Oct. 12, 1783, FO. This was the same Cary who whipped the young Isaac Granger when he didn't open the farm gates quickly enough.

incorporated it into tables—NSV, 50–52.

Madison and the weasel—Madison to TJ, June 19, 1786, FO.

17 moosey questions—TJ to William Whipple, Jan. 12, 1784, FO. John Sullivan also distributed the questionnaire to his contacts.

one enclosing moose hair—Whipple to TJ, Mar. 13, 1784, FO.

"an acquisition here more precious"—TJ to John Sullivan, William Whipple, and Archibald Cary (all separately), Jan. 7, 1786, FO. The highlighted quote was in a letter to Whipple, but it was Sullivan's men who wound up bagging the beast.

"promote useful science"—TJ to G. C. Delacoste, May 24, 1807, FO "early access" document.

"in every part of the earth"—TJ to Marc Auguste Pictet, Aug. 3, 1803, FO.

TJ's temperature readings and those of his friends—Thomson, *Jefferson's Shadow*, 179–183; Bedini, *Thomas Jefferson*, 74–77, 118–119, 201–202, 288, 448, 467–469. The Papers of Thomas Jefferson and the Center for Digital Education at UVA have collaborated to put Jefferson's weather records online at https://jefferson-weather-records.org/node/41011.

enlist the government—Lucia Stanton, "Weather Observations," TJE, https://monticello.org/site/research-and-collections/weather-observations.

the Lewis and Clark expedition—"Instructions for Meriwether Lewis," June 20, 1803, FO. TJ asked the adventurers to record the "climate, as characterized by the thermometer, by the proportion of rainy, cloudy and clear days, by lightning, hail, snow, ice, by the access and recess of frost, by the winds prevailing at different seasons, the dates at which particular plants put forth or lose their flower, or leaves, time of appearances of particular birds, reptiles, or insects."

the first physical science agency—TJ signed an 1807 act establishing the Survey of the Coast, the progenitor of today's National Oceanic and Atmospheric Agency; https://www.noaa.gov/our-history. For over sixty years, the NOAA has given out Thomas Jefferson awards to the most dedicated volunteer weather observers in the country.

Banneker's accomplishments—Silvio Bedini, *The Life of Benjamin Banneker: The First African-American Man of Science* (Baltimore: The Maryland Historical Society, 1999), 107–145, 152–154, 177–179, 182–183, 262–264.

"[How] pitiable is it to reflect"—Benjamin Banneker to TJ, Aug. 19, 1791, FO.

"doubts which have been entertained"—TJ to Banneker, Aug. 30, 1791, FO.

"puffing" up—TJ to Joel Barlow, Oct. 8, 1809, FO.

"encouraged the progress of science in all its branches"—TJ to Elbridge Gerry, Jan. 26, 1799, FO.

citizen science—Mary Ellen Hannibal's *Citizen Scientist: Searching for Heroes and Hope in an Age of Extinction* (New York: The Experiment, 2016) sees Jefferson as a touchstone for the citizen science movement (even if it arose after his time). Caren Cooper argues that Jefferson "envisioned what is nowadays called citizen science" in her blog post "Life, Liberty, and the Pursuit of Data," *Scientific American*, July 3, 2012, https://blogs.scientificamerican.com/guest-blog/life-liberty-and-the-pursuit-of-data. See also her *Citizen Science: How Ordinary People Are Changing the Face of Discovery* (New York: Abrams Press, 2016), 18–20.

"not a sprig of grass" he once wrote—TJ to Martha Jefferson Randolph, Dec. 23, 1790, FO.

"A patient pursuit of facts"—NSV, 277, n. 104.

CHAPTER TWENTY-ONE: AS IF BOTH SIDES OF THE ATLANTIC WERE NOT WARMED BY THE SAME GENIAL SUN

Jefferson explored Brittany—MB 1788, FO; Notes of a Tour into Southern Parts of France etc., 3 March–10 June, 1787, FO.

Rutledge and Short arrived there—Short to TJ, Mar. 26, Apr. 3, Apr. 20, Apr. 28, May 2, and May 4, 1789, FO; Rutledge, Jr., to TJ, Mar. 3, Apr. 3, and Apr. 27, 1789, FO. TJ had encouraged Rutledge to tack on a trip to Spain and Portugal, foreseeing that knowledge of those countries and their empires would be "useful" to the U.S. (TJ to Rutledge, Jr., Mar. 25, 1789, FO), but the young man, tired from his journey, decided to return to Paris.

Short's natural history observations—Short to TJ, Sept. 24, Oct. 2, Oct. 28, Nov. 29, and Dec. 23, 1788, and Feb. 11 and Apr. 3, 1789, FO.

"indexes of climate"—TJ to Lewis E. Beck, July 16, 1824, FO "early access" document.

Even after his thermometer broke—Lucia Stanton, "Mediterranean Journey (1787)", TJE, https://monticello.org/site/research-and-collections/mediterranean-journey-1787#footnote4_lkqfky3.

An "estimate of climate"—"Thomas Jefferson: Analysis of Weather Memorandum Book, Jan., 1807," FO.

On his French journey—Notes of a Tour into Southern Parts of France etc., 3 Mar.–10 June, 1787, FO.

Hewe's Crab and Golden Wildings—Hatch, *The Fruit and Fruit Trees of Monticello*, 74–75, 77. TJ's all-time favorite apple was the Taliaferro, which produced a champagne that came "nearer to...silky Champagne than any other." TJ to James Mease, June 29, 1814, FO.

Granger supervised apple picking and bottled cider—THM 118, 120, 122; Hatch, *The Fruit and Fruit Trees of Monticello*, 60, 64–65. His wife, Ursula, was known for her skills in bottling cider; TJ to Thomas Mann Randolph, Feb. 4, 1800, FO.

"no apple here to compare to our Newtown Pippin"—TJ to James Madison, Oct. 28, 1785. The Newtown Pippin (called the Albemarle Pippin in Jefferson country today) was sold widely, even in England in the nineteenth century. Hatch, *The Fruit and Fruit Trees of Monticello*, 70–73; Burford, *Apples of North America*, 122.

recorded apple blossoms—Notes of a Tour into Southern Parts of France etc., 3 March–10 June 1787, FO.

heard similar stories from an orchardist—The person I met with in Tuscany was Isabella Dalla Ragione, who calls herself an "arboreal archaeologist." She keeps lost species alive both in her orchard and on the page—I recommend her book *Beholding Natural Fruits: Vegetables in Cultivations, Writings, and Paintings in the Upper Tiber Valley from the 16th to the 18th century* (Città di Castello: Petruzzi Editore, 2009).

meteorology was not advancing—TJ to George F. Hopkins, Sept. 5, 1822, FO "early access" document.

He published an extensive study—NSV, 73–81; Thomson, *Jefferson's Shadow*, 183–185.

the "cheerful" climate of America—TJ to Constantin François Chasseboeuf Volney, Feb. 8, 1805, FO "early access" document.

"perpetual bank of clouds"

the Little Ice Age—Brian Fagan, *The Little Ice Age: How Climate Made History, 1300–1850* (New York: Basic Books, 2001), xiii.

8 degrees in Paris; "excessive" cold—TJ to Short, Dec. 8, 1788, FO; Short to TJ, Dec. 23, 1788, FO.

helped lead to the French Revolution—Fagan, *The Little Ice Age*, 162–164; Schama, *Citizens*, 305–307.

"A change in our climate"—NSV, 80.

"the methods invented in latter times"—"Thomas Jefferson: Analysis of Weather Memorandum Book, Jan., 1807," FO.

sea breezes traveled farther; "cleared of woods."—NSV, 76–77; Thomson, *Jefferson's Shadow*, 188–192.

"now almost entirely cleared"—TJ to Bernard McMahon, Jan. 8, 1809, FO "early access" document.

"I wish I was a despot"—Meacham, *Thomas Jefferson*, 396.

"economy" in taking wood—TJ to Edmund Bacon, Dec. 8, 1806, and May 13, 1807, FO "early access" document.

"steady attention to the thermometer"—TJ to Lewis E. Beck, July 16, 1824, FO "early access" document.

"The land gains there on the sea"—Notes of a Tour into Southern Parts of France etc., 3 March–10 June, 1787, FO.

Causes of global warming—Robert Henson, *The Rough Guide to Climate Change* (New York: Rough Guides, 2008), 20–26, 36–37; Joseph Romm, *Climate Change: What Everyone Needs to Know* (New York: Oxford University Press, 2016), 1–2, 20–22.

extreme weather patterns, ocean storm surges—Henson, *Rough Guide to Climate Change*, 58–65; Romm, *Climate Change*, 33–34, 55–56.

the polar ice caps to melt and sea levels to rise—Tim Flannery, *We Are the Weather Makers: The History of Climate Change* (Somerville: Candlewick Press, 2009 adaptation by Sally M. Walker), 139–150; Kristin Dow and Thomas E. Downing, *The Atlas of Climate Change* (Berkeley: University of California Press, 2006), 22–23.

much of this coast will be underwater—Erwan Alix, "CARTE. À quels risques climatiques votre commune est-elle exposée?," *Ouest-France*, Feb. 11, 2020.

"as if both sides"—NSV, 47.

Littoral regions, severe weather jeopardizes—Henson, *Rough Guide to Climate Change*, 66–67, 70–71, 132, 166, 168; Dow and Downing, *The Atlas of Climate Change*, 26–27, 56–61.

Rice, losing nutritional content—Chris Mooney, "Rice, the Staple Food of Billions, Could Become Less Nutritious Because of Climate Change," *The Washington Post*, May 23, 2018.

producers in Bordeaux—Claude Canellas, "*Le Vin de Bordeaux Se Prépare au Changement Climatique*," Reuters, Oct. 15, 2015.

moose dying off—Nicholas Kusnetz, "Climate Change Is Killing New England's Moose. Can Hunters Save Them?," InsideClimate News, May 29, 2017, https://www.insideclimatenews.org/news/29052017 /climate-change-ticks-killing-new-england-moose-hunters/.

"the fishy tribe"—TJ to DeWitt Clinton, Apr. 30, 1823, FO "early access" document.

"actual inspection and inquiry"—TJ to Edmund Pendleton, May 25, 1784, FO; "Queries Concerning Government, Labor, Commerce, etc.," ca. June 1, 1784, FO (see also the replies from various states); TJ to Madison, July 1, 1784; MB 1784, FO. In 2013, we toured sites Jefferson visited in Salem, Massachusetts; Newport, Rhode Island; and Portsmouth, New Hampshire (a state that Nico called New Hamster), where we sailed on a gundalow up the Piscataqua River. The cod fishing industry that was so strong in Jefferson's day—and for nearly two centuries afterward—had largely collapsed. In Rhode Island, we sailed in a schooner with Sarah Schumann, the director of a nonprofit called Eating with the Ecosystem, which promotes other fish beyond the famous species like cod, salmon, and tuna, that diners are used to but whose stocks have declined. On her boat, we tried sea robin and razor clams, both delicious.

"becalmed" for several windless days—TDLTJ, 73; MB 1784, FO.

"problematical" effects—TJ to Jean-Baptiste Le Roy, Nov. 13, 1786, FO.

"what foreign fishermen can never supply," he wrote—"VI. Replies to Queries: New Hampshire, June, 1784."

"retired" to other areas—"Report on the American Fisheries by the Secretary of State," Feb. 1, 1791, FO.

"in the warmer latitudes" off of Brazil—Jefferson's Memoranda Concerning the American, British, and French Fisheries, ca. Oct. 1788, FO.

Traveling to seaports in France—TJ to John Jay, June 21, 1787, FO; Jefferson's Memoranda Concerning the American, British, and French Fisheries, ca. Oct. 1788, FO. Jefferson himself used sperm oil candles at times but preferred ones made from myrtle wax. FB, 79–80.

open markets to whale and codfish oil—"Editorial Note: Documents Concerning the Whale Fishery," FO; TJ to Jay, June 21, 1787, FO; ROM, 38–39, 196–197.

"Science never appears so beautiful"—TJ to William Strickland, Mar. 23, 1798, FO.

the whale and its decline—Callum Roberts, *The Unnatural History of the Sea* (Washington, DC: Island Press, 2007), 90–96; Deborah Cramer, *Great Waters: An Atlantic Passage* (New York: W. W. Norton and Co., 2002), 141–149. Philip Hoare movingly deals with this subject in his *The Whale: In Search of the Giants of the Sea* (New York: Ecco, 2010).

collapse in the stock of northern cod—Mark Kurlansky, *Cod: A Biography of the Fish That Changed the World* (New York: Penguin, 1997), 182–186; Paul Greenberg, *Four Fish: The Future of the Last Wild Food* (New York: Penguin, 2010), 137–145. Many factors contributed to the collapse, including the advanced technology the trawlers used and the taking of much of the cod's prey as by-catch.

Ocean acidification—Henson, *The Rough Guide*, 124; Romm, *Climate Change*, 17–18, 118–121.

never comprehended that plants and animals could go extinct—Thomson, *Jefferson's Shadow*, 89–92.

"I like the dreams of the future"—TJ to John Adams, Aug. 1, 1816.

TJ's love of trees—See "Trees at Monticello," https://monticello.org/house-gardens/farms-gardens/landscape -features/trees-at-monticello/. TJ's letters—to Madame de Tessé and many others—are replete with refer- ences to trees, as are his Farm Book and NSV. I was fortunate enough to go with Peggy Cornett, Monticello's

Curator of Plants, on several walks where she described the history of the trees on the mountain.

planting pecan trees—The nonprofit is called Les pacaniers de Jefferson; see https://pacanierjeffersonpecan.com
/the-jefferson-pecan-project/.

Brittany plans to plant 25 million trees—Jérôme Gicquel, *"Bretagne: La région mise sur le bois et veut planter cinq
millions d'arbres d'ici à 2025," 20 Minutes,* Oct. 23, 2019.

CHAPTER TWENTY-TWO: WE'LL ALWAYS HAVE PARIS

His first trip outside of Virginia—TJ to John Page, May 25, 1766, FO; Malone, *Jefferson the Virginian,* 99–100.

Five thousand people lost their lives—Boles, *Jefferson,* 252; Clay Jenkinson, "Thomas Jefferson, Epidemics, and
His Vision for American Cities," https://governing.com/context/Thomas-Jefferson-Epidemics-and-His
-Vision-for-American-Cities.html.

"all flying who can"—TJ to Madison, Sept. 12, 1793, FO.

"danger" in remaining—TJ to Thomas Mann Randolph, Jr., Sept. 2, 1793, FO.

a house on the Schuylkill River—MB 1793, FO.

"I never before knew the value of trees"—TJ to Martha Jefferson Randolph, July 7, 1793, FO. Even before the
yellow fever outbreak, TJ spent much time in his Schuylkill house.

he returned to Monticello—TJ to Thomas Mann Randolph, Jr., Sept. 15, 1793, FO; MB 1793, FO.

had requested only a six-month sabbatical—TJ to John Jay, Nov. 19, 1788, FO.

Brought an enormous amount of baggage—List of Baggage Shipped by Jefferson from France, ca. Sept. 1, 1789, FO.

still renting—MB, 1789, FO; ROM, 207. He renewed his lease in April 1789 and paid rent for over a year.

a longer trip through Italy, a tour of Greece—George Ticknor's Account of a Visit to Monticello [4–7 Feb. 1815], FO.

nominated and confirmed as Secretary of State—Boles, *Jefferson,* 204–207.

Jefferson's political career—See in particular Meacham's *Thomas Jefferson,* which particularly focuses on TJ the
political animal.

Searching for both the Hessian fly and for allies—Editorial Note: The Northern Journey of 1791, FO; Estes,
"Jefferson as Party Leader," 131–132.

"We talked and dined"—Thomas Lee Shippen to William Shippen, Sept. 15, 1790, FO; MB 1790, FO. TJ and
Madison parted ways with Shippen in Georgetown, with the two leaders staying to explore locations for
the U.S. capital. Hayes, *Road to Monticello,* 398.

would take a daily horseback ride—TJ to Thomas Mann Randolph, Nov. 16, 1801.

"never did a prisoner"—TJ to Pierre Samuel du Pont de Nemours, Mar. 2, 1809, FO.

"mostly on horseback"—TJ to Benjamin Rush, Jan. 16, 1811, FO.

unusual plant seeds—RSE, 19–20; Peggy Cornett, "Botany and Friendship: A Circle of Transatlantic Culture
Exchange," *Twinleaf Journal,* https://monticello.org/house-gardens/center-for-historic-plants/twinleaf
-journal-online/botany-and-friendship/.

entrance hall—TJE, "Entrance hall," https://monticello.org/house-gardens/the-house/room-furnishings
/entrance-hall/; WTJ, 61–71.

a ramshackle tavern—MB 1818, FO; Wills, *Mr. Jefferson's University,* 32–35; Gene Crotty, *Jefferson's Western Travels
over Virginia's Blue Ridge Mountains* (Charlottesville: UVA Printing, 2002), 115–118. I hiked Rockfish Gap
the day of the two-hundredth anniversary of Jefferson's trip, exploring a mountain pass filled with rhododendrons and buzzing bees.

hiked the Peaks of Otter—MB 1815, FO.

"valuable addition"—TJ to Samuel Brown, Nov. 13, 1813. TJ was particularly enthused about the Texas bird pepper.

escape the crowds—Gordon-Reed and Onuf, *"Most Blessed of the Patriarchs,"* 262–264, 269; Ellis, *American
Sphinx,* 276–277.

"charged like a bee"—TJ to William Shippen, May 8, 1788, FO; TJ to John Rutledge, Sr., July 12, 1788, FO.

Shippen lived as a gentleman, suffered from disease—Paul C. Nigel, *The Lees of Virginia: Seven Generations of an American Family* (New York: Oxford University Press, 1990), 145–151.

Rutledge supported Burr—John Rutledge, Jr., to Alexander Hamilton, Jan. 10, 1801, FO.

wrote under an assumed name—John Rutledge, Jr., to TJ, Oct. 20, 1802, FO.

dying in 1819—Biographical Directory of the U.S Congress, "Rutledge, John Jr., 1766–1819," https://bioguideretro .congress.gov/Home/MemberDetails?memIndex=R000553.

remained in Paris—John Jay to TJ, June 19, 1789; TJ to John Jay, Sept. 19, 1789; Short to TJ, June 25, 1792, FO.

"unsettled vagabond kind of life"—William Short to TJ, Dec. 18, 1792, FO.

a torrid affair—Shackelford, *Jefferson's Adoptive Son*, 21; THM, 254–255. Gordon-Reed points out that Short also engaged in an affair with the teenage daughter of the family that was providing him with lodging, until around 1790, prior to his more well-known liaison with Rosalie.

Jefferson bought land for Short—TJ to Short, May 25, 1795, FO; Dumas Malone, *Jefferson and His Time: The Sage of Monticello* (Boston: Little, Brown and Co., 1981), 508–509.

"adoptive son"—TJ to John Trumbull, June 1, 1789, FO.

"Come and see"—TJ to Short, Oct. 31, 1819, FO.

Rosalie left him—Shackelford, *Jefferson's Adoptive Son*, 160.

became far wealthier than Jefferson—Shackelford, *Jefferson's Adoptive Son*, 138, 167.

travel accounts of great African cities—Short to TJ, Feb. 27, 1798, FO.

Short had no problem with racial mixture—*Id.*

"in some public way"—Short to TJ, July 18, 1816, FO. Unlike Jefferson, Short joined the abolitionist group the Société des Amis des Noirs in Paris. Shackelford, *Jefferson's Adoptive Son*, 166, 176. On another occasion, he wrote pointedly to TJ, "[a]s it will probably be a long time before the legislatures of the Southern States will take up the subject of slavery on a wide political scale, it would seem to me that influential individuals might in the meantime do good by proper examples" by gradually liberating their slaves. Short to TJ, Sept. 18, 1800, FO.

supported their efforts to emigrate to Liberia—Shackelford, *Jefferson's Adoptive Son*, 177.

CHAPTER TWENTY-THREE: THE NEVER-ENDING PURSUIT OF HAPPINESS

The trio of deeds—"TJ, Design for Tombstone and Inscription, Before 4 July, 1826," FO. Jon Meacham, tongue firmly in cheek, said in a talk once that omitting the presidency from this list was the ultimate passive-aggressive act.

A new statue—Olympia Meola, "New Statue of Jefferson Goes on Display at State Capital," *Richmond Times-Dispatch*, May 4, 2012.

Jefferson permitted the expansion of slavery—Roger Kennedy, *Mr. Jefferson's Lost Cause, Land, Farmers, Slavery, and the Louisiana Purchase* (New York: Oxford University Press, 2003), 2, 211–12.

backtracking on public support for emancipation—For the rest of his life, TJ affirmed his belief in the cause of gradual emancipation, but only in private letters, also expressing his reluctance to speak out further on the matter. See TJ to George Logan, May 11, 1805, FO "early access" document ("I have most carefully avoided every public act or manifestation" on the subject of abolition).

Joe Fossett, Sally Hemings—TWL, 219–221.

Crowds focused anger, critics started a dialogue—Bonnie Berkowitz and Adrian Blanco, "Confederate Monuments Are Falling, But Hundreds Still Stand. Here's Where," *Washington Post*, June 20, 2020; David Graham, "Where Will the Removal of Confederate Statues Stop?," *The Atlantic*, June 28, 2017 (in the article, Professor Gordon-Reed distinguishes between those "who wanted to build the United States and people who wanted to destroy it"); Jude Sheerin, "Should Washington and Jefferson Statues Come Down?," *BBC News*, Aug. 18, 2017.

"If America is right, Jefferson was right"—Parton, *Life of Thomas Jefferson*, iii, 165.

Standing in the breach—Joe Heim, "Recounting a Day of Hate, Rage, Violence, and Death," *The Washington Post*, Aug. 14, 2017; Alexis Gravely, Tim Dodson, and Daniel Hoerauf, "Torch-wielding white nationalists march at U.Va.," *Cavalier Daily*, Aug. 12, 2017.

Explored the Peaks of Otter, "subjects botanical"—TJ to Alden Partridge, Oct. 12, 1815, and Jan. 2, 1816, FO; 1815 MB, FO. Today we know the highest mountain in Virginia is Mount Rogers, in the Jefferson National Forest.

He aimed to add the height data—NSV, 20 n. 7. TJ did add it to a revised version he played around with but never published. He eventually concluded that keeping up with the data in his book was like measuring shadow "never stationary, but lengthening as the sun advances," as he wrote to John Melish on Dec. 10, 1814, FO. (When your endnotes have their own endnotes, you know it's almost time to stop.)

this never-ending pursuit of happiness—As the Final Endnote, I would like to say a few words on behalf of myself, my fellow Endnotes, and the entire Manuscript (which doesn't know I'm doing this): Thank you for reading this. It means a lot to us that you've joined us on this journey. If this story made you want to explore this world, in whatever form that might take, follow that instinct. Maybe you'll better the world along the way. You'll certainly better yourself. (Take it from me—I'll never give up on my dream of making the main text.)

Index

C

M

P

About the Author

Derek Baxter has studied Thomas Jefferson off and on his whole life, from when he played him in his fourth-grade class musical to when he attended the University of Virginia. An attorney, he lives in Fairfax, Virginia, with his wife, Liana, and children, Miranda and Nicolas. They lived quiet lives until the day they began following Jefferson's travel advice across Europe. This is his first book.